Astrology

3rd Edition

by Rae Orion

A Wiley Brand

Astrology For Dummies®, 3rd Edition

Published by: **John Wiley & Sons, Inc.**, 111 River Street, Hoboken, NJ 07030-5774, www.wiley.com

Copyright © 2020 by John Wiley & Sons, Inc., Hoboken, New Jersey

Published simultaneously in Canada

For general information on our other products and services, please contact our Customer Care Department within the U.S. at 877-762-2974, outside the U.S. at 317-572-3993, or fax 317-572-4002. For technical support, please visit https://hub.wiley.com/community/support/dummies.

Wiley publishes in a variety of print and electronic formats and by print-on-demand. Some material included with standard print versions of this book may not be included in e-books or in print-on-demand. If this book refers to media such as a CD or DVD that is not included in the version you purchased, you may download this material at http://booksupport.wiley.com. For more information about Wiley products, visit www.wiley.com.

Library of Congress Control Number: 2019920308

ISBN 978-1-119-59416-1 (pbk); ISBN 978-1-119-59415-4 (ebk); ISBN 978-1-119-59418-5 (ebk)

Manufactured in the United States of America

V10016619_122719

Contents at a Glance

Introduction 1

Part 1: Mapping Your Place in the Cosmos 7
CHAPTER 1: An Astrological Overview: The Horoscope in Brief 9
CHAPTER 2: Getting Your Precise Horoscope: The Old Way,
the Internet Way, and the Software 29
CHAPTER 3: The History of Astrology: 5,000 Years of Cosmic Ups and Downs 41

Part 2: Here Comes the Sun 59
CHAPTER 4: The Signs of Spring: Aries, Taurus, and Gemini 61
CHAPTER 5: The Signs of Summer: Cancer, Leo, and Virgo 81
CHAPTER 6: The Signs of Autumn: Libra, Scorpio, and Sagittarius 101
CHAPTER 7: The Signs of Winter: Capricorn, Aquarius, and Pisces 121

Part 3: Leafing through the Cosmic Cookbook 143
CHAPTER 8: Moon Signs: The Lunacy Factor 145
CHAPTER 9: The Personal Planets 155
CHAPTER 10: The Outer Planets (And More) 175
CHAPTER 11: What You See versus What You Get: The Rising Sign (And More) 195
CHAPTER 12: The Sun, the Moon, and the Planets in the Houses 211
CHAPTER 13: Amazing Aspects: The Secrets of Cosmic Geometry 237
CHAPTER 14: Interpreting Your Birth Chart: A Guide 267

Part 4: Using Astrology Right Now 285
CHAPTER 15: The Sun Sign Combinations 287
CHAPTER 16: The Times of Our Lives: Transits 307
CHAPTER 17: The Lunar Advantage: Using Astrology in Daily Life 333
CHAPTER 18: Retrograde Hell? The Truth Revealed 343
CHAPTER 19: Creativity and the Stars 355

Part 5: The Part of Tens 373
CHAPTER 20: Ten Talents You Can Spot in a Chart 375
CHAPTER 21: Ten (Plus One) Ways to Use Astrology in Your Life:
The Art of Timing 389

Index 399

Table of Contents

INTRODUCTION 1

About This Book. 1

Foolish Assumptions. 3

Icons Used in This Book 4

Beyond the Book. 4

Where to Go from Here 5

PART 1: MAPPING YOUR PLACE IN THE COSMOS 7

CHAPTER 1: **An Astrological Overview: The Horoscope
in Brief** 9

Looking at the Starry Sky 10

Identifying the Signs of the Zodiac 13

Understanding the Sun Signs 16

Polarity: Dividing the zodiac by two 16

Modality: Dividing the zodiac by three. 16

Elements: Dividing the zodiac by four 17

Putting the zodiac back together 18

Considering the Sun, the Moon, the Planets, and more 20

Who Rules? Discovering the Rulers of the Signs. 21

Determining Planetary Dignities. 23

Essential dignities 23

Accidental dignities 24

Assessing the Ascendant 25

Taking the House Tour 26

CHAPTER 2: **Getting Your Precise Horoscope: The Old Way,
the Internet Way, and the Software** 29

Casting Your Chart the Old-Fashioned Way 30

First Things First: Gathering the Information You Need 31

Dealing with approximate birth times 32

Coping with an absence of information. 32

Getting Your Horoscope Online for Free 33

Investing in Software. 35

Maximizing the Mac 35

Playing with the PC 36

Activating an App. 37

Wandering around Cyberspace. 38

CHAPTER 3: **The History of Astrology: 5,000 Years
of Cosmic Ups and Downs**..................................41
Looking at Early Astrology 42
Romping through Classical Times...............................43
Savoring the Romans 44
Appreciating Arabic astrologers 46
Meandering through Medieval Europe 47
Celebrating the Renaissance 49
Discovering Dr. Dee..49
A note about Nostradamus 50
Wandering through Shakespeare's star-crossed world.........51
Foreseeing disaster with William Lilly......................52
Watching the Decline of Astrology 52
Saluting Modern Times..54
Following the Sun 55
Hitler's astrologers 56
Greeting the dawn..56

PART 2: HERE COMES THE SUN 59

CHAPTER 4: **The Signs of Spring: Aries, Taurus, and Gemini**.....61
Aries the Ram: March 20–April 18................................62
The sunny side...63
The sorry side...63
Relationships 64
Work 64
Health and wellness 65
The mythology of Aries.....................................66
The constellation Aries 66
Taurus the Bull: April 19–May 20................................68
The sunny side...69
The sorry side...69
Relationships 70
Work 70
Health and wellness 71
The mythology of Taurus 72
The constellation Taurus 72
Gemini the Twins: May 21–June 20..............................74
The sunny side...75
The sorry side...75
Relationships 76
Work 76
Health and wellness 76
The mythology of Gemini...................................77
The constellation Gemini 77

CHAPTER 5: **The Signs of Summer: Cancer, Leo, and Virgo** 81

Cancer the Crab: June 21–July 22 82
    The sunny side 82
    The sorry side 83
    Relationships 83
    Work 84
    Health and wellness 84
    The mythology of Cancer 85
    The constellation Cancer 86
Leo the Lion: July 23–August 22 88
    The sunny side 89
    The sorry side 89
    Relationships 90
    Work 90
    Health and wellness 91
    The mythology of Leo 91
    The constellation Leo 92
Virgo the Virgin: August 23–September 22 94
    The sunny side 95
    The sorry side 95
    Relationships 95
    Work 96
    Health and wellness 97
    The mythology of Virgo 97
    The constellation Virgo 97

CHAPTER 6: **The Signs of Autumn: Libra, Scorpio,**
and Sagittarius 101

Libra the Scales: September 23–October 22 .102
    The sunny side 103
    The sorry side 103
    Relationships 104
    Work 104
    Health and wellness 105
    The mythology of Libra 105
    The constellation Libra 106
Scorpio the Scorpion: October 23–November 21 108
    The sunny side 108
    The sorry side 109
    Relationships 109
    Work 110
    Health and wellness 111
    The mythology of Scorpio 111
    The constellation Scorpius 111

Sagittarius the Archer: November 22–December 21 114
    The sunny side. 115
    The sorry side. 115
    Relationships 116
    Work 116
    Health and wellness 117
    The mythology of Sagittarius. 117
    The constellation Sagittarius 118

CHAPTER 7: **The Signs of Winter: Capricorn, Aquarius, and Pisces**. 121
Capricorn the Goat: December 22–January 19 122
    The sunny side. 122
    The sorry side. 123
    Relationships 124
    Work 124
    Health and wellness 125
    The mythology of Capricorn 125
    The constellation Capricorn. 126
Aquarius the Water Bearer: January 20–February 18 129
    The sunny side. 130
    The sorry side. 130
    Relationships 131
    Work 131
    Health and wellness 132
    The mythology of Aquarius 132
    The constellation Aquarius. 133
Pisces the Fish: February 19–March 19 135
    The sunny side. 136
    The sorry side. 136
    Relationships 137
    Work 137
    Health and wellness 138
    The mythology of Pisces. 138
    The constellation Pisces 139

PART 3: LEAFING THROUGH THE COSMIC COOKBOOK . . .143

CHAPTER 8: **Moon Signs: The Lunacy Factor** .145
The Mythology of the Moon. 146
The Moon in the Signs 146
The Nodes of the Moon 150
The Mythology of the Lunar Nodes 151
The Nodes in the Signs. 152

CHAPTER 9: **The Personal Planets**. 155

Locating Your Planets. 156
Mercury: Communicating with Style. 157
Venus: Love Conquers All. 160
Mars: Road Warrior. 163
Jupiter: More Is Better. 166
Saturn: Lord of the Rings 170

CHAPTER 10: **The Outer Planets (And More)**. 175

Uranus: The Rebel. 176
The myth behind the planet 177
Understanding Uranus. 178
Uranus in the signs 178
Neptune: The Dreamer. 181
The myth behind the planet 182
Assessing Neptune's influence 183
Neptune in the signs. 183
Pluto: The Power of Transformation 186
The myth behind the Planet. 187
Pinpointing Pluto's influence 188
Pluto in the signs. 188
Chiron: The Wounded Healer 190
The myth behind the . . . uh . . . small solar system body 190
Chiron's influence 191
Chiron in the signs. 191
And More 193

CHAPTER 11: **What You See versus What You Get:
The Rising Sign (And More)**. 195

Identifying Your Ascendant 196
What Your Ascendant Says about You. 197
Finding and Understanding Your Descendant 204
Looking into Your Midheaven and I.C. 206

CHAPTER 12: **The Sun, the Moon, and the Planets in
the Houses**. 211

Thinking about the Houses 213
The Sun in the Houses 214
The Moon in the Houses 215
The Nodes of the Moon in the House 217
Mercury in the Houses 219
Venus in the Houses 221
Mars in the Houses. 222
Jupiter in the Houses. 225
Saturn in the Houses 226

Uranus in the Houses 228
Neptune in the Houses. 230
Pluto in the Houses. 232
Interpreting Empty Houses 233

CHAPTER 13: **Amazing Aspects: The Secrets of Cosmic Geometry** 237
Identifying the Major Aspects 238
Figuring Out Your Aspects 240
Reading an Aspect Grid 242
A Note about Minor Aspects 243
A Word about Mutual Reception. 243
Interpreting the Aspects. 244
    Aspects to the Sun. 244
    Aspects to the Moon 249
    Aspects to Mercury 252
    Aspects to Venus 255
    Aspects to Mars 258
    Aspects to Jupiter. 260
    Aspects to Saturn. 262
    Aspects to Uranus, Neptune, and Pluto. 264

CHAPTER 14: **Interpreting Your Birth Chart: A Guide** 267
Step One: Identifying Overall Patterns. 267
    Hemisphere analysis. 268
    Pattern analysis 269
    Considering the signs 274
    Missing in Action: Elements gone AWOL 276
    Missing in Action: Modes in retreat 276
    Finding mitigating factors. 277
Step Two: Six Components of a Birth Chart 278
Step Three: Looking for Aspect Patterns .281
Step Four: Putting the Puzzle Together 284

PART 4: USING ASTROLOGY RIGHT NOW 285

CHAPTER 15: **The Sun Sign Combinations** 287
Aries in Love. 288
Taurus in Love 290
Gemini in Love. 292
Cancer in Love 293
Leo in Love 295
Virgo in Love. 297
Libra in Love. 298

Scorpio in Love. 300
Sagittarius in Love. 301
Capricorn in Love. 302
Aquarius in Love 303
Pisces in Love. 304
Finding Other Ties 304

CHAPTER 16: **The Times of Our Lives: Transits** 307
Investigating Transits 308
Visualizing transits. 309
Showing the importance of transits .309
Tracking Mars. 312
Activating Jupiter 315
Coping with Saturn 318
Unpredictable Uranus. 322
Nebulous Neptune 325
Power-Hungry Pluto 327
Warning: The Astrologer's Curse. 330

CHAPTER 17: **The Lunar Advantage: Using
Astrology in Daily Life**. 333
Timing Your Actions by the Phases of the Moon 334
Watching the Moon. 335
Taking Advantage of the Moon in the Signs 336
Tracking the Moon through the Houses .337
Making the Most of Momentous Lunar Influences 339
Avoiding the Void. 340

CHAPTER 18: **Retrograde Hell? The Truth Revealed** 343
Retrograde Revealed. 343
Successfully Handling Retrograde Mercury. 344
Making the best of it 345
Revealing the rhythm of retrograde. .346
The shadow of retrograde, decoded .348
Looking for Retrograde Venus. 349
Watching for Retrograde Mars 351
The Other Planets 352

CHAPTER 19: **Creativity and the Stars** 355
Circling the Zodiac. 355
Aries the Ram. 356
Taurus the Bull. 357
Gemini the Twins. 358
Cancer the Crab. 359

Leo the Lion 360
Virgo the Virgin. 361
Libra the Scales 362
Scorpio the Scorpion. 363
Sagittarius the Archer 364
Capricorn the Goat 365
Aquarius the Water-bearer 366
Pisces the Fish 367
Finding the Creative Heart of Every Chart 368
Signs 368
Planets. 368
Houses 369
Aspects 370

PART 5: THE PART OF TENS. 373

CHAPTER 20: **Ten Talents You Can Spot in a Chart** 375
Athletic Prowess 375
Beauty (or the Power of Attraction) 376
Celebrity Appeal. 377
Healing Hands 379
Business Savvy. 381
Making Money 383
Activist Capability. 384
Psychic Ability. 385
Becoming an Astrologer. 387
Writing. 388

CHAPTER 21: **Ten (Plus One) Ways to Use Astrology
in Your Life: The Art of Timing**. 389
Getting Married 390
Going on a First Date 391
Opening a Business. 392
Scheduling a Meeting 393
Throwing a Party 393
Purchasing Technology. 394
Buying a House 394
Having Surgery. 395
Starting a Diet or an Exercise Program 396
Writing a Novel, a Memoir, or a Screenplay 396
Laying Low 397

INDEX. 399

Introduction

Astrology can change your life. It did mine. Astrology illuminates the secret corners of the self, expands your insight into yourself and others, deepens your compassion, clarifies the past, and even offers a glimpse into the possible future. Beyond that, as with all great areas of accumulated knowledge, astrology has the power to alter perception. Once you know something about it, you never see the world in the same way again.

Blessed with a vocabulary that is simultaneously objective and poetic, astrology stimulates your intellect and fuels your curiosity. As you absorb its principles, everyone you know becomes a mystery waiting to be solved. Even public personalities and figures from the past — Frida Kahlo, say, or Vincent Van Gogh — glow more vividly when viewed through an astrological lens. Most of all, astrology offers an unrivaled method of learning about yourself, not just as a person born under one sign or another but as someone with a never-before-seen assortment of qualities and abilities, someone whose individual essence reflects the cosmos.

Many people think that astrology divides all human beings into 12 groups. How wrong they are! Astrology teaches that all human beings are subject to universal needs and desires — and that every individual is entirely and splendidly unique.

About This Book

Astrology is an ancient and evolving system that has many dimensions and appears in many forms. Western astrology is not the same as Chinese astrology or Vedic astrology. This book is about Western astrology, but even within that, there are many subdivisions. Practitioners of mundane astrology calculate horoscopes for public events and consider the fate of nations. Electional astrologers specialize in choosing dates and times for occasions such as weddings, real estate purchases, or opening night at the theatre. Financial astrologers follow the market. Horary astrologers answer questions that address everything from concerns about relationships or health to the location of lost objects. In this book, I focus on *natal astrology*, the interpretation of a birth chart to gain insight into the personality, proclivities, talents, and tribulations of an individual.

I begin by introducing you to the major components of a birth chart and showing you how to get an accurate copy of your chart via the internet. After that, I tell you how to analyze your chart's most essential features, how to compare your chart with someone else's, and how to use astrology to improve your life. It may sound extravagant to claim that astrology helps you align yourself with the universe, but it's the simple truth.

I consider astrology a tool — an objective tool — for understanding yourself and others, confronting adversity, embracing opportunity, analyzing relationships, and making basic decisions. In *Astrology For Dummies*, 3rd Edition, I show you how to use that tool for your advantage.

As you leaf through these pages, there are a few conventions to be aware of:

>> You will notice various symbols strewn across each birth chart like a handful of precious stones. Those magical-looking symbols represent the signs, planets, and other components of an astrological chart. I consider them a fundamental part of astrology's charm, and I recommend that you learn them by heart. But you don't have to because I have provided a handy Cheat Sheet that identifies every symbol and gives you a thumbnail description of each. See the "Beyond the Book" section in this Introduction to find out more about the Cheat Sheet, including how to access it.

Using the Cheat Sheet, you can translate those symbols into a language you actually speak. So if you're mulling over a birth chart and you see something that looks like this:

☿28♒05℞

you'll be able to figure out in a flash that Mercury (☿) is in Aquarius (♒) at 28 degrees 05 minutes. And, yes, it's retrograde (℞). (For more on that loaded topic, see Chapter 18.)

>> In the text, whenever I refer to a planetary position, such as the one in the preceding example, I describe it as 28°05′ Aquarius, spelling out the sign and using the international symbols for degree (°) and minute (′). In the actual charts — those round, mandala-like images scattered throughout this book — I omit those tiny indicators. Instead, the charts in this book announce their planetary positions with type: the degree number appears in a font that has been boldfaced, while the minutes are shown in a lighter, standard font. The symbol for the relevant sign of the zodiac is plunked down right in the middle, between the degree and the minutes, as follows: **28**♒05.

>> Another feature of *Astrology For Dummies*, 3rd Edition, is that you can dive in anywhere. As an author, I like to think that you'll begin in the beginning and read doggedly to the end. But I'm a realist. I know that when most people pick up astrology books, they head straight for their own Sun signs (or star signs,

as many people like to call them). I have written this book with that in mind. You can start anywhere, secure in the knowledge that if there's a fact from an earlier chapter that you absolutely must know, I will tell you. This book is filled with cross-references and reminders for just that purpose. You can jump in anywhere.

Foolish Assumptions

Despite the title of this book, I assume that you're no fool. Whether you're an absolute beginner or a long-time devotee of the cosmic art, I assume that you have enough common sense to know that astrology offers understanding — not winning lottery numbers. It can help you become your most fulfilled self. It can even make predictions, and in the hands of highly skilled practitioners, those predictions can be spot-on. But despite its association with alchemy, divination, and the occult, astrology isn't magic.

I assume that you're intrigued by the perspective astrology offers and curious about how it might apply to you, and I take it for granted that you are especially interested in your own horoscope. Most of us are, and for good reason: investigating your own chart is edifying and revealing, making it perhaps the single most instructive step you can take while learning astrology. But scrutinizing your own chart is more than an exercise for novices. Even seasoned astrologers brood over their own charts. And when they hear of a newly discovered celestial body or an ancient technique that has been resuscitated after centuries of disuse, I guarantee that they try it out first with their own charts. Exploring your personal chart is the work of a lifetime.

I assume that you have easy access to the internet. Whether you get there by way of a laptop, a smart phone, a computer in a public library, or a device that has yet to be invented, internet access will enable you to create birth charts on the spot and to track the daily positions of the Sun, the Moon, and the planets.

Finally, I assume you know that astrology isn't about fate or predestination. It's about possibility and propensity, about making the most of your strengths, recognizing your shortcomings, understanding other people, and aligning yourself with the cosmos. When I was learning astrology, I was taught that "the stars impel; they do no compel." Sir Francis Bacon (1561–1626), father of the scientific method, put it this way: "There is no fatal necessity in the stars; but that they rather incline than compel." Four centuries have passed since then, and it's still true.

Icons Used in This Book

Four icons sprinkled throughout this book serve as road signs. Here's what the icons mean:

REAL LIFE EXAMPLE

In an ideal world, every planetary placement, aspect, and transit discussed in the text would be accompanied by an example from the life of a flesh-and-blood human being. In the real world, book space is limited, so I'm able to use comparatively few such examples. This icon highlights those examples. In most cases, real-life examples feature movie stars, musicians, writers, artists, politicians, and other well-known figures, past or present. From time to time, I write about people I know personally. In those instances, the names have been changed. The astrology remains the same.

REMEMBER

Certain facts and principles are essential to reading a birth chart. I discuss most of them in the early chapters. But when you need to recall a fact in order to understand a particular facet of a birth chart, I try to remind you, gently, using this icon.

TECHNICAL STUFF

It's impossible to talk about astrology without coming smack up against astronomy and mathematics. Whenever I give a nuts-and-bolts scientific explanation of an astrological (or astronomical) phenomenon, I warn you upfront with this icon. Want to skip the explanation? Go ahead. Most of the time, you can ignore it and still be on track.

TIP

A paragraph marked with this icon may suggest an easier way of doing something. It may point you to a book, an app, or a podcast that covers material similar to that being discussed in the text. It may suggest a way to address a problem that could arise with a certain planetary configuration in a chart. Or it may tell you how to, say, seduce a Capricorn. Never let it be said that astrology isn't useful.

Beyond the Book

This book introduces you to the basics of astrology — and more. The Cheat Sheet, available online at www.dummies.com, provides a handy summary of the symbols and meanings of the signs, planets, houses, and aspects, along with a few nonessential components of your chart that might interest you. Take a look.

To get it, go to www.dummies.com and search for "Astrology For Dummies Cheat Sheet."

Where to Go from Here

There is grandeur in astrology. Using a symbolic language that brims with mythology and metaphor, it speaks to the psyche and resonates with the soul. Yet it can also be down-to-earth and specific. It covers a lot of ground and benefits from an astonishing array of techniques and approaches. That's why, if you take it up, you could be studying astrology for the rest of your life. It's that interesting. It's that fun.

So where should you begin? Chapter 1 covers the basics. Chapter 2 tells you how to get a copy of your birth chart. Once you are in possession of that essential document, you're ready to immerse yourself in the most fascinating study of human beings ever invented. I suggest that you begin by turning to Chapters 4 through 7 to read about your Sun sign and, secondarily, the signs of a few other people you know. After that, you might turn to Chapters 8, 9, and 10 to read about your Moon and your planets; to Chapter 11 to find out about your rising sign; and to Chapter 12 to read about the houses that your planets occupy. Or maybe you'd rather go directly to Chapter 15 to see how your sign is likely to hit it off with, say, Taurus. That's okay too.

Ultimately, you may end up wandering through the pages of this book in no particular order. That's not my recommendation. As far as I'm concerned, the chapters are numbered for a reason. But there's nothing wrong with hopping around. Whatever approach you take, I hope that you will rejoice in — and benefit from — the wisdom of the stars.

1

Mapping Your Place in the Cosmos

IN THIS PART . . .

Grasp the basics of astrology and see what's included in a horoscope.

Find out how to obtain your birth chart to use as a reference throughout the book.

Ramble through a brief history of astrology's ups, downs, and changing influence over the centuries.

IN THIS CHAPTER

» **Picturing the solar system**

» **Rambling through the zodiac**

» **Classifying the signs by polarity, modality, and element**

» **Contemplating the Sun, the Moon, and the planets**

» **Introducing the rulers of each sign**

» **Determining planetary dignities**

» **Discovering the Ascendant**

» **Wandering through the houses**

Chapter **1**

An Astrological Overview: The Horoscope in Brief

egend has it that Sir Isaac Newton, one of the greatest scientific geniuses of all time, may have been interested in astrology. Newton had a complex, wide-ranging mind. In addition to inventing calculus, formulating the laws of motion, and discovering the universal law of gravity, he wrote Biblical commentary and speculated about possible dates for the end of the world (all, by the way, in our current century). He experimented with the alchemical quest to turn ordinary metals into gold and may have suffered from mercury poisoning as a result. And he was interested in astrology, claiming that a book he read on the subject while a student at Cambridge University had ignited his interest in science. When his friend Edmund Halley, after whom the comet is named, made a disparaging remark about astrology, Newton, a conservative Capricorn, shot right back, "Sir, I have studied the subject. You have not." Or so the story goes.

Like every other astrologer, I like to think that story might be true. After all, astrology has faded in and out of fashion, but it has never lacked followers. Twenty-five hundred years ago, Babylonian astrologers were casting individual horoscopes. The Romans consulted astrologers regularly. Emperor Augustus visited an astrologer in 44 BCE, the year Julius Caesar was assassinated, and the orator Cicero, who spoke vehemently against astrology, numbered several well-known practitioners among his friends. In the eighth century, Charlemagne studied astrology under the auspices of an English monk. Catherine de Medici consulted Nostradamus, Queen Elizabeth I sought counsel from the astrologer John Dee, and other astrologers advised Richard the Lion-heart, Napoleon, George Washington, J. P. Morgan, and Ronald Reagan. Yet in all that time, no one has provided a satisfying explanation of why astrology works. Over the centuries, proponents of the ancient art have suggested that gravity must be the motor of astrology . . . or electromagnetism . . . or the metaphysical "law of correspondences." Carl G. Jung summarized that view when he wrote, "We are born at a given moment, in a given place, and like vintage years of wine, we have the qualities of the year and of the season in which we are born."

I don't know why astrology works any more than Sir Isaac did. I do know that the pattern the planets made when you were born — your birth chart or horoscope — describes your abilities, your challenges, and your potential. It doesn't predict your fate, though it does make some fates more easily achievable than others. The exact shape of your destiny, I believe, is up to you.

In this chapter, I give you an overview of the main components of an astrological chart: the planets, the signs, and the houses. You might think of it this way:

>> The planets represent drives, needs, and basic energies.

>> The signs represent the ways those forces express themselves.

>> And the houses represent areas of life such as career, partnership, sex, money, and health.

Looking at the Starry Sky

Picture, if you will, our solar system. In the middle is the Sun, our star. Spinning around it are the Earth and other planets along with countless asteroids, planetoids, comets, and a few lonely spacecraft. Their orbits surround the Sun roughly the way the grooves on a vinyl record album encircle the label in the center. (Although, to be clear, the orbits are not perfectly circular, and the solar system, unlike the record, is not perfectly flat.)

The idea that the planets orbit the Sun, drilled into most of us in childhood, would have astonished ancient stargazers. They never doubted that the Sun, the Moon, and the planets revolved around the Earth. And although we know better, thinking so didn't make them stupid. The Moon does revolve around the Earth — they weren't wrong there — and the Sun certainly looks as if it does. It appears to rise in the east and set in the west, and it always travels along a narrow ribbon of sky that surrounds the Earth like a giant hoop. That pathway is called the *ecliptic*. It maps the annual journey of the Sun.

TECHNICAL STUFF

Following are the most important facts about the ecliptic:

» The ecliptic represents the apparent path of the Sun around the Earth — apparent because, in reality, the Sun doesn't spin around the Earth at all. It just looks that way. The Moon and the planets seem to travel a similar path, wandering a little to the north and a little to the south of the Sun but basically following the same route.

» Like a circle, the ecliptic has 360 degrees. Those 360 degrees, divided into a dozen equal sections, comprise the signs of the zodiac. The first 30 degrees — one-twelfth of the whole — are given to Aries, the next 30 degrees belong to Taurus, and so on. Each sign receives the same amount of space.

» The stars, which are scattered like dust along the ecliptic, form the constellations of the zodiac. They are the background, a sort of celestial wallpaper against which the Sun, the Moon, and the planets move.

REMEMBER

Here comes the confusing part: The signs of the zodiac and the constellations that share their names are not the same. The signs are geometric divisions of the ecliptic, each one covering 30 degrees, each one precisely the same size. In contrast, the constellations vary in size from sprawling Virgo, the second largest constellation in the sky, to Capricorn, a faint collection of stars less than one third the size of Virgo. Although the signs of the zodiac take their names from the constellations, the signs and the stars have nothing to do with one another. I explain this sorry state of affairs in the nearby sidebar titled "The signs, the constellations, and the precession of the equinoxes."

THE SIGNS, THE CONSTELLATIONS, AND THE PRECESSION OF THE EQUINOXES

Thousands of years ago, when the Babylonians were establishing the principles of astrology, the constellations and the signs of the zodiac were roughly in alignment. On the *vernal equinox* (the first day of spring), the Sun was "in" the constellation Aries. That is, if you could observe the Sun and the stars simultaneously, you'd see the Sun amidst the stars of the Ram. In those happy days, known as the Age of Aries, the signs and the constellations more or less coincided.

Alas, this is no longer the case. On the vernal equinox today, the Sun appears amidst the (dim) stars of Pisces the Fish — a very different kettle indeed. The reason for this shift is that the Earth is not a perfect sphere. It's fatter around the middle, and its mass is distributed unequally. So it wobbles on its axis, which traces a circle in space like the spindle of a spinning top. As the Earth revolves around the Sun, the axis gradually shifts its orientation. Over the years, the constellations seem to slip backwards, a phenomenon first identified by the Greek astronomer Hipparchus in the second century BCE. The amount of slippage over a lifetime is minuscule — about one degree every 72 years — but over generations it adds up. Every equinox takes place slightly earlier in the zodiac than the one before. This process is called the *precession of the equinoxes*. It explains why the vernal equinox, which used to occur in the constellation Aries, now technically takes place in Pisces. It also explains why the signs and the constellations are no longer aligned.

One of these days, the equinox will slip back even further, to the constellation of the Water Bearer, and the Age of Aquarius will officially begin. Astrologers differ as to when that will happen because it depends on how you measure the constellations. If only they were neater! If only they were the same size! Instead, they bump into each other and overlap, and their boundaries are a matter of opinion. Do you use the artificial, right-angled, patchwork-like borders assigned to each constellation by the International Astronomical Union in 1930? Or do you look to the ecliptic, which has been artificially divided into 12 equal sections, one per sign? A Belgian astronomer, using the IAU measurements, suggests that the Age of Aquarius will begin in 2597. Another Belgian, writing in February 1890, announced that the Age of Aquarius would begin the very next month. 1844 has been nominated, along with 1962, 2012, and 3573. I cast with my vote with the English astronomer Nicholas Campion, who believes that the Age of Aquarius will begin — or has begun — between 1447 and 3596. Sounds right to me.

In short, there is no agreement except on this one point: Eventually, the equinox point will cycle backwards through the zodiac, all the way to Aries. That process takes about 25,800 years and is known as the Great Year. Our current Great Year began around 2000 BCE. Around the year 23800, the next one will begin. The vernal equinox will return to Aries. The constellations and the divisions of the ecliptic will align, and astrologers will be able to skip this entire explanation. Meanwhile, the constellations and the signs of the zodiac are not the same.

Skeptics who attack astrology — and for some reason, these wary souls can be amazingly hostile — often point to the changing position of the constellations and the precession of the equinoxes as proof that astrology is bogus. The truth is that astrologers are well aware of this phenomenon. In western astrology, the constellations are signposts or symbols. What matters is the division of the ecliptic. The stars, glorious though they are, have nothing to do with your sign.

For that reason, I avoid the term "star sign." It's an enchanting phrase, and I wish I could use it in good conscience. I don't because it misrepresents astrology as it is usually practiced. I prefer the accuracy and simplicity of "Sun sign," and that is the phrase I use in this book.

Identifying the Signs of the Zodiac

There are twelve signs in the wheel of the zodiac, each one named after a constellation, each with its own style and substance. Together they weave a narrative of human life, a progression that goes something like this:

>> **Aries** initiates the cycle with a rush of activity. Like the Big Bang, it kicks everything into motion. It is the sign of action.

>> **Taurus** calms and consolidates that ferocious energy, bringing it down to earth in a tangible form and into the body. Taurus is the sign of the senses.

>> **Gemini** activates the mind, stimulates curiosity, and forges connections through communication. It is the sign of language.

>> **Cancer** turns inward, bringing feelings into consciousness, cultivating the idea of home and family, and seeking security. It is the sign of emotion.

>> **Leo** celebrates, dramatizes, and creates. It is the sign of self-expression.

>> **Virgo** organizes, evaluates, develops techniques, and attends to details. It is the sign of analysis.

>> **Libra** reaches beyond itself, striving for balance through interaction with others and through the power of ideas. It is the sign of relationship.

>> **Scorpio** investigates the mysteries of human nature, diving deep into the inner world and the hidden self. It is the sign of transformation.

>> **Sagittarius** pursues independence, adventure, education, and the wisdom of philosophy or religion. It is the sign of the seeker.

>> **Capricorn** elevates purpose, shoulders responsibility, and creates civilization. It is the sign of structure.

> » **Aquarius** seeks liberation, focuses on society, and simultaneously supports individuality. It is the sign of community.

> » **Pisces** embodies compassion and the spiritual side of life. It is the sign of dreams and the imagination. It also oversees chaos, out of which will arise the creative fire of Aries. And so the cycle will begin anew.

OPHIUCHUS AND THE 13TH SIGN

It happens every few years, as reliable as the force of gravity: Someone announces that there are 13 constellations in the zodiac, not 12. Uproar ensues.

This folly became a story in 1970, when a book called *Astrology 14* by Steven Schmidt argued that two large constellations — Cetus the Whale, and Ophiuchus the Serpent Bearer — lie along the band of the ecliptic and therefore the zodiac should be expanded to include them. The book received enormous publicity, including a write-up in *Time* magazine, and the idea caught on, although not entirely. Cetus, which barely grazes the ecliptic, never inspired much of a following. But Ophiuchus, a large constellation squeezed in between Scorpius and Sagittarius, did.

Since then, books advocating for the addition of Ophiuchus as the13th sign have appeared with thudding regularity. In 1995, British astrologer Walter Berg published *The 13 Signs of the Zodiac*, which sold respectably in the United Kingdom but became a giant bestseller when it was translated into Japanese and published there. In 2011, the story flared up again when the Minnesota Planetarium Society announced that the constellations had moved. Ophiuchus was now part of zodiac, they said, and astrologers ought to sit up and pay attention. The BBC reported the findings. Fox news reported the findings. Even *Time*, which first publicized the story in 1970, weighed in. Their article began, "The cosmic news broke without warning."

For the zillionth time, astrologers responded. They acknowledged that due to the precession of the equinoxes, the constellations have shifted (a fact I discuss on a previous page). It's not news to astrologers.

Nor does it matter, because in western astrology, the signs are determined by the Sun's position on the ecliptic, not by the stars. On the vernal equinox, when day and night are roughly equal, the Sun enters the portion of the ecliptic known as Aries and the astrological year begins. The other signs follow, 30 degrees at a time. The stars and constellations do not determine sign.

So might you be an Ophiuchan? In a word, no. Not in this world.

REMEMBER

The sign that the Sun occupied at the instant of your birth is the most basic astrological fact about you. It defines your ego, motivations, and approach to life. But the Sun isn't the only planet, and your Sun sign isn't your only sign. (For astrological purposes, both luminaries — the Sun and the Moon — are called planets. Do yourself a favor and don't use this terminology when talking to astronomers.) Mercury, Venus, the Moon, Mars, Jupiter, Saturn, Uranus, Neptune, and Pluto represent distinct types of energy, each of which expresses itself in the style of the sign it happens to occupy. When you look at your chart, you will see that not every sign has a planet within its borders. Nonetheless, every sign is in your chart somewhere. The entire zodiac resides within each of us.

REMEMBER

Astrologically speaking, your Sun sign is the most essential fact about you. To determine your sign, use Table 1-1. But remember that the dates vary slightly from year to year. That's because a circle has 360 degrees, with each sign allotted precisely 30 degrees. But a year has 365 days, not counting leap years. Thanks to that inconvenient difference, the signs don't divide into days as neatly as one might wish, and minor variations pop up regularly. Take the first day of Cancer the Crab. Usually it's June 21. But in 2012, 2016, and occasional other years, it was June 20. The bottom line? If you were born on the first or final day of any sign — that is, if you were born "on the cusp" — I advise caution. Before you don that Sagittarian sweatshirt or invest in that Scorpio tattoo, get an accurate copy of your natal chart and check your Sun sign.

TABLE 1-1   **The Sun Signs**

Sign	Dates	Symbol
Aries the Ram	March 20–April 18	♈
Taurus the Bull	April 19–May 20	♉
Gemini the Twins	May 21–June 20	♊
Cancer the Crab	June 21–July 22	♋
Leo the Lion	July 23–August 22	♌
Virgo the Virgin	August 23–September 22	♍
Libra the Scales	September 23–October 22	♎
Scorpio the Scorpion	October 23–November 21	♏
Sagittarius the Archer	November 22–December 21	♐

(continued)

TABLE 1-1 *(continued)*

Sign	Dates	Symbol
Capricorn the Goat	December 22–January 19	♑
Aquarius the Water Bearer	January 20–February 18	♒
Pisces the Fish	February 19–March 19	♓

Understanding the Sun Signs

Like any truly satisfying system, astrology classifies and interprets its basic components in a number of ways. The twelve signs can be split into two groups, each of which is associated with a positive or negative *polarity*. They can be organized into three groups, each of which has been assigned a quality or *modality* — cardinal, fixed, or mutable. Most famously, they can be divided into four groups, each of which is associated with an *element*: fire, earth, air, or water.

Polarity: Dividing the zodiac by two

Beginning with Aries, six *positive* or *masculine* signs alternate with six *negative* or *feminine* signs. The sexist language, I regret to say, is traditional. Many astrologers use the terms yin and yang instead. Call them what you will, both qualities are part of every individual's chart. The meanings are as follows:

>> **Positive or yang** signs — Aries, Gemini, Leo, Libra, Sagittarius, and Aquarius — are more extroverted, objective, assertive, feisty, energetic, and determined.

>> **Negative or yin** signs — Taurus, Cancer, Virgo, Scorpio, Capricorn, and Pisces — are more introverted, subjective, receptive, reflective, open, and nurturing.

Modality: Dividing the zodiac by three

The zodiac can also be divided into three groups, each with its own way of interacting with the world, its own mode of operation or *modality*. The three modalities — cardinal, fixed, and mutable — occur in a repeating sequence: first a cardinal sign, then a fixed sign, then a mutable sign.

>> **The Cardinal signs** are natural leaders, enterprising and encouraging, initiating change, and making things happen. The cardinal signs are Aries, Cancer, Libra, and Capricorn.

>> **The Fixed signs** are focused, persistent, and firm. They are Taurus, Leo, Scorpio, and Aquarius.

>> **The Mutable signs** adapt and adjust. They are known for flexibility and resilience. Those signs are Gemini, Virgo, Sagittarius, and Pisces.

Elements: Dividing the zodiac by four

Allocating each sign to one of the four ancient elements of Western thought is probably the most well-known and evocative method of classification. The four elements are fire, earth, air, and water.

>> **Fire** is the first of the traditional elements, and you don't need to be an astrologer to guess what it means. Ancient astrologers associated fire with the forces of creation. That association stands. Fire brings vitality, activity, and desire. It generates heat. People born under these dynamic signs are vigorous and courageous. They're also restless and impatient. And they have trouble accepting limits — which may be why they're prone to burn out. The fire signs are Aries, Leo, and Sagittarius.

>> **Earth** signs turn the spark of fire into something tangible. Cautious where fire is bold, earth signs are sensible, productive, and materialistic — and I don't mean that in a bad way. Sensuous and responsive, they understand and respect material things, including nature. They are attuned to reality, and they get things done. The earth signs are Taurus, Virgo, and Capricorn.

>> **Air** enlivens the intellect and enhances sociability. Those born under its influence are bright, curious, versatile, and intellectually restless, always collecting information, trying out ideas, and connecting people. They revel in conversation and are supremely social. The air signs are Gemini, Libra, and Aquarius.

>> **Water** amplifies emotions and awareness. Vulnerable and receptive, those born under its influence are highly sensitive and often swamped by their feelings. They're intuitive, empathetic, and instinctively responsive to the emotional atmosphere. They also tend to have a spiritual bent. The water signs are Cancer, Scorpio, and Pisces.

Putting the zodiac back together

Once you know the order of the signs, it's easy to assign them their correct polarity, modality, and element. You don't have to bother memorizing them because those classifications always occur in sequence, as you can clearly see in Table 1-2. Even if you know nothing else about a sign, those classifications tell you a lot.

TABLE 1-2   **The Qualities of the Signs**

Sign	Polarity	Modality	Element
Aries	Positive	Cardinal	Fire
Taurus	Negative	Fixed	Earth
Gemini	Positive	Mutable	Air
Cancer	Negative	Cardinal	Water
Leo	Positive	Fixed	Fire
Virgo	Negative	Mutable	Earth
Libra	Positive	Cardinal	Air
Scorpio	Negative	Fixed	Water
Sagittarius	Positive	Mutable	Fire
Capricorn	Negative	Cardinal	Earth
Aquarius	Positive	Fixed	Air
Pisces	Negative	Mutable	Water

Consider, for example, Cancer the Crab. It's the sign of negative cardinal water. This tells you that Crabs tend to be introverted and receptive (negative or yin), with a propensity for taking the initiative (cardinal), and a profound sense of emotional awareness (water).

Or look at Leo, which lives next door to Cancer but boasts a very different personality, as is always the case with adjacent signs. Leo is the sign of positive fixed fire. Its natives tend to be outgoing and assertive (positive or yang), determined (fixed), warm, and full of personality (fire).

REMEMBER

The polarity, modality, and element provide a rudimentary sense of what each sign is about. For a detailed description of the signs, turn to Part 2.

THE ZODIAC AND THE BODY

The zodiac arcs across the cosmos, huge and impossibly remote. Its symbolic equivalent, small and incredibly close, is the human form. About two thousand years ago, the Roman astrologer Marcus Manilius correlated each sign of the zodiac with a part of the body in a sequence that starts at the head with Aries and runs down to the feet, which belong to Pisces. Medieval art, both European and Islamic, includes many fine renderings of the so-called Zodiac Man, a figure that also appears in ancient medical texts. Indeed, medicine as it was once practiced looked to astrology not only for an understanding of disease — the Black Death that swept across Europe between 1347 and 1351 was widely blamed on a planetary conjunction and an eclipse — but also for cures. Throughout the Middle Ages (and beyond), medical students at the University of Bologna and elsewhere were required to study astrology.

I have concerns about medical astrology. I have seen cases in which astrological diagnosis has proven to be weirdly accurate. Still, it's not a sport for amateurs. To make an accurate diagnosis through astrology requires serious expertise. I love this diagram anyway because it reminds us that the spectrum of experience represented by the signs of the zodiac is universal and lives in each one of us.

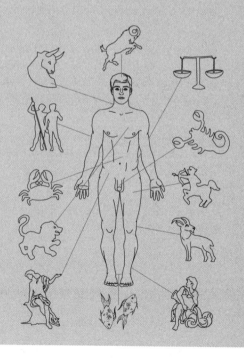

Considering the Sun, the Moon, the Planets, and more

The Sun, the Moon, and the planets play individual parts in your horoscope. Each one carries a certain kind of energy and represents a different facet of what it means to be human. Their meanings are as follows:

>> **The Sun** represents your essential self, will, and individuality. More than any other celestial body, it represents who you are.

>> **The Moon** represents your emotions, subconscious, instincts, habits, and memory.

>> **Mercury** symbolizes your approach to communication, your reasoning ability, the way you think, and your curiosity.

>> **Venus** represents your approach to love, attraction, beauty, money, possessions, and the arts.

>> **Mars** is the planet of action, desire, and aggression. It represents your physical energy, combativeness, enterprise, and courage.

>> **Jupiter** is the planet of expansion and good fortune. It represents growth, prosperity, abundance, generosity, religion, philosophy, and wisdom. (Jupiter is said to represent the "higher mind" while Mercury, the planet of gossip and word games, must make do with the "lower mind.") Jupiter's position in a horoscope tells you where you're lucky and where your efforts are most likely to be rewarded.

>> **Saturn** represents limitation, caution, organization, endurance, and discipline. It tells you where you have to face your fears — and also where you're ambitious.

>> **Uranus** represents rebellion, revolutionary change, originality, independence, and everything unexpected or unconventional. It also represents technology, electricity, and invention.

>> **Neptune** represents spirituality, dreams, psychic ability, intuition, disintegration, compassion, self-sacrifice, deception, illusion, and imagination.

>> **Pluto**, which was officially relegated to a dwarf planet in 2006 but maintains its status within the astrological community, represents destruction, regeneration, renewal, and transformation.

Besides the planets, many astrologers sneak a few other celestial bodies into their charts. The most notable is Chiron, which was discovered in 1977. It has been classified as an asteroid, a minor planet, a comet, and finally a centaur. Like the mythological half man/half horse for whom they are named, centaurs are hybrids, part asteroid and part comet. **Chiron** represents past wounds and pathways to healing. Many astrologers associate it with holistic medicine.

REMEMBER

In every chart, some planets are more powerful than others. But every chart includes every planet, and every planet has its own meaning. One way to summarize all this is to associate a single word with each planet. These keywords appear in Table 1-3.

TABLE 1-3 **Keywords for the Planets**

Planet	Keyword	Symbol
Sun	Self	☉
Moon	Emotion	☽
Mercury	Communication	☿
Venus	Love	♀
Mars	Action	♂
Jupiter	Expansion	♃
Saturn	Restriction	♄
Uranus	Revolution	♅
Neptune	Imagination	♆
Pluto	Transformation	♇
Chiron	Healing	⚷

Who Rules? Discovering the Rulers of the Signs

In an ideal universe, each planet would function perfectly well in each sign. But astrologers have long noted that some placements seem to work better than others. The sign in which a planet is most effective — that is, the sign with which it shares the greatest affinity, the sign whose style is most like its own — is the sign that it is said to rule. Two thousand years ago, when astrologers only had to worry about the Sun, the Moon, and five planets, they connected the planets and the signs this way:

>> The Sun ruled Leo.

>> The Moon ruled Cancer.

>> Mercury ruled Gemini and Virgo.

>> Venus ruled Taurus and Libra.

>> Mars ruled Aries and Scorpio.

>> Jupiter ruled Pisces and Sagittarius.

>> Saturn ruled Aquarius and Capricorn.

After Uranus was discovered in 1781, followed by Neptune in 1846 and Pluto in 1930, astrologers modified the system, allotting one sign to each of the newly discovered planets. Uranus was designated the ruler of Aquarius, Neptune was pronounced the lord of Pisces, and Pluto was delegated to Scorpio. Mercury and Venus continued to rule two signs each. Until recently, the most commonly accepted planetary rulers were as follows:

>> The Sun rules Leo.

>> The Moon rules Cancer.

>> Mercury rules Gemini and Virgo.

>> Venus rules Taurus and Libra.

>> Mars rules Aries.

>> Jupiter rules Sagittarius.

>> Saturn rules Capricorn.

>> Uranus rules Aquarius.

>> Neptune rules Pisces.

>> Pluto rules Scorpio.

Today, the consensus surrounding rulers has begun to unravel, with many astrologers giving more weight to traditional rulers than was the fashion only a few decades ago. Some astrologers have reverted entirely to the pre-industrial rulers, eliminating Uranus, Neptune and Pluto. Other astrologers have decided to keep the old rulers plus the new planets. The signs most affected by that approach are Scorpio, Aquarius, and Pisces, each of which can now boast two rulers, one traditional and one modern:

>> Scorpio is ruled by Mars, its traditional ruler, and Pluto.

>> Aquarius is ruled by Saturn, its traditional ruler, and Uranus.

>> Pisces is ruled by Jupiter, its traditional ruler, and Neptune.

As for Chiron, some astrologers believe that it rules Virgo, Pisces, or both. Others associate it with Sagittarius. Many don't bother with it at all, and it has not been officially assigned to a sign. The same is true for other asteroids, dwarf planets, and astronomical points. Astrologers might pop them into a chart, but they have not given them dominion over particular signs.

Determining Planetary Dignities

Astrological tradition holds that, in addition to the sign it rules, each planet earns high grades in another sign — the sign of its *exaltation*. The planet operates less well in two other signs: the sign of its *detriment*, which is opposite the sign it rules, and the sign of its *fall*, which opposes the sign of its exaltation. Table 1-4 gives you the details.

How does this affect your chart? A planet exalted or in its home sign (or domicile) expresses itself with ease and is accorded "dignity." A planet in its detriment or fall — positions sometimes referred to as debilities — may feel impeded or weak. Take Mars. In Aries, Mars has no trouble being assertive. Aries supports that. In diplomatic Libra, the opposite sign, the warrior spirit of Mars feels tamped down, stifled. Each planet is happiest in the signs where it can best express its essential nature.

A planet can gain dignity in at least five ways. I'm only going to consider two: essential dignity, which depends upon the sign the planet occupies, and accidental dignity, which depends upon the house placement.

Essential dignities

This isn't the first thing to consider when doing a chart. But it does provide an additional bit of information, another point to consider. I pay particular attention when a planet occupies its home sign or sign of exaltation. No matter what else is happening with that planet, it is stronger than it might appear. The dignities are listed in Table 1-4.

TABLE 1-4 **Table of Essential Planetary Dignities**

Planet	Rulership	Detriment	Exaltation	Fall
Sun	Leo	Aquarius	Aries	Libra
Moon	Cancer	Capricorn	Taurus	Scorpio
Mercury	Gemini	Sagittarius	Aquarius	Leo
	Virgo	Pisces		
Venus	Taurus	Scorpio	Pisces	Virgo
	Libra	Aries		
Mars	Aries	Libra	Capricorn	Cancer
	Scorpio	Taurus		
Jupiter	Sagittarius	Gemini	Cancer	Capricorn
	Pisces	Virgo		
Saturn	Capricorn	Cancer	Libra	Aries
	Aquarius	Leo		
Uranus*	Aquarius	Leo		
Neptune*	Pisces	Virgo		
Pluto*	Scorpio	Taurus		

* Although astrologers have confidently named Uranus, Neptune, and Pluto as rulers or co-rulers of Aquarius, Pisces, and Scorpio, those planets have not been given signs of exaltation or fall. These things take time.

Accidental dignities

Another way to dignify a planet is by house placement. Imagine that the first house is equivalent to Aries, the first sign. If Mars, the ruler of Aries, happens to be in the first house, it is accidentally dignified, regardless of the sign it occupies. Similarly, Saturn is the ruler of Capricorn, the tenth sign, so it is accidentally dignified in the tenth house, no matter what sign it's in. Table 1-5 shows you where each planet is accidentally dignified.

REAL LIFE EXAMPLE

What do Muhammad Ali, Albert Einstein, and Kim Kardashian have in common? On the face of it, not much. But all three have Saturn accidentally dignified in the tenth house, a placement that correlates with success, public recognition, and fame.

TABLE 1-5   ## Table of Accidental Planetary Dignities

House	Accidental planetary dignity
1	Mars
2	Venus
3	Mercury
4	Moon
5	Sun
6	Mercury
7	Venus
8	Mars and Pluto
9	Jupiter
10	Saturn
11	Saturn and Uranus
12	Neptune and Jupiter

Assessing the Ascendant

Another major component of your chart is the *Ascendant* or *rising sign* — the sign that was climbing over the eastern horizon at the moment of your birth. It describes your mask or persona, the surface personality that you show the world.

Have you ever had a friend who was Miss Congeniality — until you got to know her? Did you ever encounter anyone who seemed standoffish and cold at first but warmed up later on? Do you know anyone whose devil-may-care, lighthearted attitude masks a calculating, manipulative mind? And have you ever wondered how you strike other people, especially when they don't know you well? Your horoscope provides the answer. While your Sun sign may not be apparent to people, they definitely notice your Ascendant. It's your image, your facade, your surface. Whether it clashes or harmonizes with your Sun sign, it describes the way people see you and the impression that you make. Indeed, some astrologers consider the ruler of the Ascendant — that is, the planet that rules your rising sign — to be the overall ruler of your chart.

No matter what your Sun sign is, any one of the 12 signs might have been rising over the eastern horizon at the moment of your birth. If you were born at dawn, when the Sun was just peeking over the horizon, you already know your rising sign: It's the same as your Sun sign. If you were born at any other time of day, your rising sign and Sun sign differ.

For those people whose Sun signs and rising signs are identical, the surface and the substance are the same. For everyone else, what you see isn't necessarily what you get.

REAL LIFE
EXAMPLE

Consider the artist Vincent Van Gogh. With Cancer rising, his emotional sensitivity was obvious. We can see it even now in the wary expression (and bandaged ear) of his many self-portraits. But his extreme vulnerability was only part of his nature. Beneath the insecurity, he was an Aries, restless, competitive, and courageous. His pioneering, energetic nature is clearly visible in the confident, quick brushstrokes, churning colors, and wild vigor of his groundbreaking canvases.

REMEMBER

If you have a copy of your chart, it's easy to figure out your Ascendant: it's the sign at the nine o'clock spot on the wheel. If you don't have your chart, you can get one by going to one of the websites listed in Chapter 2 and entering your birth data as instructed. And if you don't have a reliable birth time? Don't worry about it. Even without a correct Ascendant, your birth chart is a map of your deepest self, and it offers whole continents of information to be explored.

Taking the House Tour

Whether you're a workaholic Virgo or a spiritually inclined Pisces, you still have to deal with money, work, health, siblings, and everything else that's part of life. Those areas are described by the *houses*. The houses slice the sky into 12 parts, beginning with the Ascendant and the first house. Their meanings are described in Table 1-6.

Just as every chart includes all the planets, every horoscope has all 12 houses. Not every house will be occupied by a planet. But every house will have a sign on the *cusp*, or beginning of the house, that describes your approach to the concerns of that house. For instance, if Taurus is on the cusp of your sixth house of health and work, you are likely to be dependable, productive, and patient on the job, even if that house is empty. You're a hard worker. And one more thing: you'd probably enjoy having a dog.

REMEMBER

The word *cusp* is used in two ways in astrology. When astrologers refer to the cusp of a house, they are talking about the gateway to that house, the place where it begins. When people say they were born "on the cusp," they usually mean that their birthday falls at the end of one sign or the start of another, and they're not sure what sign is theirs, an issue I discuss in the nearby sidebar "Questlove on the cusp."

Now you've got the basics. Together, the signs, planets, and houses make up the basic vocabulary of astrology. There's more. (There's always more.) But for now, you have everything you need to begin the excavation of your chart. If you don't have a copy of it, the next chapter will tell you how to remedy that situation.

TABLE 1-6 ## Houses and Their Significance

House	Areas of Concern
First house	Appearance, surface personality, and the impression you make on others
Second house	Money, possessions, wealth; the things you value; your urge to acquire
Third house	Communication, language, short journeys, brothers and sisters, neighbors, early education, attitude toward learning
Fourth house	Home, roots, real estate, security, one parent (usually the mother); also, circumstances at the end of life
Fifth house	Romance, children, recreation, creativity, self-expression
Sixth house	Work, health and healing, service, habits and routines; also, pets
Seventh house	Relationships, partnerships, open enemies, and the general public
Eighth house	Sex, death, transformation, joint resources, other people's money, mystery, magic, and occult interests
Ninth house	Higher education, long journeys, travel, religion, philosophy, and publishing
Tenth house	Career, vocation, status, reputation, one parent (usually the father)
Eleventh house	Friends, community, teamwork, hopes, wishes, and aspirations
Twelfth house	Seclusion, secrets, the subconscious, hidden enemies, spiritual interests

QUESTLOVE ON THE CUSP

Take the case of Ahmir Khalib Thompson, aka Questlove, the Grammy-winning drummer and co-founder of The Roots, the hip-hop house band for *The Tonight Show Starring Jimmy Fallon*. He is a DJ, a record producer, an entrepreneurial foodie, an author, an adjunct professor, and more. But what's his sign? He was born on January 20, 1971, time unknown. And therein lies the problem. Is he a goal-oriented, disciplined Capricorn, a sign known for its work ethic, or a rebellious, iconoclastic Aquarian? He can't be both . . . or can he?

If he was born before 12:13 p.m., he's a Capricorn, which would certainly explain his ambition and productivity. If he was born after 12:13, he's a freedom-loving, highly individual Aquarian.

So which is it? The variety of his accomplishments, musical and otherwise, and his interest in collaboration argue in favor of Aquarius. Compared to Capricorn, Aquarius is quirkier and more individualistic, the sign of the maverick and the avant-garde. On paper, it sounds hipper and more creative. I suspect the man himself might prefer it.

On the other hand, he did not come to music as a form of rebellion. On the contrary, music was, in his phrase, the "family business." (His father was a well-known doo-wop singer.) He came to it as a responsible Capricorn, not a rebellious Aquarian. An indefatigable worker, he has built his brand with care, touring relentlessly and aligning himself with established institutions such as *The Tonight Show* and New York University.

So what's his sign? In the absence of a complete birth certificate, a clarifying word from his mother, or a rectification by an astrologer who specializes in that technique, only he can decide which sign sounds more like the person he knows himself to be.

If your situation is similar, the same holds true for you. Astrologers will tell you that your Sun is in one sign or the other, not both. That's true. But there are other planets, and they also bring something to the party. Questlove has Mercury in Capricorn and the North Node of the Moon in Aquarius. Even without the Sun, he has a touch of both signs. So where is his Sun? In his heart of hearts, he probably knows.

IN THIS CHAPTER

» Creating your chart the old-fashioned way

» Assembling your birth information

» Getting your chart online for free

» Considering astrological software

» Assessing apps

» Wandering around the web

Chapter **2**

Getting Your Precise Horoscope: The Old Way, the Internet Way, and the Software

What could be more fabulously arcane than an astrological chart? Well, lots of things: alchemical sigils, kabalistic diagrams, magical amulets — you name it. But this book isn't about them. It's about astrology, which may seem esoteric at first glance but actually is not. That's because an astrological chart, for all its mysterious-looking symbols and mandala-like shape, has nothing mystical about it. It's a simple representation of the real world — a picture, in streamlined form, of the solar system at the time of your birth. The interpretation may be complicated and nuanced, but the image itself is straightforward.

To visualize the cosmos as it was when you were born, imagine standing on the Earth at that precise instant. Imagine, too, that you're facing south and looking at a gigantic clock face that has been superimposed on the sky. To your left, in the nine o'clock position, is the eastern horizon. That's your Ascendant. If you were born around dawn, that's where the Sun is. If you were born around midday, your Sun is high in the sky in front of you, near the twelve o'clock mark. To your right, in the three o'clock position, lies the western horizon. If you were born around dusk, that's where your Sun is. And if you came into this world around midnight, when your part of the world was dark and the other side of the planet was awash in daylight, your Sun can be found near the bottom of your chart, somewhere around the six o'clock spot.

If you happen to know the phase of the Moon at your birth, you can locate it in a similar way. Were you born under a new moon? Then your Moon and Sun are in roughly the same place. Born under a full moon? Then the Sun and Moon are opposite each other — 180° apart. If one is rising, the other is setting.

The point is this: Your natal chart is neither a metaphysical construct nor a mystical diagram. It's a stylized map of the heavens that shows the Sun, the Moon, and the planets at a precise moment in time from a specific place. The astrologer's task is to interpret all that information. But first, you have to get an accurate copy of your chart.

Casting Your Chart the Old-Fashioned Way

In the past, before the computer and related technology infiltrated every molecule of human existence, casting a chart was more than a challenge. It was a commitment. It required hours of free time, a fearless attitude towards mathematics, the ability to concentrate on minutiae, and a willingness to grapple with longitude, latitude, standard meridians, local time, daylight saving time, universal time, sidereal time, and a table of proportional logarithms. If you made a mistake — and it was easy to do that, adding when you should have subtracted or copying the wrong numbers from a page entirely covered with rows and columns of numbers — well, you had to start all over again. Most people didn't have the patience.

I felt differently. I liked staying up late with a pot of tea and all my astrological supplies: a planetary almanac or ephemeris, a heavy atlas, a book of time zones and time changes, a *Table of Houses* (my battered hardcover — it must be around here somewhere — had a copyright date of 1893), pads of yellow paper, and the special horoscope blanks I bought at a metaphysical bookstore. As I calculated each planetary position and house cusp, drew the symbols of the signs and planets onto the wheel of the chart, figured out the geometrical relationships among the planets, and counted up how many were in fire signs, in earth signs, and so on, the chart — and the person — slowly grew clear in my mind.

That process takes time, and I don't do it anymore. I use a computer, like every other astrologer. With a computer or a smart phone anyone can generate an accurate chart in less time than it takes to sharpen a pencil. It's a satisfying form of instant gratification, which is why, as nostalgic as I occasionally feel for those long-ago evenings of computation and revelation, I wouldn't go back.

In those days, many people who were fascinated by astrology never learned it because they were put off by the math or by the amount of time required. Those issues no longer exist. In the rest of this chapter I tell you how to get an accurate copy of your chart the easy way — via the internet.

First Things First: Gathering the Information You Need

Before you can gaze in wonder at the wonders of your chart, you need the following information:

>> The month, day, and year of your birth

>> The place of your birth

>> The precise time of your birth

Most people know the month, day, year, and place of their birth. If there's a problem, it's usually with time. Time matters because it determines your rising sign (see Chapter 11) as well as the house positions for your planets (see Chapter 12). Without a birth time, those components of your chart are unknowable. Having an accurate time is also important if one of your planets changed signs on the day you were born. Is your Moon in Leo or in Virgo? There's a big difference. That's why I recommend that you corroborate your birth time through the official record, your birth certificate.

TIP

If you don't already have a copy of your birth certificate, the most reliable way to get one is to go to the National Center for Health Statistics at http://www.cdc.gov/nchs/index.htm and click on "National Vital Statistics System" followed by "How to get a birth, death, marriage, or divorce certificate." That will send you to a list of U.S. states and territories (plus "foreign or high-seas events," for those whose birth stories are more dramatic than most). Click on the place of your birth, follow instructions, and be prepared to pay a fee, different in every location.

Once you have your birth certificate, you can be confident that the information on it is more or less correct, although I marvel at the vast number of people who, according to their birth certificates, were born exactly on the hour or half hour. Statistically speaking, there are way too many of us. Still, the time on your birth certificate, rounded off though it may be, has to be considered the gold standard.

If you don't have a birth certificate, do some sleuthing. Start by asking your mother. But don't be surprised if her memory of what must surely have been the highlight of her life turns out to be spotty. It's shocking how many parents can't remember when their children were born. They know the date — birthdays are easy — but the time is another story. They can't recall if it was 2:05 or 5:02. They don't know if it was a.m. or p.m. One mother confessed to me that she wasn't sure who was born at 10:06 a.m.: her daughter or herself. As every courtroom attorney knows, eyewitness testimony is notoriously unreliable. This is just another instance of that truth.

Dealing with approximate birth times

It can happen, especially if you were born in the United Kingdom, Ireland, Australia, Canada, or India, that a birth certificate will not include a time. In that case, you may have to rely on family legend. Maybe you've been told that you were born after breakfast or in the middle of *Saturday Night Live*. If that is your situation, take the information and run with it. When you're ready to get your chart, choose a time that corresponds to the legend. Born in the middle of rush hour? Figure that for 6:00 p.m. and carry on.

Coping with an absence of information

A more significant problem arises if you have no idea whatsoever of your time of birth, and no way to find it out. I have a beloved friend, one of many children, who never knew her birth time. And then one day, things got rapidly worse. During an astonishing conversation with an older sister, she discovered that no one in her family could vouch with 100 percent certainty for the day of her birth — or even the month. Suddenly she wasn't sure whether she was a Libra (no way) or a Scorpio (yes). This rare state of affairs is an astrologer's worst-case scenario.

If your birth time is irretrievably lost, your ascendant and house placements are unknowable. You also face a small additional problem: what to do when an astrological website or piece of software requires you to fill in a birth time. Here are three ways to handle that:

>> Assume you were born at noon. That way, the calculations can't be more than 12 hours off. Even the moon, which spins through the entire zodiac in a month, can't be more than about six and a half degrees off. So the planetary positions will be roughly correct. But the house positions won't be, which means that the Sun isn't really at the top of your chart (unless, by coincidence, you really were born around noon). It just looks that way.

>> Assume you were born at sunrise. Not all astrology websites allow that possibility, but many do. Just choose the sunrise option and proceed. As with noon charts, remember that the Sun probably isn't in the first house (unless you really were born at dawn), and the house positions are only a guess. (If you were born via C-section but don't know exactly when, you might want to assume that you were born at 8:00 a.m., which is statistically the most common birth time in the United States, entirely due to C-section deliveries.)

>> Use what are known as "natural houses." With natural houses, Aries always occupies the whole of the first house, Taurus occupies the second, and so on, all the way to Pisces, which encompasses the entire twelfth house. Thus, if you were born under Libra, which is the seventh sign of the zodiac, your Sun will be in the seventh house. Again, since you don't know when you were born, these house positions are only provisional. But without them, you'd be looking at little more than a list. By using natural houses, you can see how the planets are arranged, what signs they are in, and how they interact with each other — and that's a wealth of information.

Finally, if your birth time truly is lost, there is one more option. You can commission a professional astrologer to *rectify* your chart. Rectification is a complex, laborious process. It involves working backwards from major events in your life (such as marriage, divorce, the birth of a child, or the death of a parent) to make an educated guess about your probable birth time. Some astrology software includes rectification modules, making it possible to do this yourself. But I would advise against that; it's too easy to let wishful thinking influence your results. Ask a seasoned professional, someone who has considerable experience with this specific technique. Rectification isn't a sure bet, especially in the hands of amateurs. But when it works, it works.

Getting Your Horoscope Online for Free

Someday, should you resolve to quit your day job and become a professional astrologer, you may want to learn how to cast a chart the old-fashioned way. It wouldn't be a waste of effort, and if you decide to become a certified astrologer through one of the official astrological organizations, such as the American

Federation of Astrologers, you'll be required to master that skill. At the moment, though, there's no need to climb that particular mountain because you can obtain a copy of your chart for free just by going to an astrological website and entering the date, time, and place of your birth. Many websites offer free horoscopes. Here are a few of the best:

>> **Astrolabe** (`https://alabe.com`): Astrolabe provides a no-frills birth chart with two or three pages of interpretation. Its resources and services are not as extensive as those of some other websites, and its charts are not as lovely. But if you go to this website, look for "Free Astro Chart" (or words to that effect), enter your birth data, and hit "submit," your natal chart will instantly wing its way back to you. Astrolabe does not tempt you with too many bells and whistles. (Don't worry, I tell you in the following bullet points where to satisfy that craving.) But if you want an easy-to-read birth chart with some basic interpretation, you can get it here — fast and free.

>> **Astro-charts** (`https://astro-charts.com`): The first thing you'll see here are the words "Welcome to the home of beautiful astrology charts." That's an exaggeration, but the charts do look good, and they are accompanied by lists of planetary placements, aspects, and chart patterns. (See Chapter 14 for more on that subject.) They are not, however, accompanied by interpretation. For that, you have to pay. One other caveat: this website requires a birth time. There is neither an "unknown" option nor a sunrise option. If you don't know the time of your birth, I recommend that you create a noon chart by entering 12:00 p.m. as your time.

>> **Café Astrology** (`https://cafeastrology.com`): "Where do I begin?" asks the home page. A line or two below you will see the words "How to obtain my natal chart." Click on that, follow the instructions, and you will obtain an analysis of your chart. The chart itself does not appear until the end of the report. Keep scrolling past the multi-colored introductory tables, past the interpretative paragraphs, almost to the end. It's a pretty chart, but you'll have to look carefully for the house cusps, which are indicated with Roman numerals and delicate dashes. Cafe Astrology also offers dozens of articles, daily horoscopes, yearly overviews, all kinds of forecasts you can purchase, and a free yearly horoscope based on the day of your birth. Look for "If Today Is Your Birthday," even if today is not your birthday. A few extra clicks will bring you where you want to go.

>> **Astrodienst** (`www.astro.com`): And so we arrive at the oldest, most respected, and most professional astrological website. At Astrodienst, a Swiss site founded in 1980, you can do more than entertain yourself; you can

educate yourself. But navigating this site can be a challenge. Here's how to get your free natal chart:

1. Go to "Free Horoscopes," visible at the top of the home page on the left. Let the cursor hover over "Free Horoscopes." A menu will appear. One of the items (on the right-hand side, as of this writing) is "Natal Chart/Ascendant." Click on that.

2. Now you're on a page welcoming guest users and registered users. For the moment, count yourself a guest. Click on the words "click here to go to the data entry page."

3. On the data entry page, tick the box accepting their privacy policy. Then fill in your birth data and click "continue." Your chart will magically appear. To print it out on a page of its own, sans ads, click on the small circle in the middle.

Now you can go to town. You might browse through the section called "Free Horoscopes." Want a report on Love, Flirtation, and Sex, as reflected in your chart? A Psychological Portrait? A Yearly Horoscope Analysis? A Color Oracle? (Fun, though what this has to do with astrology, I do not know.) For a full report, you'll have to pay. Fortunately, the folks at Astrodienst are giving away free samples, and although those samples are abridged, they are perceptive and interesting. Also available are astrology lessons, a huge library of articles from multiple sources, daily and weekly forecasts, and an Astro-Databank of 56,611 public figures (and counting). The more you bop around this site, the more you'll discover.

REMEMBER

These are only a few of the websites that offer free natal charts. To assess some of the others, just Google "free birth chart" or "free natal chart" and shop around.

Investing in Software

Nothing in the astrological world is more fun that being able to cast charts for anyone at a moment's notice. Astrological software is endlessly diverting, but it isn't cheap. If you decide it's worth the investment, here are a few recommendations.

Maximizing the Mac

To this day, despite the genius of the late Steve Jobs and the unstoppable expansion of Apple products into every coffee shop on the planet, Macintosh users — and we are legion — have remarkably limited choices for astrological software. Supposedly, by the time this book is published, that will have changed. May it be so. Meanwhile, I recommend these programs:

>> **TimePassages:** Henry Seltzer, the founder of Astrograph Software, designed this software as a universal tool, usable with both Mac and Windows. In addition to calculating birth charts, transits, comparison charts, and more, it offers one irresistible feature, especially for novices. After you generate a chart, you can click on anything within it — a planet, a house cusp, an aspect line running between two planets, or a symbol on the aspect grid — and an interpretation will pop up. Not sure what it means to have Moon in the tenth house,? Or a Grand Trine, which he is also fortunate enough to have? One click generates a paragraph of explanation. For a free demo, go to `https://www.astrograph.com`.

>> **Io Programs:** Time Cycles Research Programs offers this software for the professional, but you don't need to be professional to use it. Io Edition, their core program, calculates charts; Io Interpreter provides analysis; Io Forecast, Io Solar Return, and Io Lunar Return peer into the future; Io Body and Soul offers a holistic astrological approach to health and wellness. And there are additional options. You can reach Time Cycles by e-mail at `astrology@timecycles.com`, or on the Web at `www.timecycles.com`.

>> **Solar Fire.** This ambitious, top-of-the-line program has long been available for Windows only. By the time this book is published, I'm told, it will also be available for Macintosh computers. To find out what Solar Fire can do (short answer: it can do almost everything), read on.

TIP

If you decide to invest in astrological software but feel the need for counsel from a recognized expert, there's only one way to go: Contact astrologer Hank Friedman, longtime software reviewer for *Mountain Astrologer* and other periodicals. The consultation is free, and he sells all the software at a discount. You can e-mail him at `stars@soulhealing.com` or visit his website at `https://www.soulhealing.com`. There you will find information about software, links to free software demos, more than a hundred fifty free tutorials on western and Vedic astrology, and an impressive array of recipes involving chocolate.

Playing with the PC

The software options for PC are too numerous to do justice to here. I asked Hank Friedman to make a few suggestions. His recommendations include the following:

>> **Solar Fire Gold.** A huge range of capabilities makes Solar Fire the most popular program for professional astrologers. It supports virtually any kind of calculation imaginable, and its graphic design features are spectacular. You can customize everything. In addition to natal charts, transits, an astrological encyclopedia, and all the usual features, you can work with eclipse cycles, hypothetical planets (yes), geocentric or heliocentric charts, relocation charts, Vedic astrology, Medieval astrology, mundane astrology, financial astrology, esoteric astrology, midpoints, over a thousand asteroids and minor planets, and eighteen(!) varieties of prenatal chart.

Using Solar Fire, you can cast a horoscope for anyone born from 5401 BCE to 5399 CE. That's a lot of years and a lot of information. If you suspect that this is more than you could possibly want or digest — and, trust me, I'm only showing you a partial catalog — you could decide to consider Solar Fire aspirational and pass on it, at least for now. On the other hand, if that list, truncated though it is, excites your curiosity, go to Hank's website at www.soulhealing.com asap, and read all about it.

>> **Janus 5.** This versatile software is not as powerful as Solar Fire, but it costs less and still has more capability than most people will ever need. In addition to traditional natal astrology, transits, and so on, it offers Vedic astrology, electional astrology, horary astrology, relocation charts, and much, much more. Hank Friedman calls Janus 5 "a Swiss army knife of a program." You can't get more useful than that. For more information, go to www.soulhealing.com.

REMEMBER

Mundane astrology addresses politics, history, and national concerns. *Electional* astrology is the art of choosing dates for events such as the start of a campaign, a wedding, or the opening of a business. *Horary* astrology is the art of answering questions, whether they are vitally important or utterly trivial.

Activating an App

It's great to have a serious piece of software installed on your laptop, but having it in your pocket or on your iPad can be even better. There are many apps, at many price points. Here are two worth considering:

>> **AstroGold.** Made by the same people who brought you Solar Fire, this is a professional piece of software with options galore. A great app to have if you're interested in doing astrology at an advanced level, it is available for Android, iPhone, and iPad, and is fully compatible with Solar Fire's desktop version. To get it, contact Hank Friedman at www.soulhealing.com or, if you're using an Apple device, go to the iTunes store.

>> **TimePassages Pro**. This is a well-designed App for anyone who wants to create charts on the fly, and you can download it free. (Right now it's available only for the iPhone, but an Android version is in the works.) You get your birth chart, a daily chart showing where the planets are now, and lots of supporting interpretations. There's a small charge to add charts, or you can skip those incremental fees and spring for a full upgrade to Timepassages Pro. As of this writing, it costs $29.99 — and it's totally worth it. I probably look at this app every day. Where is the moon? Is Mercury still retrograde? Should my friend J. make an offer on that house? And what's going on with my doctor (yes), who just asked me to look at his chart? TimePassages Pro to the rescue.

Wandering around Cyberspace

Like bell-bottom jeans or gladiator sandals, astrology fades in and out of fashion. When I learned astrology, it was in the air and on the pop charts. For the first time, an astrology book — *Linda Goodman's Sun Signs* — had climbed atop the *New York Times* best-seller list, and all the people I met, including those who claimed to be skeptics, seemed to know their sign. I landed a part-time job casting horoscopes for a metaphysical bookstore and another — believe it or not — teaching astrology at an alternative public high school. It was the heyday of astrology, I thought.

But I was wrong. This is the heyday of astrology, right now. Besides books, magazines (*The Mountain Astrologer* in particular), an endless stream of e-mail horoscopes, and a growing community of astrologers, there are websites, webinars, conferences and retreats, videos, apps, and podcasts, not to mention starry postings on Facebook, Twitter, Instagram, and whatever social media I have inadvertently omitted. Among them are Hellenistic astrologer Chris Brennan (@chrisbrennan7); Astro Butterfly (@Astro_Butterfly); Mary English and her delightful homemade podcast, *Learn Astrology with Mary English*; the AstroTwins, Ophira and Tali Odit, and their website, https://astrostyle.com; and the following:

>> **Anne Ortelee.** On her down-to-earth weekly podcast, she imagines the planetary dance as a sort of reality show, full of demanding personalities and shifting alliances. Similar energies, she explains, will be manifest in situations you might (and in my experience, almost certainly will) encounter in the week ahead. Check her out on Twitter (@AnneOrtelee) or listen to her podcast, Anne Ortelee Weekly Weather.

>> **Susan Miller.** Her popularity is worldwide, and not just because that she's a top-notch astrologer, although she is. Her optimism and warmth, her sense of possibility, her deep knowledge of the subject, and her practical view of the world are what distinguish her. She writes long, and her monthly forecasts can be downright uncanny. She also explains the significance of eclipses, delves into retrograde Mercury, offers daily forecasts, produces a yearly wall calendar and an annual book of predictions, and is all over cyberspace. Her followers adore her. Connect with Susan on her website (astrologyzone.com), on Facebook (Susan Miller's Astrology Zone), on Twitter and Instagram (@Astrologyzone), and via her mobile app, Daily Horoscope Astrology Zone, available for iOs, Windows, and Apple Watch. As with many other apps, there's a free version and there's a more substantial one that you pay for. For free, you get daily forecasts, a lengthy monthly forecast for your sign, Sun sign profiles, access to Susan's tweets, and a nice little calendar describing key astrological events for the next few months. For a fee, you get more. You can't lose.

>> **Rob Brezsny.** His horoscopes, available through `freewillastrology.com`, are like no others. Instead of talking signs and planets, he describes a scene in a film, quotes a poet, ponders a cultural ritual or a scientific discovery, recounts an anecdote from the biography of a historical figure or an unknown musical genius. And then, as a master of metaphor, he ties it into your life. The stories don't always resonate. But usually they do, and when that happens, you feel as if a door has just swung open and all you have to do is walk through it and breathe the fresh air. His horoscopes are more than empathetic and descriptive; they're motivating. Plus, he provides plenty of reading material, including a regularly updated chronicle of good news — imagine that! — from around the globe. I like his brand: Free Will Astrology. That's exactly the way I see things, and I hope you will too.

>> **Chani Nicholas.** Chani is a social justice, mythologically informed, LGBTQ-aware feminist activist whose smart, perceptive astrological work springs from that politically engaged platform. She calls it "astrology for radical, political, critical mystics." You can follow her on Instagram or Twitter (@chaninicholas) or go to her website (`https://chaninicholas.com`) to mull over her monthly New Moon horoscopes and guided meditations, admire her well-crafted collages, and purchase workshops, classes, and individual readings. As someone who has been called a goddess, a rock star, and a cult favorite, she has been featured in newspapers and magazines including *Vogue, Vanity Fair, Oprah, Out,* and *Rolling Stone.* Her most original offering as an astrologer appears monthly as up-to-date, thematically chosen "horoscopes in the form of playlists," available through Spotify. It's not your usual horoscope, but why should it be? Astrology for the 21st century. At last.

IN THIS CHAPTER

» **Appreciating early astrology**

» **Considering classical times**

» **Meandering through the Middle Ages**

» **Relishing the Renaissance**

» **Witnessing the waning of astrology**

» **Welcoming the modern revival**

Chapter **3**

The History of Astrology: 5,000 Years of Cosmic Ups and Downs

n 410 BCE, a Babylonian astrologer cast a horoscope for a child born on April 29th. That chart, the nativity of one "son of Shuma-usur, son of Shumaiddina, a descendant of Deke," is the oldest natal chart we have. It's easy to imagine the astrologer speaking reassuring words to the child's parents (assuming it was they who commissioned this horoscope). He would have seen that the Sun was in Taurus and the Moon in Libra, a peaceful, pleasure-loving combination. Venus in Taurus and Jupiter in Pisces would have delighted him, for both planets were strongly placed in signs they rule: good omens in anyone's estimation. The chart had its challenges — no chart is without them — but by and large, he might have thought it an agreeable horoscope. Surely the child's parents would have been glad to hear his assessment — that is, unless they were hoping for a military leader. This chart leans toward the arts.

By the fifth century BCE, when this chart was drawn up, astrology was thriving. In this chapter, I take you through the story of astrology in the western world, its periods of popularity in classical times and the Renaissance, the centuries of censure when it was denigrated and dismissed, and the times when it came roaring back to life, as in our own day.

Looking at Early Astrology

Ancient peoples watched the sky as we do not: with attention. About 34,000 years ago, Stone Age observers recorded the cycle of the Moon on pieces of bone and antler. Some 17,000 years later, their descendants painted the bull of Taurus and the star cluster of the Pleiades — there can be no mistaking those identifications — on the walls of a cave in what is now France. In China, astrological activity dates back to the fifth millennium BCE. The most concentrated astronomical activity in the western world was in Mesopotamia. By 3,000 BCE, Babylonian stargazers had mapped the constellations, determined the length of the lunar month (a little more than twenty-nine and a half days), charted the cycle of Venus, marked the appearance of comets, meteors, rainbows, storms, and cloud formations, and sought correlations between celestial goings-on and events here on Earth. During the second millennium BCE, they recorded their findings on dozens of clay tablets collectively known as the *Enuma Anu Enlil*, which translates as "*When Anu and Enlil*" and refers to the sky god Anu and his son Enlil, lord of air and weather. This was not astrology as we know it. It was not personality analysis in any sense. Rather, it was a collection of useful omens. These are typical:

>> When Jupiter goes out from behind the Moon, there will be hostility in the land.

>> When the fiery light of Venus illuminates the breast of Scorpio, then rain and floods will ravage the land.

>> When Mercury is visible in Kislew, there will be robbers in the land.

>> When Mercury approaches Spica, the crops of the land will prosper, the cattle will be numerous in the fields, the king will grow strong. Sesame and dates will prosper.

These pronouncements were messages from the gods. They were political or weather-related, focused on war and peace, floods and famine. Vague and often portentous, they were heralds of catastrophe or — less often — prosperity. But they were not personal (unless you were the king).

By the middle of the first millennium BCE, Western astronomers and astrologers — there was no difference — had settled upon the zodiac as we know it, whittling it down from 18 constellations to 12. Equally important, they had identified the ecliptic, the path followed by the Sun as it rolls across the sky, and divided it into 12 sections, each 30 degrees long. This advance allowed for the creation of the signs (as distinct from the constellations), each one equal in duration, length, and value. Thus the seeds of modern astrology were strewn in ancient Babylonia. From there, they wafted into Egypt, into Greece, and throughout Mesopotamia all the way down to Chaldea, a small area in the southeast where observers recorded eclipses and other celestial phenomena. In time, as Chaldea was absorbed into the larger, more powerful Babylonia, the word "Chaldean" gradually came to mean one thing: astrologer.

Romping through Classical Times

Political changes swept across the ancient world during the first millennium BCE. In 539 BCE, the Persians under Cyrus the Great conquered Mesopotamia and the rest of the Middle East. Two hundred years later, Alexander the Great vanquished the same area and ventured beyond it into Egypt and to the border of India.

The shattering aftermath of these invasions — the Persians from the east in 539, and the Greeks from the west in 331 — was not just military or political. It was cultural. Throughout the conquered region, Greek became the common language and cross-cultural pollination became the norm, to the benefit of astrology. Egyptian astrologers offered a solar calendar along with an emphasis on the angles of the horoscope and whatever was rising, be it star or constellation. Babylonian astrology provided the zodiac, tables of planetary movement, an endless supply of lunar and planetary lore, and the idea that the planets were gods. The Greeks, who valued astronomy and mathematics but had never done much with astrology, soaked it up. Even Plato, who had his reservations, was curious enough to study it in his old age with — yes — a Chaldean.

Why did the Greeks, who supposedly prized lucidity and reason, respond so strongly to a subject that skeptics think of as possessing neither of those qualities? Because it struck them as scientific, structured, and based on precise measurements, unlike methods of divination such as interpreting the flight of birds or trying to decipher the utterances of an oracle inhaling vapors from a cauldron, as at Delphi. Like geometry, astrology looked supremely rational, and the intellectual class accepted it. It took a while to filter down to the shipbuilders and the shepherds. But filter down it did.

To learn astrology in ancient Greece, you went to the island of Kos, birthplace of the physician Hippocrates. In 280 BCE, a Babylonian named Berossus who was an astrologer, a historian, and a priest of the goddess Bel Marduk, founded a school of astrology there and cast thousands of horoscopes, not one of which has survived. Pliny the Elder, the Roman naturalist who died in the eruption of Mount Vesuvius in 79 CE, reported that Berossus was so admired that after his death, the citizens of Athens erected a statue of him with a golden tongue.

The most important classical contribution to astrology came from an Egyptian geographer, mathematician, astronomer, and astrologer named Claudius Ptolemy who lived in Alexandria. Born around 100 CE, Ptolemy wrote two books of interest to astrologers: the *Almagest*, an astronomy book that includes tables and detailed mathematical instructions for determining planetary and house positions; and the *Tetrabiblos*, the most influential astrology book ever written (in four parts: hence the title). It explained elements, aspects, fixed stars, the astrology of nations, of birth defects, of parents, brothers and sisters, twins, disease, death, and more. As late as the seventeenth century, Ptolemy's *Tetrabiblos* was being taught in universities. It has been described as the Bible of astrology.

Savoring the Romans

In the Roman Empire, astrology and divination were the cat's meow. Romans paid attention to portents, and there were portents aplenty: comets, dreams, lightning, snakes, lamps that abruptly flickered out (a good omen, or so thought Tiberius), laughing statues, decapitated statues, trees growing in unexpected directions, and birds — ravens, eagles, vultures, doves, wrens, and sacred chickens — behaving badly. Not everyone supported astrology. Cicero, for one, questioned it. But emperors consulted astrologers, and they did so on a regular basis.

In 44 BCE, Shakespeare tells us, Julius Caesar foolishly ignored a soothsayer's advice to "Beware the Ides of March." That seer, according to Cicero, was Vestritius Spurinna, who could read the future in the stars and in the entrails of sacrificed animals.

Caesar's successor was his adopted son Augustus, who in his youth visited the astrologer Theogenes with his friend Agrippa. Theogenes prophesized such wondrous good fortune for Agrippa that Augustus was certain that he would suffer in comparison. But after Theogenes cast his chart, he threw himself at Augustus's feet. Augustus was so heartened that he had his horoscope published and issued coins emblazoned with the symbol of Capricorn, thereby sending historians into a tizzy that has lasted over 2000 years. (See sidebar.)

WAS AUGUSTUS A CAPRICORN?

He was not, although he liked the symbol. The Roman historian Suetonius reports that Augustus was born before sunrise on September 23 in 63 BCE. Do the chart for that day, and you will see that Augustus was a Virgo (not a Libran) with the Moon in Capricorn. But astrology in those days did not rise and set with the Sun. Other planets were equal in importance. So his allegiance to Capricorn could allude to his Moon sign. Or it could be a nod to his conception, an event Roman astrologers deemed to have occurred 273 days prior to birth, in which case Augustus would have been conceived in late December — in Capricorn. Or maybe Augustus just wanted to capitalize on the imperial grandeur of Capricorn. Perhaps his regard for the sea-goat was a form of branding. The seventeenth-century astronomer Johannes Kepler, who was a full-fledged astrologer, investigated the matter for Emperor Rudolph II, hoping to figure out why the emperor favored the sign. He never reached a conclusion, and scholars are still mulling it over.

After Augustus came Tiberius, whom Pliny the Elder considered "the gloomiest of men." Tiberius believed in astrology but didn't trust astrologers, so he tested them. He and the astrologer, accompanied by a powerfully built freedman, would climb to the top of a cliff high above the sea where the astrologer would interpret his chart. If Tiberius felt deceived or dissatisfied, the freedman pitched the astrologer over the cliff.

So when the astrologer Thrasyllus was asked to give a cliff-side consultation, he predicted a glorious future for Tiberius. Then the emperor asked how he saw his own prospects. Tiberius cast a chart and, trembling, exclaimed that a perilous, possibly fatal crisis was looming over him. Tiberius, who knew this to be true because he was indeed thinking about that cliff, congratulated the astrologer on his perspicacity and embraced him as a member of his household. They became close friends but after a while, Tiberius started to lose faith. One day, as he and Thrasyllus strolled along the cliff, the astrologer spotted a distant ship and announced that it would bring good news. For once, he was right: "a lucky stroke," says Suetonius, "which persuaded Tiberius of his trustworthiness."

The reality was that most Romans believed in astrology, but they associated it with the heavy hand of fate. So it fascinated and frightened them, and from time to time they acted on that ambivalence. On at least eight occasions between 139 BCE and 175 CE, disgruntled dignitaries expelled astrologers en masse (even if they found ways to allow their personal seers to remain). Belief in astrology was almost universal. But astrologers had no job security. They were always on probation.

NERO'S HOROSCOPE

When Nero was born on December 15, 37 CE, the astrologer on duty took one look at the infant's chart and promptly fainted. Why was he so rattled? Nero had bellicose Mars, one of the two "malefic" planets, rising in Sagittarius closely conjunct the Sun and Ascendant, and square the other malefic, Saturn — an aggressive, defensive, quick-tempered, hard-hearted combination. His Moon in flamboyant Leo was square Jupiter in Scorpio, magnifying his arrogance, extravagance, and attention-getting ways. The Moon and Jupiter were both semi-square Saturn, for a touch of insecurity, pessimism, and suspicion. And unbeknownst to the astrologer, Pluto (which would not be discovered for nearly 1900 years) was exactly conjunct his Sun, adding a tyrannical, obsessive quality to an arrogant, violence-prone chart.

To be fair, the notion that Nero fiddled while Rome burned is a myth. He didn't start the fire, Tacitus claims, because he wasn't even in town. Other Roman writers insist that he did start it, possibly to clear space for a palace he wanted to build. All agree that he worked to rebuild the devastated city and that he blamed the Christians, many of whom he executed in horrific ways. Nor were they the only people he killed. His astrologer — who predicted correctly that he would murder his mother — would not have been surprised.

As Christianity gained strength, astrology lost it. After Constantine converted to Christianity in 312 CE, ancient practices were gradually outlawed, as were divination and astrology, which were linked to paganism and thought to deny free will. Around 364 CE, an assembly of clerics condemned magic and astrology. Even St. Augustine, who converted to Christianity in 386 CE, piled on. He held that the Christmas star heralded the end of astrology. He was wrong. But that didn't matter. The heyday of astrology in the West was over.

Appreciating Arabic astrologers

After the Roman Empire collapsed in 476 CE, the golden aura of astrology dimmed in Europe and what had been the Roman Empire. In the Byzantine Empire, in Arabic lands, and throughout the Middle East, it continued to glow. Astrology could be found everywhere from the shipyards to the courts, where astrologers held official positions and received salaries. Even so, astrology did not meet with universal approval, especially after the rise of Islam in the seventh century. Muslim religious leaders, who felt that only God could predict the future, attacked astrology, as did a number of influential philosophers and poets. And still, the "science of the decrees of the stars," as it was called, continued to attract adherents.

In the year 762, leaders of the Abbasid Caliphate founded a new capital city on the Tigris River with the help of astrologers, among them an Arab Jew named Masha'Allah, who chose an auspicious time to begin construction. A few years later, Baghdad's first astrology school opened. The philosopher al-Kindi, whose writings ranged from cryptography to music to how to make perfume, was the first head of that school. He wrote about the 960-year Jupiter-Saturn cycle; the 97 so-called Arabic parts or lots, imaginary points derived according to formulae and symbolizing just about everything; and the stellar rays that he believed explained the power of the stars.

Throughout this period, tremendous work was being done in astrology, philosophy, mathematics, astronomy and other disciplines. Still, there was always debate about astrology. In the ninth century, an astrologer named Abū Ma'shar (aka Albumasar) wrote a vigorous defense with an introduction that was translated into Greek and Latin, distributed widely, and pored over for centuries. In the eleventh century, the brilliant Muhammad ibn Ahmad al-Bīrūni was asked to create a textbook on astrology. He did so, covering the entire enterprise of Islamic astrology. But at the same time, mindful of possible criticism, he protected himself, explaining that he was only trying to show the intelligent reader what to avoid and to assist the indigent astronomer in making a living.

During the Golden Age of Islam, extending roughly from the eighth century through the thirteenth, mathematicians, engineers, astrologers, astronomers and other scientists made tremendous advances, the invention of algebra being one example. But the most important work done during this period was translation. Arabic scholars translated classical writers such as Aristotle, Ptolemy, his contemporary Vettius Valens, and the Hellenistic astrologer/poet Dorotheus of Sidon into Arabic from Greek, Sanskrit, Persian, Indian and other languages. Later, when many of those classical works were lost in Europe, Arabic translations allowed them to be reclaimed. Centuries of Arabic scholarship kept learning alive.

Meandering through Medieval Europe

In the twelfth century, Ptolemy's *Tetrabiblos*, written in Greek, was translated from the Arabic into Latin, and the revival of astrology began. Planetary tables put together in Toledo, Spain, by Arabic astrologers appeared on the desks of astrologers in France and England. European Kings sought the counsel of learned Arabic astrologers such as the Jewish physician and astrologer Abrahan ibn Ezra. Universities offered courses in astrology and medicine. And the greatest writers of the age took notice.

DANTE'S *INFERNO*

The Italian poet Dante Alighieri (c. 1265 to 1321) has a fine time in his *Inferno* punishing wrong-doers. As he travels through the nine circles of hell with his imaginary guide, the Roman poet Virgil, he observes souls in torment everywhere — the lustful, the gluttonous, the wrathful, the misers, the thieves, and so on. They are all being tortured in hideous, imaginative ways — and the punishment always fits the crime. In the eighth circle Dante finds two astrologers, weeping. They are Guido Bonatti (c. 1207 to c. 1296), the foremost astrologer of the age, and Michael Scot (1175 to 1234), a Scottish astrologer who worked for popes and emperors and, according to Dante, "truly knew the game of magic fraud." Their heads are twisted backwards; having tried to peer into the future, they can now only look behind them.

But Scot and Bonatti may have been stand-ins for the astrologer who really got under Dante's skin: Cecco d'Ascoli (1257-1327), a professor of astrology at the University of Bologna who criticized Dante's use of fictional devices and sought to "correct" Dante's literary errors with a poem of his own while simultaneously trying to strike up a correspondence with him. Although D'Ascoli worked for Pope John XXII, he had ideas that did not sit well with the church, as a result of which he was put on trial for heresy and instructed not to teach. He failed to get the message. A few years later, teaching once again, he cast a horoscope for Jesus Christ, thereby implying that the stars, rather than God, controlled Christ's fate. For this, he was burned at the stake, the only astrologer and the first university professor to be so punished.

Astrology fully infiltrated medieval life. When the Black Death raced across Europe in 1348, wiping out at least a third of the population, the King of France asked the medical faculty at the University of Paris to look into it. They soon determined that the bubonic plague was a result of a spectacular conjunction of Jupiter, Saturn, and Mars in March 1345. A lunar eclipse that same month only heightened the cosmic malevolence. Although people had other theories about the cause of the plague, this one made the most sense and was widely accepted, even if the conjunction preceded the plague by a full three years. The doctors had diagnosed the problem.

In the centuries that followed, astrology permeated every corner of society, and every castle. At times there was controversy. Astrologers were feted by some and condemned by others. They consulted with popes and kings, chose propitious times for battles and coronations, were caught up in royal scandals, debated with theologians and philosophers, were knighted, and once — in England in 1441 — drawn and quartered. But that unfortunate astrologer had cast a chart that foresaw the death of the king. In other words, he had committed treason.

Celebrating the Renaissance

During the Renaissance, astrology continued to thrive even as science became more prominent. Astrologers enjoyed social prestige and, with it, access to the rich and powerful.

In Florence, the philosopher Marsilio Ficino (1433–1499) translated the works of Plato and other Greek writers into Latin. An astrologer, physician, and Catholic priest, he headed an academy that aimed to replicate Plato's academy in Athens and was largely responsible for the revival of classical learning in the Renaissance. But in 1489, someone reported him to Pope Innocent VIII, accusing him of heresy and magic. Ficino had influential friends — an ambassador, an archbishop — who were able to plead his case with the pope. He was not charged, and the pope asked to meet with him. Whether the meeting occurred is unknown. But Ficino must have been considering it, because he asked the archbishop to send him a description of the pope's horoscope, temperament, and state of health, and he promised to prepare a beneficial medication.

Discovering Dr. Dee

In England, John Dee (1527–1608) also knew people in high places. He was a mathematician, a magician, a mapmaker, a master of stage craft, a philosopher, a bibliophile who compiled the best private library in England, a collector of astronomical and mathematical instruments, an astronomer who supported the radical theory that the Sun, not the Earth, was the center of the universe, and an astrologer who was accused of treason for casting charts for Queen Mary, her husband, and her half-sister Elizabeth, a charge he was somehow able to dodge.

When Elizabeth became queen, he became her advisor, the role for which he is best known. Dee tutored her in astrology, chose the time for her coronation in 1559, advised her regarding foreign policy, calmed her fears about a large comet, and received her more than once at his home, although he never received quite the recognition he wanted from her, or the money.

In 1582, Dee became embroiled with a charismatic medium, alchemist, and convicted forger named Edward Kelley. An aficionado of the occult, Dee had long tried to see images in crystals and to communicate with angels, skills he longed to possess. Kelley, a flamboyant Leo with an eighth house Sun, assured him that he had those gifts. And so began a drama-filled association that developed in England, migrated for several years to eastern Europe, and was dominated by angelic communiqués. Once, for instance, Kelley had visions — a message on a scroll, a scantily clad angel — which he understood to mean that Kelley and Dee must share their wives. This was a spiritual crisis for Dee, but he went along, and nine months later his wife Jane gave birth to a child they named Theodore: gift of God. When Dee returned to England shortly thereafter, he discovered that his famous library had been vandalized: a crushing blow. He never saw Kelley again but he learned that his former compatriot had been knighted by Emperor Rudolf II in Prague and later, when his alchemical skills proved inadequate, imprisoned. Dee returned to casting horoscopes. He never ceased trying to communicate with the angels.

A note about Nostradamus

John Dee was far from the only Renaissance astrologer to serve royalty. Another such seer was Michel de Nostradame (1503–1566), astrologer to Catherine de Medici, queen of France. Nostradamus was the author of a collection of 942 inscrutable prophesies in verse form. Although making predictions using these ambiguous verses has proven to be a formidable task, applying them to events that have already occurred is another story, the opacity of the verses being easily pierced with wild interpretative leaps, anagrams, numerology, and mistranslations. The prophecies are also easily imitated. Despite multiple hoaxes perpetrated in his name, including a quatrain invented by a college student that supposedly predicted the events of 9/11, Nostradamus continues to mystify and intrigue.

DR. DEE AND 007

With the Sun, Mercury, and Jupiter in the eighth house of mysteries and Mars in Scorpio in the twelfth house of hidden things, John Dee could not resist the lure of anything arcane. He loved crystals, magic mirrors, and secret symbols, a few of which he invented. Among them:

- A capital letter E with a crown on top that he used to represent Queen Elizabeth.

- Two symbols that he used to represent himself: a Greek delta (Δ) and a complicated design that combined symbols for the Sun, the Moon, the elements, and fire. It looks something like the glyph of Mercury and also resembles the image invented by the musician Prince (who also had an eighth-house Sun and plenty of Scorpio).

- A symbol he used in correspondence with Queen Elizabeth that looked like a numeral seven with two zeroes tucked beneath its extended roof, signifying that this letter was for her eyes only. Centuries after Dee's death, that symbol caught the attention of the novelist Ian Fleming, creator of James Bond, and 007 was reborn.

Was he at least a good astrologer? Catherine de Medici didn't seem to think so; she preferred someone else. But certainly he knew something about astrology, for his prophecies are filled with specific planetary references. One such prophecy inspired Orson Welles to predict a 1988 earthquake in Southern California. You could argue that it's not that hard to predict an earthquake in California. And this one didn't even happen. But there *was* an earthquake in Northern California the following year, so if you want to believe. . .

Wandering through Shakespeare's star-crossed world

In the Renaissance, astrology saturated everyday life, so it's no surprise that the plays of Williams Shakespeare (1564–1616) are pumped full of comets, eclipses, Suns, Moons, planets, and stars, few of which arrive without an adjective. In addition to being constant, blazing, shining, shooting, sparkling, wandering, fixed, and Earth-treading, Shakespeare's stars are auspicious, charitable, chaste, comfortable, fair, favorable, glorious, good, happy, jovial, and lucky — or angry, bad, revolting, base, mortal, thwarting, homely, inauspicious, malignant and ill-boding. But astrology's primary influence on Shakespeare is more than a matter of description. He thinks astrologically. His plays are shaped by signs (Scorpio and *Macbeth*; Cancer and *A Midsummer Night's Dream*; Gemini and *Romeo and Juliet*). His characters are molded in the light of the four elements or modeled after planets such as quick-witted Mercury (Romeo's friend Mercutio) or melancholy Saturn (King Lear). Even his plots are shaped by astrology. In Shakespeare's plays, portents are never false alarms. When a prediction is uttered, it comes true. And while several characters speak against astrology and in favor of free will, those characters are not the ones we generally like. "The fault, dear Brutus, is not in our stars but in ourselves," states Cassius in an oft-quoted remark. But Cassius is the one who has a lean and hungry look, the one who engineers the assassination of Caesar, and the one who — in a work of literature from another era — ends up in Dante's ninth circle of hell along with Brutus, his fellow assassin, and Judas Iscariot: betrayers all.

Whether Shakespeare believed in astrology personally is probably unknowable. That he knew astrology is without question. In *All's Well That Ends Well*, two characters even josh about the effect of retrograde Mars. Shakespeare found in astrology an organizing principle — and an opportunity for humor. "Saturn and Venus this year in conjunction!" says Prince Hal in *Henry IV Part II* as he watches an aging Falstaff romance a saucy wench. As Priscilla Costello points out in *Shakespeare and the Stars*, everyone would have caught the planetary references and laughed; it was a bit of a dirty joke. Shakespeare was a man of his times.

TIP

I've seen almost every Shakespeare play, and I've read them all. But not until I discovered Priscilla Costello's miraculous book, *Shakespeare and the Stars: The Hidden Astrological Keys to Understanding the World's Greatest Playwright* (Ibis Press, 2016) did I understand the magnitude of astrology's influence on the bard. A must-read.

Foreseeing disaster with William Lilly

Another man of his times was William Lilly (1602–1680), the most influential astrologer of the seventeenth century. His book, *Christian Astrology* — a misleading title, nothing in it being especially Christian — is full of advice for the studious astrologer on topics such as how to calculate the length of life (it's dauntingly complex) and how to answer run-of-the-mill questions about finding lost objects, renting a house, identifying a thief, predicting the course of an illness, or determining whether you will be repaid money you are owed. These problems were assessed through horary astrology, according to which the astrologer casts a chart for the moment the client asks a question, and that chart contains within it the answer.

Lilly was a master at this. He could answer any query and accurately predict the outcome of a battle or political conflict. He is most famous for predicting, seventeen years before the actual events, that in 1665 ("or near that year . . . more or less of that time") the city of London would suffer from "a consuming plague" and "sundry fires." And that's what happened. In 1664, fleas carrying bubonic plague invaded London, and the death toll began to mount. By September of 1665, as many as seven thousand people a week were dying, and everyone who could leave, left. Close to one quarter of the population died.

A year later, a fire broke out in a baker's house on Pudding Lane and set the town ablaze. In four days, four fifths of London was destroyed. Lilly was called before the House of Commons and questioned. He was acquitted of any wrongdoing. Nevertheless, with the city a ruin, he moved to the country, took up medicine, and contented himself with publishing a yearly almanac. His prediction retains its status as one of astrology's great moments.

Watching the Decline of Astrology

For a long time, astronomy and astrology were braided together. Even the most important scientists of the age knew how to cast horoscopes — and some of them did it very well.

>> Nicolaus Copernicus (1473–1543) started the Scientific Revolution by arguing that the Earth revolved around the Sun, not the other way around. He also studied astrology and had exalted, ecstatic feelings about the Sun that were about as far from scientific as you can get.

>> Galileo Galilei (1564–1642) discovered the four largest moons of Jupiter, thus proving that all celestial bodies do not revolve around the Earth. This earned the ire of the Church, which accused him of heresy and sentenced him to house arrest for the rest of his life, all because he supported Copernicus. Galileo willingly cast horoscopes for his daughter, for himself — and for clients.

>> Johannes Kepler (1572–1630) determined the laws of planetary motion, bemoaned the importance people gave to astrology, and nonetheless cast more than eight hundred horoscopes, many with astute commentary and chillingly accurate predictions.

>> Even Isaac Newton (1642–1726), who discovered the universal law of gravity, entertained a certain curiosity about astrology, though he found alchemy more compelling. Newton is a transitional figure. He was so immersed in the search for the philosopher's stone that he may have died from mercury poisoning, a side effect of his alchemical experiments, and yet his scientific and mathematical contributions were so essential that he is considered a founding father of the Age of Reason.

By the eighteenth century, the Enlightenment or Age of Reason was upon us, and astrology was often the object of ridicule. In 1708, the English satirist Jonathan Swift, author of *Gulliver's Travels*, pretty much ruined the life of John Partridge, a former shoemaker, almanac writer, and astrologer whose death he "predicted" and then "reported" on the appointed date. Writing under the pseudonym Isaac Bickerstaff, Swift even composed an elegy for the man with a brief epitaph in rhyming couplets. "Here, five feet deep, lies on his back / A cobbler, star-monger, and quack," it began. Partridge had to turn away his would-be embalmers at the door.

Nevertheless, astrology was part of everyday life, as the continuing sale of almanacs suggests. They included useful facts about weather, tides, and so on. But they were also filled with celestial information. In the British colonies of North America, Benjamin Franklin published his *Poor Richard's Almanack* under the pseudonym Richard Saunders, an homage to an English astrologer who died before Franklin was born (and whose books were found in Isaac Newton's library). *Poor Richard's Almanack*, published from 1733 to 1758, sold well. Although it is known primarily for Franklin's sensible aphorisms ("No gains without pains"), it also provides an enormous quantity of astrological data. In the very first issue, in direct imitation of Swift, Franklin predicts the death of a living person — in this case, Titan Leeds, his competitor in almanac publication. Leeds would die, Franklin wrote, "on Oct. 17. 1733. 3 ho. 29 m. P. M. at the very instant of the ♂ of ☉ and ☿." He knew the language of astrology, even if he mocked it.

Attitudes were changing, assisted by scientific advances. In 1781, William Herschel spotted Uranus, the first new planet discovered in recorded history. Twenty years later, astronomers discovered Ceres, originally thought to be a planet but later classified as an asteroid (although recently upgraded to dwarf planet). After Ceres came Pallas, Juno, Vesta — and eventually millions of small celestial bodies. In 1832, Neptune was discovered. And in 1835, almost three centuries after publication, the book that started it all, Copernicus's *On the Revolutions of the Heavenly Orbs*, was taken off the Catholic Church's Index of Forbidden Books. By then, astrology was no longer in fashion. Universities didn't even offer courses in it.

Saluting Modern Times

Wrenching change is what the nineteenth century was about. There were revolutions everywhere: wars of independence in Latin America, democratic revolutions in Europe, and in the United States, slavery, the Civil War, and the failed attempt at Reconstruction. There were astounding inventions — railroads, the telegraph, the electric light — and medical advances such as the first vaccines. Music, art, and literature flourished, and feminism arose at last. Early in the century, there was Romanticism, with its emphasis on emotion and its preference for the intuitive over the rational. Later in the century, there was Spiritualism, with its séances and otherworldly spirits, and a resurgence of interest in the occult. Amidst all that, astrology sprang to life.

One person responsible for its resurgence was an Englishman named William Frederick Allan, a Leo who renamed himself Alan Leo, it being the style among astrologers to adopt celestial or angelic pseudonyms. In 1890, Leo began publishing *The Astrologer's Magazine*. A few years later, when he changed its name to *Modern Astrology* and began offering free horoscopes to subscribers, the magazine took off. The books he wrote — basic texts emphasizing the Sun — were widely read, by Carl G. Jung among others. Many are still in print.

In 1914, Leo was charged with fortune telling under the Witchcraft Act. Although he was acquitted on a technicality, he hoped to avoid future legal showdowns by focusing on psychological analysis and spiritual development rather than on prediction. Quoting Heraclitus, he wrote a brochure called *Character is Destiny*. And that is how Alan Leo became "the father of modern astrology." Not that the authorities cared; in 1917, he was again accused of fortune telling, and this time he was convicted and fined. He died a month later.

In the United States, similar conflicts occurred, but at least once, the outcome was different. The astrologer in question was Evangeline Adams. In 1899, she checked into the fashionable Windsor Hotel in New York City in 1899, scrutinized the proprietor's horoscope, and warned that he was in immediate danger. The next afternoon, his hotel went up in flames. Evangeline Adams never had to search for clients again. Working out of an office suite above Carnegie Hall, she counted among her clients Charlie Chaplin, Tallulah Bankhead, Joseph Campbell, and J. P. Morgan. "Millionaires don't use astrology," Morgan supposedly said (though evidence is scant). "Billionaires do."

In 1914, the same year Alan Leo was first taken to court, Evangeline Adams was accused of fortune-telling. At her trial, to prove her expertise, she agreed to cast the chart of someone she did not know. The subject of that blind reading turned out to be the judge's son. "The defendant raises astrology to the dignity of an exact science," the judge announced, and she was acquitted. "I have Mars conjunct my natal Sun in the 12th house," she said. "I will always triumph over my enemies."

Astrology was becoming more visible and changing emphasis, becoming symbolic, psychological, and solar. Early in the twentieth century, the psychologist Carl Gustav Jung studied the mix of images, archetypes, and myths he found in astrology. To explain astrology's power, he promoted the idea of synchronicity, an "acausal connecting principle" whereby seeming coincidences are resonant with meaning. It's still a satisfying explanation in many ways. And although Jung tried without success to sell astrology to his mentor, Sigmund Freud, from whom he later broke, his astrological musings have done much to shape contemporary astrology.

Following the Sun

In August 1930, something unprecedented took place in the astrological world. In London, the editor of the *Sunday Express* asked the astrologer Cheiro (aka William John Warner) to write about the horoscope of the new royal baby, Margaret. When Cheiro declined, his assistant, R. H. Naylor, stepped in. He foresaw "an eventful life" for the little princess with "events of tremendous importance to the Royal Family and the nation" in her seventh year. A few weeks later, he predicted problems for British aircraft between October 8 and 15. On the fifth, a large airship — a hydrogen-filled dirigible — crashed and exploded in France, killing 48 people. It was a few days early, but never mind: Like Evangeline Adams and William Lilly before him, Naylor benefitted from predicting a disaster. The editor asked him to write a regular column with predictions for everyone. Naylor did this based on birthdays — that is, on Sun signs. This had not been done before, and it was an immediate hit. Circulation rocketed up, and rival publications hired their own astrologers to write similar columns. And so the horoscope column, based on Sun sign, became a regular part of the daily paper. When King Edward VIII, aka the Duke of Windsor, abdicated the throne of England during Margaret's seventh year in order to marry a divorced American, a scandal that riveted the entire world, Naylor's reputation was secured. His later predictions — so, so wrong — mattered not a whit.

Hitler's astrologers

Adolf Hitler was not a fan of astrology, although it was popular in Germany. In 1923, an astrologer named Elsbeth Ebertin wrote in her almanac, *A Glance into the Future*, that "a man of action born on 20 April 1889" — everyone knew who that was — should exercise caution that November. Annoyed, Hitler forged ahead with his plan to seize power in Munich. When the Beer Hall Putsch, as it was called, failed, Hitler was sentenced to five years in prison. He served nine months — just long enough to complete *Mein Kampf*.

In 1933, when he became chancellor, his birth chart was widely discussed, and not always favorably, with the result that by 1934, astrology was essentially banned. But as the Romans learned centuries before, astrology never disappears for long. In 1939, a Swiss astrologer named Karl Ernst Krafft, a staunch supporter of the Third Reich, alerted a friend in Germany that between November 7 and 10, Hitler's life would be in danger. And sure enough: an assassination attempt was made, a bomb exploded. Hitler was unharmed, having left the building earlier than expected, but Krafft was dragged in for questioning. He convinced the authorities that he had not been involved and he ended up in Berlin, working for the Nazis. They directed him to parse the prophecies of Nostradamus to see what lay ahead. He found that the quatrains augured well for the future of Nazi Germany.

But no one was safe in Nazi Germany, including Krafft. When one of Hitler's henchmen, Rudolf Hess, took off in a small plane and crash-landed in Scotland in 1941, the Nazis blamed his unofficial solo flight on his unhinged mental state and his interest in astrology. Another crackdown followed. Astrologers were arrested and their libraries confiscated. Most were only forced to stop practicing, but a few, including Krafft, were imprisoned and sent to concentration camps. After a year in solitary, Krafft died in January 1945 while being transferred to Buchenwald.

Meanwhile, astrology may have been banned, but members of Hitler's inner circle were consumed by it. In April 1945, joseph Goebbels examined Hitler's chart and that of the Third Reich and announced that a turn-around in the war was imminent. When Franklin Roosevelt died in office later that month, he was jubilant, certain that this meant victory. It did not. Within weeks, Goebbels and Hitler committed suicide, and Germany surrendered. Astrology is still recovering from the embarrassment of the association.

Greeting the dawn

In late April 1968, the rock musical *Hair* with its opening number, "Aquarius," premiered on Broadway. Six months later, *Linda Goodman's Sun Signs* was published, the first astrology book ever to hit the bestseller list. "What's your sign?" became first a pick-up line, then a cliché, and finally the least cool thing a person could possibly say, even if it was what everyone wanted to know. In those days, there were astrological bookstores galore; classes in living rooms and coffee shops; discussion groups that convened in hipster movie theatres; paperback books with state-by-state listings of professional astrologers you could call on the phone, numbers included. If this wasn't the dawning of the Age of Aquarius, what was?

Astrology reached a peak of visibility in 1988, when a former member of Ronald Reagan's administration revealed that President Reagan and his wife, Nancy, regularly consulted an astrologer who timed their every move. The mockery was relentless. And it had an effect. Over the next decade, here and there, horoscope columns disappeared. Metaphysical bookstores closed their doors. If you weren't looking, you might have thought that astrology was fading.

In fact, astrology was on the cusp of a fantastic blossoming, a Renaissance. The internet was part of it, as was the development of software that anyone could use. But the larger change wasn't about the method of delivery or the ease of access. It was about expanding the worldview of astrology and reclaiming its history.

Astrologers began to examine traditions outside of western astrology such as Chinese, Meso-American, and Vedic astrology, the astrology of India. Also known as Jyotish, Vedic astrology has been particularly influential. It shares a chunk of its DNA with western astrology but veers off in other directions, using a sidereal zodiac based on the constellations rather than the ecliptic and relying on techniques unknown in western astrology.

Astrologers have also burrowed into the history of western astrology. In a decades-long effort spearheaded by astrologer Robert Hand, Project Hindsight, and the Archive for the Retrieval of Historical Astrological Texts or ARHAT (that being a Buddhist term for a person moving toward enlightenment), astrologers have translated ancient and medieval manuscripts and revived neglected techniques from centuries ago. Initially, this looked like an arcane interest shared by a tiny cadre of scholarly astrologers. But the excitement generated by their pursuit has rippled through the astrological community. Today, there is widespread interest in ancient techniques, particularly those of Hellenistic astrology, which was used through the Roman Empire and is currently undergoing an astonishing revival.

So astrology has changed. In the space of only a few decades, astrology has deepened and broadened, expanded its vocabulary, welcomed new celestial bodies into its cosmos, and incorporated ancient techniques of timing and analysis that most western astrologers knew nothing of — until recently. As unlikely as it seems, everything old is new again.

There are many excellent books about the history of astrology. Here are a few of my favorites:

A History of Western Astrology, Volumes I and II, by Nicholas Campion (Bloomsbury Academic, 2008). A magisterial, scholarly work.

The Secrets of the Vaulted Sky: Astrology and the Art of Prediction by David Berlinkski (Harcourt, Inc., 2003). Entertaining, evocative, and full of attitude.

Astrology: A History by Peter Whitfield (Harry N. Abrams, 2001). Nicely written and, unlike other books on the topic, profusely, gorgeously illustrated.

The Fated Sky: Astrology in History by Benson Bobrick (Simon & Schuster, 2005). Brilliant, fascinating, full of fantastic details. I recommend it without hesitation.

2

Here Comes the Sun

IN THIS PART . . .

Get the scoop on the signs of spring: Aries, Taurus, and Gemini.

Check out the signs of summer: Cancer, Leo, and Virgo.

Contemplate the signs of autumn: Libra, Scorpio, and Sagittarius.

Wrap up with the signs of winter: Capricorn, Aquarius, and Pisces.

Chapter **4**

The Signs of Spring: Aries, Taurus, and Gemini

W hen I was in college, I bought my first astrology book in a train station, and by the end of the ride, my understanding of life had been transformed. The book — it was one of many by Zolar, a name used by a succession of astrologers — described the people I knew with uncanny accuracy, based solely on their Sun signs. My parents, my roommate, my so-called boyfriend — all were there, in stunning detail. Later, I learned that every chart also includes the Moon, eight planets, twelve houses, and more. But the core of almost every horoscope is the Sun.

The Sun begins its journey through the signs and the seasons on or about March 20, when it enters Aries. On that day, the Vernal Equinox, day and night are approximately equal. But soon the balance shifts. For three months, the night grows shorter and the day progressively longer as the Sun spins through the signs of spring — the most youthful signs of the zodiac. When the day reaches its maximum length, spring is over. The three signs of spring are:

» Aries the Ram (March 20 to April 18), the sign of positive (or yang) cardinal fire. Aries is bold, energetic, youthful, and gifted at setting things into motion.

» Taurus the Bull (April 19 to May 20), the sign of negative (or yin) fixed earth. Taurus is tenacious, pragmatic, resourceful, and — in case you thought that earth signs are only about practicality — talented, sensuous, and pleasure-loving.

>> Gemini the Twins (May 21 to June 20), the sign of positive (or yang) mutable air. Gemini is spontaneous, curious, quick-witted, restless, sociable, and capricious.

If your birthday falls into one of those signs, you are in the right place.

REMEMBER

The Sun's placement in the sky at the moment of your birth determines your sign. If you have any doubt about your Sun sign, perhaps because you were born at the beginning or end of a sign, turn to Chapter 2 without delay. It will tell you how to get a free, accurate copy of your birth chart. Once you have that, you'll know for sure.

REMEMBER

Figure 4-1 represents the Sun. In ancient cultures, the Sun always symbolized something big, like life and death. The Incas thought of the Sun as a divine ancestor. The Egyptians and other civilizations considered the Sun a god. The astrological symbol reflects that importance. The outer circle represents infinity, the universe, and your cosmic potential. The dot within it represents your human individuality.

FIGURE 4-1:
The symbol
of the Sun.

© John Wiley & Sons, Inc.

Each sign has a polarity (positive or negative, yang or yin), an element (fire, earth, air, or water), and a quality or modality (cardinal, fixed, or mutable). For more on those terms, turn to Chapter 1.

Aries the Ram: March 20–April 18

As the first sign of the year, Aries the Ram is spirited, straightforward, courageous, enterprising, and filled with vitality. Yours is the sign of new beginnings.

Your planetary ruler is Mars. Named after the Roman god of war, Mars is associated with action, energy, assertiveness, anger, and desire.

The *glyph* or written symbol of Aries appears in Figure 4-2. It signifies the head of the ram with its fabulously curved horns; a gushing fountain of fresh water; or the eyebrows and nose of a human being — a part of the face that's well-defined and graceful on a typical Aries.

FIGURE 4-2:
The symbol of
Aries the Ram.

© John Wiley & Sons, Inc.

The sunny side

Aries is a force of nature like no other. Blessed with boundless energy and a bold, exhilarating personality, you have a zest for life that other signs can only envy. You're a firebrand — intrepid, enthusiastic, passionate, and courageous. Unconventional and joyously individualistic, you display a robust sense of who you are and an eagerness to forge your own path. You have a sense of purpose and a distinct personal style, and you refuse to let others define you. Often a creature of extremes, you react quickly and make instantaneous decisions. You believe in action and proudly stand up for what you know is right, even if it conflicts with commonly held notions. Neither a joiner nor a follower, you're a natural-born leader because you have a clear, decisive mind combined with total faith in your own reactions and plans.

At your audacious best, you're untiring, ardent, thoroughly original, and filled with joie de vivre You're an activist on your own behalf, a risk-taker with a pioneering spirit and a deep need to prove yourself. So when a fresh idea or a groundbreaking mission captures your imagination, you rush in. Later on, if your interest falters or your hopes don't pan out, you move on, undaunted. Life is too short to waste on anything that fails to interest you.

The sorry side

Like a child, you can be self-centered, inconsiderate, and intent on doing things your way. When you really want something, you can be combative, brash, and even ruthless in your efforts to get it. You're willing to do a lot of rule breaking, a trait that doesn't always work to your benefit. Rather than bending to someone else's requirements, you prefer to simply obey your instincts. You have initiative, but at times you exhibit a woeful lack of foresight, and you often lack diligence. Although your enthusiasms are many, you're restless, and your initial interest may fizzle. Your impatience is legendary. For that reason, you find greater satisfaction with short-term ventures than with lengthy ones.

Emotionally, you find it difficult to imagine how other people feel. You can strike people as insensitive, egocentric, and self-absorbed. And there's no avoiding the fact that you have a volcanic temper: It comes and goes in a flash, but when it appears, you're terrifying. You hold strong opinions, and you're not afraid to express them, no matter how impolitic (or impolite) they may be. You figure it this way: If expressing your views causes others discomfort, let them nurse their fragile sensibilities on their own. You have too much to do to sit around obsessing over hurt feelings or petty criticism.

Relationships

Anyone who knows you, from friends and family to the most casual of acquaintances, knows where you stand. Outspoken and direct, you don't hesitate to express yourself, and you have little patience for those who can't take the heat or require a lot of coddling. Self-sufficient and independent, you prefer your friends to be as on-the-move as you are, and you can't bear whining. As for love, you're an exciting person to be around. Although you suffer from jealousy and can be competitive, you enjoy the chase — not that you let it drag on for too long. You're not a game player. You know what you like, and when you find it, you go for it. And did I mention that you're sexually ravenous?

At the same time, you're an idealist who's fully prepared to hold out for the real thing. You demand equality, and if you don't get it, you make your displeasure clear. With Mars, the warrior planet, as your ruler, you seldom shy away from confrontation. And even though you don't mean to be contentious, at times you can't help yourself. You're not one to suppress your feelings or to spend endless hours delving into the intricacies of your own — or anyone else's — psyche. You'd rather face the issues head-on. Your combustible, intimidating exterior may mask feelings of inferiority, but most people won't realize that. All they know is that you're a force to be reckoned with.

For information on your relationships with other signs of the zodiac, flip to Chapter 15.

Work

With your executive decision-making ability and general verve, you're a self-starter and an effective leader who likes to initiate change. Ambitious and competitive, you rise to a challenge. But you're a sprinter, not a long-distance runner. You love the unmistakable thrill that comes at the beginning of an undertaking, when creative momentum is high and the possibilities are wide open. You're happy to experiment and innovate. But once things have settled into a routine and the endeavor becomes weighted down with procedures, precedents, and supervisors, your excitement wanes. You find it dispiriting to spend time focusing on details or doing standard maintenance tasks. Quitting too soon is one of your worst and most frequent mistakes.

Aries craves autonomy. Independent and feisty, you're a solo act, most contented working on your own or being the boss, preferably in an enterprise that allows you to set your own schedule. When that's not possible, you benefit from physical activity and the opportunity to participate in a variety of tasks. You're easily bored, and your need to express yourself is stronger than your need for security.

Pie-in-the-sky careers include being a film director like Francis Ford Coppola, Quentin Tarantino, or Akira Kurosawa, all Aries; a talk show host like David Letterman, Conan O'Brien, or Rosie O'Donnell; an entrepreneur like Larry Page, cofounder of Google; and anything that feels dangerous or has a high excitement quotient, such as being a stuntman or working in an emergency room. Surgery is said to be an Aries profession, as is anything that involves fire (such as cooking) or the military. I know Aries who are devoted activists, artists, attorneys, educators, musicians, writers, and entrepreneurs. Whatever your calling, it's not something you choose for money or prestige. You're drawn to it because it offers you a way to make an impact on the world and to express your incomparable, adventurous self.

TIP

If you work for an Aries, be aware that your boss will most likely be impatient with anyone who can't keep up or requires excessive supervision. Your best move is to work independently and quickly — and don't take those angry explosions personally.

Health and wellness

As the first sign of the zodiac, Aries has immense vitality and a strong constitution. You heal quickly and can get by on little sleep. When something new excites you, you dive in. But tedium undoes you, and "slow progress" feels like a contradiction in terms to you. Having a goal is motivating, but if your new diet or supplement or gym class or therapy doesn't show results fairly quickly, you're unlikely to stick with it. You'd rather give something else a try.

In traditional western astrology, Aries is associated with the head, making you prone to headaches, earaches, eyestrain, and related woes. You are also ruled by Mars, the planet of war. His aggressive tendencies can spark angry, adrenalin-fueled outbursts and occasional accidents. That's why the number one health tip for Aries is simple: calm down. Close your eyes, take a deep breath, stretch. A few minutes of meditation before you grab your lance and gallop into the fray can be restorative. The number two health tip: when engaged in an activity that might require headgear such as jousting or skateboarding or bicycling, don't be obstinate. Wear the helmet. Also useful: head massages, facial acupressure, cranial-sacral massage, a sleep mask for those occasions when you don't get to bed until sun-up.

REMEMBER

A Sun sign description of health is, by necessity, a generality. When seasoned medical astrologers do individual health readings, they assess your chart in detail. Nevertheless, an astrological reading does not replace a check-up. If you're concerned about your health, see a physician.

The mythology of Aries

The Egyptians of 3500 years ago saw this constellation as a ram, just as we do, but the myth most associated with Aries comes from Greece. It starts with Queen Ino, who resented her stepchildren, Phrixus and Helle, and devised a plan to get rid of them. She began by causing the harvest to fail. Fearing famine, her husband, King Athamas, sent for advice from the Delphic oracle, but Ino persuaded the messenger to ignore whatever the oracle said and instead instruct Athamas to sacrifice his son, Phrixus. Like the Biblical patriarch Abraham, Athamas agreed. He was just about to cut his son's throat when a winged ram, sent by Hermes (aka Mercury), appeared out of nowhere. The children scrambled on top of the creature and off they flew. Helle lost her grip and tumbled into the narrow strait, once known as the Hellespont, that separates Europe from Asia Minor. But Phrixus held on. After they landed, he sacrificed the ram to Zeus and nailed its golden fleece to an oak tree in a sacred grove. But that's another story.

The constellation Aries

As a sign of the zodiac, Aries is fiery and exciting. As a constellation, it is small and unremarkable. Its brightest star, Hamal (Arabic for lamb), is the 50th brightest star in the sky.

Aries: The Basic Facts

Polarity: Positive	Favorable Colors: Red and white
Quality: Cardinal	Lucky Gem: Diamond
Element: Fire	Part of the Body: The head
Symbol: The Ram	Metal: Iron
Ruling Planet: Mars	Key Phrase: I am
Opposite Sign: Libra	Major Traits: Energetic, impetuous

LADY GAGA: ARIES IN ACTION

There is nothing mild in Stefani Germanotta's chart. With her Sun and Venus in fiery Aries, she is intrepid, as her fearless self-presentation — think of the meat dress — clearly demonstrates. Competitive and enterprising, she does not stand still. Her foray into acting in *A Star is Born* could have bombed, but with a Moon/Pluto conjunction in the fifth house, she really does have theatrical talent; her recording of American Songbook standards with Tony Bennett, 60 years her senior, could have dimmed her pop luster, but two planets in Capricorn enabled her to establish a link to traditional material and older people; a shattered hip and chronic pain might have derailed her career – and with Saturn in the sixth house opposite Chiron (and Uranus transiting over her Sun at that time), her health issues were not minor. She managed to avoid all those dangers. Her moon in Scorpio, conjunct Pluto, gives her willpower to burn and an intense emotional nature. Half a dozen mutable placements (including the Ascendant and Midheaven) give her the ability to adapt to circumstances. But is she, as an early album title suggests, a fame monster? Could be. Jupiter and Mercury at the top of her chart stimulate her need for public acclaim and boost her ability to attract it. But it is her dynamic Aries Sun that gives her the audacity and authenticity that define her. She really was born that way.

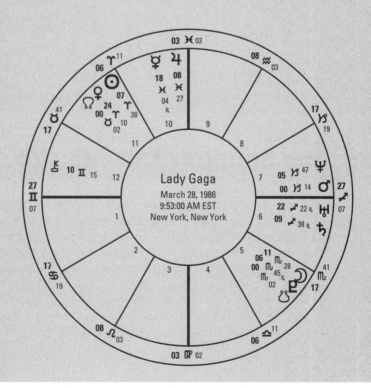

MORE CLASSIC ARIES

- Marlon Brando, Booker T. Washington, Danica Patrick, Iris Chang (Moon in Aries)

- Norah Jones, Quentin Tarantino, Diana Ross, Robert Downey, Jr. (Moon in Taurus)

- Reba McIntyre, Harry Houdini, Jackie Chan, Mario Vargas Llosa (Moon in Gemini)

- Charles Baudelaire, Aretha Franklin, Robert Frost, astronaut Judith Resnick (Moon in Cancer)

- Joseph Campbell, Gloria Steinem, Patricia Arquette, Andrew Lloyd Webber (Moon in Leo)

- Emmylou Harris, William Wordsworth, Marvin Gaye, Michael Fassbender (Moon in Virgo)

- Rosie O'Donnell, Steven Tyler, Maya Angelou, Susan Boyle (Moon in Libra)

- Eric Clapton, Francis Ford Coppola, Edie Sedgwick, Nancy Pelosi (Moon in Scorpio)

- Thomas Jefferson, Vincent Van Gogh, Emma Watson, Cynthia Nixon (Moon in Sagittarius)

- Al Gore, David Letterman, Sarah Jessica Parker, Keri Russell (Moon in Capricorn)

- Steve McQueen, Conan O'Brien, Seamus Heaney, Tennessee Williams (Moon in Aquarius)

- Kareem Abdul-Jabbar, César Chávez, Herb Alpert, Rachel Maddow (Moon in Pisces)

Taurus the Bull: April 19–May 20

When Harry Truman was president, a sign in the oval office read "The buck stops here." That's just what you might expect from a Taurus. In good times and bad, you're steadfast, dependable, and willing to accept responsibility. But Taurus also has a pleasure-loving side, for it is ruled by Venus, the guardian of love and art. Truman knew something about that side of life too. A devoted husband and fiercely protective father, he was a gifted pianist who thought about becoming a professional musician. He decided that he didn't have what it takes. "A good music-hall piano player is about the best I'd have ever been," he said. "So I went into politics and became President of the United States." Taurus has the stamina and the persistence to make something like that possible.

The glyph of Taurus, shown in Figure 4-3, represents the head and horns of the Bull — or the womb and the fallopian tubes — or, according to the most esoteric interpretation, the circle of potential topped by the crescent of receptivity.

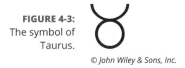
The sunny side

In the cycle of the zodiac, Aries, the pioneer, arrives first, spewing energy in every direction. Taurus, the second sign, brings that energy down to earth and uses it to build something solid. As a fixed earth sign, you're cautious, grounded in reality, steady on your feet, and utterly reliable. Because you have an intense need for security, both emotional and financial, you make conservative choices and try to avoid change. You hold on tightly, only giving up when there's no other option. Once you've made a decision, nothing can convince you to change your mind. Your tenacity is legendary. Concrete goals make the most sense to you. You pursue them quietly and with single-minded determination. It's true that you may not reach your destination quickly, but like the legendary tortoise to which you're often compared, you do get there.

As an earth sign, you're at home in your body and attuned to your environment. Romantic and sensuous, kind and gentle, you're responsive to comforts of every kind, and your senses are wide open. You love slow, languid sex; the textures of silk, velvet, and expensive lotions; the taste and smell of freshly baked bread, full-bodied red wine; nature in all its seasons; and handcrafted objects, which you acquire with ease and never cease to enjoy. You love — and require — beauty, and you're not averse to luxury. Taurus is also creatively gifted. Chances are you have talent in one or more of the arts, including music, dance, sculpture, painting, design, architecture, cooking, gardening, and the fine art of relaxing.

The sorry side

Although your dedication is impressive, your leisurely pace can drive other people to distraction. You start slowly and refuse to be rushed. You can be stodgy at an early age, and you can easily fall into a rut. Plus, you're incredibly stubborn. Your well-known tenacity is a positive trait when it means sticking up for moral principles (think of Coretta Scott King or Bono, the Taurus rock singer who was nominated for a Nobel Peace Prize). Too often, though, it means refusing to change, no matter what the circumstances. I've seen Taureans cling to outmoded, self-destructive patterns for years just because they didn't want to risk trying something new. That's what being bull-headed can mean.

As long as we're discussing negative traits, let me add that you can be greedy, status conscious, acquisitive, gluttonous, self-indulgent, and self-pitying. Normally, you're hard-working and persevering, but when you're down, you become apathetic. You can also be possessive, dependent, jealous, insensitive and, at your worst, a user. You don't intend to exploit other people. But, you know, things happen.

One more point: Taurus, unlike Aries, doesn't get angry easily, for which the rest of the world is grateful. But when you do blow up . . . let's just say that some of the worst mass murderers and dictators in history — men like Hitler, Lenin, Pol Pot, Ho Chi Minh, Saddam Hussein, and cult leader Jim Jones — were born under the sign of the Bull.

Relationships

With Venus as your ruling planet, you're appealing and affectionate, and you effortlessly attract friends, lovers, and sidekicks. Romance is hugely important to you, but (with rare exceptions) you won't go after it aggressively. Quietly seductive, you give subtle signals, and if the object of your desire turns out to be immune, you look elsewhere.

Your feelings run deep, but it's not excitement you seek; it's sanctuary. In your heart, familiarity breeds contentment. You relish the small domestic rituals that accompany the security of a long-running relationship. When you're in a secure partnership, you hold on tightly. You're loyal, loving, protective, and supportive, even if you're also dependent and possessive.

Although you dislike conflict and try to avoid it, you don't back down either. If a relationship is on shaky ground, you can hardly bear the tension. Some people (Leo and Scorpio, for example) get all caught up in those romantic ups and downs. They throw themselves into the drama and even find it titillating. Not Taurus. Sincere and intense, you play for keeps because you're not playing. For you, love isn't a game.

For the lowdown on your relationships with other signs, turn to Chapter 15.

Work

Because you adore the creature comforts and lack that manic hit that often characterizes high achievers, people may assume that you're lazy. They couldn't be more wrong. Though your ability to lounge around on weekends is without equal, you're diligent, productive, and organized when you want to be, with an inborn need to do something constructive. Security is essential to you, whether that means money in the bank, real estate, a first-rate pension plan, or all of the above. And yet, that's not where you live. At bottom, it's more important for you to believe in what you're doing and to find a modicum of creative expression. When you identify an area that satisfies those needs, you're willing to make financial sacrifices.

Whatever you choose, you work at a steady pace. And unlike other signs, you aren't constantly trying to elbow your way into the spotlight. Naturally, people come to rely on you. And yes, it sometimes feels as though you're doing more than your share of the work for less than your share of the recognition. That's one of the drawbacks of being an earth sign.

TIP

Working with Taurus natives is easier if you accept the fact that they know what they want and are unlikely to change. They value productivity, follow-through, loyalty, and the ability to stay cool. As for those brilliant thoughts you have about how to shake things up, keep them to yourself. Those ideas will only make your Taurus boss distrust your judgment.

Health and wellness

Perhaps more than any other sign, Taurus is attuned to the physical world and the body. You are patient (or at least you try to be) and persistent, and your endurance is enviable. At your best you are sturdy and grounded, especially if you spend sufficient time outdoors. Being in nature is more than a diversion for you; it is healing. It reduces stress and brings you pleasure — and that is where the danger lies. As someone who is ruled by the planet Venus, you respond to beauty, art, and all the senses, starting with touch. No one loves to eat and drink more than Taurus, and you struggle with a tendency to overindulge. But trying to alter your habits via extreme measures is never going to work with you. The only way is slow and steady. It's not exciting, but it will get you there.

In traditional astrology, Taurus rules the neck, thyroid, and throat. Sore throats and laryngitis can be bothersome, and you store tension in your shoulders and neck. Stretching, chanting, and simple yoga asanas can be beneficial. So can aromatherapy; it may not work for everyone, but it will work for you. Massage offers definite relief. Also helpful: running, hiking, gardening, bicycling, and any exercise you can stick with, including the treadmill, the elliptical machine, and the stationary bike. The best remedy of all: spending time in nature.

The mythology of Taurus

Mythology and religion teem with sacred bulls. So which one is Taurus? Is it the Egyptian bull god Apis? The immortal Nandi, loyal mount of the Hindu god Shiva? The Bull of Heaven, who fought with Gilgamesh in the great Sumerian epic? The Minotaur, who was imprisoned in a labyrinth? Medieval European astrologers looked to the sky god Zeus, who took the shape of a snow-white bull and approached the princess Europa as she dallied on the shore. Charmed by his seemingly gentle ways, Europa festooned him with flowers and playfully climbed onto his back. That was when he plunged into the Mediterranean and swam to Crete, Europa clinging to his back as he plowed through the waves. Ultimately, she gave her name to the continent, and Zeus cemented his reputation as a symbol of power and patriarchy.

The constellation Taurus

One of the most majestic constellations in the sky, Taurus has three distinguishing features: the bright star Aldebaran, which marks the eye of the bull; the Pleiades, a hazy star cluster often called the Seven Sisters (although even the Greeks could only pick out six); and another cluster, the Hyades, the half-sisters of the Pleiades. On a clear autumn night, you can see the blur of the Pleiades, the V-shape of the Hyades that forms the face of the bull, and the faintly orange glow of Aldebaran.

Taurus: The Basic Facts

Polarity: Negative	Favorable Colors: Greens and browns
Quality: Fixed	Lucky Gem: Emerald
Element: Earth	Parts of the Body: Neck and throat
Symbol: The Bull	Metal: Copper
Ruling Planet: Venus	Key Phrase: I build
Opposite Sign: Scorpio	Major Traits: Productive, obstinate

GEORGE CLOONEY: TAURUS IN ACTION

Like many attractive people, award-winning actor/director George Clooney, once considered Hollywood's most eligible bachelor, has Venus rising in the first house. With Mars in the house of romance, and Neptune, ruler of his Pisces ascendant, in the eighth house of sex, it's no surprise that *People* Magazine twice dubbed him the Sexiest Man Alive. A pleasure-loving Taurus, he is also a loyal and generous friend, and an outrageous prankster. With his Sun in the second house of money, he values security and has built a considerable fortune, with the real estate to prove it. His wealth comes partly from his film career and partly from a business he started with friends (one word: tequila) and sold at a huge profit. But beneath his easy-going affability beats the heart of a serious man. A Saturn-Moon conjunction in austere Capricorn encourages him to muffle his emotions but also supports his work ethic. With those two planets in the eleventh house of community and humanitarian goals, plus Jupiter in idealistic Aquarius, he is also a longtime social activist focused on international crises, disaster relief, and other progressive causes. When he married an acclaimed international human rights lawyer, his choice surprised many people. It shouldn't have.

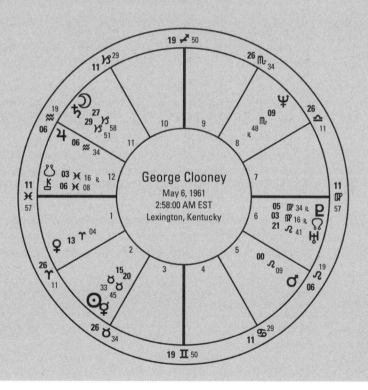

George Clooney
May 6, 1961
2:58:00 AM EST
Lexington, Kentucky

MORE CLASSIC TAURUS

- Stevie Wonder, Cate Blanchett, Salvador Dali, Dev Patel (Moon in Aries)
- Katharine Hepburn, Kelly Clarkson, Karl Marx, Bernie Madoff (Moon in Taurus)
- Sigmund Freud, Fred Astaire, Ella Fitzgerald, Stephen Colbert (Moon in Gemini)
- Benjamin Spock, Ulysses S. Grant, Penelope Cruz, Poet Laureate Natasha Tretheway (Moon in Cancer)
- Barbra Streisand, Renee Zellweger, James Brown, Kirsten Dunst (Moon in Leo)
- Jack Nicholson, Shirley MacLaine, Adrienne Rich, Rami Malek (Moon in Virgo)
- William Shakespeare (maybe), Billy Joel, Rosario Dawson, Tina Fey (Moon in Libra)
- Harry S. Truman, Bono, Keith Haring, Mark Zuckerberg (Moon in Scorpio)
- Frank Capra, Al Pacino, Sue Grafton, Adele (Moon in Sagittarius)
- Cher, David Byrne, David Beckham, Dwayne Johnson (Moon in Capricorn)
- NIcolo Machiavelli, Charlotte Brontë, George Lucas, Gigi Hadid (Moon in Aquarius)
- Audrey Hepburn, Jerry Seinfeld, Chè Guevara, Charles Mingus (Moon in Pisces)

Gemini the Twins: May 21–June 20

Agile and articulate, Gemini is lively, bright, thoroughly engaged, and incredibly persuasive. That's because you're ruled by quick-witted Mercury, the trickster god who could talk his way out of anything.

The two pillars of Gemini (see the glyph in Figure 4-4) represent the mythological twins: Castor, the human son of a man, and Pollux, the immortal son of Zeus, king of the gods. They also symbolize the two sides of your double-sided nature.

FIGURE 4-4:
The symbol of
Gemini.

© John Wiley & Sons, Inc.

The sunny side

Forever young, they say. You're intelligent, quick, inquisitive, gregarious, and cheerful — and it shows in your face. In your never-ending quest for stimulation, you habitually veer off in unexpected directions. Your mind is always working. Effervescent and up-to-date, you're invigorated by the newest friend, the latest fad, the most incredible news story, and the juiciest gossip. Excited by everything life has to offer, you are thrilled to explore new interests and meet new people. When you step into a new world, you feel renewed.

To fend off the ever-present threat of ennui, it reassures you to have two (or more) novels on your bedside table, two jobs (preferably part-time), two love affairs (or a main one and a backup), and at least two email addresses and social media accounts. You maintain an ever-expanding legion of friends. Your enthusiasm is infectious, and nothing pleases you more than forging connections between unexpected people or unrelated ideas. You're in constant motion, and you make a point of cultivating spontaneity, at least in theory. In reality, you sometimes load yourself down with so many activities that spontaneity becomes essentially impossible. Inevitably, you end up doing a lot of juggling. Yet the truth is this: When you're overcommitted and slightly frazzled, much as you might complain, you feel at home in the world.

The sorry side

A hostage to hyperactivity, you squander your resources because you can't resist the immediate gratification of conversing, cavorting with the cat, or feeding your addiction to your phone. If you could, you'd be in two places at once. Impatient, inconstant, and easily distracted, you have a short span of attention and too often drop the ball. You often find it difficult to concentrate — or even to sit still. When you find something that excites you, you accelerate into overdrive. But you can kill your enthusiasm by talking it into the ground. You don't hesitate to sing your own praises. And although you may not notice, your intense focus on whatever you're interested in can be draining.

At your worst, you can be deceptive, superficial, and fickle — the living, breathing incarnation of hot air. Astrologers (and jilted lovers) often accuse you of being emotionally shallow. Actually, you experience real emotions — just not for long. When troubles come, you see no point in dwelling on them. Instead, you push your feelings aside and adapt to the changed circumstances — and you do it with stunning ease. A lover breaks up with you? Your supervisor locks your computer and escorts you to the Exit sign? No worries. You rewrite history, and pretty soon you're the one who walked. You'll deal with the repercussions down the road (if at all). Meanwhile, you may be a bundle of nerves, but you're busy writing a new chapter. Like Gemini Bob Dylan, you don't look back.

Relationships

Those who have been burnt in a relationship with a Gemini often accuse members of your sign of being unfeeling and fickle. This is unfair. I know Geminis who have enjoyed monogamous relationships for decades. There are many factors in a horoscope, and the Sun is only one of them.

But I've also known Geminis who fit the stereotype to a T. Playful and engaging, you love the excitement of making conquests. The banter of courtship amuses you but you're restless and may soon grow disenchanted. The ideal partner for you is multifaceted enough to provide the stimulation you seek, confident enough to let you have the freedom you enjoy, and witty enough to make you laugh. You can't help responding to someone who presents a challenge. An on-again, off-again relationship, I'm sorry to say, arouses your curiosity. The reality is, you don't need a profound emotional connection. You also don't need off-the-charts sex (which is not to say that you don't appreciate it). What you need is a lively connection that generates sparks and engages your mind.

For details about your relationships with other signs, turn to Chapter 15.

Work

Versatile and cerebral, you have fine motor skills and are often a wizard with words. You're stimulated by everything, and ideas readily come to you. Smart and buoyant, you pick things up so fast that you practically don't *have* a learning curve. But in work (as in love), you grow quickly bored and are easily distracted. Jobs that require a lot of repetition, no matter how outwardly rewarding, are a mistake for you. You require mental stimulation, plenty of opportunities to socialize, and a mixture of responsibilities. The best professions for you offer variety rather than routine and take advantage of your ability to communicate. Classic Gemini careers include education, travel, writing, and anything connected with newspapers, magazines, radio, TV, or social media. Twitter was made for you. Inventive and entrepreneurial, you're skilled at creating original business ventures. Even though the freelancer's life isn't for everyone, you bask in its variety and manage the challenges (no security, no predictability) with confidence. Just make sure you hire a sensible Taurus or a Capricorn to look after your finances. Handling money is *not* your strength.

Health and wellness

Who invented multi-tasking anyway? It must have been a Gemini. You are active, engaged, quick on the uptake, and full of enthusiasm for anything that piques your interest — and what could be more intriguing than something new? You don't need a lot of sleep, which is fortunate, since it pleases you to have a host of friends and to juggle multiple projects. But insomnia can stalk you nevertheless. You are high-strung and easily distracted, and although you are a master at setting goals, the path from A to B often meanders, to your dismay. Maybe that's why your greatest health challenge is learning to focus, quiet your nerves, and manage stress.

The parts of the body associated with Gemini are primarily the lungs, arms, hands, and shoulders. According to traditional astrology, you may be prone to bronchitis and other respiratory issues, to injuries to your arms or hands, and to anxiety. The remedies are just what you might guess. Meditation, deep breathing, and breathing techniques such as pranayama soothe and balance, even if you only do them for a few minutes. Exercise classes are good for your body as well as your social life, especially if you vary them. Calming teas such as lemon balm or chamomile can help quiet your mind and reduce anxiety. Finally, keeping a diary will help you focus your intentions and give you a place to vent: a fine restorative for your mental health.

The mythology of Gemini

Sumerians looked at the stars of Gemini and saw a pile of bricks. Egyptians pictured a couple of sprouting plants. But most ancient peoples saw twins. In classical mythology, their story starts with Leda, who was approached on her wedding day by Zeus in the shape of a swan. Soon she gave birth to — or, to use the technical term, hatched — four children from two eggs. Helen and Pollux were fathered by Zeus, the king of the gods, and were therefore immortal. Castor and Clytemnestra were the children of Leda's husband, the human king of Sparta, and were therefore mortals, doomed to die. Despite that difference, Castor and Pollux enjoyed innumerable adventures together. But one day, Castor was pierced by a spear. Distraught, Pollux begged Zeus to let his brother live. Zeus complied, allowing the two brothers to share the immortality that by rights belonged only to one of them. The catch was that they had to divide their time between Olympus, the home of the gods, and the underworld. Thus the twins shuttle between two homes, a situation many Geminis might consider ideal.

The constellation Gemini

It's hard to see a ram in the stars of Aries, but looking at Gemini, it's easy to picture its brightest stars, Castor and Pollux, as the heads of twins. Castor is a stellar community comprising three hot bluish-white stars, each of which is a double: six stars in all. Pollux is cooler, a red giant about ten times the size of the Sun orbited by a large planet discovered in 2006 by a Gemini astronomer.

Gemini: The Basic Facts

Polarity: Positive	Favorable Color: Yellow
Quality: Mutable	Lucky Gem: Agate
Element: Air	Parts of the Body: Arms, shoulders, lungs
Symbol: The Twins	Metal: Mercury
Ruling Planet: Mercury	Key Phrase: I think
Opposite Sign: Sagittarius	Major Traits: Clever, superficial

REAL LIFE EXAMPLE

DONALD J. TRUMP: GEMINI IN ACTION

Like many prominent people, Donald Trump was born with the Sun near the top of his chart, giving him leadership ability and a drive for public recognition and authority. His Sun is conjunct both the North Node of the Moon, an aspect that brings many blessings but also encourages narcissism, and Uranus, the planet of rebellion, upheaval, and social media. That Sun/Uranus combination makes him a natural non-conformist, a rebel with an idiosyncratic style who trusts his own intuition above all else and resists authority, even as he longs to possess it. As a Gemini, he has a style of communication and a way with words that is uniquely his own, with a square between Mercury and Neptune blurring the distinction between wishful thinking and reality. Other components of his chart amplify his vivid, unruly personality. Born on the day of a lunar eclipse, he has a full moon in independent Sagittarius opposite his Sun. That's an exciting, vital aspect, and many people are drawn to its energy. But it also causes him to feel pulled in multiple directions and to externalize his conflicts. An unexpected key to his chart can be found in Pluto. Tucked away in the twelfth house of hidden enemies and the unconscious, it does not make a major aspect with another planet. So although his will is strong, his Plutonian drive for power is unconstrained and compulsive. Megalomania is a possibility, but so too are feelings of powerlessness. Moreover, Pluto is located midway between Saturn and Mars, thickening the brew of frustration, suspicion, and pent-up rage roiling beneath the surface. Finally, Trump has Leo rising. Leo is, metaphorically, the quintessence of gold. It explains his taste, his tan, his confidence, the enjoyment he takes in performance, and his love of the spotlight. But with pugnacious Mars conjunct the ascendant, his anger and aggression are equally on display. Quarrelsome and willful, he will never be a peacemaker. That's the simple, astrological truth.

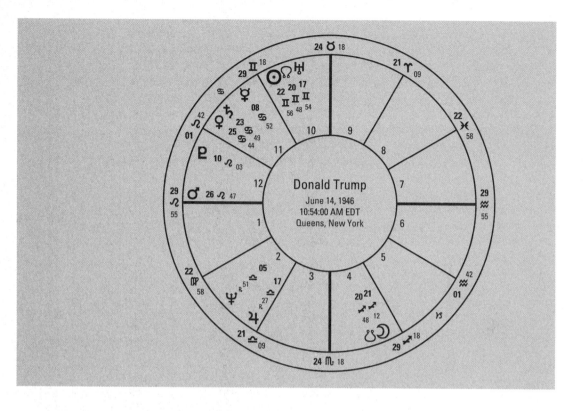

Donald Trump
June 14, 1946
10:54:00 AM EDT
Queens, New York

CLASSIC TWINS

- Anderson Cooper, Angelina Jolie, Raymond Carver, Jeffrey Toobin (Moon in Aries)

- Bob Dylan, Ian Fleming, Aaron Sorkin, Peter Dinklage (Moon in Taurus)

- Queen Victoria, Brooke Shields, Salmon Rushdie, Gwendolyn Brooks (Moon in Gemini)

- Cole Porter, Roseanne Cash, Colin Farrell, Prince William (Moon in Cancer)

- Anne Frank, Venus Williams, Clint Eastwood, Paul McCartney (Moon in Leo)

- Marquis de Sade, Frank Lloyd Wright, John F. Kennedy, Natalie Portman (Moon in Virgo)

- Henry Kissinger, Aung San Suu Kyi, George H. W. Bush (Moon in Libra)

- G. K. Chesterton, Miles Davis, John Wayne, Alanis Morissette (Moon in Scorpio)

- Judy Garland, Nicole Kidman, Naomi Campbell, Orham Pamuk (Moon in Sagittarius)

- Johnny Depp, Stevie Nicks, Charles Aznavour, Mehmet Oz (Moon in Capricorn)

- Arthur Conan Doyle, William Butler Yeats, Marilyn Monroe (Moon in Aquarius)

- Allen Ginsberg, Kanye West, Kendrick Lamar, Prince (Moon in Pisces)

Chapter **5**

The Signs of Summer: Cancer, Leo, and Virgo

I t always feels odd to me that the first day of summer, when the Sun rises to its maximum height, is the longest day of the year and simultaneously the start of the slow descent into winter. After that glorious Summer Solstice, the days dwindle down, becoming progressively shorter while the nights grow long. When day and night are roughly equal in length, summer's over. But while it lasts, summer is surely the most exhilarating season of the year.

The three signs of summer are:

» Cancer the Crab (June 21 to July 22), the sign of cardinal water. Cancer is known for its emotional acuity, sympathetic nature, and love of all things domestic.

» Leo the Lion (July 23 to August 22), the sign of fixed fire. It's vibrant, confident, determined, and brimming with personality.

» Virgo the Virgin (August 23 to September 22), the sign of mutable earth. Virgo is famed for its intelligence, analytical mind, attention to detail, and tendency to be a perfectionist.

TIP

The position of the Sun at the time of your birth determines your sign. If you are unsure of your sign, possibly because you were born at the beginning or end of a sign, turn to Chapter 2 and read the section "Getting Your Horoscope Online." In most cases, getting your chart online will result in a clear verdict about your sign. Why wonder what you are? Find out now.

REMEMBER

Each sign has a polarity (positive or negative), an element (fire, earth, air, or water), and a quality or modality (cardinal, fixed, or mutable). For more about these terms, go back to Chapter 1.

Cancer the Crab: June 21–July 22

Ruled by the ever-changing Moon, you're introspective, intuitive, security-conscious, and exceedingly aware of your emotional environment. But Cancer is not just a stagnant puddle of emotions, even if that's how you sometimes feel. As a cardinal sign, there's nothing stagnant about you. You're determined to conquer your vulnerabilities and achieve your goals.

The glyph of Cancer (see Figure 5-1) represents the breasts (and hence the mother), the claws of the crab, and the fluid nature of feeling. Its slight resemblance to the yin-yang symbol hints at your desire to embrace all of life and achieve awareness.

FIGURE 5-1:
The symbol of
Cancer the Crab.

© *John Wiley & Sons, Inc.*

The sunny side

You embody an intriguing paradox. As a water sign, you're emotionally wide open with an intense inner focus. As a cardinal sign, you're enterprising and ambitious, with a strong interest in the outer world. No wonder you're known for your fluctuating moods. Your emotional sensitivity is one of your greatest assets. It serves as a barometer to the atmosphere around you, and the more tuned into it you are, the better. You're shrewd and insightful. When you trust your intuition enough to act in accordance with it, you can navigate through the roughest storm.

You also maintain a strong tie to the past, both personal and historical, and you have a powerful longing for home, family, domestic tranquility, and emotional security. Loyal, affectionate, kind, and supportive, you never give up on someone you love — and if that means clinging or being overprotective, so be it. Your ability to nurture others parallels your need to care for and comfort yourself.

At the same time, you're intent on initiating activity. Whatever your emotions may be, you don't let them stop you from setting far-reaching goals and resolutely going after them. Your determination is extraordinary. Despite your doubts and insecurities, you forge ahead valiantly, though not without some tears along the way. At your best, your internal awareness supports your outer ambition, just as your knowledge of the past forms a sturdy foundation for your forays into the future. The fact that you have the best memory on the planet is yet another strength.

The sorry side

Picture the crab. Vulnerable and soft within its protective armor, it approaches its target sideways and, when frightened, scuttles back into its shell. You do the same. Fretful and high-strung, hesitant to address a problem directly, you defend yourself effectively but occasionally to your own detriment. You can be possessive and demanding, or so defensive, so imprisoned by anxiety, that movement becomes impossible. You withdraw or enter a state of denial, where you become unreachable. At your worst, your need for security paralyzes you.

Yet there's no avoiding your powerful emotions, which can wash over you as suddenly as a rogue wave. Those moments are an indelible part of who you are, and you don't always deal with them well. Spurred by your fear of being abandoned, stranded, or without resources, you cling ferociously, holding on to relationships — and jobs — way past their expiration dates. Avoiding the quicksand of insecurity and the snake pit of depression are challenges you must confront; uprooting your fears is another.

Relationships

As the most maternal sign in the zodiac, Cancer has an instinct for closeness. The family you were born into never ceases to play a central role in your consciousness, whether positive or negative (or, more likely, a perplexing amalgamation of both). You lavish attention on friends and lovers alike, and in the absence of a committed romantic partner, you turn friends into family. Children claim a special place in your heart.

Love affairs absorb you, but you're most comfortable in a committed, traditional relationship. Shyer than you appear, you long for someone with whom you share a soul connection. When you feel cherished, you're utterly devoted and supportive. When you feel insecure, it's another matter. Fearful of being alone and yet unwilling to engage in conflict, you hold on too tightly for too long. When a relationship falls apart, you're devastated, even if you're the one who made the decision. You withdraw into the safety of your shell. Many tears are shed. And then — it's amazing — you're fine. Although astrologers always say that the Crab moves sideways (and I've said it myself), it's not always true. Sometimes you move forward with giant strides. I have seen Cancer soar from abject misery to honeymoon cruise within a matter of months. In romance, as in other areas, your ability to take action and recognize opportunities pays off.

For more on your relationships with other signs, turn to Chapter 15.

Work

It's true that yours is the sign of domesticity. That doesn't mean you want to stay home making tea and crumpets. As a cardinal sign, you're happiest when you're actively involved in the world. You shine in fields that rely on your emotional sensitivity. You excel in medicine, teaching, social work, child psychology, marriage counseling, and any of the healing arts. Because you have a deep love of home (and house), you can succeed at real estate, architecture, landscape design, and anything connected to food. Finally, thanks to your interest in the past, you're drawn to history, antiques, and museum work. You're great with children. You're also supremely responsive to the elderly and would thrive in geriatrics. Whatever you do, it must offer emotional fulfillment as well as material security. Your occupation needs to captivate you, and there's no reason to settle for anything less.

Despite your doubts and hesitations, taking the initiative is your best move. Within an organization, you quickly form alliances and rise to a position of leadership. But you become emotionally involved in your work, and you tend to take it home with you. It helps to find a mentor. Establishing a tie with someone who has the authority and expertise you lack can be reassuring and helpful. Similarly, after you have accumulated some experience, you find it gratifying to become a mentor.

TIP

If you work with or for a Cancerian, be prepared to give your all. Crabs want to create family, even at the office. They try to forge strong connections and generate a positive atmosphere. At least in theory, the office door will be open, and criticism will be constructive. If you need help, say so. If you have a legitimate complaint, address it in a private meeting. But don't sneak around complaining behind your boss's back. Cancerians may hide their emotions, but they're astute enough to sense dissatisfaction. And don't spread rumors; they will see it as betrayal.

Health and wellness

Intuition leads you in the right direction. As a water sign, your feelings are primary, and you have probably learned to trust them, with one possible exception: You tend to exaggerate your fears. As a cardinal sign, your wellbeing rests on your ability to quiet those terrors and take action. It helps to be with supportive people — the ones who contribute to your peace of mind, not the ones who undermine your confidence or reinforce negative patterns — and it also helps to incorporate periods of silence and solitude into your routine. Exercise can be a pathway to serenity, as with tai chi, dance, yoga, or swimming. Spending time in or near water is restorative. Finally, if you feel overwhelmed, consider therapy. You are an excellent candidate for almost any form of it because you are brave enough to bring the secrets that have been in shadow into the light.

In traditional astrology, Cancer rules the breasts and the stomach, making how and what you eat of supreme importance (especially if you happen to be breast-feeding). So eat your greens and do it in a mindful way. A few deep breaths before a meal soothe the unsettled spirit. The more conscious you are, the more vibrant you feel.

REMEMBER

A Sun sign description of health is by definition an over-simplification. Legitimate medical astrologers would never rely solely on your Sun sign, and neither should you. If you're worried about your health, please see a doctor.

The mythology of Cancer

Heracles (aka Hercules), a hero of classical mythology, was not a hero to Hera, the wife of Zeus. He was proof of Zeus's infidelity, and she despised him. She tried to prevent his birth, and when that effort failed, she hid two venomous snakes in his cradle, hoping they would kill him. Heracles strangled them both. Later, when he was grown, Hera drove him mad. In his frenzy, he murdered his family. Among his punishments, he was ordered to slay the many-headed hydra. It was a daunting task, since each time he sliced off a head, two more sprang up in its place – and in addition, one of the heads was immortal. The battle was fierce, but to Hera's dismay, he held his own. So she sent a giant crab into the fracas. It sank its claws into Heracles' foot to distract him, but he crushed it. Soon afterward, with the assistance of his nephew, who cauterized the wound after each beheading, thereby preventing the hydra from sprouting another head, Heracles slew the hydra and buried its immortal head under a rock. In recognition of the hydra's mighty struggle and the crab's bravery, Hera lifted them into the sky as constellations.

This story alludes to a distant age when Hera was the Great Mother goddess, and Heracles — which means "Glory of Hera" — was her mate. When invaders swept into Greece with their new gods, they reshaped the culture and, along with it, the mythology. Zeus became king, Hera was demoted to wife, and Heracles became her nemesis. In Hera's struggle against Heracles, the crab was her ally, as was the hydra. Their presence in the sky is a reminder of a remote, matriarchal past.

The constellation Cancer

Cancer is the most inconspicuous constellation in the zodiac. Its most notable feature is a faint smudge known as the Beehive. When Galileo viewed it through a telescope in 1609, he discovered that it was not a gas cloud, as had been thought, but a cluster of stars. Galileo counted 36. There are more than 1,000.

Bordering Cancer is Hydra, the largest constellation in the heavens. It is not on the ecliptic and hence is not part of the zodiac.

Cancer: The Basic Facts

Polarity: Negative	Favorable Colors: White and silver
Quality: Cardinal	Lucky Gems: Pearls and moonstones
Element: Water	Parts of the Body: Stomach and breasts
Symbol: The Crab	Metal: Silver
Ruling Planet: The Moon	Key Phrase: I feel
Opposite Sign: Capricorn	Major Traits: Intuitive, moody

REAL LIFE EXAMPLE

FRIDA KAHLO: CANCER IN ACTION

Frida Kahlo's disquieting, colorful, surrealistic paintings reflect her passionate, pain-wracked life. As a child, she contracted polio, causing one leg to be shorter than the other, an imperfection that prompted her in later life to favor floor-length skirts. When she was eighteen, a trolley plowed into the bus she was riding, fracturing her pelvis, injuring her spine, crushing her foot, and impaling her through the abdomen with an iron rod. Immobilized for months in a full-torso cast, she borrowed her father's paint box, which she had secretly been eyeing, and began to paint. Her first subject was herself.

Artistic ability is all over her chart. Her Cancer Sun conjuncts Neptune, the planet of the imagination, with nearby Jupiter magnifying her talent. Venus, ruling art, conjuncts Pluto, the planet of transformation. Her Moon in earthy Taurus in the tenth house stimulated her love of beauty and her yearning for recognition. Leo rising gave her pride, incomparable style, and a gift for self-expression.

There's more, because exceptional ability tends to appear in multiple places. In Frida's fifth house, hot-blooded Mars and unconventional Uranus — an explosive pair — spiked her creative vision with a shot of dazzling originality. They also drew her into turbulent relationships with, among others, her husband, the artist Diego Rivera. (She married him twice.) And because Mars, the planet of war, and Uranus, the planet of the unexpected, opposed her Sun, they introduced the possibility of violent accidents.

Overseeing all this was Frida's Sun in Cancer, the sign of domesticity. Although she lived with Diego in various places (Detroit, for example), her base was the blue house — *la Casa Azul* — in Coyoacán, Mexico City, where she grew up and where she died. Though her injuries prevented her from having a child, which was a profound sorrow, and brought her more than thirty surgeries, agonizing pain, and serious bouts of depression and alcoholism, she never lost the gift of joy. She hosted dinner parties and holiday celebrations, and she loved to cook in her festive, mood-elevating kitchen. Did she commit suicide? Probably. Nonetheless, her last painting, finished a week before she died, is a cheerful image of sliced watermelons emblazoned with the words "Viva la Vida." Long live life.

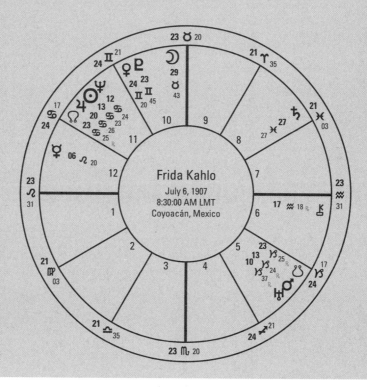

MORE CLASSIC CRABS

- Kevin Bacon, Pamela Lee Anderson, Sonia Sotomayor, Benedict Cumberbatch (Moon in Aries)

- Meryl Streep, Elizabeth Warren, Frances McDormand, Chiwetel Ejiofor, (Moon in Taurus)

- Robert A. Heinlein, Florence Ballard, Priyanka Chopra, Khloe Kardashian (Moon in Gemini)

- Pablo Neruda, Harrison Ford, Courtney Love, Sandra Oh, Mindy Kaling (Moon in Cancer)

- Thurgood Marshall, Ringo Starr, Tom Hanks, Antoine de Saint-Exupéry (Moon in Leo)

- The Dalai Lama, Anjelica Huston, Jhumpa Lahiri, Elon Musk (Moon in Virgo)

- Twyla Tharp, Ariana Grande, Derek Jeter, Alan Turing (Moon in Libra)

- Rembrandt van Rijn, Nelson Mandela, Gisele Bundchen, Wendy Williams (Moon in Scorpio)

- Gerald Ford, Mike Tyson, Michael Phelps, Kevin Hart (Moon in Sagittarius)

- Edgar Degas, Ernest Hemingway, Anthony Bourdain (Moon in Capricorn)

- Mel Brooks, Linda Ronstadt, Solange Knowles, Diana, Princess of Wales (Moon in Aquarius)

- Herman Hesse, Helen Keller, Robin Williams, Debbie Harry (Moon in Pisces)

Leo the Lion: July 23–August 22

I used to imagine that I was somehow unique in having so many Leo friends. But I'm not unique in the least; everyone has Leo friends because Leos are so outgoing and warm that they accumulate friends the way other people collect shoes.

The swirling glyph of Leo (see Figure 5-2) represents the lion's tail, the lion's mane, or the creative force of the Sun.

FIGURE 5-2:
The glyph of Leo.

© John Wiley & Sons, Inc.

The sunny side

You've got flair. If you're a typical Leo, you're outgoing, loyal, determined, cheerful, and genial. You're active, with a busy social calendar and a pile of responsibilities. Whatever you do for a living, your schedule is crammed full. You aim to live life to the fullest and have a good time while you're at it. You often fall into the role of entertaining other people because you love to be the center of attention — and with the Sun as your ruling planet, you really do light up the room. Equipped with a lively sense of humor, vividly rendered opinions, and the ability to enjoy yourself even under adverse conditions, you present yourself with confidence and pizazz. Radiant and proud, you are the embodiment of charisma.

You also have a king-of-the-jungle sense of dignity and a regal sense of entitlement to go with it. You appreciate luxury and glamour in all their forms. Yet despite your aristocratic ways and your need to be pampered, you respect hard work and are willing to shoulder more than your share of the responsibility. Although you can be demanding, you value loyalty and return it in kind. You're helpful and generous, a staunch supporter of an underdog or a friend in distress. And you bring the party with you. Naturally, you want to be acknowledged. What's wrong with that?

The sorry side

Beneath your flamboyant exterior, you would be humiliated if anyone knew how hard you try or how vulnerable you feel. You want to please people, and you want to be seen in a flattering light. In your efforts to achieve those aims, you're inclined to tell people what you think they want to hear, which is a nice way of saying that you are manipulative and you sometimes lie. Your motivation is pure: You want what's best for everyone, and you certainly don't want anyone's feelings to be hurt. You're more protective of others than you often get credit for. But in the end, you're not willing to tamp down your personality or repress your opinions. If you care about something, you will eventually speak your mind. You can be adamant about the tiniest things — shampoo, say. Or barbecue sauce. Or what other people ought to do with their lives. One way or another, you have to express yourself. And if you have to exaggerate in order to make your point, so what?

At your worst, you can be controlling, overbearing, vain, self-aggrandizing, demanding, and histrionic — a drama queen and a know-it-all who finds it difficult to admit mistakes, at least publicly (though you have no problem castigating yourself in the privacy of your thoughts). The good news is that you are seldom at your worst. When you calm down and stop trying to control things, your warmth and generosity come through, along with your good intentions, and you effortlessly command the adoration that you crave.

Relationships

Your self-assurance and easy-going humor draw a crowd. The center of any social scene, you're an accomplished party-thrower and a sought-after dinner guest. Although you prefer to maintain the upper hand in a relationship, and you rely on the attentions of others to keep your ego in shape, you also know how to bestow affection and admiration. People feel privileged to be your friend.

As for romance, Leo loves to be in love and believes in everything symbolic of that state — from Saturday night (which is sacred) to flowers, frequent contacts, breakfast in bed, plenty of sex, and enviable presents. (I've known Leos to leave marked-up copies of the Tiffany catalogue on the breakfast table, just to make sure the message gets across.) You're definitely high maintenance, though you undoubtedly think otherwise. When times are good, you're passionate, accommodating, supportive, and adoring. When things are falling apart, you do too, becoming domineering, arrogant, and jealous. Should a hot affair cool into dull predictability, you may stir things up, just to keep life interesting. But when your beloved hits a rough patch or suffers a setback, you're devastated, even if you don't let it show. For all your bluster, you have a tender heart.

Finally, I want to add a note about animals. In traditional astrological lore, pets are not associated with Leo. But I have noticed that the people who treat their pets like family, cart them around in Louis Vuitton cases, purchase wardrobes for them, publish books about them, or appear on television with squirming bulldogs on their laps to protest against puppy mills, are overwhelmingly Leos. Not every Leo has a pet, and some wouldn't dream of it. (They don't want to be upstaged.) But those who do value their four-legged friends invest themselves fully in the relationship.

For information on Leo's relationships with other signs, take a look at Chapter 15.

Work

Because Leos enjoy basking in the limelight, people occasionally assume that you aren't hard-working. This judgment couldn't be further from the truth. Leos are hugely ambitious. You're resourceful and productive, a skilled organizer with a sharp business sense. You seek recognition more than most, fantasize about fame, and can be somewhat opportunistic, but you are willing to work at maximum intensity. If you are employed within a large organization, you can succeed working with a team, especially if you're the captain. When you're at the top of the heap, you feel powerful and magnanimous. You happily make room for others, and you're not afraid to get your hands dirty. But if you feel fenced in by too many layers of authority, you may rebel. It is exceedingly difficult for you to lack control. Many Leos would rather work on their own as solo practitioners, freelancers, day traders, or entrepreneurs, than submit to the requirements of a corporate culture.

But no matter how gratifying your job may be in other respects, you can't exist without a little razzle-dazzle. Ideal careers are musician, actor, clothing designer, politician, and anything that's likely to put you in front of a camera or a group of people. Fifth-grade teacher? Fine. Lawyer? Sure, especially if you can strut your stuff in court. President of anything? Absolutely. Star of screen and stage? Now you're talking.

TIP

If your boss is a Leo, be prepared to make your job your top priority, to shower him or her with respect and compliments, and to step politely aside whenever the spotlight is turned on. Your allegiance and skill will be recognized and rewarded. Leo is warm and generous. But remember, Leo rules. The term of art here is "benevolent despot."

Health and wellness

Ruled by the Sun, you have vitality to burn — but perhaps not as much as you wish you had. You are ambitious and full of brio, with a lengthy To Do list, a demanding social life, and a fondness for spontaneous outings. You take on a lot and often wear yourself out, which is why your first health challenge is to get a good night's sleep. Naps can help. An early bedtime can help. Substances probably can't. Also beneficial, both to your sleep cycle and your overall health: sunlight (with sunscreen); restful vacations; and vigorous exercise, especially if you do it in the company of others. That neglected treadmill in the attic will never tempt you. If you must exercise alone, try walking the dog. Better yet, don't exercise alone. Take a class. The music will energize you, and the presence of others will motivate you to push yourself.

The parts of the body associated with Leo are the heart and the spine. To maintain your back, try Pilates. As for the heart, you know what to do: no smoking, a pox on junk food, and so on. That crazy-sounding new diet? Please. Although you might wish it were otherwise, the road to wellness runs through fields of moderation.

REMEMBER

Your Sun sign only describes certain aspects of health. If you have health concerns, please see a medical doctor.

The mythology of Leo

After Heracles killed his family (see the mythology of Cancer for more about that), he was sentenced to perform a series of seemingly impossible tasks known as the Twelve Labors. The first of these was to kill the Lion of Nemea, which had fallen to Earth from the Moon and was terrorizing the countryside. Seemingly invincible, the lion had thick fur that neither iron, bronze, nor stone could pierce. Denied these weapons, Heracles cornered the beast, strangled it with his bare hands, and skinned it, using the lion's own claw as a knife. Some stories say he lost a finger in the process. If so, it was a small loss compared to what he gained when he completed all twelve labors: immortality.

The constellation Leo

Leo is an impressive collection of stars that, unlike most constellations, marginally resembles the thing for which it is named. On a dark night in spring, the front portion of Leo is splayed against the sky like a huge backwards question mark — or, if you use your imagination, the head and mane of the lion (though the Chinese saw this constellation as a horse). At the bottom, like the dot at the base of the question mark, sits the bright star Regulus — "the little king." It represents the lion's heart.

Leo: The Basic Facts

Polarity: Positive	Favorable Colors: Gold and orange
Quality: Fixed	Lucky Gem: Ruby
Element: Fire	Parts of the Body: Heart and spine
Symbol: The Lion	Metal: Gold
Ruling Planet: The Sun	Key Phrase: I will
Opposite Sign: Aquarius	Major Traits: Extroverted, demanding

REAL LIFE EXAMPLE

MEGHAN MARKLE: LEO IN ACTION

When Meghan Markle, Duchess of Sussex, gave birth in 2019, her ascendant in Cancer, the sign of all things maternal, was on display. Around the world, people were fascinated by the new mother and the royal baby, just as they were riveted by her wedding the previous year. But Meghan doesn't need a baby or a handsome prince to command attention. Thanks to the Sun, Mercury, and North Node in Leo in the first house, her star quality is baked in.

So too is her ability to communicate. A triple conjunction of the Moon, Saturn, and Jupiter in the third house of communication gives her a lively intellect and a complex emotional nature that combines the ability to set boundaries and control expression with the ability to emote. Therein lies her acting talent — and also her ability to write. At age eleven, she wrote a letter complaining about a sexist advertisement to Procter &

Gamble (and also to then First Lady Hilary Clinton and attorney Gloria Allred). It resulted in a new, improved ad — and landed her on television for the first time. Thanks to Venus, her writing ability is quite literal. As an aspiring actress, she worked as a calligrapher — a prototypical illustration of Venus, the planet of beauty, in the house of writing. She also collaborated with a Canadian retailer to design an affordable fashion line, and she created a blog — another third-house activity — that won her an invitation from the United Nations to join a program promoting gender equality. Well before she met Harry, she spoke to audiences around the world, addressing issues such as social justice (and making productive use of her double major in college: theatre and international studies).

But no chart is perfect. Pluto in the fourth house implies power struggles in her family of origin. Hot-blooded Mars in watery Cancer in her twelfth house of secrets can be passive-aggressive, with an insecure, prickly edge. Mars also stirs up considerable hostility, squaring both the Midheaven, which represents her public image, and the triple conjunction in her house of siblings. Despite the unpleasantness, she has initiative, and in irrepressible Leo form, will carry on.

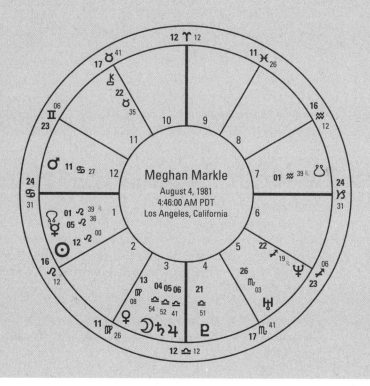

MORE CLASSIC LEOS

- Jacqueline Kennedy Onassis, Andy Warhol, Tom Brady (Moon in Aries)
- Carl Jung, Bill Clinton, Mick Jagger, Ted Hughes, Monica Lewinsky (Moon in Taurus)
- Amelia Earhart, Tony Bennett, Greta Gerwig, Barack Obama (Moon in Gemini)
- Emily Brontë, Annie Oakley, Sean Penn, Steve Wozniak (Moon in Cancer)
- Charlize Theron, Halle Berry, Alison Kraus, Maria Popova (Moon in Leo)
- Madonna, Dustin Hoffman, J. K. Rowling, Elizabeth Moss (Moon in Virgo)
- Fidel Castro, Julia Child, Belinda Carlisle, Michelle Yeoh (Moon in Libra)
- Alfred Hitchcock, Ben Affleck, Steve Martin, Jennifer Lopez, Kylie Jenner (Moon in Scorpio)
- Herman Melville, T. E. Lawrence, Neil Armstrong, Kacey Musgraves (Moon in Sagittarius)
- Napoleon Bonaparte, Lucille Ball, Gene Kelly, Yves St. Laurent, Arnold Schwarzenegger (Moon in Capricorn)
- Sandra Bullock, Beatrix Potter, Helen Mirren, Viola Davis, Cara Delavigne (Moon in Aquarius)
- Coco Chanel, Robert De Niro, Alex Rodriguez, Usain Bolt (Moon in Pisces)

Virgo the Virgin: August 23–September 22

The mind of a Virgo is a wondrous thing. Thanks to Mercury, the planet named after the quick-witted god of communication, you're observant, insightful, capable, and articulate. You're also discriminating and critical, especially of yourself. Constantly in search of self-improvement, you consider yourself a work in progress.

The symbol of Virgo the Virgin (see Figure 5-3) resembles an M with a closed-in loop. It signifies the small intestine and female genitalia, in contrast to Scorpio, which represents the male.

FIGURE 5-3:
The symbol
of Virgo.

© John Wiley & Sons, Inc.

The sunny side

Nothing sneaks past you. You have an eye for detail, an inborn sense of efficiency, and a supreme sensitivity to the implications of language. Smart, funny, and engaging, you can claim extraordinary analytical abilities, a rare clarity of mind, an enviable capacity for concentration, and a love of learning that isn't just for show. On top of that, you're considerate and appealingly modest. You know you're not perfect — but you're doing just about everything you can to get there. Like the other earth signs, you're conscientious and efficient. Unlike them, you're also an idealist. You know how things ought to be, and you're certain that you can make them that way, one detail at a time. You're organized and disciplined, ready to push yourself to the limit. You're equally willing to assist other people, an offer that extends way beyond your immediate circle. You have a strong moral core and can be helpful to the point of selflessness. People often forget that Virgo is the sign of service. Acting on behalf of others makes you feel good about yourself.

The sorry side

You're too hard on everyone, yourself included. You can't distinguish between that which is acceptable (your spouse) and that which is ideal (your spouse, if only he or she would shape up). You can be incredibly demanding — and incredibly disappointed when your demands aren't met. At times you act the part of the martyr compelled to put up with the inadequacies of others, but you also suffer from spasms of guilt, inferiority, shyness, and anxiety. You worry about the air, the water, global warming, politics, the homeless person you passed on the street, the insensitive remark you're afraid you may have made, your investments, and your body.

A note on neatness: No matter what you may have heard, not all Virgos are neatness fiends. Not that it doesn't happen: I've known Virgos who can't rest unless everything in the refrigerator is arranged parallel to the door. I've known Virgos who have genuine opinions about tile cleansers. I've also known Virgos who are incapable of throwing things out. Their intention is to do something useful with all that stuff. Meanwhile, they don't look compulsively neat in the least; they look like hoarders.

Relationships

You'd think that a sign supposedly as critical as Virgo would have trouble making friends. But this isn't the case. Virgos love to converse, excel at analyzing other people, dote on exploring new ideas, and maintain a multitude of interests. Conversation with a Virgo is never dull. Virgos remember birthdays, bring chicken soup to ailing friends, and generally extend themselves. So you don't lack for a busy social life — even if you are a little heavy-handed with the advice from time to time.

In a committed relationship, you're most comfortable when your role and responsibilities are clearly defined. When you don't know what to expect or those roles are shifting, you become jittery, insomniac, withholding, and — your worst mistake — controlling. You don't mean to be — you just want to make sure that everything is on track. You have a powerful sense of the way things should be, and when reality conflicts with your high standards, you may slip into a state of denial and see what you want to see. When breakups occur, you're stunned. For all your good sense, a Virgo with a broken heart is a pathetic creature indeed. Fortunately, you aren't one to spend your life sobbing into your limited-edition designer brew. Inevitably, you find a way to turn things around. You have no trouble attracting admirers, for Virgo can be incredibly seductive, despite its virginal image. (Iconic Virgo sex symbols include Sean Connery, Sophia Loren, Idris Elba, and Beyoncé.) But that's not what helps you get through tough times. It's your mental ability to reframe a situation. Sure, things may look bad from one angle. But from another . . .

For the scoop on Virgo's relationships with other signs, check out Chapter 15.

Work

It's difficult to imagine an organization that wouldn't benefit from having a Virgo or two around. The master of multi-tasking, you easily juggle dozens of details and conflicting demands. Organized and meticulous, you're skilled at teaching, writing (and other forms of communication), and anything that requires rigorous analysis. But no matter what you do, more work ends up on your desk than on anyone else's because, guess what? You're more efficient than anyone else. That's why the powers-that-be keep calling on you. No one else is up to the job — and you may not want to do it either. Even so, you produce accurate, timely results because you can't resist rising to a challenge. Might as well admit the truth: You can't resist the compliment, and you take secret pleasure in tucking in every last loose end. You're the ideal employee, like it or not — which may be why Virgos often fantasize about owning their own businesses. The degree of control you gain as an entrepreneur is tonic for your soul.

TIP

If you work for a Virgo, follow instructions to the letter and obey the unstated rules of the workplace. On the surface, the environment may be casual and egalitarian. Nonetheless, the standards are strict. So go ahead and request instruction and clarification when you need it. Virgo will respect you for asking. Similarly, feel free to ask for feedback. But understand that after you receive advice, you must follow it. Otherwise, Virgo may perceive your request as a waste of time. And take my word for it: You don't want to waste a Virgo's time.

Health and wellness

It's not easy being a Virgo. Even under the sunniest of circumstances, there's anxiety to contend with. That ache in your shoulder: Is it an athletic injury? Or a symptom of something worse? And what about those split ends: an indication that you need a haircut? Or a warning of a nutritional deficiency, possibly connected to an autoimmune disease? For many Virgos, anxiety in the form of hypochondria is a dragon you have to slay again and again, which is not to say that you aren't occasionally beset by real health issues. Telling the difference can be a challenge, which is why learning to counter fearful thoughts is your number one health priority. You benefit from a regular schedule, holistic medicine, positive affirmations, hypnosis, and companions who refuse to get rattled by your fears.

Traditionally, Virgo rules the small intestine, the pancreas, and the nervous system. Your anxieties find expression in your digestive tract or your nervous system, leading to the inadvertent creation of all manner of minor discomforts. Low-key physical activities such as walking, hiking, bicycling, and cross-country skiing ease your mind. Herbal teas, a meditation routine, and a few drops of Rescue Remedy from time to time are healing.

The mythology of Virgo

Life on earth was terrible and getting worse, each age more dreadful than the one preceding it. The Golden Age of harmony gave way to the Silver Age, which brought in bad weather; then to the Bronze Age, when weapons were invented; and finally to the Iron Age, an abysmal era — our own era — of war and crime. When the gods and goddesses of classical mythology could no longer tolerate the misery, they turned their backs on Earth and fled. Only the goddess Astraea remained behind, hoping that humanity would find a way to live in peace. When her patience ran out, she threw up her hands in despair and abandoned the Earth, the last immortal to do so. This constellation honors her. Other contenders for the Virgo crown include Ishtar, Demeter, Persephone, Urania, the Greek muse of astronomy, and Dike, the goddess of luck and dice.

The constellation Virgo

Virgo is the largest constellation in the zodiac, and the second largest in the night sky. Its brightest star is Spica, representing the spike of wheat carried by Demeter, the goddess of grain. Finding it is easy. First, locate the Big Dipper. Follow the line of its handle to the bright star Arcturus — or, as they say in astronomical circles, arc to Arcturus. Then, continuing on, follow that imaginary curve to the next bright star, Spica. You will have covered half the night sky, and you will have found Virgo, the only constellation in the zodiac identified as a woman.

Virgo: The Basic Facts

Polarity: Negative	Favorable Colors: Navy and neutrals
Quality: Mutable	Lucky Gem: Peridot
Element: Earth	Part of the Body: Small intestine, pancreas, and nervous system
Symbol: The Virgin	Metal: Mercury
Ruling Planet: Mercury	Key Phrase: I analyze
Opposite Sign: Pisces	Major Traits: Analytical, faultfinding

REAL LIFE EXAMPLE

VIRGO IN ACTION: BEYONCÉ KNOWLES

Is there a more electrifying performer than Beyoncé? There is not. She can do everything. No surprise, then, that her horoscope is formidable. All ten planets reside on the left side of her chart, so the control she wields over the direction of her life is considerable. A pile-up of planets in artistic Libra, including a tight conjunction of Venus, Pluto, and her Ascendant, imparts beauty, power, and unstoppable charisma. Her Moon is conjunct Uranus in Scorpio, so her emotions — love, rage, ecstasy, the whole spectrum — are volatile and deeply felt. Since both planets are in the second house, financial independence is important to her. Although she spends lavishly and has the proven ability to earn enormous amounts, money remains a highly charged element in her life. Mars in Leo at top of her chart conjunct her Midheaven and North Node supplies ambition and a competitive streak, and also describes her mate.

But the essence of her horoscope can be found in her Sun. Because it occupies the eleventh house of community, she puts a high value on friendship and has concerns that transcend the personal, such as commitments to African American culture and to feminism. And although Libra might seem to be the dominant influence in her chart, her Sun in Virgo stands alone and is tremendously powerful. Beyoncé embodies everything you might associate with that sign, from her Vegan-ish diet and flawless appearance to her relentless work ethic and propensity to micromanage. "I personally selected each dancer, every light, the material on the steps, the height of the pyramid, the shape of the pyramid," she explains in a documentary about Coachella 2018. "Every tiny detail had an intention." That's classic Virgo.

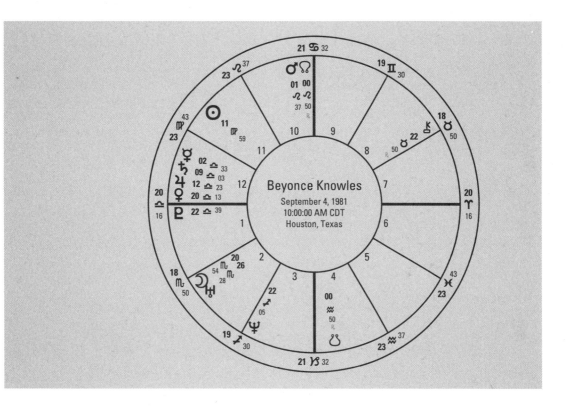

MORE CLASSIC VIRGOS

- Lauren Bacall, Leonard Bernstein, Bernie Sanders, George R. R. Martin (Moon in Aries)
- Oliver Stone, Mother Theresa, Prince Harry, Colin Firth (Moon in Taurus)
- Cathy Guisewite, Karl Lagerfeld, Buddy Holly, Jeanette Winterson (Moon in Gemini)
- Julio Iglesias, Dave Chapelle, Melissa McCarthy, Stella McCartney (Moon in Cancer)
- William *"Lord of the Flies"* Golding, Idris Elba, Amy Poehler, Andrew Lloyd Webber (Moon in Leo)
- Sean Connery, Michelle Williams, Fiona Apple, Padma Lakshmi (Moon in Virgo)
- Ivan the Terrible, D. H. Lawrence, Agatha Christie, Ray Charles (Moon in Libra)
- Bruno Bettleheim, A. S. Byatt, Jimmy Fallon, Julio Cortázar (Moon in Scorpio)
- Mary *"Frankenstein"* Shelley, Stephen King, Warren Buffet (Moon in Sagittarius)
- Dorothy Parker, Brian de Palma, Amy Winehouse, Louis C. K. (Moon in Capricorn)
- Sophia Loren, Samuel Goldwyn, Joan Jett, Temple Grandin (Moon in Aquarius)
- Michael Jackson, Leonard Cohen, Ava DuVernay, Sheryl Sandberg (Moon in Pisces)

Chapter **6**

The Signs of Autumn: Libra, Scorpio, and Sagittarius

The first six signs of the zodiac, according to traditional astrology, are youthful and subjective, signs of self and individual development. The last six signs are other-oriented, more invested in relationship, community, and the world.

Well, that's one way to look at the circle of the zodiac. Another way would be to think of it as a hero's journey, a mythological tale that starts with an Aries adventure and ends with Piscean enchantment, though that too is an over-simplification. Still, that's something reassuring about the notion that the signs tell a story by building on each other. Take the signs of Autumn, which shine a light first on relationships (that's Libra's responsibility); then on sex, death, and regeneration (that's Scorpio's weighty mission); and finally on the urge to explore the world in search of wisdom (the eternal quest of Sagittarius).

The three signs of autumn are:

>> Libra the Scales (September 23 to October 22), the sign of cardinal air. Libra is recognized for its intellect, sense of fairness, and aesthetic sensitivity, as well as for the importance it places on relationships.

>> Scorpio the Scorpion (October 23 to November 21), the sign of fixed water. Scorpio is known for its intensity, magnetism, instinct, and strategic intelligence.

>> Sagittarius the Archer (November 22 to December 21), the sign of mutable fire. The archer is independent, adventurous, expansive, and philosophically inclined.

TIP

The Sun sign dates in this book (and every other astrology book) are only approximate because, from year to year, there's always a bit of variation. So if your birthday falls at the beginning or end of a sign, you need a mathematically correct horoscope. To make sure that you've got one, collect your birth data and go online. In Chapter 2, the section "Getting Your Horoscope Online" will tell you what to do.

REMEMBER

Each sign has an element (fire, earth, air, or water), a polarity (positive or negative) and a quality or modality (cardinal, fixed, or mutable). For more on those terms, see Chapter 1.

Libra the Scales: September 23–October 22

I grew up surrounded by Librans, and I can tell you this: Libra is the sign of civilization. Ruled by Venus, the planet of love and beauty, you act rationally, believe in fairness, and are usually easy to be around.

The glyph of Libra (see Figure 6-1) represents a simple balance or the scales of justice. It also suggests the setting Sun, which reflects the fact that the first day of Libra is the fall equinox, when day and night reach a point of perfect equilibrium.

FIGURE 6-1:
Libra's glyph.

© John Wiley & Sons, Inc.

The sunny side

Where elegance meets cool, and sense meets sensibility, that's Libra. Refined and even-tempered, amiable and observant, you're the ultimate diplomat (when you want to be). You seek serenity, respond strongly to art and music, and thrive in aesthetically agreeable surroundings (though ordinary nuisances like noise make you tense and tired). Your artistic sensibility is highly developed, your social sense even more so. Easy-going, graceful, smart, and charming, you're a sought-after dinner party guest who very much wants to be liked. And although you can't stop being flirtatious, you're also a committed partner for whom relationships are indispensable.

At the same time, as an air sign, you have a sophisticated intellect and you pride yourself on your sensible approach to life. You seek out information and opposing points of view, and you do your best not to jump to conclusions, often arguing a point just to work your way around all sides of an issue. (Plus, let it be said that you enjoy a good debate.) Because reason is a high value for you, you naturally try to be objective. That's the meaning of the scales, your symbol, which represents your ability to weigh both sides of an issue as well as your need to achieve emotional balance. Most of the time, your thoughtful, objective approach works. The harmony and balance that you seek are achievable.

The sorry side

As Eleanor Roosevelt, a classic Libran, once said, "Nobody can make you feel inferior without your consent." Well, no problem: You consent. Your amiable personality may conceal a festering dissatisfaction and a terrible struggle with emotional complexities. You have a deeply ingrained predisposition to worry, combined with — at your sorriest — a woeful lack of confidence. (If you have planets in Virgo, as many Librans do, you're undoubtedly your own harshest critic.) Anxious for the good opinion of others, you may try too hard to satisfy. And yet in other ways, you don't try hard enough. When you're down, you can be vague, dependent, self-indulgent, and withdrawn, and your refined sensibilities are so easily injured that it's sometimes laughable.

You can't bear squabbles — and yet you're more than capable of generating them. Like Librans Mahatma Gandhi, the prophet of nonviolence, and John Lennon, the antiwar rock star, you're more contentious than your reputation or image suggests.

And as much as you need balance, you have trouble maintaining it. Because you're a serious thinker, you can be indecisive to the point of paralysis, especially when you need to make a consequential choice. Uncertainty undoes you. You wobble back and forth, balancing pros and cons. You compare and contrast. You work yourself up into a tizzy, becoming distant, argumentative, or obsessed. Making up your mind so that you can move forward can be your greatest challenge. In your search for peace, beauty, and equilibrium, you can wear yourself out. Your best approach is the Roman one: Moderation in all things.

Relationships

What a bundle of contradictions Libra can be. On the one hand, you're ruled by seductive Venus, and relationships are essential to you. Longing for love, you instinctively look to romantic partners to balance your inadequacies and stabilize you. On the other hand, you're an air sign, ruled by your head — not your heart. Thanks to your refined sensibilities and visceral distaste for tear-soaked melo-dramas, you unconsciously preserve a distance meant to protect you from conflict and emotional chaos. In relationships, as in other areas of life, you often end up in an internal tug-of-war, first drawing close to the object of your affection, and then pulling away. It's a form of balance. Not surprisingly, that ambivalence may strike the other person as manipulative.

And what is it that you seek? The right partner has to come equipped with the whole package: looks, brains, energy, style, manners, and a dash — or more than a dash — of status. When you find that person, as most Librans do, you're loyal, loving, generous, and proud. Meanwhile, thanks to your ineffable charm and your ability to keep the conversation interesting, you need never dine alone.

For insight into your relationships with other signs, go to Chapter 15.

Work

For Libra, life would be much more pleasant without the irksome necessity of work. Because your aesthetic sense is directly related to your mood, it's imperative that your workspace be clean and airy with plenty of opportunities for face-to-face socializing. Finding an environment that supports you both intellectually and socially is equally important. You aren't enormously ambitious, perhaps because you underrate yourself. Money is seldom your chief motivation, but you know what you're worth, and you're confident enough to ask for the recognition you deserve. Still, the day-to-day quality of your work is what matters most.

Ideal fields include all aspects of the arts, including the visual arts, theater, dance, and music. Cultural organizations are natural spots for you. You can also express your artistic talents in fashion, graphic design, interior decoration, architecture, photography, cinema, and related fields. Other areas for which you are equally well suited include diplomacy, mediation and negotiation, the law (Libra makes a fine judge), and anything that requires making contact with the public.

TIP

If you work with or for a Libra, you have the opportunity to observe the power of reason close up. Libra respects rational decision-making and analysis. Gifted with poise and intelligence, Libra values your input, tries to be fair, and expects you to share in the spirit of compromise. It's true that Libran decision-making can be a lengthy process. But after a decision has been reached, Libra moves with dispatch. Two pieces of advice: Present your ideas calmly and logically. And look your best. Libra may pretend that appearance doesn't matter. Don't believe it.

Health and wellness

No matter the question, the answer for Libra is always the same: Seek balance. It is your remedy, your therapy, your consolation. But it is also your challenge because, in real life, incorporating a balanced diet and regular exercise into your schedule is not always easy. Two caveats. Number one: Because Libra is an air sign, your diet, like your exercise routine, has to make rational sense to you. If it sounds even a tiny bit crazy, it's not for you. Number two: Because Libra is ruled by Venus, you're most responsive to exercise that verges on art (such as skating or dance), has a social component, and offers a chance to spend time in a beautiful setting. Those grueling, sweat-drenched workouts people brag about: Why? Finally, treat sleep with respect. Get as much as you need, and it will benefit you immensely.

The parts of the body most associated with Libra are the kidneys, the skin, and the lower back. To keep the kidneys reliably filtering out impurities, drink plenty of water and stay hydrated. To protect of your skin, use sunscreen and visit a top-notch dermatologist regularly. Finally, lower back pain can be an obstinate but ultimately solvable problem. Try yoga postures such as Tree Pose, Tai Chi, or bodywork such as the Zero Balancing technique.

REMEMBER

A Sun sign description of health can only suggest tendencies. A medical astrologer can tell you more. But even the most brilliant medical astrologer does not, for example, do surgery. Or command an X-ray machine. If you have a question about your health, please see a physician.

The mythology of Libra

Along among the constellations of the zodiac, only Libra is perceived not as an animal, a person, or an imaginary figure but as a thing: an ordinary scale or balance, an object with no story attached. Four thousand years ago, the Sumerians saw it as the "balance of heaven" and the fulcrum of the year, marking the moment when the Sun is midway through its yearly passage. The Greeks didn't think of Libra as a separate constellation. Instead, they attached it to the adjacent constellation and referred to the stars of Libra as the claws of the Scorpion. The Romans, who had a special fondness for Libra, preferred the Sumerian image and associated the constellation with the goddess who holds the scales of justice. Cicero reported that Rome was founded when the moon was in Libra. Thus, according to Marcus Manilius, a Roman astrologer and poet of the first century CE, "Italy belongs to the balance, her rightful sign."

The constellation Libra

The image of the scale or balance triumphed long ago over the notion that the stars of Libra could represent the claws of the Scorpion. And yet that idea lives on in the Arabic names of Libra's brightest stars: Zubenelgenubi, the southern claw, and Zubeneschemali, the northern claw. To most people, Zubeneschemali looks like an ordinary white star. But for observers with especially acute vision, it is also the only bright star in the sky sometimes described as green.

Libra: The Basic Facts

Polarity: Positive	Favorable Colors: Blues and pastels
Quality: Cardinal	Lucky Gems: Sapphire, jade, and opal
Element: Air	Parts of the Body: Kidneys and skin
Symbol: The Scales	Metal: Copper
Ruling Planet: Venus	Key Phrase: I balance
Opposite Sign: Aries	Major Traits: Cosmopolitan, indecisive

REAL LIFE EXAMPLE

LIBRA IN ACTION: BRUCE SPRINGSTEEN

On the surface, Bruce Springsteen is the most macho of rock 'n' roll icons. But in his autobiography and Broadway play, he talks about his introverted, anxiety-ridden childhood, his conflicts with his father ("my hero and my greatest foe"), his struggles with depression, and the difference between his image and the person he feels himself to be. His ascendant is in restless, garrulous Gemini, sign of the wordsmith. Rising in the first house is freedom-loving, rebellious Uranus. Those influences shape his persona. A deeper source of strength lives in his fifth house of creativity and entertainment, where a cluster of planets in Libra tugs him toward the arts. It would have been hard to resist that pull, and he did not. Early on, Springsteen determined that neither his voice nor his instrumental skill would bring him the greatness he craved. It had to be writing. Several factors support that insight. His Gemini ascendant gives him a flair for storytelling and turning a phrase. Mercury, ruler of Gemini and thus his ruling planet, occupies the fifth house and is retrograde — which I hope puts to rest the misguided belief that retrograde Mercury is a fearful thing in a natal chart. It is not. It deepens his intellect and sharpens his insight. Finally, Mars and Pluto, located in the third house of communication and in Leo, sign of the performer, give him infinite drive and a commanding aura: hence, the Boss. The hard rock style, melodramatic tales, and ferocious emotion filtered through his work are gifts of that adrenaline-fueled duo. Every element of an astrological chart can be used in a positive or negative way. In Springsteen's case, he has turned turmoil into art.

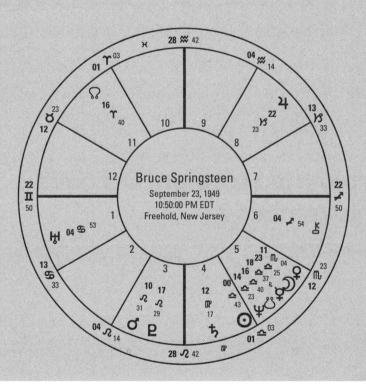

MORE CLASSIC LIBRANS

- Giuseppe Verdi, E. E. Cummings, Martina Navratilova, Cardi B (Moon in Aries)
- F. Scott Fitzgerald, Sigourney Weaver, Carrie Fisher, Jesse Jackson (Moon in Taurus)
- Gwyneth Paltrow, T. S. Eliot, Ursula K. LeGuin, Hugh Jackman (Moon in Gemini)
- Paul Simon, Gwen Stefani, Neil deGrasse Tyson, Eleanor Roosevelt (Moon in Cancer)
- Mahatma Gandhi, Oscar Wilde, Elmore Leonard, David Benioff (Moon in Leo)
- Serena Williams, Lenny Bruce, Bella Hadid, Ang Lee (Moon in Virgo)
- Arthur Rimbaud, Kate Winslet, Doris Lessing, Kelly Ripa (Moon in Libra)
- Will Smith, Jimmy Carter, Ralph Lauren, Brie Larson (Moon in Scorpio)
- Friedrich Nietzsche, Richard Meier, Christopher Reeve, Dakota Johnson (Moon in Sagittarius)
- Susan Sarandon, Wally Lamb, Matt Damon, Michael Douglas (Moon in Capricorn)
- George Gershwin, John Lennon, Annie Leibovitz, Eminem (Moon in Aquarius)
- Eugene O'Neill, Chuck Berry, Kim Kardashian (Moon in Pisces)

Scorpio the Scorpion: October 23–November 21

Intensity is the key to Scorpio. Ruled by Pluto, the (dwarf) planet of transformation, you're a compelling personality — and a creature of extremes. Emotionally or otherwise, in fact or in fantasy, you live on the edge.

The glyph of Scorpio (see Figure 6-2) represents the male genitals or the piercing barb of the Scorpion's tail.

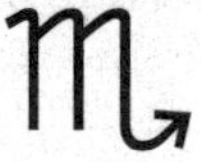

FIGURE 6-2: The symbol of the Scorpion.

The sunny side

You are vibrant, magnetic, passionate, perceptive, and sensual: A person of depth and complexity who participates fully and courageously in life and whose insights into human psychology are discerning. You are aware of the spoken message as well as the subtext and the body language, and you can't help relishing the melodrama of it all. Your mood seesaws between ecstatic heights and nightmarish depths, and there's hardly an emotion that you haven't felt right down to your soul. You're also curious about other people. Although you value your privacy and are often quite reticent, you're skilled at ferreting out the secrets of others. Mysteries fascinate you, which is why astrology books inevitably recommend that Scorpios become detectives or spies.

Here's another positive trait: You're determined. When you apply yourself, your willpower is astonishing (although you can also take it too far: Eating disorders are a blight on your sign). You're resourceful, too. You make careful plans, and if the time's not right, you wait. You don't ever give up. You aim for the highest — or the lowest. That's why, unlike any other sign, Scorpio has three symbols: the scorpion, which crawls through the dust; the eagle, which soars through the air; and the phoenix, which burns itself up in the heat of its passion and is reborn. Like that mythical bird, you have the ability to rejuvenate yourself.

The sorry side

Let me be honest: Scorpio has some deeply nasty traits. You can be obsessive, jealous, secretive, manipulative, and arrogant. You have an exceedingly wicked tongue. You know how to wound, and if you're backed into a corner, you don't hesitate to do so. Once you decide that you've been crossed, you're unforgiving. You can be vengeful, spiteful, and disturbingly cold-hearted — or so it appears. When Scorpio (sign of Charles Manson) is bad, it's downright scary.

But in my experience, most Scorpions keep that side of their personalities under wraps. Instead, you struggle with depression. When times are tough, you plummet to the bottom of the sea. Other signs don't begin to comprehend the bleak despair that pulls you down. Yet this is an essential component of being a Scorpio. It works like this: You sink into darkness, claw your way through the underworld of the psyche, and wrestle with your own worst qualities and darkest fears. And then you emerge. Before Pluto was discovered in 1930, astrologers regarded Mars, the planet of war and desire, as the ruler of Scorpio. And it is, for you pursue your demons like a warrior, fighting relentlessly, even against addiction and other tribulations. Pluto adds an element of renewal and transformation. In your quest for that, you're unflinching.

Relationships

No one said relationships were easy. That's because casual liaisons don't satisfy you. Even your friendships are serious. Growing up, you understood the concept of blood brothers or sisters (even if you never found a friend who qualified), and you longed for that kind of connection. As an adult, you still want to bond on the deepest level. That's especially true in your romantic life. Ardent and mysterious, you long for blazing sex, conversation that breaks all barriers, and total immersion. When you fall in love, it's theatrical and impassioned — a drama for the ages.

At its finest, that intensity helps you create the kind of fully intertwined partnership you crave. At its worst, it causes you to become suspicious, possessive, and resentful. Issues of power and control arise, and you can become painfully obsessive. When you feel injured or when a relationship is disintegrating, you unleash the deadly sting for which the scorpion is famous. If you cut someone off, it's forever. No one feels ecstasy the way you do; and no one suffers more.

Finally, I want to point out that, despite your desire to mind-meld with another human being, Scorpio also requires privacy. Without it, your peace of mind unravels, something anyone involved with you must understand. Solitude, like sex, is a necessity.

Wondering how you get along with other signs? Turn to Chapter 15.

Work

Scorpio brings energy and ambition to the workplace, and your goals are generally of the highest order (though, for the record, Scorpios can also be adept as scam artists, drug dealers, and low-level thugs). Astute and insightful, you make a fantastic advocate for anyone in need. Plus, you're a fighter. You're fascinated by power and money, which gives you the motivation to excel at business (think of Bill Gates) or politics (consider Hillary Clinton, Robert F. Kennedy, or Joe Biden). Whatever field you're in, trivialities don't interest you. Nor do you have to be center stage (unless, of course, you have a lot of Leo in your chart). But you do need to be involved in an enterprise that matters. Scientific research, surgery, counseling, community organizing, investigative reporting, investment banking, politics, and psychology all come to mind. As I noted earlier, detective and spy are two positions traditionally considered Scorpionic. But did I mention magician? Mortician? Obituary writer? Mystery novelist? Guru? Poet? Greatest artist of the 20th century (Picasso)? And the list goes on.

TIP

If you work with or for a Scorpio, you'll see what it means to be committed. Scorpios are industrious, disciplined, and demanding. They know how to concentrate (unless, of course, they can't, in which case, you get to see the miserable, sulky Scorpio). They also know how to keep a secret, which means you can trust Scorpios with yours. But they're inscrutable. They nurture their accomplices — and demolish their enemies. If you have a Scorpio boss, do your best — and don't try any fancy stuff. A Scorpio will see it coming, and you'll pay for your presumption. No one, and I mean no one, wants to have a Scorpio for an enemy.

Health and wellness

Mars and Pluto, Scorpio's ruling planets, bring you a robust constitution and a forceful will. With Scorpio, determination is all. It's true that your intensity can turn against you when it slides into obsession, and you may struggle with addictive behaviors. That's a problem many Scorpios face — and conquer. More often, your intensity works in your favor. Self-discipline and commitment are within your command, and you're not afraid to do what needs to be done, whether than means quitting smoking (start when the Moon is new), putting your diet in order, or getting psychological help. Finally, serious exercise is essential. Strolling in the park, while pleasant, doesn't count. You require something more intense, like rock-climbing, boot camps, martial arts, working out with weights, training for marathons, or vinyasa yoga. As a water sign, you also benefit from swimming, surfing, and restorative saltwater baths. You may prefer to exercise on your own, rather than in a class. The bottom line is this: Anything you're passionate about is something you will stick with. That's the right exercise for you.

Traditionally, the body parts associated with Scorpio are the reproductive organs and the colon. So you're smart to schedule regular visits to the appropriate specialists — including, after a certain age, regular colonoscopies.

REMEMBER

A Sun sign description of health only offers an overview. An experienced medical astrologer delves deeper and can tell you more. But if you're truly worried about your health, please consult a medical doctor.

The mythology of Scorpio

The giant Orion bragged to Artemis, the Greek goddess of the hunt, that he could kill every animal on the planet. When Gaia, goddess of Earth, heard his threat, she sent a Scorpion darting up through a crack in the ground to attack him. As the venom coursed through his body, Orion raised his club and smashed it down on the Scorpion, killing it. Afterwards, Zeus lifted both Orion and his assailant into the heavens, but because they were enemies, he placed them as far from each other as possible. That's why all variations on this myth end the same way: When one constellation is rising over the horizon, the other is setting.

The constellation Scorpius

Of all the astrological constellations, Scorpius is the only one that looks the way it ought to look, with a distinctively curved body and a red star, Antares, in just the spot where the Scorpion's heart would be. One summer's night, find a dark spot far from the city's glare, look south, and you will see it, easily the most dramatic constellation in the zodiac.

Scorpio: The Basic Facts

Polarity: Negative	Favorable Colors: Dark reds and black
Quality: Fixed	Lucky Gem: Opal
Element: Water	Part of the Body: Reproductive organs
Symbol: the Scorpion	Metal: Steel or iron
Ruling Planets: Mars and Pluto	Key Phrase: I desire
Opposite Sign: Taurus	Major Traits: Passionate, obsessive

REAL LIFE EXAMPLE

SCORPIO IN ACTION: ANA MENDIETA

Ana Mendieta, a Cuban-American artist who died young just as her enigmatic art began receiving the recognition it deserved, was a Scorpio through and through. When she was 12, Uranus, the lord of disruption, squared her Scorpio Sun. Not every transit expresses itself dramatically, but this one did. Her parents, foreseeing trouble from Fidel Castro's newly formed government, sent Ana and her sister, Raquelin, to the United States, where they were shuttled among refugee camps, foster homes, reform schools, and other institutions. That upheaval tore her from her cultural roots, stirring feelings of loss and alienation that never disappeared. Her life became a search, conducted with typical Scorpio intensity, for identity and healing. That quest, supported by the conjunction of her Sun with Chiron, the asteroid of healing, is clearly visible in her art.

Studying at the University of Iowa, she was drawn to avant-garde, interdisciplinary art; to non-traditional materials; to feminist themes; and to spiritual, Earth-centered rituals. Using blood, mud, sand, moss, ice, fire, gunpowder, and her naked body, she staged raw tableaux addressing violence against women; carved images of Afro-Cuban goddesses into the walls of a jungle cave; and made hundreds of films and "siluetas" featuring her body — or its silhouette — melding into a tree, a rock, or a river bed, blanketed with flowers or feathers, and merging with the Earth. In short, she repeatedly transformed herself, which is the mission of her sign. The images she created are disquieting, hinting at forces unseen and pushing boundaries, including that of gender. Like other Scorpios, she enjoyed breaking taboos. "She had that spark," her sister said. "She was never afraid of anything."

At 35, her career on the rise, she married the sculptor Carl Andre. One night they argued and, somehow, Ana fell from the window of their 34th-floor apartment. Andre was charged with murder. He was acquitted for insufficient evidence but in the court of public opinion, the jury is still out. What really happened? In death as in life, mystery surrounds her.

Note: Unlike the other chart in this book, Ana Medieta's chart was calculated using an arbitrary time — dawn — and "whole sign" houses. That's one of the few options when the time of birth is unknown. So we cannot know her Ascendant or houses, and they should be totally ignored in the interpretation. Fortunately no matter what time she was born, her planets, including the Moon, occupy the same signs and make the same aspects. So, for example, her Jupiter is opposite Uranus, making her an independent spirit, restless and innovative. That is true no matter what time she was born. Her Venus is in Libra, an ideal placement for an artist. Plus, it was widely conjunct Neptune, inspiring her imagination but also, perhaps, skewing her romantic judgment. Might those planets be in her house of marriage? We just don't know.

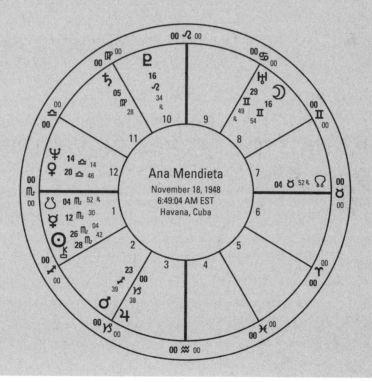

MORE CLASSIC SCORPIONS

- Bill Gates, Jamie Lee Curtis, Jimmy Kimmel, Kendall Jenner (Moon in Aries)
- Demi Moore, Prince Charles, Joe Biden, Adam Driver (Moon in Taurus)
- Fyodor Dostoyevsky, Bonnie Raitt, Tilda Swinton, Roseanne Barr (Moon in Gemini)
- Condoleezza Rice, Kris Jenner, Mark Ruffalo, Drake (Moon in Cancer)
- Julia Roberts, Kurt Vonnegut, Nail Gaiman, Hedy Lamarr (Moon in Leo)
- Sean Combs, Matthew McConaughey, k.d. lang, Lorde (Moon in Virgo)
- Marie Antoinette, Leonardo DiCaprio, Billie Jean King, Sylvia Plath (Moon in Libra)
- Whoopi Goldberg, Ryan Reynolds, Katy Perry, RuPaul (Moon in Scorpio)
- Pablo Picasso, Rock Hudson, Kelly Osbourne, Ivanka Trump (Moon in Sagittarius)
- George Eliot, Indira Gandhi, Robert F. Kennedy, Bernard-Henri Lévy (Moon in Capricorn)
- Albert Camus, Dylan Thomas, Neil Young, Caitlyn Jenner (Moon in Aquarius)
- Marie Curie, Hillary Rodham Clinton, Laura Bush, Joni Mitchell, Jonas Salk (Moon in Pisces)

Sagittarius the Archer: November 22–December 21

Independent, energetic, and filled with an irrepressible sense of possibility, you feel most vibrantly alive when you're having an adventure or exploring the world. For that you can thank Jupiter, your ruler, the planet of expansion and good fortune.

The glyph of Sagittarius (see Figure 6-3) represents the centaur's arrow and your high aspirations.

FIGURE 6-3:
The symbol of
Sagittarius.

© John Wiley & Sons, Inc.

The sunny side

At your happiest and best, you're a free spirit, a cheerful wanderer, an honest and intelligent companion, and a philosopher who likes to ponder the big questions — preferably with a few pals and a plentiful supply of snacks. You see life as an ongoing quest for experience and wisdom, not as a search for security. Restless and excitable, with a rapid-fire wit, you chafe under restriction and demand autonomy, which you happily extend to others.

In your eternal quest for experience and knowledge, you pursue a multitude of interests and you set ambitious, wide-ranging goals for yourself. Brimming with curiosity, you want to see the world and understand it, which is why your sign rules travel, philosophy, religion, law, and abstractions of all kinds. Sagittarius is free-thinking, casual, open-minded, and optimistic (though a couple of planets in Scorpio can dampen your spirits and add a touch of melancholy). You connect easily with all kinds of people and are said to be lucky. The truth is that your spontaneous decisions and out-there gambles occasionally pay off, but what benefits you the most is your fearless attitude. Sure, troubles may come. No one is immune to that. But ultimately, buoyed by your belief in the future, you bounce back. You look at it this way: What other choice is there?

The sorry side

Like the centaur, your half-human, half-horse symbol, you're divided. Part of you aspires to party into the night (that's the quadruped half). The other part of you aims high, longing to expand your mind and explore the infinite reaches of the spirit. Sounds good, but you can be a blowhard — and without a target, you flounder. Impractical and disorganized, you're easily sidetracked and must battle a tendency to procrastinate. You fritter away endless amounts of time and energy (and money). Moreover, you can be unreliable, with a regrettable tendency to promise more than you can deliver. You don't mean to misrepresent yourself; it's just that your innate optimism causes you to overestimate your ability.

A peculiar fact about Sagittarius is that although you supposedly love the outdoors, you may not spend much time there. And though you thrive on exercise, you can be physically clumsy. More significantly, you can be dogmatic and fanatical, with an exasperating propensity to preach. Finally, there's your legendary tactlessness. You haven't learned to lie, even when it's a kindness to do so. A friend shows up with badly cropped hair or a hideous new outfit? You blurt out the unflattering truth. (Or maybe you're more subtle than that, and your silence says it all). It's the flip side of your honesty — and it's nothing to be proud of.

Relationships

Funny, generous, enthusiastic, talkative, and direct, the Archer makes friends easily. Stimulating conversation and a clever sense of humor carry a lot of weight with you. You also prize personal freedom, making romance trickier than friendship. Despite a tendency to take risks in other areas, you hold back romantically and are famous for being resistant to commitment. Whether you come across as a Don Juan, an inconstant lover, or a monk-in-training, you usually manage to maintain your independence, even at the cost of occasional loneliness. Besides, you're an optimist (though you may think otherwise). So why settle for someone who's less than perfect when a single swipe might bring you someone who is? No wonder it's hard to choose. Denizens of other signs may rush to the altar, anxious to pair up and settle down. You have fantasies aplenty — but they're not about weddings, gift registries, mortgages, or twins. You'd just as soon see the world and develop some of your own talents.

When you do ultimately connect (and fear not, it happens all the time), you sincerely hope that the relationship will lead to a larger, more fulfilling life — not a more constrained one. You have nothing against domesticity, but it is not your dream, and neither is stability your guiding principle. You seek a life of adventure, be it geographic, intellectual, or spiritual, with plenty of laughs along the way — and an active, accomplished companion who doesn't mind being with someone as independent as you. Even in a fully committed, passionate relationship, Sagittarius needs space.

For the lowdown on the Archer's relationships with other signs, turn to Chapter 15.

Work

Sagittarius rules higher education, and the professions associated with the sign reflect that. Blessed with a love of learning and a yearning to do something that matters, you're well suited for teaching, publishing, journalism, law, religion, communications, and anything involving international relations or travel. You dislike bureaucracy, grow restless in a rigidly structured organization, and may have time management issues. Whatever you do, your intellect needs to be engaged. Versatile and quick, you're easily distracted and may accept a hodge-podge of assignments just to keep things interesting. Big projects and high ideals excite you. Bookkeeping doesn't. And delegating makes you uncomfortable. A natural egalitarian, you hate asking others to perform routine tasks, even though you're better off handing small stuff to someone else. Learn to delegate. Your success depends on it.

If you work for a Sagittarian, your task is to make sure things are moving in the right direction. If that is happening, the Archer won't nitpick. Sagittarius expects you to be independent and generally doesn't micromanage. On the other hand, if you need help with something specific, you may not get it. After all, you already received a rundown of the overall situation — right? And be prepared: Sagittarius doesn't object to working late. If you're a strict 9-to-5er, the Archer may question your commitment.

Health and wellness

It's a funny thing about Sagittarius: You earn kudos for being athletic and out-doorsy, yet you get mocked for being a klutz. Crazy — but it makes sense. As a fire sign, exercise is essential to your wellbeing. Working out builds your endurance and energizes you. But that endorphin-fueled exuberance can cause you to stumble over pebbles or take a turn too fast. Plus, you're distractible. You can improve your odds of avoiding mishaps by getting sufficient rest, by incorporating stress-relief techniques like meditation into your schedule (even if you don't exactly have a schedule), and by putting down your phone. You only think you can text while running. Just don't do it. Also, Sagittarius is ruled by Jupiter, the planet of expansion. Since that can be an all-too-literal description, it behooves you to watch what you eat.

Sagittarius is traditionally assigned the hips and thighs. I always thought of that as a figurative association related to the anatomy of the centaur (who, after all, has twice as many thighs as the rest of us). Then one Sagittarian friend injured herself falling off a horse and another stumbled and broke a femur, and I began to rethink. Sometimes, astrology is not metaphorical. Sometimes it's literal. So please, Sagittarius: Watch where you're going. Take a deep breath. And take care.

A Sun sign description of health can only suggest basic tendencies. If you're concerned about your health in any way, just see a doctor.

The mythology of Sagittarius

There is no doubt that Sagittarius is a centaur. But which one? He is not one of the rowdy band of centaurs, half man and half horse, who became known for their lascivious ways and savage battles. Nor is he Chiron, the beloved tutor who is represented by the constellation Centaurus, which is not in the zodiac. That leaves Crotus, the Sagittarian archer, whose mother, Eupheme, was the nurse of the muses and whose father was Pan, the flute-playing woodland god with the hindquarters of a goat. Crotus (or Krotos) invented archery and was the first to applaud after a song, an innovation that earned him a place in the heavens.

The constellation Sagittarius

The figure of Sagittarius as depicted in antique celestial maps is a marvel, showing a star-spangled centaur aiming a bow and arrow, a wreath at his foot. In real life, if you gaze at the sky on a summer's eve, you may have trouble locating the Archer because it doesn't resemble a centaur. It resembles a teapot — handle, spout, and all. It's a cozy image, but you should know: When you're looking at Sagittarius, you are looking at the ravenous black hole in the center of our galaxy.

Sagittarius: The Basic Facts

Polarity: Positive	Favorable Colors: Purple and blue
Quality: Mutable	Lucky Gem: Turquoise
Element: Fire	Parts of the Body: Hips and thighs
Symbol: The Centaur	Metal: Tin
Ruling Planet: Jupiter	Key Phrase: I see
Opposite Sign: Gemini	Major Traits: Adventurous, independent

REAL LIFE EXAMPLE

SAGITTARIUS IN ACTION: LUDWIG VAN BEETHOVEN

What makes a composer for the ages? Why does Ludwig van Beethoven still get standing ovations two centuries after his death? The answer is obvious: Beethoven had not just the spark but the raging flame of genius. He was born a day before the new moon, with the Sun and Moon in Sagittarius. One lunar cycle was winding down, another about to begin. This echoes the way scholars see him — as one of the last great composers of the classical era and the first of the romantic. Three planets in Sagittarius opposing Mars made him determined and volatile. Three planets in Capricorn brought that firepower down to earth and inspired a love of structure. If his birth time is accurate, he has Scorpio rising, which explains the penetrating gaze of his late portraits, and four planets in the second house of money, the source of never-ending financial struggles, despite his success as a composer.

Beethoven's talent was recognized in childhood. His alcoholic father taught him music so harshly that he made little Ludwig weep, and there were other teachers as well. He published his first composition when he was 12. With Saturn forming a helpful trine to his Sagittarian planets, he received support and recognition from people in high places.

But he himself was a commoner with a weakly aspected Venus, and his love life suffered accordingly. His friendships were often contentious. He could be rude, coarse, and paranoid, with atrocious table manners and a volcanic temper. His profound tragedy was that he went deaf, a condition that led him to consider suicide. It did not stop him from composing some of the most majestic, jubilant, heartrending music ever written. Yet, with the exception of that Scorpio ascendant, Beethoven had not a drop of water in his chart, making it difficult for him to deal with emotions. In his music, he found a way. He died during a storm. Observers said that, at the instant of his death, a clap of thunder rang out. The story sounds apocryphal. But it's easy to believe.

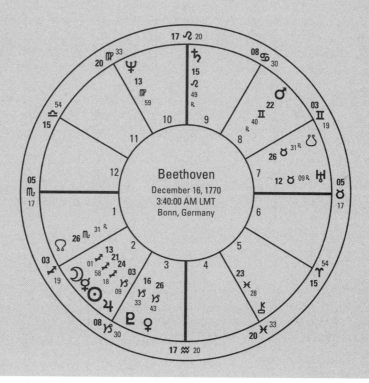

MORE CLASSIC SAGITTARIANS

- Mark Twain, Tyra Banks, Pablo Escobar, Jean-Pierre Foucault (Moon in Aries)
- Lucy Liu, Jim Morrison, Diego Rivera, Jamie Foxx, Felicity Huffman (Moon in Taurus)
- Jeff Bridges, Edith Piaf, Tina Turner, Caroline Myss, Tiffany Haddish (Moon in Gemini)
- William Blake, Jimi Hendrix, Taylor Swift, Chrissy Teigen (Moon in Cancer)
- Gustave Flaubert, Shirley Jackson, Winston Churchill, Sara Bareilles (Moon in Leo)
- Keith Richards, Jane Birkin, Kenneth Branagh, Zoë Kravitz (Moon in Virgo)
- Jane Austen, Emily Dickinson, Sinéad O'Connor, Jay–Z (Moon in Libra)
- Scarlett Johansson, Bruce Lee, Steven Spielberg, Miley Cyrus (Moon in Scorpio)
- Joan Didion, Jon Stewart, Ronan Farrow, Gael García Bernal (Moon in Sagittarius)
- Mary Queen of Scots, Brad Pitt, Richard Pryor, Sarah Silverman (Moon in Capricorn)
- Rainer Maria Rilke, Woody Allen, Pope Francis, Sarah Paulson (Moon in Aquarius)
- Joe DiMaggio, Frank Sinatra, Aleksandr Solzhenitsyn, Gianni Versace (Moon in Pisces)

Chapter **7**

The Signs of Winter: Capricorn, Aquarius, and Pisces

The zodiac is more than a magnificent ribbon of stars seemingly wrapped around our planet. Astrologers see it as a mirror of human experience. It commences with the birth of the individual, evolves into family and other relationships, and culminates, symbolically, with the establishment of civilization (that's Capricorn); the quest for a nobler world (that's Aquarius); and the ascent into realms of the spirit (that's Pisces, at least in theory). After that, the Earth keeps spinning, so it's back to the beginning. The cycle never ends.

What makes this design so enthralling is that we carry within us all twelve signs, each one equally commendable — and equally pitiful. Even if you have nothing — not a planet, not an asteroid, not even an angle — in any of the three signs of winter, they still live within you, part of your cosmic DNA.

Here are the signs of the winter, the last three on the cosmic wheel:

» Capricorn the Goat (December 22 to January 19), the sign of cardinal earth. The Goat is resourceful, conscientious, steadfast, and ambitious.

> » Aquarius the Water Bearer (January 20 to February 18), the sign of fixed air. Aquarius is forward-looking, innovative, altruistic, and an avatar for change.
>
> » Pisces the Fish (February 19 to March 19), the sign of mutable water. Pisces is sensitive, compassionate, intuitive, imaginative, and spiritual.

If you were born between the Winter Solstice and the Spring Equinox — that is, if you are a Capricorn, an Aquarian, or a Pisces — this is the chapter for you.

REMEMBER

Each sign has an element (fire, earth, air, or water), a polarity (positive or negative), and a quality or modality (cardinal, fixed, or mutable). For more on those terms, see Chapter 1.

TIP

If you were born at the very beginning or end of a sign (that is, if you were born on the cusp), you need to obtain a mathematically accurate copy of your chart if you want to be sure of your sign. To do that, turn to Chapter 2 and follow the instructions there.

Capricorn the Goat: December 22–January 19

Somebody has to uphold tradition. Somebody has to follow the rules. For that matter, somebody has to write them. With somber Saturn, the planet of structure, as your ruler, it may as well be you.

The glyph of Capricorn (see Figure 7-1) represents either the mountain goat with its curling horns or the mythical sea-goat who is a goat above and a fish below.

FIGURE 7-1: The symbol of Capricorn.

© John Wiley & Sons, Inc.

The sunny side

You're productive, responsible, competitive, and mature. You're an adult — even as a child. Capricorn often has a tough time as a youngster because you're more serious than most people. You come into your own in adulthood, and you age beautifully. Although there may be occasional dips along the way, it's a well-recognized phenomenon that the older you get, the happier you become. It's the miracle of Capricorn.

You're ambitious. Like the mountain goat that clambers over rocky terrain to reach the summit, you have your eye on a distant peak — and you've figured out how to get there. Patient, industrious, and thrifty, you bravely weather any difficulties you encounter along the way. Society depends on Capricorn because you have the ability to step outside yourself, to recognize the needs of others, and to develop realistic strategies for fulfilling those needs. You're a natural leader.

Though you may panic internally during times of stress, externally you stay calm. Unlike other signs I can name (Sagittarius, say, or Pisces), you know how to apply self-discipline — and you can do so without making a fetish of it. Your control is obvious in every cell of your body. You're cool, reserved, dignified, and authoritative. As an earth sign, you see what needs to be done and act accordingly. And though you often have trouble loosening up, you have that earth-sign sensuality to indulge in. You respond to timeless art, true love, and the pleasures of the kitchen, the bedroom, and the boardroom — up to and including a nice, fat investment portfolio. Say what you will, money does provide security.

The sorry side

A natural-born conservative, no matter what your politics may be, you have a plan (and a budget) for everything. Status-conscious and money-minded, you can be fearful, repressed, and pessimistic. You have such a deep sense of purpose that you find it difficult to relax. Taking time off feels like breaking stride to you, and you don't want to do it. After all, there's more to be done — much more. You're frustrated by your slow progress. The truth is that if it weren't for other people, you'd live on the treadmill. You're the least spontaneous sign of the zodiac. A little resilience would lighten your considerable load, but it isn't easy for you to bend. I hesitate to say "You work too hard" only because I know that you will agree — and secretly take it as a compliment.

Here's another problem: Emotional issues can be threatening to a Capricorn. Even with friends, you'd rather not discuss feelings at all, thank you. No one likes to reveal weakness, but for you it's especially painful. So you suffer in silence and are prone to denial. Why see what you don't want to see? What's the point of gazing into the heart of darkness — or the void at the center of a deteriorating relationship — if you aren't prepared to do anything about it? It may be better not to know. Right?

Right. Except that sometimes facing the truth is the only way to make things better.

Relationships

Begin by acknowledging that Capricorn has a strong sense of privacy, propriety, and emotional reserve. Even your oldest friends don't get too close. You admire them for their accomplishments and sympathize with them for their troubles. You're not unkind. But you're uncomfortable with emotional displays and would just as soon not have to be there during times of major crisis. (You would rather help by doing something practical.) In love, too, you go out of your way to avoid pyrotechnics. You just can't stand it.

On the other hand, you're a traditionalist with a strong sex drive and a deep need to be comforted, admired, and connected. Your ideal partner is accomplished, well put-together, and worthy in the eyes of the world. You can't help responding to the confidence that success brings. What's so terrible about that?

When you find the right person — and it can take a while — you're faithful and supportive. Playing around isn't your style. Trouble is, you're an earnest person, and playing in any form can be a stretch for you. A pillow fight on a weeknight? No way! You need 7.5 hours of sleep, and not a nanosecond less. An afternoon tryst with your beloved? Are you joking? You have a job! In Capricorn relationships, it's generally the other person who tries to provide the laughs (and the spontaneity). Someone's gotta lighten things up — and it probably won't be you.

For specifics on the Goat's interactions with other signs, flip to Chapter 15.

Work

Can you say workaholic? Capricorn is the most ambitious, competitive, industrious sign of the zodiac. You accept responsibility without complaint. You know how to operate within an organization, large or small, and when structure is lacking, you know how to provide it. You may not like bureaucracy, but you understand it, and you're at home in a corporation. Naturally you crave recognition. Awards and accolades are nice. But let's face it: Although recognition comes in many guises, its primary form is money. You understand the stuff. Occasionally, you even become preoccupied with it because money is proof of accomplishment — and you want credit for what you're achieved. "I'm not a paranoid, deranged millionaire," the obsessive-compulsive tycoon Howard Hughes once said. "Goddamit, I'm a billionaire."

So, yes, some Capricorns are covetous and materialistic. Most are not. And many of you have a little-recognized ability to put the good of others ahead of your selfish desires. Not for nothing was Martin Luther King, Jr., a Capricorn. Those born under the sign of the Goat, despite a reputation for capitalist venality, often have a social conscience. They just don't think they should have to suffer for it.

TIP

If you work for a Capricorn, everything you ever learned about how to behave at work applies: Be on time, dress for the next level up, anticipate your boss's needs, be organized, and so forth. Avoid office pranks. Don't post anything stupid on social media. And make sure that nothing suspect appears on your computer screen — and that includes solitaire. Remember: Capricorns wrote the rules. You'd be a fool to break them.

Health and wellness

As the most responsible sign of the zodiac, Capricorn plays it straight. You are dignified and resolute. So one might assume that you'd take care of yourself. But do you? I'm not so sure. On the one hand, Capricorn excels at establishing routines, a quality that all by itself can help ensure good health. On the other hand, for all your enviable qualities, Capricorns are rigid rather then resilient, and so tuned into external targets that you may miss internal signals. Given a choice, Capricorn would rather repress uncomfortable emotions than acknowledge them, leading to melancholy and possible digestive distress. Managing stress is not your high card. Your key challenge is to convince yourself that relaxing is not the same as wasting time.

Given that Capricorn's ruler is Saturn, the guardian of structure, it's no surprise that the primary body parts associated with your sign are the most solid: the skeleton and the teeth. Calcium and other bone-building nutrients are essential to keep them strong. Also helpful: weight training and anything that will support flexibility. Be especially careful concerning your knees, traditionally an area of weakness for Capricorn. And remember: It's not always smart to run through pain. Sometimes the smart thing to do is to stop running.

REMEMBER

A medical astrologer can give you tremendous insight into your health. But if you're worried about something in particular, see a doctor. Of all the signs, you are the one who will feel most reassured knowing that a certified medical professional has given you a clean bill of health.

The mythology of Capricorn

Thousands of years ago in Mesopotamia, the stars of Capricorn were said to form the figure of Enki, later known as Ea, a god of wisdom, water, sorcery, crafts, and creation. Splendid in a horned crown and the skin of a fish, he could claim three symbols: the goat, the fish, and the amalgamation of the two — the goat-fish or sea-goat, the badge of Capricorn.

Over time, stories arose to explain the existence of such a bizarre creature. One such tale, coming out of Egypt but recounted by a Roman in the first century BCE, went like this: Some gods were lounging on the banks of the Nile when the many-headed giant Typhon attacked. Terrified, the gods scattered and, to protect themselves from the monster, turned into animals. Apollo shape-shifted into a raven. Mercury became a long-legged ibis. Diana, goddess of the hunt, transformed herself into a cat. But the goat-god Pan — from whom we get the word "panic" — froze. What animal should he become? He couldn't decide. Only when the giant was almost upon him did he leap into action. He jumped into the Nile feet first, and at that instant, the metamorphosis occurred. The part of him that was already underwater became a fish, while the rest retained its goat-like form. The symbol of Capricorn stems from this image. (Nor is Capricorn the only astrological sign that can trace its lineage back to Typhon. For another example, flip forward to Pisces.)

The constellation Capricorn

Capricorn is not the most dazzling constellation in the heavens. There's a double star here, a globular cluster there, but by and large, it's nothing special — except that this is where, thousands of years ago, the Winter Solstice took place. That's why the Mesopotamians called this little patch of stars the "Gate of the Gods." Through that secret door in the cosmos, that entrance to eternity, the souls of the dead could leave the earth behind and wend their way to the afterlife.

Capricorn: The Basic Facts

Polarity: Negative	Favorable Colors: Dark green and brown
Quality: Cardinal	Lucky Gem: Onyx
Element: Earth	Parts of the Body: Bones and teeth
Symbol: The Goat	Metal: Silver
Ruling Planet: Saturn	Key Phrase: I use
Opposite Sign: Cancer	Major Traits: Goal-oriented, rigid

REAL LIFE EXAMPLE

CAPRICORN IN ACTION: LIN-MANUEL MIRANDA

When Lin-Manuel Miranda was writing his audacious hip-hop musical *Hamilton*, he was filled with self-doubt. He needn't have worried. From an astrological point of view there was never an ounce of uncertainty about his possible success. Born on the last day of a lunar cycle, he has the Sun, Moon, and Mercury in Capricorn, all in or near the tenth house of reputation and success, making him ambitious, hardworking, disciplined, and delighted to be in the public eye. Looking at his chart, any astrologer would have predicted success.

And there are other indications of achievement. Mars, the ruler of his robust Aries ascendant and hence of his entire chart, is in Virgo in the sixth house of work, along with Jupiter and Saturn. So he cares about work, pays attention to details, and tackles difficult projects — the kind he prefers — with enthusiasm and persistence. Is he workaholic? Could be. But working brings him joy, thanks to optimistic Jupiter, which, together with Mars, forms a Grand Trine with the Moon, the Midheaven, and Chiron.

His theatrical and creative abilities are also built in. The North Node of the Moon, representing the direction his soul wishes to take, is in Leo in the fifth house of entertainment. Venus, the planet of the arts, is in musical Pisces, where it expresses itself with ease. And nimble Mercury, bringer of verbal dexterity, is well placed at the top of his chart, where it is also in mutual reception with Saturn (a concept I discuss in Chapter 13).

But the strongest force in his chart has less to do with the arts and more to do with his unrelenting urge to accomplish something and be recognized for it. Miranda's musical gifts were always blazingly apparent. But if, in some alternate universe, he had chosen another field, he would have been successful there too (although not as satisfied). Five planets in earth signs in the tenth and sixth houses — plus the Moon conjunct the Midheaven — give him ambition to burn and an extraordinary work ethic. He was bound to succeed.

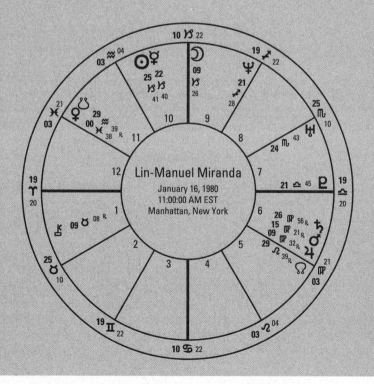

LIN-MANUEL MIRANDA AND ALEXANDER HAMILTON: A MATCH MADE IN THE HEAVENS

In high school, Lin-Manual Miranda wrote a paper about Alexander Hamilton but not until his late twenties did he have his legendary epiphany. While on the beach reading Ron Chernow's acclaimed biography of Hamilton, it struck him that the founding father's eighteenth-century life would be a superb vehicle for twenty-first century hip-hop. Eight years later, when *Hamilton*, the musical, opened on Broadway, it was an instant phenomenon. *Rolling Stone* called it "the cultural event of our time."

What drew Miranda to Hamilton? He claims that Hamilton reminded him of his father and of Tupac Shakur. That may be. But surely the attraction was also internal, for Hamilton had a sensibility that resembled his own. Both Hamilton and Miranda have the Sun, Moon, and Mercury in Capricorn, and both have Jupiter in Virgo. The first Treasury Secretary and the creator of the musical that restored him to his rightful place in the American pantheon are astrological soulmates.

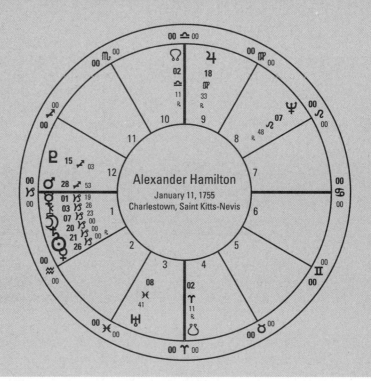

MORE CLASSIC CAPRICORNS

- Albert Schweitzer, Diane von Furstenberg, Shonda Rhimes, LeBron James (Moon in Aries)

- Carlos Casteneda, Naomi Judd, Isaac Asimov, Kellyanne Conway (Moon in Taurus)

- Joan Baez, Jim Carrey, Haruki Murakami, Gelsey Kirkland (Moon in Gemini)

- Mary Tyler Moore, Janis Joplin, Jimmy Page, Kate Middleton, Duchess of Cambridge (Moon in Cancer)

- David Bowie, Mao Zedong, Marilyn Manson, Christine Lagarde (Moon in Leo)

- Tycho Brahe, David Lynch, Yukio Mishima, Dolly Parton (Moon in Virgo)

- Chet Baker, Bradley Cooper, Sean Hannity, Christian Louboutin (Moon in Libra)

- Henry Miller, Orlando Bloom, Pat Benatar, Kate Moss (Moon in Scorpio)

- Henri Matisse, Tiger Woods, Julia Louis-Dreyfus, John Legend (Moon in Sagittarius)

- Clara Barton, A. A. Milne, Federico Fellini, Zooey Deschanel (Moon in Capricorn)

- Cary Grant, Richard M. Nixon, Denzel Washington, Muhammad Ali (Moon in Aquarius)

- Martin Luther King, Jr., Elvis Presley, J. R. R. Tolkien, Patti Smith (Moon in Pisces)

Aquarius the Water Bearer: January 20–February 18

You're an original. With unpredictable Uranus as your ruler, you're progressive, future-oriented, and prone to dazzling flashes of insight. You're also more idiosyncratic than you may realize.

The glyph of Aquarius the Water Bearer (see Figure 7-2) represents the waves of water, sound, electricity, or light. It is derived from an Egyptian hieroglyph that looks like a horizontal zigzag and illustrates the ripple of water.

FIGURE 7-2:
The symbol of
Aquarius.

© John Wiley & Sons, Inc.

The sunny side

Very much a member of your generation, you're a natural visionary and a humanitarian of the first order — at least in theory. You have high-minded principles, and you try to live by them. Altruistic and issue-oriented, you believe in the equality of all human beings, and you're interested in everyone, regardless of race, class, age, sexual orientation, or any of the myriad concerns that shape our lives and sometimes divide us. You are exquisitely aware of the impact those factors often have, and the terrible things that happen in the world appall and animate you. But when you wonder what is to be done, you draw your own conclusions. You have a capacious brain, and you think for yourself.

A maverick with a lively, inventive intelligence, you have an off-beat set of interests and habits. Science fiction and technology are Aquarian; so is video art and everything indie. But whether you resonate to those particular areas isn't the point. (After all, not every Cancer loves to cook.) The point is that you lean into the future, not away from it. Current developments and new inventions excite you. Unafraid and intrigued by everything that is unconventional and experimental, you're utterly contemporary, a composition in avant-garde — or in any case, that which is innovative and fresh to you. You're also affable and charismatic. You accumulate a remarkable variety of friends (and to your perverse joy, they often disapprove of each other). Your likeable personality and open-minded intelligence are the draw.

The sorry side

Your unconventional, independent outlook can morph into eccentricity, thoughtlessness, pointless rebellion, and regrettable tattoos. You can be contrary and childish, a foot-stomping rebel who's never willing to go along. As a fixed sign, you tend to be stubborn, and it's rare for you to give up a cherished idea, no matter how outlandish it may be. And your famous humanity, perhaps your finest trait, can seem false. You may strike people as distant and aloof, despite your reputation for empathy and general wokeness, because you sometimes recoil from intimacy and may even go out of your way to erect barriers against it. For you, detachment is a natural state. More comfortable with ideas than with emotions, you can be warm on the surface but chilly underneath, a criticism often lobbed at Aquarians. You're a visitor to spaceship Earth — alert and curious but uninvolved. Although your idealism runs deep, and you truly want the best for yourself and others, you don't necessarily express these thoughts in a positive way. Emotionally, you may strike people as peculiarly insensitive, even as they strike you as inexplicably thin-skinned. The truth is that you just don't get it. At your worst, I'm sorry to say, you're an android.

And there's another element to you that's easily overlooked. Beneath the razzle-dazzle of your personality and your remarkable, inventive mind, you can be stunningly insecure. Other people may not notice this. They may think, instead, that you have an overinflated ego. In fact, your self-doubt hampers you and is something to fight.

Relationships

Given that Aquarius is the sign of humanity, you might imagine that your relationships would be models for the rest of the world. And in some ways, they are. Fair and friendly, you're interested in people from every corner of society and every part of the globe. So what if you eventually drop most of these relationships? You also maintain a few friendships for life.

Romance is more complicated. Although you pride yourself on your tolerance, certain established customs — getting engaged, for instance, or reserving Saturday night for your beloved —seem phony or old-fashioned to you. You're often astonished by the conventional expectations that people continue to hold dear, and you resent having to go along with those antiquated notions. It amazes you when people misinterpret your independent ways, taking them as rejection. Those needy folks probably strike you as unreasonable and demanding. You understand that intimate relationships have their own rhythm, which sometimes requires you to behave according to accepted norms, outmoded though they may be. It's just that you don't like feeling constrained.

For the lowdown on your relationships with other signs, flip to Chapter 15.

Work

Why would anyone want to follow the beaten path? Striking out for terra incognita is much more entertaining. Ideally, you'd like to set your own goals and create your own schedule. You're willing to work hard. You just don't want to do it under someone else's command. And much as you despair of mind-numbing tasks and banal co-workers, what matters most is that your job has purpose and is focused on the future. That's where you find the most personal satisfaction. Fields that are a fit for Aquarius include social work, politics, science, medicine, academia, environmentalism, civil rights, and anything that pushes the boundaries in a progressive direction. Politicians like Abraham Lincoln, thinkers like Charles Darwin, and inventors like Thomas Edison demonstrate the impact that your sign can make. Innovative Aquarius sees the future before anyone else and knows how to react to it. Technology, by the way, is oxygen to your soul, assuming you don't overdo it. Even if you think you don't like modern technology — maybe you're an aficionado of vinyl or a collector of portable typewriters — you still benefit from it.

If you work with or for an Aquarian, be prepared to argue your viewpoint effectively and to do your job without prodding. Aquarius wants to be independent and is glad to grant the same privilege to you — assuming you don't take advantage. Don't force a showdown.

Health and wellness

Aquarians are advocates of new-fangled everything, including health care. A deeper understanding of the human body combined with radical new approaches to cure and prevention: That's the way you would like health care to operate. Incompetent insurance agents, doctors who can't see you until three years from now, medications with unpleasant side effects — these are anathema to the Aquarian vision, and they make you angry besides. Whatever style of health care you might prefer — conventional, as per your traditional Saturn ruler, or alternative, as per your modern ruler, Uranus — you don't want to be limited, and you don't want to be lectured. The whole wide spectrum is available to you, and you want to keep it that way.

With unpredictable Uranus as your ruler, energy is always coursing through your body and your mind is always churning. Movement in the form of active team sports, tennis, and cycling can help. Remember, though, that Aquarius rules the ankles, so be sure to wear protective footwear, especially when running. Because Aquarius also rules the circulatory system, acupuncture, Reiki, and other techniques designed to move energy will help reduce stress and regulate your sleep cycle.

Finally, the Aquarian affinity for technology is a definite advantage, except when it's not. Which is to say, don't go overboard. Disconnecting from time to time will boost your mood, refresh your brain, and give your eyes a rest.

Are you worried about your health? If so, it may help to talk to a medical astrologer. You'll learn a lot. For that matter, see a shaman or any other kind of healer. And then, just to be on the safe side, see a doctor. I mean, why not?

The mythology of Aquarius

To us, the spattering of stars in Aquarius looks like nothing in particular. The ancients imagined a figure pouring water from a large urn or bucket. In Mesopotamia, this figure was Enki or Ea, the mischievous god of water. In Egypt, it was the god Hapi, who poured water into the Nile, causing it to flood. And in Greece, it was Ganymede, a mortal shepherd whose beauty so captivated Zeus that the king of the gods turned into an eagle and abducted him. Ganymede became the cupbearer to the gods, meaning that he poured the nectar. As a reward, he was lifted into the skies as a constellation and given immortality.

The constellation Aquarius

Aquarius is distinguished by three stars that are traditionally considered lucky and two planetary nebulae, bubbles of hot gas emitted from dying stars. They are the Saturn Nebula, which vaguely resembles that planet, and the Helix Nebula, which has been called the Eye of God. To find out why, go to nasa.gov.helixnebula and take a look.

Aquarius: The Basic Facts

Polarity: Positive	Favorable Colors: Electric blue and glow-in-the-dark shades
Quality: Fixed	Lucky Gem: Amethyst
Element: Air	Parts of the Body: Ankles, circulatory system
Symbol: The Water Bearer	Metal: Aluminum
Ruling Planets: Uranus (modern) and Saturn (traditional)	Key Phrase: I know
Opposite Sign: Leo	Major Traits: Progressive, rebellious

REAL LIFE EXAMPLE

AQUARIUS IN ACTION: OPRAH WINFREY

Growing up in poverty in rural Mississippi and Milwaukee, Oprah Winfrey learned to read and gained a reputation for public speaking while still a toddler. With her Sun and Mercury in visionary Aquarius, and her Moon and Ascendant in effusive, philosophizing Sagittarius, she always loved to talk, and not about the small stuff.

But Oprah has an exact square between her Sun and Venus in Aquarius, and Saturn, and her circumstances were grim. She was shuttled from here to there, mocked for her potato sack dresses, and, beginning at age 9, repeatedly raped. At 14 she gave birth to a premature baby who soon died. The next stop was a detention center. But when the center had no vacancy, her mother shipped her off to her father, a barber. It was, says Oprah, "my saving grace." With her progressed Sun (see Chapter 16) precisely opposing her Pluto in the eighth house of regeneration — and transiting Jupiter, bringer of opportunity, lighting up the same area — the trajectory of her life changed.

Under her father's strict supervision, she became an honors student, was elected "most popular," went to a White House conference, and was crowned Miss Black Tennessee, which led to a job as a radio newscaster. Radio led to TV. Nashville led to Baltimore. And then she was fired. To soften the blow, the station gave her a failing morning talk show. And so she found her place in the world.

(continued)

(continued)

Five years later, in Chicago, she premiered the Oprah Winfrey Show, an empathy-fueled, self help-oriented, literature-promoting, confessional gabfest that outran the competition for 25 years and made her one of the most influential women of our time. In addition to being an award-winning actress, producer, publisher, and philanthropist, she is the first black female billionaire. Her success can be traced to her tenth house of reputation and profession, which holds Neptune, the ruler of her third house of communication. The third house is empty, but Neptune at the top of her chart gives it prominence. Neptune also brings a touch of mysticism to her career. Meanwhile, the ruler of that career — her Midheaven — is Venus, the money planet, conveniently located in Aquarius in her second house of finances and values. She made her fortune via revealing conversations and a long-running exploration of issues and values. With the assist of her Ascendant in Sagittarius, she has aimed for authenticity, for awareness, for honesty and optimism, and for a larger, more inclusive conversation. In that, she has been a true Aquarian.

(For more about Oprah's relationships, see Chapter 15).

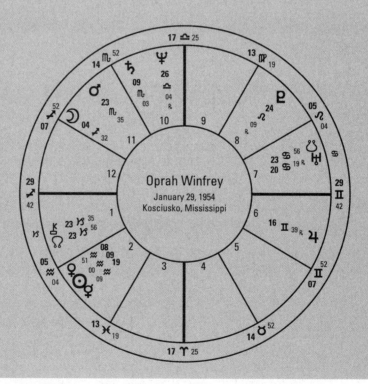

MORE CLASSIC AQUARIANS

- Virginia Woolf, Renata Tebaldi, Anton Chekhov, Ellen DeGeneres (Moon in Aries)
- Bill Maher, Sheryl Crow, Jackson Pollock, Ronald Reagan (Moon in Taurus)
- Jack Benny, Leontyne Price, William Burroughs, Patton Oswalt (Moon in Gemini)
- Lord Byron, Mischa Barton, Franklin D. Roosevelt, Michael B. Jordan, actor (Moon in Cancer)
- James Joyce, Judy Blume, Paris Hilton, Cristiano Ronaldo (Moon in Leo)
- John Travolta, Vanessa Redgrave, Gertrude Stein, Mena Suvari (Moon in Virgo)
- Natalie Cole, Stonewall Jackson, Edouard Manet, Dr. Dre (Moon in Libra)
- James Dean, Bob Marley, Etta James, The Weeknd (Moon in Scorpio)
- Wolfgang Amadeus Mozart, Lewis Carroll, Kenzaburo Oe, Michael Jordan, athlete (Moon in Sagittarius)
- Charles Darwin, Thomas Alva Edison, Abraham Lincoln, Betty Friedan (Moon in Capricorn)
- Jackie Robinson, Angela Davis, Ashton Kutcher, Francois Truffaut (Moon in Aquarius)
- Susan B. Anthony, Toni Morrison, Paul Newman, Laura Dern (Moon in Pisces)

Pisces the Fish: February 19–March 19

Yours is the sign of dreams, imagination, compassion, and matters of the spirit. Ruled by mysterious Neptune, the planet of glamour and illusion, your challenge is to find a way to live in a workaday world when you have an out-of-this-world sensibility.

The glyph of Pisces (see Figure 7-3), considered abstractly, connotes a connection between two forms of experience, internal and external. Alternatively, it represents two fish tied together. When they cooperate, they navigate their watery domain with ease. When they pull in opposite directions, neither gets anywhere.

FIGURE 7-3:
The symbol of
Pisces the Fish.

The sunny side

You want sensitive? Pisces is sensitive. Every tiny bounce in the emotional weather sends your internal compass into a spin. Sympathetic and receptive, you receive a constant barrage of impressions and information, and you can be weirdly psychic. But protecting yourself is difficult because you lack boundaries. All your membranes are permeable. When the people upstairs have a fight, you feel battered. When bad things happen to good people, you're horrified. And when good things happen to people you love, you rejoice. (It's one of your most magnificent traits.) You're generous, big-hearted, insightful, and truly compassionate. You're also innately spiritual.

Another strength is your powerful imagination. Your dreams and daydreams can be a vivid source of inspiration and even problem-solving. Your intuition is equally powerful. You sense what's going on way before it registers on the seismograph. At your intuitive best, your refusal to get hung up on the limitations of reality enables you to bounce right over obstacles and to make surprising breakthroughs and turnarounds. Unlike more "realistic" signs, you embrace change and are willing to take enormous risks. You've got faith in yourself, and often your gambles succeed. When they don't, you're philosophical about it. As Albert Einstein, a prototypical Pisces, said, "A person who never made a mistake never tried anything new."

The sorry side

But you can also become trapped in a web of illusion. At your out-to-lunch worst, you're gullible in the extreme, irrational, and so vulnerable that you're practically an open wound. Because the requirements of ordinary life can overwhelm you, you're prone to wishful thinking and outright fantasy, often combined with a sense of entitlement that boggles the mind. At your worst, you're indecisive, weak, and readily deceived.

But that's not the most serious problem. More often, you delude yourself. At your worst, your grasp of reality can be tenuous, and you may refuse to accept even a drop of responsibility for your situation. Worse, you may stubbornly refuse to do anything about it. Even when you're miserable, your passivity can bypass all reason. Instead of taking action when you're feeling trapped, you wait to be rescued, sinking into a melancholy pattern of brooding and procrastination. Moreover, when your efforts come to nothing or your dreams are thwarted, you tend to be overcome by lethargy, self-pity, depression, guilt, anger, or resentment. Sleep — too little or, more commonly, too much — can defeat your most heartfelt resolutions. And did I mention substance abuse? Let's just say that you're susceptible. More than most, you're your own worst enemy. And more than most, as the sign of mutable water, you have the capacity to be flexible, or reframe your feelings and change your attitude, and to turn your circumstances around.

Relationships

A faithful, generous friend, a whimsical, starry-eyed lover, and a tender spouse, you have a sweetness that can't be denied, and your ability to love is without equal. You see the best in those you care for, even when they don't see it themselves. You delight in cheering them on, in part because you crave that kind of encouragement yourself, and when they succeed, you are legitimately happy for them.

A genuine romantic, you yearn to be swept away in true Hollywood style. You're also capable of falling for a homeless bum just because you sense the potential beneath the plastic poncho. Friends may object. But once your feelings are engaged, your ability to make rational judgments evaporates like mist. As you wander around in the fog of infatuation, totally lost, you spin a fantasy that enables you to ignore unmistakable flaws (alcoholism and infidelity, say) and to believe in the least likely of lottery-winning outcomes. It's a strange phenomenon: You're supremely responsive to other people. When you sit down with friends to analyze their relationships, your intuition is flawless. Yet when it comes to looking squarely at your own, you suffer from a dangerous Piscean malady: a deep-seated, willful refusal to face reality. For Pisces, seeing clearly is always a worthy goal.

For a glance at your relationships with other signs, turn to Chapter 15.

Work

In Utopia, these are a few of the jobs that Pisces would happily hold: poet, artist, musician, member of the clergy, clairvoyant, palm reader, sailor, filmmaker, actor, wine taster, spiritual healer, hypnotist, herbalist, florist, yoga teacher, and anything concerning tropical fish or ballet.

Given those career choices, you might expect Pisces to be a failure in the real world. But you'd be wrong. It turns out that Pisces is strangely adept at generating vast sums of money. A study conducted by *Forbes Magazine* in 1995 found that more of the 400 richest Americans were Pisceans than any other sign. (In a 2019 study of the world's billionaires, Pisces fell to second place, right behind Libra. But such fluctuations are normal. And, in any case, second place still wins the silver.) Pisces is a major moneymaker because you have a truly creative mind. It's not just a matter of coloring outside the lines; you have the ability to toss the book aside and design something completely original. (Not for nothing was Steve Jobs a Pisces.) Plus, unlike more pragmatic signs (Capricorn, for example, which comes in last among billionaires), you dream big. If you can harness that vision to an old-fashioned work ethic, you can accomplish anything. If your job also benefits humanity, all the better. Pisces aspires to be of service. That's why, besides the utopian trades in the previous paragraph, you may also want to consider medicine, social work, philanthropy, education, environmentalism, oceanography, and — yes — finance.

If you work with or for a Pisces, stay tuned — and I mean every minute. Any bad vibes you detect, Pisces notices too. Sympathetic and broad-minded, Pisceans support their staff and don't get stuck on minor points. But they're strivers, both more opportunistic and less secure than they may appear. If a Piscean senses dissension in the ranks or anything less than total loyalty, you'll be fish food.

Health and wellness

Do something! As every Pisces knows, that's easier said than done, especially when the issue is your own wellness. Even the most competent, master-of-the-universe Pisceans can fail to take care of themselves. Yet once you gather your courage and make a move, the results are likely to be immediate. What should you do? You benefit hugely from taking a holistic, cross-cultural, spiritually attuned approach to health care. Techniques that are too subtle for grosser souls can be game changing for you and you respond quickly. Just do something.

In antique images of the so-called Zodiac Man (see Chapter 1), Pisces receives dominion over the feet. So you benefit from foot massage and techniques such as reflexology; from wearing shoes that actually fit; from visiting a skilled podiatrist should a problem arise; and from long walks, preferably on a sandy beach or a shady country lane.

But there's more to your health than just taking care of your feet. Pisces also rules your immune system. To strengthen your resistance and keep your system functioning at its best, try Qigong, Tai Chi, or chakra-balancing, which refreshes every part of the body. Finally, exercise is essential, but it needn't be — shouldn't be — brutal. Devote yourself instead to something uplifting, rejuvenating, or just plain pleasant. Afterwards, you should feel revitalized — not exhausted

If alternative techniques and astrological counsel aren't enough to calm your fears, that's the time to see a doctor.

The mythology of Pisces

The earliest images associated with Pisces date back to deities such as Derke or Derketo, an ancient Syrian fertility goddess who had the tail of a fish — a mermaid, one might say. Only a fragment of her power remains in the stories bequeathed to us by classical mythology. In one such story, which resembles the myth of Capricorn, Venus and her son Cupid (Aphrodite and Eros to the Greeks) were lounging by the shores of the Euphrates when the fearsome monster Typhon, with his many heads and snake-like fingers, attacked. To save themselves, Venus and Cupid dove into the river and turned into fish. To make sure they didn't lose one another, they tied their tails together with a length of flaxen cord.

The constellation Pisces

In the constellation Pisces, the V-shaped cord that links the two fish is long and straggly, with a neat oval of stars called the "Circlet of Pisces" on one end and a loose scatter at the other end. In the middle of the cord, at the base of the V, is a blue-white binary star called Alrisha (Arabic for "the cord"). It represents the spot where ancient starwatchers, their eyes so much sharper than our own (and their skies so much darker), imagined a knot in the cord.

Pisces: The Basic Facts

Polarity: Negative	Favorable Colors: Sea green and lavender
Quality: Mutable	Lucky Gem: Aquamarine
Element: Water	Parts of the Body: Feet and immune system
Symbol: The Fish	Metal: Platinum
Ruling Planets: Neptune (modern) and Jupiter (traditional)	Key Phrase: I believe
Opposite Sign: Virgo	Major Traits: Sensitive, escapist

REAL LIFE EXAMPLE

PISCES IN ACTION: ALBERT EINSTEIN

Pisces is the sign of the imagination writ large. Great Piscean artists (Michelangelo), writers (Gabriel Garcia Marquez), far-seeing politicians (George Washington, Abraham Lincoln), inventors (Alexander Graham Bell), and billionaires (Steve Jobs) possess the ability to see beyond their immediate circumstances and imagine something new to the world. But there has never been an imagination like that of Albert Einstein, who re-imagined time, space, and the cosmos, not in a sci-fi or artistic context, but for real. And he got it right.

He imagined a clock whizzing through space at the speed of light, and it caused him to reassess the nature of time. He imagined being stuck in an elevator in the emptiness of space, and that led him to a new theory of gravity. He predicted that light whizzing past a massive object like the Sun wouldn't go in a straight line but would be bent by that object's gravitational field. Measurements taken during a solar eclipse in 1919 proved him correct. "Lights All Askew in the Heavens," headlined the *New York Times*. "Einstein Theory Triumphs." From then on, he was world famous. With four planets in the tenth house, including his Pisces Sun, his celebrity never faded.

(continued)

(continued)

To this day, his name is synonymous with genius. A close Mercury/Saturn conjunction kept him from speaking until he was three, and he never did particularly well in school. But that same conjunction gave him a serious, systematic mind and the power of deep concentration. Mercury in Aries gave him intellectual daring and quickness. Uranus in the third house brought him revolutionary ideas and lightning flashes of intuition. Jupiter in the ninth house — its most natural placement — encouraged his love of knowledge. It also brought him good fortune through publication and, once he arrived in the United States in 1933, it found him a permanent academic job in Princeton.

As an impressionistic Pisces with Neptune in Taurus, Einstein also had a strong connection to music. He played the violin beginning at age six and was especially fond of Mozart. After the 1919 eclipse, he celebrated the confirmation of his theory by buying himself a new violin. "I live my daydreams in music," he said. "I see my life in terms of music." And he averred that, had he not been a physicist, he would have become a musician. You can't get more Piscean than that.

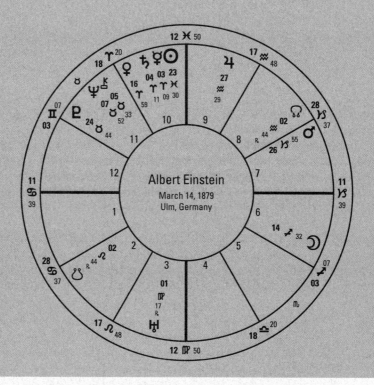

MORE CLASSIC PISCEANS

- Gabriel Garcia Márquez, Steve Jobs, Rihanna, Daniel Craig (Moon in Aries)

- Edgar Casey, Bobby Fischer, Jerry Lewis, Rob Lowe (Moon in Taurus)

- Benicio del Toro, W. H. Auden, Jessica Biel, Simone Biles (Moon in Gemini)

- Kurt Cobain, Drew Barrymore, Emily Blunt, Aziz Ansari (Moon in Cancer)

- Antonio Vivaldi, Queen Latifah, Dakota Fanning, Javier Bardem (Moon in Leo)

- Jack Kerouac, Chaz Bono, Lou Reed, Chelsea Handler (Moon in Virgo)

- Elizabeth Barrett Browning, Nat King Cole, Rudolph Nureyev, Trevor Noah (Moon in Libra)

- Elizabeth Taylor, Johnny Cash, John Steinbeck, Ruth Bader Ginsburg (Moon in Scorpio)

- Nicolaus Copernicus, Victor Hugo, Luis Buñuel, Amy Tan (Moon in Sagittarius)

- Anaïs Nin, Philip Roth, Nina Simone, Frederic Chopin, Bryan Cranston (Moon in Capricorn)

- Glenn Close, Diane Arbus, Harry Belafonte, Robert Kardashian (Moon in Aquarius)

- Michelangelo, Stedman Graham, Erykah Badu, Rachel Weisz (Moon in Pisces)

3 Leafing through the Cosmic Cookbook

IN THIS PART . . .

Behold the Moon and its implications.

Learn about Mercury, Venus, Mars, Jupiter, and Saturn.

Explore the distant worlds of Neptune, Uranus, Pluto, and Chiron.

Identify your Ascendant and play the angles of your chart.

Survey the houses of your chart.

Decipher your planetary aspects.

Weave it all together and interpret your chart.

Chapter **8**

Moon Signs: The Lunacy Factor

S trange but true: To an Earthling gazing at the sky, the Sun and Moon appear to be the same size. In reality, the Sun is about 400 times larger than the Moon. But visually, the two are equal. Ancient peoples incorporated that seeming equality into their mythologies, turning the Sun and Moon into deities and associating them with squabbling lovers or competing siblings.

Astrologers picture the Sun and the Moon as partners who may or may not play well together. The Sun represents your basic essence, vitality, and conscious self, while the inconstant Moon with its many phases and regular disappearances signifies your emotional style, reactions, instincts, habits, and unconscious.

If the Sun and Moon occupied compatible signs at your birth, you're in luck. Your (solar) will and (lunar) emotions, your conscious awareness and your unconscious, moony self, are in sync. That must be nice — I wouldn't know. If your luminaries are in clashing signs, you'll experience conflicting needs and desires. Well, that's life. Astrology just reflects it.

REMEMBER

The Moon, which shines by the light of the Sun, is symbolized by the crescent of receptivity (see Figure 8-1).

FIGURE 8-1:
The symbol of the
Moon.

The Mythology of the Moon

More than any other object in the heavens, the Moon is associated with a host of deities. There's Yemoja, the Yoruban goddess of water, women, and the Moon; Coyolxāuhqui, the Aztec goddess whose head became the Moon after her brother, the Sun god, chopped her into pieces; Ch'ang-o, the Chinese goddess who swallowed the pill of immortality and now dwells on the Moon full-time, receiving visits from her husband on every full Moon; and the triple goddesses of classical and Celtic mythology. One such trio comprises Artemis, the Greek goddess of the hunt and the Moon, and the protector of girls; Selene, who drove the chariot of the Moon across the heavens; and Hecate, the goddess of witchcraft, the night, and the underworld. Those goddesses represented three stages of a woman's life — maiden, mother, and crone — and three phases of the lunar cycle: the waxing Moon, the full Moon, and the waning Moon.

REMEMBER

It takes the Sun a year to travel through all twelve signs of the zodiac. The Moon completes that same journey in a little under a month, swinging from one sign to the next every two or three days. If you happen to be born on a day when the Moon changed signs, the only way you can be certain which sign is yours is to consult an accurate chart cast for the time and place of your birth. If you are not in possession of such a chart, please turn to Chapter 2 and follow the instructions about how to get your chart on the internet.

For a description of the Moon in the houses, turn to Chapter 12.

The Moon in the Signs

The sign that the Moon occupied at your birth describes your emotional nature and needs, your subconscious, and your instincts. It defines an area of fluctuation and instability in your chart, and it also represents women in general and your mother in particular. Here's how the Moon operates in each of the signs:

>> **Moon in Aries:** Instinctive and spontaneous, you form judgments instantly. Your enthusiasm is easily aroused, as is your anger. You may come across as self-absorbed and independent, and you're often remarkably competitive, but you're more insecure than you let on. You're feisty and decisive (sometimes

foolishly so). You can also be irritable and impatient. Quick-tempered and impetuous, you make sure your needs are met at the earliest possible moment. The chances are that, when you were a child, your mother reacted promptly to your insistent, fiery demands. She had no choice. As a result, you got what you wanted — and you learned to be independent, direct, and courageous.

» **Moon in Taurus:** You yearn for security, emotional and material, and you do everything you can to achieve it. Steady and stubborn, patient and affection-ate, you approach change cautiously because nothing makes you more apprehensive. You value stability and comfort, and you try to curb emotional excesses. But once you understand that change is inevitable, you do what you have to do. Trustworthy and congenial, you're charming, attractive, warm, faithful, and possessive. As a child, you desperately needed the security that comes from having loving, reliable parents. You still crave the pleasures of predictability, security, love, and comfortable surroundings.

» **Moon in Gemini:** You're flighty, friendly, dashing. You express yourself with verve, even if you strike people as glib or superficial. Nervous and high-strung, you take an essentially mental approach to affairs of the heart. Although you occasionally panic, that reaction is fleeting. After the feathers settle, you look around objectively and analyze your situation, which brings you a measure of calm. A first-rate rationalizer, you don't hesitate to move on. You're adaptable. As a child, you were restless and easily distracted. During stressful moments, your mother (or whoever took on that role) found it easy to divert you. Diversion still strikes you as a reasonable strategy during hard times.

» **Moon in Cancer:** The Moon rules the sign of the Crab, so no matter what else is in your chart, you're a lunar person: moody, receptive, vulnerable, and supremely aware of the ebb and flow of emotions. Tears spring to your eyes with little provocation, and you may need to withdraw to soothe your surging feelings. You're also gentle and caring, the kind of person who likes to turn friends into family. But, like people born with the Moon in Taurus, you have a rough time letting go. As a child, you were extraordinarily responsive to your mother, which is why, when you have children, you're likely to be an excep-tionally loving, occasionally overinvolved parent.

» **Moon in Leo:** A Leo Moon adds warmth and exuberance to any Sun sign. Generous, devoted, and lively, you love to laugh and are gifted with joie de vivre. Although your considerable pride is easily injured (especially if you feel ignored), you're usually confident and upbeat. One way or another, you love to perform, and the world loves to respond. But when things are going badly or when you feel downhearted or insecure, you cover up your doubts and ambivalence with emotional fireworks. You picked up this dramatic pattern from your mother, who was somewhat of a drama queen herself. She taught you to seek recognition, and she gave you the confidence to set ambitious goals.

>> **Moon in Virgo:** Emotionally timid and inhibited, you'd rather repress your emotions than articulate them. You find it difficult to confront serious issues head-on. Instead, you distract yourself with minutiae or by working so hard you barely have a chance to breathe. You're industrious and reliable, and it pleases you to be of practical service. But you can also be fussy and hard to satisfy. Without a doubt, you're your own harshest critic. Where does this reprehensible quality come from? You guessed it — your mother (or whoever played that role in your life). Although her criticism, implicit or explicit, made an impact on you, she also deserves credit for several of your virtues, including the value you place on efficiency and organization, and your heartfelt desire to relieve the suffering of others.

>> **Moon in Libra:** You're gracious, romantic, and artistic. You shun vulgarity, value courtesy and elegance, and try to convey your feelings in a calm, diplomatic manner. Peace is essential to you, and you will do anything to attain it. As a child, you learned to maintain appearances, even if you were abused. Your even temper drew praise, and people came to expect it of you. Now, as an adult, you seem unflappable. Love and relationships are fundamental to your well-being. If you're single, you feel bereft without a partner; if you're mated, you can scarcely imagine any other scenario and may be fearful of being alone. Either way, you detest confrontation. So problems may remain unresolved; your desire for peace and harmony surpasses all other needs.

>> **Moon in Scorpio:** Willful, intense, easily injured, and occasionally self-destructive, your emotions — to quote Herman Melville — rush like "herds of walruses and whales" beneath the surface of your personality. Your tendency is to protect yourself by keeping those emotions hidden. If that requires dissembling and secrecy, well, too bad. Not that you mean to be manipulative — you just can't help it. Covering up your feelings is something you learned growing up. Even if your childhood looked enviable from afar, you were afraid of abandonment or rejection and were well aware of the suppressed needs and subterranean conflicts within your family. You learned to keep quiet about your own concerns. Your silence is a form of protection — and hiding. Although some people with this placement nurse fantasies of retaliation for long-ago wrongs, most simply continue to hide their feelings. Those walruses and whales may still be down there, but the surface looks smooth.

>> **Moon in Sagittarius:** You're philosophical, outspoken, cheerful, uninhibited, well-intentioned, unrealistic and, at times, pathetically idealistic. Your optimism runs deep. As a result, you're a risk-taker, always prepared to gallop off on a quest or to commit yourself to a cause other people deem hopeless. Intellectually and emotionally, you cherish your independence above all else. Lengthy relationship discussions make you squirm. More comfortable with action than with analysis, you can be self-righteous and inadvertently hurtful,

and you tend to justify your own misdeeds without blinking. Yet you mean well. And people sense that about you. Even as a child, whenever you radiated good cheer, your mother responded positively. To encourage that sort of reaction, you convey your enjoyment more readily than your pain and, like her, you shrink from emotional displays.

>> **Moon in Capricorn:** You're steady, reserved, self-reliant, dependable, and well-disciplined. Even when you were small, you were serious, and the playfulness of childhood may have eluded you. Now, ever the realist, you recognize your strengths and limitations, one of which, you suspect, is the inability to loosen up. From time to time you descend into depression and pessimism, perhaps because your mother suffered similarly. Sensing her gloom, you pulled back. You're emotionally reserved and self-conscious, especially in the face of other people's melodramatic outbursts. You can't bear those scenes. Success steadies you. You willingly accept significant responsibilities because you feel more grounded, as well as more powerful and peaceful, when you have a sense of purpose and the authority to go with it. Somebody's got to take control. It may as well be you.

>> **Moon in Aquarius:** In your mind's eye, you're out to improve the world. You have a gift for friendship, an instinctive affection for unconventional people, and strong sense of being part of a community. Social connections and group membership mean a lot to you. But at a certain point, you disappear because on some level, intimacy makes you uneasy. You shy away from closeness and are drawn instead to the world of the intellect. Thank your mom. Even if your early years were marred by turmoil, she encouraged you to use your intelligence and express your individuality. She was less comfortable with your emotional needs. You're the same way. You find it taxing to delve into your emotions. You'd rather pretend they aren't there — and this technique works . . . at least for a while.

>> **Moon in Pisces:** No matter how you may appear to others, internally you are ultrasensitive. Easily wounded and often shy, you feel like a hostage to your feelings, which are constantly changing and difficult to control, though you do try. At your best, you pay close attention to your instincts and hunches and can be virtually psychic. The world of the spirit calls to you, and you're also likely to be artistically talented. But you can be gullible, hopelessly unrealistic, and self-indulgent. And you may have trouble standing up for yourself. This goes back to childhood. Ever alert to your mother's many moods, you learned to do what you could to improve the emotional atmosphere — even if that meant disregarding your own needs. Your continuing challenge is to be as compassionate to yourself as you are to others.

The Nodes of the Moon

To astrologers in India (and Vedic astrologers everywhere), the Nodes of the Moon are a vital part of every horoscope, as fundamental as the Sun or Moon. But when I began to study astrology, my teachers barely mentioned the Nodes. Even now, many introductory astrology books refer to them only in passing, if at all. One reason for this neglect is that even though the Nodes occupy sensitive degrees in your chart, there's no celestial body at either spot. In a strictly physical sense, the Nodes of the Moon don't exist. Nevertheless, they have a long and splendid astrological history.

TECHNICAL STUFF

The lunar Nodes are the points where the Moon, in its monthly orbit around the Earth, crosses the *ecliptic,* which is the apparent path of the Sun across the sky. The spot where the Moon climbs over the ecliptic is the *North Node;* the point where it sinks below the ecliptic is the *South Node.* The Nodes, which are exactly 180° apart, usually move in a retrograde fashion, gradually shifting backwards. They spend about a year and a half in each sign and travel through the whole zodiac in about 19 years.

To ancient astrologers, the North Node (or Dragon's Head) was beneficial, allied with prosperity and luck, while the South Node (or Dragon's Tail) was Saturnian in flavor, a point of loss or adversity. Well into the 20th century, some astrologers still described the South Node as evil — a distressing comment to anyone with the South Node in a prominent position.

Practitioners of Western astrology generally agree that the North Node illuminates your spiritual path and the constructive yet demanding choices that promote growth. For those who believe in reincarnation, the North Node suggests an evolutionary journey for which you may feel unprepared because it's a trip into the unknown. In contrast, the South Node supports habit over effort, stagnation over growth, staying put over exploration. It's your default mode. It feels comfortable because you've been there before, perhaps in an earlier life.

I concede that the South Node's reputation isn't good. When it's in a prominent position in your chart, it can trigger doubt along with a sense of insecurity, of being overlooked or invisible. But it also represents a set of habits and skills you've mastered. The danger lies not in using those skills but in placing undue emphasis on them and falling back on old habits that no longer serve you, thus retreating from greater challenges, which are represented by the North Node. Although it may seem more positive and encouraging, it too has a downside. A strong North Node can bring ambition, success, and charisma — or an inflated ego with more than a touch of narcissism. The point is that both Nodes are in your chart. The South Node is your launching pad; the North Node is your destination.

The North Node or Dragon's Head (see the horseshoe-shaped left-hand image in Figure 8-2) is a point of expansion, potential, and growth. Among Vedic astrologers, it is called *Rahu*. The South Node or Dragon's Tail (see the image on the right in Figure 8-2), known to Vedic astrologers as *Ketu*, symbolizes deeply entrenched patterns and habits that no longer profit you.

FIGURE 8-2:
The North and South Nodes, also known as the Dragon's Head or *Rahu* and the Dragon's Tail or *Ketu*.

© John Wiley & Sons, Inc.

The Mythology of the Lunar Nodes

Ancient Hindu texts report that the gods and the demons once joined together for a mighty purpose: to churn the ocean and obtain the nectar of immortality. They carried out this task with the aid of an uprooted mountain, which became their churning stick, and a colossal serpent they wrapped around the mountain and used as a rope, with the demons clutching the head and the gods gripping the tail. Back and forth they went, the gods pulling in one direction and the demons in the other. At last, the water turned to milk and released a stream of gifts including herbs, gems, various goddesses, magical creatures, and a bowl filled with the nectar. The great Vishnu, preserver of the universe, favored the gods and so handed the bowl to them. But a demon called Rahuketu disguised himself as a god and took a sip. The Sun and Moon reported this violation to Vishnu, who flung a discus at the demon and decapitated him. The head rose into the sky and became Rahu, the North Node, the dragon's head. The rest of him crashed into the earth and became Ketu, the South Node, known as the dragon's tail.

Some astrological services, for reasons that escape me, choose to pop the North Node into a chart without the South Node. If your chart has fallen victim to this quirk of astrological editing, fear not. Once you know where your North Node is, you can quickly locate your South Node because it's always exactly 180° away. The Nodes inhabit opposite signs. To wit:

If one Node is in . . .	The other Node is in . . .
Aries	Libra
Taurus	Scorpio
Gemini	Sagittarius

If one Node is in . . .	The other Node is in . . .
Cancer	Capricorn
Leo	Aquarius
Virgo	Pisces

The Nodes in the Signs

The Sun, the Moon, and the planets are substantial, massive objects. Whether they're solid and rocky like the Moon and Mars, or gas giants like Jupiter and Neptune, they're distinct, visible worlds with their own geography and their own chemistry. This isn't so of the Nodes. The Nodes are points in space — not physical bodies. They lack features of any kind. Nonetheless, they carry meaning.

REMEMBER

The North Node and the South Node are a matched pair, equal but opposite. They are always located in opposite signs and opposite houses. (For information on the Nodes in the houses, turn to Chapter 12.)

The following list identifies the areas of growth and habit marked by the North and South Nodes of the Moon:

>> **North Node in Aries/South Node in Libra:** You yearn to move in the Aries direction, toward assertiveness, self-sufficiency, and action. When you obey those impulses, you flourish. But all too often, you give your power away to others. You may fear that if you assert yourself, you'll never find the relationship you want (or you'll destroy the relationship you have). On the contrary: Submerging your identity in another person is a mistake. The more independent you are, the more contented you will be, whether you're in a relationship or not.

>> **North Node in Taurus/South Node in Scorpio:** Sex, lies, manipulation, and other people's money fascinate you, as do the melodramatic relationships you often attract. Trouble is, after a while, those soap operas go stale. Rather than plunging into the dark fascination of your obsessions, you gain from building a secure base in the real world. Your best moves are to gather the material resources you need, to learn to manage money effectively, to cultivate patience (and possibly a garden), and to let your values be your guide. What you need above all is self-worth.

>> **North Node in Gemini/South Node in Sagittarius:** How delightful to sit around theorizing about life, death, and the meaning of existence. How nice to know it all. And what a pleasure to convey your brilliant thoughts to your

grateful friends and family. Sadly, it's a waste of energy. With your unstoppable curiosity and ability to communicate, you benefit from accumulating information and employing it for useful purposes. You're a journalist, an artist, a teacher, a communicator. You're interested in ideas, but not inclined to listen to those of others. That needs to change. Don't just trust your intuition or your philosophical musings. Seek the views of others. And get the facts.

» **North Node in Cancer/South Node in Capricorn:** Ambitious and controlling, you readily assume responsibility because you're intent on gaining respect and admiration from others. Yet that's not where your greatest joy lies. Despite your thirst for authority and status, you have a more compelling need for home, family, and emotional authenticity. Although revealing your hopes and fears may cause you to feel distressingly vulnerable, the key to your evolution rests in your ability to trust, to release your need for control, to accept the shifting tides of your feelings, and to act in a caring fashion toward others.

» **North Node in Leo/South Node in Aquarius:** Globally, these are hard times. Many problems need to be addressed, and you'd like to devote yourself to the greater good. At least you think you'd like that. In fact, dedicating yourself to a cause won't bring you the satisfaction you seek, however noble that cause may be. Your fulfillment lies elsewhere. To be the person you were meant to be, you must risk expressing your individuality and your personal desires. You need an outlet for creative self-expression — a way to proclaim who you are, quirks and all.

» **North Node in Virgo/South Node in Pisces:** The realm of the spirit has an irresistible pull for you. But immersing yourself in that world can feed your escapist tendencies. You're better off putting away your Ouija board and attending to the routine concerns that vex us all. Your need to be a victim or a martyr limits your possibilities, as does your sense of inferiority. True happiness lies in a more mundane direction: getting organized and taking care of business. Helping others is admirable, but you don't need to sacrifice yourself. You need to focus. Pay attention to the small stuff, and you'll be amazed at how contented you will feel.

» **North Node in Libra/South Node in Aries:** You're courageous, impulsive, and resourceful. You're comfortable asserting yourself (even if you do have a temper), and you're an effective leader and decision-maker. But you're also self-centered, and the advantages of a loving partnership may elude you, which is too bad because relationship is central to your wellbeing. Your challenge is to cooperate, to share, to be supportive, and to acknowledge the circumstances of other people's lives. By balancing their needs with your own, you move in the direction of inner peace.

» **North Node in Scorpio/South Node in Taurus:** You may think of yourself as a person who values comfort and believes that material security provides the foundation for psychological strength. In fact, your deepest fulfillment has little to do with the material possessions or sensual pleasures, much as you appreciate them. Instead, you benefit from digging into your psyche and overcoming your resistance to change. "Want the change," wrote the poet Rainer Maria Rilke. "Be inspired by the flame." Deep down, you crave nothing short of total metamorphosis.

>> **North Node in Sagittarius/South Node in Gemini:** It's easy for you to stumble into a life of trivial pursuits or to get lost in a maze of rumor-mongering Websites, Sudoku, and random chat. But frittering away your time will not benefit you. With your North Node in the sign of religion, law, travel, and higher education, you need to wrap your mind around the big questions. Seek knowledge. Learn a language. Explore ideas. Find a cause or a philosophy. On antique maps, uncharted areas were decorated with images of sea monsters, meant to warn travelers away. You need to trust your intuition, put down your phone, and sail into those unknown waters, monsters and all. That's where you can find the balm you most need: adventure in the big world — and in the life of the mind.

>> **North Node in Capricorn/South Node in Cancer:** You have a love of the past and a lively appreciation for the pleasures of domesticity. But much as you adore your home and family, you won't find contentment sipping tea in the parlor. That's not your path. You require real-world accomplishments, the kind that are born in ambition, shaped through self-discipline, and rewarded with money and prestige. You need to exercise your talents — despite your moods and insecurities. You have the ability to achieve a great deal. Knowing that the fates are with you may boost your confidence and help you recognize opportunities.

>> **North Node in Aquarius/South Node in Leo:** Creative self-expression comes easily to you, and you attract the kind of notice that many people crave and never get. You have drive. But you're inclined to take over, and you overwhelm people with your need for attention. For real growth, you need to broaden your vision, team up with others, and get involved in something that can make a difference. By attaching your urge for self-expression to a cause that's larger than yourself, you transcend your ego and move in the direction of fulfillment.

>> **North Node in Pisces/South Node in Virgo:** Work we must: That's your motto. You do your best to maintain order, but you get so caught up in your ordinary tasks that there's no room for anything else. You feel like you should work harder, but you tell yourself — wisely — that there's only so much you can do. And besides, you may think, you don't want to drift. And yet, drift you must. By putting aside your dreaded to-do list and letting your mind wander, you allow yourself to explore the province of the spirit. Reading and writing poetry, doing yoga, and meditating are possible tools. Your goal is to become a fully conscious being.

Chapter **9**

The Personal Planets

The Sun and the Moon carry masses of information. All by themselves, they provide a skeleton key to your psyche. But to fully grasp the complexity of your own horoscope, you need to include the planets.

To ancient astrologers, that meant noting the positions of Mercury, Venus, Mars, Jupiter, and Saturn — the only planets easily visible from Earth. For thousands of years, stargazers assumed that there were no other planets. Then, in 1781, a professional musician — a church organist and composer — who was also an amateur astronomer discovered another planet, Uranus, and the race was on. Neptune was discovered next, then Pluto. Asteroids and dwarf planets joined the list of celestial bodies that orbit the Sun. Soon a simple question — how many planets are in the solar system? — turned out to have an ambiguous answer.

Astrologers agree that the five planets you can see for yourself in the night sky (and sometimes during the day), are the most important. Astrologers regard those five planets as having the most immediate impact on the individual. That's why Mercury, Venus, Mars, Jupiter, and Saturn are known as the *personal planets.* The *outer planets,* which aren't visible without a telescope, are less personality-driven and more generational in their effects.

Locating Your Planets

If you have slogged your way through Chapters 1 and 2, you probably have a copy of your chart in hand, in which case you already know your planetary placements. If you don't yet have an accurate copy of your chart, turn to Chapter 2, go online, and download a copy of your chart once and for all.

To figure out what your planetary placements mean, list your planets by sign and by house and then look them up in this chapter (for the personal planets), Chapter 10 (for the outer planets), and Chapter 12 (for house placements).

REMEMBER

Each planet performs a different function in your horoscope and in your life, and each planet has at least one *keyword* that summarizes its essential meaning. Table 9-1 lists those keywords, along with the mysterious little symbols that represent the planets.

TABLE 9-1

Planetary Keywords and Symbols

Planet	Keyword	Symbol
Mercury	Communication	☿
Venus	Love	♀
Mars	Activity	♂
Jupiter	Expansion	♃
Saturn	Restriction	♄
Chiron	Healing	⚷
Uranus	Revolution	♅
Neptune	Imagination	♆
Pluto	Transformation	♇
North Node	Potential	☊
South Node	The past	☋

You will note that a few items on this list don't technically qualify as planets. Pluto, for instance: after its discovery in 1930, it was officially counted as the ninth planet in the solar system. But in 2006, the International Astronomical Union reclassified it as a dwarf planet, a demotion that astrologers have ignored. As far as we're concerned, it's still a planet.

Chiron is another non-planetary entry on this list. Not long after it was discovered in 1977, astrologers began popping it into charts, even though it was initially classified as an asteroid. Since then, it has been reclassified several times. As of now, it is considered a minor planet, which is not the same as a dwarf planet. But never mind. Chiron has been embraced by the astrological community, myself included, and so here it is.

Finally, the North and South Nodes of the moon are on this list. The Nodes mark the spots where the path of the Moon crosses the ecliptic, although neither one has a physical body attached to it. For a long time, only Eastern astrologers paid serious attention to them. That is changing. The Nodes are on this list because they play an important role astrologically.

As you analyze the planetary placements on your chart, do not fret if you notice occasional contradictions. They're inevitable. We all have them. As Walt Whitman, a Gemini, wrote, "Do I contradict myself? Very well then I contradict myself, (I am large, I contain multitudes.)" What matters more than the occasional inconsistencies are the patterns that show up again and again in a natal chart. Once you begin to identify those repeating themes, you're on your way to becoming an astrologer.

Mercury: Communicating with Style

How do you process information? How do you communicate? Mercury has the answers.

TECHNICAL STUFF

In astronomy, the little planet Mercury is distinguished by its rapid pace — it whirls around the Sun in a mere 88 days — and its proximity to the Sun. Mercury orbits our star so closely that it is always either in the same sign as the Sun or in an adjacent sign — and in no case is it ever more than 28° away.

In mythology, the Roman god Mercury, known to the Greeks as Hermes, is recognized for his speed. Clad in his winged sandals and cap, and holding a snake-wrapped staff or caduceus, he was the messenger of the gods as well as a thief, musician, trickster, accomplished liar, and master of spin who could talk his way out of anything. The ancients worshipped him as the god of speech, writing, travel, roads, boundaries, crossroads, sleep, dreams, and the nameless places that fall between here and there. Two of those in-between spots deserve special mention: the shadowy realm between wakefulness and sleep, and the transition between life and death. In classical mythology, it was Mercury who escorted the souls of the dead to the banks of the River Styx, whence they would be ferried to the underworld.

REMEMBER

Astrologers see Mercury as the symbol of learning, reason, intelligence, business, commerce, and everything associated with communication. Its position in your birth chart determines the way you think, the speed with which you gather facts and process information, the style with which you express yourself, and your ability to give a speech, use language, and tell a story, truthful or otherwise.

Mercury's symbol has three metaphysical components: the cross of earth or matter, the circle of spirit, and, perched on top, the crescent of personality looking like a tiny satellite dish, ready to receive information.

For a description of the way your mind operates, find Mercury in your chart and read the appropriate paragraph:

>> **Mercury in Aries:** Never slow to jump to conclusions, you have a lightning-fast mind and a direct, forceful way of expressing yourself. Though you can be impatient and competitive (and often find it difficult to concentrate), you're never dull or wishy-washy. You're willing to lay down the law if you must. You express yourself assertively. You want to make sure people know what you think — and they do.

>> **Mercury in Taurus:** You're thoughtful and levelheaded. You gather your facts, construct a careful argument, and present it diplomatically. After that, you only appear to consider other points of view. In fact, having reached a reasoned decision with all deliberate speed, you see no reason to alter your opinion. You tend to be inflexible, and it's difficult to argue with you, in part because you have the facts, and in part because opening up to fresh ideas is not easy for you. You already know what you think.

>> **Mercury in Gemini:** You're smart, inquisitive, perceptive, persuasive, humorous, and hurried. Your intellectual agility is extraordinary. Your curious mind engages easily, you juggle a multitude of interests, you talk like the wind — and you bend with the wind. All too adaptable, you quickly adjust to circumstances and you can pretty much rationalize anything. Still, this is an enviable placement. Mercury rules Gemini (and Virgo), so it works very effectively here.

>> **Mercury in Cancer:** Sensitive and empathetic, you're insightful and reflective. Most of all, you are exceedingly well tuned-in, often sensing things before you consciously know them. You can communicate with verve and compassion, and you absorb information with ease. You have an amazing memory and a remarkably intuitive mind. But there are times when your moods swamp your better judgment, and you are prone to wishful thinking.

>> **Mercury in Leo:** Dramatic, dignified, and ambitious, you think creatively, express yourself vividly, and are confident in your views. No wonder you're an opinion leader. You are organized in your thinking, winning in your

presentation and, when you're at your best, eloquent in your style of communication. But you can also be dogmatic and boastful, with a tendency to exaggerate, which could explain why Mercury is in its fall in Leo. As often happens with Leo placements, you sometimes go overboard, but in the end, your sincere enthusiasm makes up for your excesses and carries the day.

» **Mercury in Virgo:** You're smart, subtle, persistent, knowledgeable, analytical, and seriously intelligent. Nothing escapes your notice, including logical inconsistencies. A secret idealist who bemoans the yawning gap between how things are and how they ought to be, you can be a nitpicker, a critic, or a prosecuting attorney. At the same time, you are a brilliant thinker and a first-rate conversationalist. Mercury rules Virgo so this placement works exceptionally well. As an added bonus, you excel at crafts and anything that requires fine motor skills and hand-eye coordination.

» **Mercury in Libra:** Rational and intelligent, you seek a balanced, objective viewpoint and intuitively understand that the best solution is generally the simplest. Because you are attuned to the nuances of language, you express yourself with elegance and charm. You fully understand the link between discretion and diplomacy. You're careful not to offend. And yet you love to debate. But in the privacy of your mind, you bounce up and down on the seesaw of uncertainty, and because you try to consider all sides of a question, it takes a while for you to reach a conclusion.

» **Mercury in Scorpio:** You have a penetrating mind that continually probes beneath the surface. At your best, you're an eagle-eyed observer and a profound thinker. You take nothing at face value, which makes you a superb researcher but also makes you warm and suspicious. You're analytical, shrewd, incisive, and capable of digging out all sorts of information. But you also have a biting, sarcastic wit and a persistent tendency to use words as weapons. This is a superlative position for a detective, a research scientist, a therapist, a long-form journalist, or anyone who is mesmerized by the tics and truths of human nature.

» **Mercury in Sagittarius:** You have a searching intellect and an entertaining conversational style. You can be inspired in your insights and in your philosophizing. You can also be grandiose, dogmatic, hypocritical, weak when it comes to details, and direct to the point of tactlessness, which is why traditional astrology considers Mercury in its detriment in Sagittarius. Evangeline Adams, celebrated astrologer of the early 20th century, complained in *Astrology for Everyone* that people with this placement fail to keep their promises due to the "discontinuous and flitterbat quality" of their minds. Your sense of humor is your salvation.

» **Mercury in Capricorn:** Methodical, realistic, and organized, you're a systematic thinker who knows how to focus and acts like an adult. Though you can be conventional and rigid, you try to be even-handed in reaching conclusions, even when that means overcoming your own biases. A serious thinker who values practical information, you're responsible enough to collect the facts before you reach a conclusion, and you communicate clearly and responsibly.

» **Mercury in Aquarius:** Fueled by ideas, you have an inventive, often brilliant mind (think of Thomas Edison, Steve Jobs, or Wolfgang Amadeus Mozart). No wonder Mercury is said to be exalted here. Happiest when committed to a cause, a theory, or a scientific quest, you express yourself in unique ways and often gain your greatest insight in momentary flashes of inspiration. Though you run the risk of getting carried away, your ideas are original, and your excitement about it all is one of your most endearing qualities.

» **Mercury in Pisces:** Any planet in Pisces leads to the triumph of feeling over fact, which is why Mercury is in its detriment here. In reality, people with this placement are savvy both as thinkers and as communicators. You respond to people and situations instinctively, often making the right decision without knowing why. And you find it easy to adapt to changing circumstances. Your mind is receptive, subtle, empathetic, and imaginative. Although you can get lost in a daydream, your reveries often bring realizations. In the end, you rely on your intuition, which runs like a river through your conscious thoughts and is one of your strongest assets.

Venus: Love Conquers All

Whether it appears as the Morning Star or the Evening Star, Venus, the second planet from the Sun, outshines every object in the sky except for the Sun and the Moon.

TECHNICAL STUFF

Astronomers report that Venus, the planet nearest our own, is a hothouse hell, its fractured plains and ancient volcanoes smothered beneath thick blankets of poisonous clouds. With a surface temperature of 900° Fahrenheit, a totally toxic atmosphere, and a surface pressure 100 times higher than that on Earth, it's uninhabitable, as unlovely a place as you can imagine.

In many ancient cultures, people associated the brightest planet with the goddess of love, sex, and beauty. In ancient Sumer and Mesopotamia, she was known as Ishtar or Inanna. In Greece, she was called Aphrodite, and in Rome, Venus. She was the lover of Adonis (and others); the constant companion of her son, the winged god Eros (known as Cupid in Rome); and the unfaithful wife of Hephaestus (known to the Romans as Vulcan), who caught her in bed with her favorite paramour — Ares (Mars to the Romans), the god of war.

REMEMBER

Astrologers associate Venus with love, flirtation, seduction, beauty, art, luxury, harmony, and pleasure. Venus rules the force of attraction, sexual and otherwise. It describes the quality of your interactions with others, the way you express your affections, your artistic impulses, and, strangely enough, the way you handle money.

The symbol for Venus includes two components from the metaphysical tradition: the cross of earth or matter, and, rising above it, the circle of spirit — or love. People also associate the symbol of Venus with the biological symbol for woman.

In your horoscope Venus represents your romantic tendencies, values, and response to beauty, art, money, and possessions. Viewed from Earth, Venus can never be more than 48° from the Sun. That translates to a maximum distance of two signs between Venus and the Sun. Here's how it operates in each of the 12 signs:

>> **Venus in Aries:** Excitable, enthusiastic, and impulsive, you like to think of yourself as a romantic adventurer. You fall in love impetuously and at first sight — and fall out equally fast. More demanding than you realize (and more self-centered), you are ardent and easily aroused. You will readily make the first move — and the last. Even though you ultimately require mental compatibility, what gets you going in the first place is physical appearance.

>> **Venus in Taurus:** As the ruler of Taurus, Venus is completely at home here, making you demonstrative, artistic, and sensual. All the comforts of life appeal to you, starting with rich food and ending with long, luscious sexual encounters, preferably with the same person every time. You value consistency, and though you're capable of fooling around, it's not your natural mode. You require security, comfort, cuddling, beautiful objects, an occasional push to get you moving, a committed partner, and a healthy bank account. Not to mention roses, pastry, and sheets with as high a thread count as you can possibly afford.

>> **Venus in Gemini:** The planet of love in the sign of the inconstant mind produces witty banter, lots of light-hearted flirtation, endless texting (especially if Mercury is also in Gemini), many happy hours of conversation and bookstore browsing, and an irresistible attraction to people who are smart and quick. You are easily swayed, and you're more than capable of carrying on a love affair entirely via app. The challenge is to distinguish between what ought to be a fine romance (it sounds like a great idea) and actual love.

>> **Venus in Cancer:** A natural nester, you find your deepest pleasures in home and family. You're kind, sympathetic, sentimental, loyal, devoted, popular, and a terrific cook (or you'd like to be anyway). You look like the epitome of self-confidence. Yet you require more than a little psychological support. Your fear of rejection, however you try to disguise it, may cause you to hold on too long to both lovers and friends. You don't mean to cling. It's just that when you love someone, you want it to last forever.

>> **Venus in Leo:** You're in love with love. Outgoing and self-dramatizing, loyal and loving, you feel deeply and express yourself flamboyantly. Love is an essential part of your nature, and you tend to define yourself through it. You want to adore and be adored. A lover of the arts, you are creative enough to need an artistic outlet, and you enjoy having friends in the arts. That doesn't mean you're about to run away with a would-be indie filmmaker or an unpublished poet — not unless said artiste has a trust fund. Let's face facts: you love luxury, and you're happiest when the cash flows freely.

>> **Venus in Virgo:** When you're in love, you pay full attention, analyzing every utterance to make sure you've grasped the nuances. You have a strong sense of responsibility and will do anything for your lovers. But you can be critical and controlling, full of opinions about how other people ought to act (which is why this placement is said to show Venus in its fall). Some people with Venus in Virgo have flashy personalities (those with the Sun in Leo, for instance). Most are modest and slightly inhibited. You long to give yourself to your lover, body and soul, if only it were as easy as it sounds.

>> **Venus in Libra:** You're affectionate, charming, and willing to please — a true romantic. Venus rules Libra, making this an exceptionally desirable position. Yet because you idealize love, you often have trouble adapting to the rough spots of a real relationship. When disappointment sets in, you take it hard for a while, and then you get moving. You're highly attractive to other people, and there's usually someone who's circling around you. This position brings a love of beauty and a strong aesthetic sensibility.

>> **Venus in Scorpio:** Thanks to Scorpio's infamous sexiness, this placement sounds like a ticket to ecstasy. And sometimes it is. You are aroused by the presence of mystery and will always respond to a hint of the taboo. You're prone to deep longing, both sexual and emotional, and your love life tends to be stormy. At your best, you're devoted and passionate. But when feeling unappreciated, you're capable of pulling back and isolating yourself behind an invisible shield. At your worst, you can be jealous and vengeful, which is why Venus is in its detriment here.

>> **Venus in Sagittarius:** Animated and excitable, you see love as an adventure — not as a way to nail down a secure future. You cherish your freedom, and your ideal lover is someone who inspires you to explore the world and experience more of life — not someone who constricts your activities or limits your options. You are drawn to people with high ideals who hale from backgrounds unlike your own. Such people intrigue you, and if you happen to fall for someone like that, you feel enlarged in the best possible way. And if it shocks the folks, that's an additional benefit.

>> **Venus in Capricorn:** You're sensual in your sexual liaisons, constant in your affections, and cautious about revealing your emotions. You value stability, propriety, and rectitude. The messiness of emotional free-for-alls terrifies you,

so you keep your feelings under wraps. In art, as in love, you understand the need for control and admire anything classic. You are serious and sophisticated, and sometimes you're accused of privileging status over humbler values. But what's wrong with that? You know that in the real world, status matters.

>> **Venus in Aquarius:** You're drawn to mavericks and rebels, and you like having a multitude of friends. Although you are open-minded and friendly, you are not the most passionate person on the planet, and you tend to enjoy a stimulating intellectual companionship more than a romantic one. Ideas and causes appeal to you. Emotional displays do not. On top of that, you need a certain amount of solitude. Ultimately, you're an independent sort, and your heart is difficult to capture.

>> **Venus in Pisces:** You're sentimental, artistic, devoted, and willing to do anything for your beloved, which is probably why Venus is considered exalted in this sign. You truly seek union with your lovers, but you have no idea what's reasonable and what's not. Other people find it easy to abuse you, in part because you shrug your shoulders and accept crumbs. Eventually, that makes you angry, which is why you can become emotionally abusive, often in a passive-aggressive way. You truly know how to love. That's not the problem. The problem is that you're sometimes too willing to sacrifice your own needs to those of others.

Mars: Road Warrior

What a terrible reputation Mars has. Because it glows red in the sky (a result of the iron oxide in its rocky soil), the Babylonians associated it with death and destruction, Pacific Islanders thought of it as the home of a giant red pig, and New Jerseyites, listening to Orson Welles on the radio in 1938, ran screaming from their homes in fear of invading Martians. Yet people have always fantasized about living on the red planet.

TECHNICAL STUFF

The fourth planet from the Sun, Mars takes almost two years — 687 days, to be exact — to spin through the zodiac. In general, it spends approximately two months in a sign. But once every year and a half, its pattern changes, and it lingers in one section of the sky, sometimes moving forward, sometimes retrograde, giving that particular sign an extra jolt of Martian energy.

In every chart, Mercury and Venus are always relatively close to the Sun. Mars is the first planet to break away from that restriction. No matter what your Sun sign is, Mars can occupy any of the 12 signs of the zodiac.

To the ancient Romans, Mars was the god of war, and many festivals were held in his honor. Ares, the Greek equivalent, was not admired. Throughout Greek mythology, Ares is constantly put down by the other gods — except for Aphrodite (Venus), the goddess of love, who adores him.

REMEMBER

Early astrologers saw Mars as the planet of violence and bad temper. As late as the 15th century, astrologers associated it with theft, murder, battle, lechery, dishonesty, and seething malice of all sorts. Astrologers continue to associate Mars with anger, accidents, and injury. That's the negative side of the planet of war. The positive side sees Mars as the planet of action and desire. It brings will, endurance, drive, strength, energy, and the courage to go after what you want. Mars makes things happen.

The metaphysical symbol for Mars, like the symbol for Venus, has two parts: the circle of spirit, and the cross — or the arrow, or the spear — of matter. In the case of Venus, spirit triumphs over matter. Mars is the opposite, showing matter — and the urge for action — prevailing over spirit. In biology, this figure represents the male, just as the symbol for Venus represent the female. Whether that usage will continue in this age of gender fluidity remains to be seen.

The position of Mars by sign describes the way in which you take the initiative and dive into a new endeavor. It represents your drive, energy, and desires. To find out what sign your Mars is in, look for its symbol on your chart. (If you don't have a chart, go to Chapter 2 for tips on how to get one.) Then check out the appropriate paragraph on this list:

>> **Mars in Aries:** You are forceful, impulsive, brave, and sometimes foolhardy. As the ruler of Aries, Mars endows its natives with energy and an occasionally explosive temper that you must learn to manage. Fortunately, you don't hold on to your anger. After you explode, your fury evaporates. Enthusiastic and daring, you're a natural leader who commands attention even without seeking it. It helps that you have sexual charisma to burn.

>> **Mars in Taurus:** Hard-working and down-to-earth, you are blessed with stamina. Although you can be distracted by the desires of the flesh, you are determined and persistent, slow to anger and equally slow to let it go. When you commit yourself to something, whether it's a relationship or a job, you're in it for the long haul — and for the comfort that it could provide. Born with a serious practical streak, you care about material possessions and status, often more than you're willing to admit.

>> **Mars in Gemini:** With the planet of aggression in the sign of the twins, you're high-spirited, argumentative, nervous, spontaneous, and irritable. Your energy waxes and wanes, sometimes with startling speed. And although you love to debate, you aren't always able to distinguish between major principles and

minor points. Still, you enjoy the back-and-forth. You have a lively, ingenious mind, and you're loads of fun.

» **Mars in Cancer:** You're an inherently emotional, moody, sympathetic person who shies away from confronting others. In good times, you are responsive, protective, and devoted. But when times are tough and you need to have a difficult conversation, you may sulk or project signals so subtle that people miss them. Confrontation is not your strength — proof that Mars is in its fall here. Regardless of your Sun sign, you stew. You become anxious (and might feel the effects in your digestive system). You bury your emotions and, like a crab, retreat into your shell, addressing problems indirectly when you ought to tackle them head-on.

» **Mars in Leo:** Impassioned, and tireless, you have presence and real follow-through. When committed to a cause or an activity, you're virtually unstoppable. Your high spirits and self-assurance are contagious. True, you can be egotistical and arrogant, and your need for an audience can be wearing. Nevertheless, your bravura willingness to take the initiative and step into the fray brings you many admirers. You create excitement.

» **Mars in Virgo:** Control is your issue. When you have it, you are scrupulous, reliable, methodical, and content. When you don't have it, you look reality dead in the eye and detach. You might continue to be involved in whatever it is, but you have separated yourself emotionally. That underrated characteristic — the ability to compartmentalize — may sound dull but it will take you far by helping you strategize under stressful conditions. Military leaders who share this placement include Alexander the Great, Joan of Arc, Napoleon Bonaparte, and General George Patton.

» **Mars in Libra:** You're friendly, flirtatious, stylish, and happiest when you have a partner. But Mars in peace-loving Libra is in its detriment, so asserting yourself can be a challenge. You'd rather advocate for peace and justice than fight a war, and persuasion is your mode of argument. You always seek balance and harmony. But because you try to examine all sides of a question, you find it difficult to reach a conclusion, even when the question is as basic as, what do I want?

» **Mars in Scorpio:** You're courageous, cunning, determined, and self-sufficient. Blessed with fierce willpower and unwavering desires, you're highly sexed and intensely emotional. You struggle with jealousy and the desire for revenge. Although adapting to changing circumstances isn't easy, you have a reliable source of internal energy and a mountain of personal power. Mars is the traditional ruler of Scorpio, so this is a beneficial placement.

» **Mars in Sagittarius:** You have strong convictions, a love of the outdoors, and a deep desire for independence. But you can be slapdash and defiant, and your idealistic campaigns, so eagerly launched, sometimes run aground. The astrologer Evangeline Adams, never one to pull her punches, claims that this placement makes people "scintillating rather than solid, dashing rather than enduring." Phrased that way, it may sound negative. But who wouldn't want to be scintillating and dashing? You're also fair and direct, and you can gather your energy quickly — especially when you're galloping off on another escapade.

» **Mars in Capricorn:** Your desires, sexual and otherwise, are strong, your ambitions focused, your actions deliberate. When you feel recognized, your energy is disciplined and steady. Efficient and systematic, you respect tradition, understand hierarchies, and often rise to the top. You have a natural sense of authority and in many ways are a born leader. When you feel thwarted, your vitality fades and you have trouble repressing your anger. But Mars is exalted in Capricorn, giving you the ability to power through discouragement and stick to your goals.

» **Mars in Aquarius:** Whenever possible, you prefer the road less traveled. You're enterprising, impatient, willful, and sometimes eccentric. Convention bores you because it suggests stagnation. Independent and idealistic, you disdain predictability and would rather take a risk in search of something new and improved. Ideas — and ideals — excite you but emotionally, you can be on the chilly side, and you occasionally rebel just for the pleasure of making a statement.

» **Mars in Pisces:** You fall deeply in love. You're generous, moody, restless, and highly intuitive, which is perhaps your greatest asset. But when the emotional din becomes more than you can tolerate, you shut down. When that happens, your willpower evaporates, you have trouble getting motivated, you drive friends insane with your passivity, and your physical energy evaporates. One of the central challenges of your life is regulating your energy. It's not easy to do. But you have the capacity to reach a level of cosmic awareness that is beyond the ability of most people to even imagine.

Jupiter: More Is Better

Looking for luck? Your search is over. Auspicious Jupiter is the lord of luck, the guardian of good fortune, and the champion of getting an even break.

TECHNICAL STUFF

Jupiter is the largest planet in the solar system by far. More massive than all the other planets combined, it could devour 1,330 Earths and still have room to burp. Its most famous feature is the Great Red Spot, a 300-year-old high-pressure storm — an anti-cycle, to be specific — that's double the size of the Earth and has been churning away for close to two centuries.

Not surprisingly, the biggest planet in our solar system was named for the king of the gods, known in Greece as Zeus and in Rome as Jove or Jupiter Optimus Maximus — the biggest and the best, even if he was punitive and promiscuous. The Greeks depicted him as bearded, dignified, and powerful — Zeus the father figure, surveying the universe from his home on snowy Mount Olympus.

REMEMBER

Astrologers associate Jupiter with opportunity, expansion, growth, abundance, learning, success, optimism, and good cheer. Whatever Jupiter touches, it expands. Of course, like every planet, it can express itself positively or negatively. At its best, it brings luck, generosity, and the ability to seize an opportunity. When it's tied to other planets through tension-producing aspects, such as squares and oppositions (discussed in Chapter 13), it expresses its shadow side by indulging in gluttony, laziness, and excess of all kinds.

Rejoice when you see this symbol in your chart, for it marks an area of opportunity. In the metaphysical tradition, the symbol has two parts: the cross of matter and, rising above it like a sail, the curve of personality, indicating the expansive unfurling of the self. That's one way to remember it. Or you can think of it as looking like a highly stylized number four.

GALILEO AND THE MOONS OF JUPITER

About one hundred years after the birth of Christ, the astronomer Ptolemy wrote a book asserting what everyone already knew: That the Earth was the center of the universe, and that everything else — the Sun, the Moon, the stars, and the planets — revolved around it.

Over a millennium later, in 1453, Copernicus proved Ptolemy wrong. He showed that the Earth orbited the Sun, not the other way around. His observations were not widely accepted. Martin Luther referred to him as an "upstart astrologer" (and in fact he was an astrologer, as were most astronomers). Most people continued to put their faith in Ptolemy. Few doubted that the Earth was the center of the universe.

A century and a half later, Galileo trained his telescope upon distant Jupiter and discovered that it was orbited by a population of moons. (He saw four; scientists have now found 79, and counting.) His announcement was greeted with distress, particularly by the church, because if those four moons were orbiting around Jupiter, then by definition, not everything revolved around the Earth and the Ptolemaic system was flawed. Galileo was accused of heresy. He ended up spending the rest of his life under house arrest for his role in promoting this new view of the heavens. His ideas triumphed. In 1992, 350 years after Galileo's death, the Vatican acknowledged its mistake. Thus, Jupiter and its many moons opened up a new way to see the cosmos. In an astrological chart, Jupiter has a similar function. It opens things up; it expands the possibilities.

Jupiter takes about 12 years to spin through the zodiac, spending about a year in each sign. Its position by sign describes ways you can broaden your horizons and areas where you're more likely to be lucky.

>> **Jupiter in Aries:** You have confidence, energy, and zest. Although you have many interests, you may not sustain them over the long run. You easily get fired up, and you have an egocentric tendency to get overly wound up in your own concerns and to lose control of the details. On the other hand, you are a pioneering soul with the audacity to strike out into new territory. Do your gambles pay off? Often, they do. Case in point: Sally Ride, the first female astronaut. Or Jeff Bezos, founder of Amazon and the richest man on Earth. Say what you will, from a business point of view his radical venture has been a rousing success.

>> **Jupiter in Taurus:** You're devoted and kind. A lover of material objects and physical pleasures, you can easily slip into self-indulgence. You're great in bed, relaxed and sensuous, but you may be plagued by excess weight or other afflictions of the Epicurean kind. Fortunately, you value the practical amenities, such as a well-padded bank account, and you have the patience to build it. When it comes to the bottom line, your judgment is sound.

>> **Jupiter in Gemini:** You're clever, multitalented, and easily engrossed. Nothing fires you up more than an unusual idea. You are never happier (or luckier) than when you're immersed in a subject or activity that fascinates you. But you struggle with distractibility, which is why Jupiter is in detriment here. Still, your potential is huge. You benefit from anything that involves writing, be it keeping a journal or working in a bookstore or being a journalist or practicing calligraphy. One tip: Beware of losing your interest in a topic by talking it to death.

>> **Jupiter in Cancer:** You're openhearted, benevolent, intuitive, protective, and sympathetic — the ultimate Earth mother, even if you're a man. Understanding and forgiving (sometimes pathetically so), you love the pleasures of home, property, and parenthood. Traditional astrology holds that Jupiter is exalted in this position, and experience shows that it tends to bring luck in real estate. Look for a spacious kitchen, all the better to experience the joy of cooking.

>> **Jupiter in Leo:** You're magnanimous, compassionate, exuberant, and dramatic, with enormous vitality and a deep need for recognition, respect, and power. When you entertain, you do so lavishly. Though you can be overbearing, you're openhearted and well liked, which is one reason that this position often brings success.

>> **Jupiter in Virgo:** You're organized and practical, with a sharp intellect, a serious work ethic, and a tendency to put in too many hours in pursuit of perfection. When your efforts produce concrete results, as often happens, you feel content and proud. Yet Jupiter is an expansive force while Virgo is restrictive, so this placement — Jupiter in its detriment — can give rise to internal tension. But so what? Any placement in Virgo tends to stir up a little anxiety. That's the price of excellence.

>> **Jupiter in Libra:** You're likable, sympathetic, fair, and popular, with an innate attraction to the arts. Gifted with natural charm, you benefit from working with other people and are happiest when you have a partner. When you sense that things aren't going well, you may be too eager to please. Self-indulgence is another possible problem. Finally, you may wrestle with the classic Libran challenge: making decisions, important or not. You can spend forever balancing the pros and the cons. Finding a way to shorten that process will ease your mind and bring you good fortune.

>> **Jupiter in Scorpio:** You have huge passions, a magnetic intensity that other people can sense, and a strongly sexual nature. Though you may be reserved, you're observant, and you have a sincere interest in investigating whatever's under that rock. Ambitious and sometimes aggressive, you have great personal pride and a ferocious willpower that can help you achieve your dreams.

>> **Jupiter in Sagittarius:** Because Jupiter rules Sagittarius, this is considered a favorable placement. Sagittarius brings out the best in Jupiter, making you genial, optimistic, generous, broad-minded, and philosophical. With your eye on the big picture, you know enough to avoid obsessing over minutiae — at least most of the time. A skilled teacher, you're drawn to foreign travel, higher education, and large, all-encompassing theories and ideas. But beware: You can be a blowhard, which means that, after a while, no one wants to hear you lecture, no matter how worthy the subject.

>> **Jupiter in Capricorn:** With the planet of expansion in cautious Capricorn, you're ambitious, dutiful, honest, serious-minded, realistic, and disciplined. When you set a goal, your chances of achieving it are excellent. But optimistic Jupiter is in its fall in constricting Capricorn, so along the way you may have to combat pessimism. You also have a tough time relaxing. Fortunately, you have the sense to be in the right place at the right time, and it's not dumb luck, no matter how it may appear. Like the great Capricorn scientist Louis Pasteur, you understand that "chance favors the prepared mind." So you do your homework, and when good fortune comes along, you're ready.

>> **Jupiter in Aquarius:** Open-minded, altruistic, and innovative, you take an interest in everything that's cutting edge and everyone whose ideals point in the direction of a better, more just world. Blessed with originality, vision, and

humanitarian beliefs, you enjoy working within a community, even if you're sometimes scornful of individuals. You can easily imagine an ideal society. But you don't deal with disappointment well, and you can become egotistical and overbearing.

» **Jupiter in Pisces:** Traditionally, Jupiter rules Pisces, making this an auspicious placement. Born with powerful intuitive and imaginative faculties, you absorb everything going on around you. A forgiving and empathetic person, you cherish the notion that you can make things better, even to the point of self-sacrifice. But when you feel overwhelmed, as happens from time to time, you need to withdraw. Everyone needs to escape once in a while. In your case, solitude lets you soothe your battered ego, and spiritual pursuits sustain you.

Saturn: Lord of the Rings

Before the invention of the telescope, Saturn was the most distant planet that anyone could see. It marked the end of the solar system. Naturally, it came to represent limits. Today, it remains the most distant planet that's easily visible with the naked eye, so that meaning still applies. But its image has improved. Thanks to the telescope and the Voyager space missions, everyone knows what Saturn looks like. Even people who have never peered through a telescope have seen pictures of its dazzling ring structure. And they know that Saturn is the most beautiful planet in the solar system.

TECHNICAL STUFF

The second largest planet (after Jupiter), Saturn is a gas giant surrounded by a broad collar of icy rings, at least 62 moons, and more than 1.5 million moonlets embedded in the rings. Saturn is so large that 95 Earths could fit inside it. But its density is so low that, if there were an ocean large enough to hold the entire planet, Saturn would float.

Saturn takes 29½ years to travel through the zodiac and spends about 2½ years in each sign.

In mythology, Saturn was originally an Italian corn god whose winter festival, the Saturnalia, was a raucous time of abundance in which masters became servants and feasting was non-stop. The Romans identified Saturn with the Greek god Kronos, who overthrew his father, Uranus, but then, fearful of being similarly attacked, swallowed his own children. Needless to say, he could not escape his fate and was vanquished by his own sons and daughters. His son Zeus became king of the gods. Kronos, also known as Father Time, symbolizes the past and the old order, both of which are associated with Saturn and Capricorn.

In astrology, Saturn represents the established order. It brings structure, organization, discipline, limitations, boundaries, responsibility, duty, perseverance, and fear. A serious, even somber influence, it tests people and forces them to confront reality. As a result, Saturn has a frightful reputation, one that has been nurtured by generations of astrologers, including the great Evangeline Adams. In *Astrology for Everyone,* she explains that Saturn "blights all that he gazes on. He is the curse of disappointment, not of anger. He freezes the water-springs; he is the dry-rot and the death of the ungodly. He looks upon the Sun, despairs; in cynic bitterness his draught is brewed, and he drinks it, wishing it were poison. His breath withers up love; his word is malediction . . . But in each one of us this principle exists; it is the most inescapable of all our fates."

With publicity like that, it's no wonder that followers of astrology came to fear Saturn. Yet its reputation isn't entirely deserved because, although Saturn can trigger a cascade of difficulties, it also helps create order. Saturn's influence enables you to conquer your fears and to combat your inertia. If it forces you to struggle with depression, disappointment, poverty, and other obstacles, it does so by compelling you to seek solutions, set goals, get organized, and work harder than you ever thought you could. Saturn is, in short, the planet of accomplishment.

The symbol of Saturn, wherever you find it in your chart, identifies your greatest trials and challenges. Metaphysical astrologers describe it as the cross of matter and circumstances rising out of the crescent of personality, which suggests that we create our own limitations and must find ways to confront them. An easier way to remember the symbol is that it resembles a curvy lowercase "h" (for "hardship" or "humbled") with a slash mark across it like that in a French "7."

Saturn's placement by sign determines your sense of inadequacy, your fears and hesitations, the obstacles and liabilities that block your path, and the ways in which you try to overcome them.

>> **Saturn in Aries:** You're an independent thinker but expressing your individuality doesn't come easily. You fear losing your independence, so you can't stand following the leader, but neither are you comfortable directing other people. Though you're entrepreneurial and determined, you can be inconsiderate. Learning to assert yourself in a constructive way is part of your challenge. You resist following the dictates of others, but once you determine for yourself a goal and a game plan, you do well. And it may reassure you to know that the worst difficulties you face come when you are young.

>> **Saturn in Taurus:** Images of the poorhouse dance in your head. You have an intense need for economic and emotional stability, so you learn to manage your resources and try to avoid the trauma of moving or making other major changes. You're industrious and cautious, with tremendous willpower.

The downside? You lack spontaneity. In your need for security, you can become avaricious or jealous. And enjoying the physical side of life in a healthy, non-obsessive way is something you may have to learn.

» **Saturn in Gemini:** You're smart, serious, and well-spoken despite your fear of being considered intellectually inferior. An excellent problem-solver, you are adept at mastering new subjects. When you're learning a language or developing a skill you never thought you could master, you feel motivated and alert. (Learning, for you, is a remedy against boredom and melancholy.) As with any planet in the sign of the Twins, Saturn in Gemini can reveal itself in a number of ways. At your worst, you can convince yourself of anything. When you're at the top of your game, your ability to concentrate, absorb information, and communicate is impressive.

» **Saturn in Cancer:** Not an easy placement, Saturn in Cancer often brings a difficult childhood with at least one parent who's cold or withholding. As a result, you may be insecure and inhibited, with a yearning for emotional control and understanding. Your attempt to win the love and warmth you lacked as a child can become the quest of a lifetime. Some people with this placement become clingy or cover up their fear of vulnerability by acting overly confident or pretending to be indifferent, a disguise that seldom fools anyone. Most aim to create in adulthood what they lacked in childhood by becoming tolerant, protective, and loving, especially as parents.

» **Saturn in Leo:** Determined and dignified, you long to be creative but are afraid of expressing yourself and terrified of being considered mediocre. If that sounds like a description of writer's block, welcome to Saturn in Leo. The same principle applies to romance. Finding the right match may take a while because, much as you yearn for love, you fear being rejected. That's the Catch-22 you must overcome. Self-doubt wears you down and gets you nowhere. The challenge of this position is to acknowledge, not bury, your longing for love, your creative urges, and your need for recognition. It's not necessary to repress your personality to achieve those things. On the contrary: dare to be dramatic. You'll be much happier.

» **Saturn in Virgo:** You're analytical, precise, diligent, and drawn to solitude. (In a previous life, according to one of my first astrology teachers, you may have been a medieval monk.) Negative thinking is your nemesis. Fearing loss of control and apprehensive about the future, you try to fend off the apocalypse by managing the small stuff. Your challenge is to remember that the vast majority of the things you worry about — 85 percent, according to one commonly cited study — never happen at all. Here's a reminder from the Dalai Lama: "There is no benefit in worrying whatsoever."

>> **Saturn in Libra:** This position — Saturn in its exaltation — makes you rational, reliable, discreet, and concerned about relationships. You're critical of the relationships you have, which you may deem unsatisfying for one reason or another, and yet you fear being alone, which causes you to feel uncomfortable when you try to connect. Though it may take longer than you wish, you most certainly will connect. Have you ever known someone who simply will not settle, even in the most inconsequential way? That's not you. You value — or learn to value — fairness, loyalty, sincerity, and character, and you have a robust sense of proportion. This may not sound romantic, but here goes: you will be far happier when you make the sensible choice.

>> **Saturn in Scorpio:** You're resourceful and powerful, with strong convictions and a deep sense of purpose, but dependency issues can trip you up. Although you have undeniable sexual needs, sex is complicated for you. You may struggle to define yourself as an individual while maintaining a relationship, and you're prone to jealousy and resentment. Beneath it all, you are fearless. You have the courage to deal with your passions and conquer your fears, including fear of death. Mysteries fascinate you, and none more than the mystery of your own psyche.

>> **Saturn in Sagittarius:** Because you dislike constraints and limitations, you seek to broaden your horizons, literally and figuratively. But unless you find a structured approach to achieving your goals, circumstances may conspire to keep you from reaching them. Even though you may fantasize about being independent and footloose, what you actually need is to find meaning in your daily activities, to travel widely and with purpose, and to study in a serious way those aspects of religion, law, philosophy, and other cultures that most interest you. Sagittarius wants to move swiftly. Saturn doesn't. Learn to persevere.

>> **Saturn in Capricorn:** You're capable, ambitious, and pragmatic, with natural authority and obvious competence. Because you crave recognition and are secretly afraid that you won't get it, you doggedly pursue your objectives, making sure to follow the rules — even if you have to lose your own ideas along the way. You don't like restrictions any more than the next person, but you know how to deal with them and can function within a structure. You don't flail around, hoping to be rescued. You figure out the necessary steps, and you take them. Saturn rules Capricorn, so this is considered a superb placement.

>> **Saturn in Aquarius:** With Saturn ruling Aquarius, this is an enviable position. Your number one asset is that you have a clear and original mind and, along with it, the ability to influence others. Liberal-minded and unselfish, you conceive of yourself as a member of society, a small part of a larger whole.

And you're a person of principle. It's essential for your happiness and self-respect that you live in accordance with your ideals, which are typically of the noblest sort. Material success isn't a motivating force in your life. Other values matter more.

» **Saturn in Pisces:** You're sympathetic and intuitive, with a sweet vulnerability that makes you appealing to others. Spiritual pursuits brings you satisfaction. But you're afraid of chaos and isolation, and you struggle to stave off those terrors. A stumbling block is that you wrestle with more than your share of anxieties, baseless apprehensions, and — I'm sorry to say — self-pity. Though you understand how other humans operate, you may be at a loss when it comes to solving your own problems, especially if substance abuse happens to be among them. Establishing boundaries is a skill you need to practice. Expressing yourself through poetry or music is one way to allay your fears and advance one of your greatest assets: your imagination.

IN THIS CHAPTER

» Plugging into Uranus, the planet of revolution

» Imagining visionary Neptune

» Brooding over Pluto, the dwarf planet of transformation

» Checking out Chiron, the centaur of healing

» Acknowledging other celestial bodies

Chapter **10**

The Outer Planets (And More)

U ntil 1781, astrologers cast horoscopes using the Sun, the Moon, and the five planets easily visible from Earth: Mercury, Venus, Mars, Jupiter, and Saturn. Then William Herschel, a professional musician and amateur telescope maker in Bath, England, made a momentous breakthrough. After years of staying up late with his devoted sister and obsessively (he was a Scorpio) mapping the heavens, he became the first human in history to train a telescope on the night sky and find a planet. That discovery — of the planet Uranus — rocked the astronomical world. Occurring in the midst of the American War of Independence and just a few years before the French Revolution, it overturned the commonly held view of the solar system. Eventually it changed astrology too, becoming associated with upheavals of all kinds — personal, political, and scientific.

Studying Uranus, scientists found anomalies in its orbit that they thought might indicate the presence of still another planet. In 1846, after a search marked by total confusion (in keeping with the nature of the planet), European astronomers found that mysterious body and named it Neptune. A third discovery further expanded the solar system in 1930, when Clyde Tombaugh, a 24-year-old amateur working at the Lowell Observatory in Arizona, located Pluto.

These celestial bodies differ from the visible planets of antiquity. The Sun, the Moon, Mercury, Venus, and Mars reflect individual disposition and are known as personal planets. Jupiter and Saturn are social planets. Uranus, Neptune, and Pluto, which inhabit the outer reaches of the solar system, are known as transpersonal planets. Whereas the Sun swings through all 12 signs in a year, it takes Uranus 84 years, Neptune 165 years, and tiny Pluto almost two and a half centuries to make the same trip. These planets have relatively minor impact on day-to-day activities. Instead, they define generations; spark momentous events and cultural shifts; mold the collective unconscious; and act as harbingers of change. They shake you up (unpredictable Uranus), inspire and bewilder you (enigmatic Neptune), and push you to the brink (take-no-prisoners Pluto). They represent the invincible, unstoppable, cosmic forces of change.

TIP

The generational dates given in parentheses later in this chapter for these planetary placements are not exact; they're fuzzy around the edges. What actually happens when Neptune, Uranus, or Pluto enters a new sign is that for about a year, the planet appears to ricochet back and forth between the old sign and the new one. As a result, if you were born during (or close to) the first or final year of a planet's journey through a sign, the only way to know for sure where each planet was when you were born is to examine an accurate copy of your chart. Chapter 2 tells you how to get one.

Uranus: The Rebel

Uranus is the planet of revolution and the modern age. It rules invention, technology, and everything on the cutting edge. Its action is unpredictable. It can barrel into your life like a rogue wave, with all the terror and excitement that implies. Or it can slip past with scarcely a splash. Known as the Great Awakener, Uranus is the planet of astrology.

Arguably the most electrifying planet out there, Uranus represents the part of you that's original and inventive, that shuns convention, craves freedom, and attracts — or creates — abrupt change. It can stir up senseless disruption, studied eccentricity, restlessness, turmoil, and agitated states of mind. It can also herald unexpected, life-altering events, typically in areas where you haven't been paying attention. Uranus, it must be said, can shatter your world.

Uranus also generates bright flashes of insight and fresh ideas when you need them the most. It's the iconoclastic lord of genius, ingenuity, and everything that captures you by surprise. When lightning strikes, be it in the form of an out-of-the-blue pink slip or a surprise promotion, love at first swipe or an unforeseen break-up, a lottery win or a housing catastrophe, you can bet that Uranus, the emissary of disruption, is at work.

It takes 84 years — a human lifetime — for Uranus and its 27 moons (and counting) to revolve around the Sun. Like Neptune, Uranus is an ice giant. It has a few rings, darker and sparser than Saturn's. And its poles point to the Sun, meaning that Uranus, alone among all the planets, seems to roll around on its side.

The myth behind the planet

Mythology is seldom pretty, as the story of Uranus demonstrates. In Greek mythology, Uranus (Sky) and Gaia (Earth) — heaven and earth — mated and gave birth to dozens of offspring. After a while, Uranus felt so threatened by his progeny that he began pushing them back into Gaia's womb. When Gaia could stand it no longer, she gave a sickle to her son Kronos and begged him to stop his father. Kronos — Saturn, to the Romans — did so in spectacular fashion. He castrated his father and tossed the severed genitals into the sea, which frothed up around them. Out of the foam emerged Aphrodite, the goddess of love and beauty. Thus Uranus, overthrown by his son, is associated with insurrection, even if he himself caused it with his paranoia and punishing behavior.

Uranus is the only planet named after a Greek mythological figure rather than a Roman one. But if William Herschel had had his way, there would have been no mythology at all. He believed that he was living in modern times and he wanted the planet's name to reflect that. He suggested that it be called Georgium Sidus, George's Star, after King George III of England. A French astronomer objected, and wiser heads prevailed. But what if Herschel had succeeded? Would a different name have made a difference astrologically? George III experienced bouts of mania and derangement. (Historians think he suffered from a hereditary blood disorder exacerbated by unintentional arsenic poisoning.) So Georgium Sidus might have come to indicate eccentric ways of thinking. George III collected mathematical and scientific instruments. So Georgium Sidus might have been linked with technology. Most of all, George III is the king against whom American colonists revolted. Without a doubt, then, Georgium Sidus would have come to signify revolution. Astrologically, the meaning of the planet would have remained roughly the same. It doesn't matter whether you look at Uranus through the lens of mythology or history or science. Its time had come.

The most commonly used glyph of Uranus (see Figure 10-1) looks like an antiquated TV antenna — an apt image for the planet associated with electricity, technology, and the future. It also incorporates the letter H, a nod to William Herschel, the first human being (but not the last) to discover a planet.

FIGURE 10-1:
The symbol of
Uranus.

© John Wiley & Sons, Inc.

Some astrologers use another glyph: a circle with a dot (like the symbol of the Sun) and an arrow attached to the top pointing straight up. I don't use this glyph because I find the similarity between it and the symbol of Mars to be distracting. But this glyph has many advocates, and if you patronize certain websites, you will see it.

Understanding Uranus

Uranus spends about seven years in each sign. Like Neptune and Pluto, it makes its biggest impact on generations. In an individual chart, its influence is usually subtle. But when it's prominent in a birth chart, Uranus is the mark of geniuses, idealists, iconoclasts, eccentrics, inventors, revolutionaries, and astrologers. It lights up the places where you struggle against convention. This is where you are reluctant to conform. This is where you resist.

And when, over the course of its 84-year cycle, it approaches the Sun, the Moon, the other planets in your birth chart and the major angles, it can beget tumultuous turn-arounds, idiotic accidents, hair-raising relationship dramas, mind-boggling job shifts, and — in brief — whatever mayhem it takes to loosen you up and liberate you.

Uranus, like the other outer planets, primarily influences generations rather than individuals — unless it happens to occupy an important position in your natal chart. It is prominent in your horoscope if

>> It occupies an angle — that is, it is located in the first, fourth, seventh, or tenth house of your chart. It's most powerful if it's within approximately 8° of your Ascendant or Midheaven. The closer it is, the stronger its impact. (See Chapter 11 for more on Ascendants and Midheavens.)

>> It makes several close aspects to other planets and, in particular, to the Sun, the Moon, or the planet that rules your Ascendant. (See Chapter 13 for a discussion of aspects.)

>> You have one or more planets in Aquarius.

Uranus in the signs

The sign that Uranus occupies in your birth chart determines the way you and other members of your generation shake off the burden of expectation, stand up against the established order, release yourself from fear, and express your most idiosyncratic, singular self.

» **Uranus in Aries (1927 to 1935; 2011 to 2018):** You're feisty, indomitable, and impatient, and you value your freedom more than most. A pioneering spirit, you are brave at your core. When change is called for, you rush in, preferring the risks of being impulsive to the so-called safety of the slow-and-sensible approach. You're intrepid and inventive, even if your enthusiasms do flicker on and off. Change invigorates you.

» **Uranus in Taurus (1935 to 1942; 2018 to 2025):** Once you admit that you want something and begin going after it, nothing can stop you. Your willpower helps you overcome all obstacles. You have a unique appreciation of things and gravitate toward concrete, innovative methods of making money, although you may undergo financial ups and downs.

» **Uranus in Gemini (1942 to 1949; 2025 to 2032):** You're clever, inquisitive, chatty, versatile, and mentally restless. When faced with unwanted change, you try to reframe it because you'd rather feel like an unconscious architect of your own fate than like a victim of circumstance. But you can also lie to yourself. You gravitate toward original ideas and have a tendency to procrastinate or to be easily distracted.

» **Uranus in Cancer (1949 to 1956; 2032 to 2039):** You have an active imagination, a sensitive disposition, and an atypical family life. You may live in unusual places or experience disruptions in your home life. Much as you long for the security of a nuclear family, you also feel hemmed in by its restrictions. When you're in a traditional family (or even a standard-issue house), you may alter its structure. Home, to your mind, is a concept that needs to be shaken up and redefined.

» **Uranus in Leo (1956 to 1962; 2039 to 2046):** Assertive and freewheeling, ardent and talented, you enthusiastically throw yourself into creative endeavors and projects that sound exciting. Offbeat love affairs (the more reckless the better) entice you, and you wade into times of change with gusto. But you can also be egotistical, imperious, and full of yourself.

» **Uranus in Virgo (1962 to 1969; 2046 to 2053):** Because you have an acute and analytical mind, you relish novel approaches and rebel against monotony — especially on the job, where your need for freedom is not always an advantage. You have little patience for following directions. You prefer to develop your own procedures and devise your own routines, especially in terms of health, work, and daily life.

» **Uranus in Libra (1969 to 1975; 2053 to 2059):** You're imaginative and artistic, although members of other generations may be appalled at your taste. They may also be befuddled by your relationships, romantic and otherwise, because you're drawn to unusual people and situations.

In many ways your generation is forging an innovative approach to relationships — one that incorporates a high degree of personal freedom. Still, in times of stress, you're happiest with a companion by your side.

» **Uranus in Scorpio (1975 to 1981; 2059 to 2066):** Deeply intuitive and strong-willed, you're charismatic, determined, and more than willing to break taboos. Long-term fixations and fleeting infatuations may plague you; you may be perpetually absorbed by thoughts of sex or death; and finances may absorb you, especially during crazy economic times. But you're resourceful and unafraid, and when change is afoot, you choose to run with it, always keeping an eye on the future. Is Uranus exalted in Scorpio? Some astrologers think it is.

» **Uranus in Sagittarius (1981 to 1988; 2066 to 2072):** You're optimistic and free-spirited, with large aspirations. You resent naysayers who denigrate your dreams, and you refuse to be constrained by practical matters. You'd like to see the world, but not by following someone else's itinerary. You'd like to achieve enlightenment, but standard orthodoxies seem outdated and stale to you. Travel and education motivate you, and you feel liberated by the winds of change.

» **Uranus in Capricorn (1988 to 1996):** You're ambitious, responsible, and methodical. Yet you instinctively shun the prescribed curriculum, which means that your career can take surprising twists. If you can express your individuality within an organization or a system, fine. If not, your discomfort with the hierarchy makes you want to bring it to its knees (or to fantasize same). You're a force for constructive change.

» **Uranus in Aquarius (1996 to 2003):** You're tolerant and selfless, idealistic yet unsentimental. A nonconformist and idealist at heart, you celebrate individuality and number many an oddball among your friends. Incredible coincidences and strokes of luck animate your life. Uranus is the ruler of Aquarius, which means that it works well here. So when you embrace change, your world opens up. When you try to contain change, unhappiness follows. Activist involvement in causes that speak to you can kindle the liberation you seek. This is also an auspicious placement for scientific and technological explorations.

» **Uranus in Pisces (2003 to 2011):** Intuitive and talented, you're susceptible to convoluted dreams and psychic flashes that really might be trying to tell you something. You have deep compassion for others, although you may occasionally feel swamped by self-pity or loneliness. At such times, volunteering or being of service in some way can help you get back on track. Music, art, and out-of-the-ordinary spiritual pursuits help you maintain composure and express your inalienable uniqueness.

THE SECRET OF THE 1960S

Why are some decades more memorable than others? The outer planets are usually to blame. They travel slowly through the zodiac. When they combine their considerable energies by moving in tandem, things start to cook.

In the 1960s, for example, freedom-loving Uranus and Pluto, the planet of transformation, were aligned in the same sign of the zodiac (Virgo) for the first time in over a century. The previous time was around 1848, when a wave of revolutions swept across Europe. In the 1960s, that same energy was at work. Together, Uranus and Pluto egged each other on, turning Uranian defiance into something that transformed society. The civil rights movement, the antiwar movement, the student movement, the Black Power movement, feminism, the sexual revolution, the Stonewall Riots, the Moon Walk, and even the horrific assassinations that characterized the decade are all manifestations of unpredictable Uranian energy deepened by the transformative power of Pluto. Nor was this solely an American phenomenon. There were strikes, protests, and civil unrest in France, Mexico, Czechoslovakia, West Germany, Spain, and elsewhere. It was an era of uprising.

At the time, cultural touchstones such as Woodstock, LSD, communes, be-ins, the Weather Underground, and *Be Here Now* (for example) seemed fraught with cosmic resonance. Not only did they epitomize the Uranian urge to rise up against the repressive adult society of the 1950s, they took on the profundity of Pluto and the weight of philosophy — or so it seemed. And if, in retrospect, more than a few expressions of the era look ridiculous, it's also true that many repercussions of those long-ago, tie-dyed days will simply not fade away.

If you were born between 1962 and 1969, you have both unruly Uranus and transformative Pluto in Virgo. Although the impracticality of much of what went down in the 1960s probably irritates you, on some level you're deeply in sync with the urge to break away from old forms, alter the hidebound assumptions of mainstream society, and give peace a chance.

Neptune: The Dreamer

In 1612, Galileo gazed through his little telescope (practically a toy by today's standards) and saw what looked like a dim star — except that, unlike the other stars, it moved. He even drew a picture of it, and if he'd been thinking, he would have realized that it was a planet. Alas, he didn't put two and two together, and he missed the opportunity to identify Neptune.

More than two hundred years later, Neptune continued to elude discovery, although two scientists, one French and one English, working separately, had pinpointed the planet's theoretical location. But neither could gain access to a large telescope to confirm it. If they had, they would have found it in precisely the predicted spot (in Aquarius). But neither had the wherewithal to make that happen. Finally, in 1846, one of them asked astronomers in Germany to undertake a search for the new planet. Johann Galle, a young assistant at the Berlin Observatory, found it within an hour.

In a chart, impressionistic Neptune promotes intuition, dreams and visions, psychic ability, artistic talent, imagination, glamour, and everything that flows. Neptune finds expression in dance, music, poetry, and daydreams. It stimulates compassion, dissolves boundaries, and sensitizes anything it touches. But it also has a dark side. Despite its idealism and spiritual nature, Neptune is the planet of illusion and deceit. Under negative conditions, it accentuates the tendency to drift and increases the threat of addiction, hypochondria, escapism, and a refusal to confront reality.

TECHNICAL
STUFF

In NASA photographs, Neptune looks like a luminous turquoise marble — a swirl here, a wisp of white there, and otherwise nothing. Astronomers classify Neptune as an ice giant (like Uranus), meaning that it's essentially a ball of chemical ices packed around a rocky core. It sports a dim halo of barely visible rings and has at least 14 moons, including Triton — the coldest place in the solar system.

The myth behind the planet

Saturn, like his father, was threatened by his offspring. To protect himself, he swallowed them at birth, to the dismay of his wife, Rhea. The sixth time she gave birth, she spirited the baby away to be raised elsewhere. Then she handed Saturn a stone wrapped in swaddling clothes, and he swallowed it. His fears were realized when that child — Jupiter to the Romans, Zeus to the Greeks — returned to vanquish his father and free his siblings. Jupiter became the principal god of classical mythology, ruling the heavens from Mount Olympus while his brother Pluto (Hades) ruled the underworld, and Neptune (Poseidon) became lord of the sea. Neptune was a stormy, aggressive god who lived in a palace made of coral on the ocean floor and had dominion over earthquakes. In astrology, Neptune is associated with gentler stuff. The myth reminds us that the inspiration behind all things Neptunian does not come from lilacs and sunsets. It bubbles up from the turbulent depths of the unconscious.

REMEMBER

Neptune is named after the Roman god of the sea. Its symbol (see Figure 10-2) evokes that god's three-pronged trident.

FIGURE 10-2:
The symbol of
Neptune.

© John Wiley & Sons, Inc.

Assessing Neptune's influence

Neptune spends an average of about 14 years in a sign. Neptune stimulates intuition, imagination, dreams, spirituality, and artistic expression. But it also erases boundaries and can generate confusion and wishful thinking.

REMEMBER

Neptune doesn't affect everyone equally. Like the other outer planets, it tends to influence generations more than individuals. But in some charts, Neptune has exceptional power. How can you tell if you possess such a chart? Neptune occupies a prominent position in your birth chart if

>> It occupies an angle — that is, it's in the first, fourth, seventh, or tenth house of your chart. It is strongest if it's near your Ascendant or Midheaven. (See Chapter 11 for more on that topic.)

>> It closely aspects other planets and, in particular, the Sun, the Moon, or the planet that rules your Ascendant. (See Chapter 13 for a discussion of aspects.)

>> You have one or more planets in Pisces.

Neptune in the signs

Neptune's position by sign describes the ways your generation is most idealistic — and most unrealistic. Its position in your horoscope represents an area of imagination, idealism, and spirituality (on the positive side), and aimless drifting, passivity, misapprehension, and deception (on the negative side).

>> **Neptune in Aries (1861 to 1875; 2026 to 2038):** Members of this generation had an intuitive sense of self and took an active approach to their spiritual life. They could be wildly inconsiderate and had trouble regulating their aggression, being at times too weak (like Neville Chamberlain) and at other times too reckless (like Winston Churchill at Gallipoli or the anarchist Emma Goldman). But one member of this generation, expressing Neptune in Aries at its most rarefied, altered the nature of conflict: Mahatma Gandhi, the prophet of nonviolence (who was nonetheless assassinated in 1948). Neptune returns to this position in 2026.

>> **Neptune in Taurus (1875 to 1889; 2038 to 2052):** People born with this placement love art and architecture, rich food, the abundance of nature, and all sensual comforts. It's no coincidence that the most famous lover of all time — Giacomo Casanova, born in 1725 — had this placement. People with Neptune in Taurus are attuned to the physical world and respond instinctively to the needs of the body, though they may have trouble dealing with practicalities. Examples include Isadora Duncan, Virginia Woolf, and Albert Einstein. Neptune returns to the sign of the bull in 2038.

>> **Neptune in Gemini (1889 to 1902, 2052 to 2065):** People born during the last decade or so of the Gilded Age had subtle, clever, complicated minds and a knack for language, as illustrated by brilliant wordsmiths such as Dorothy Parker, Cole Porter, Ira Gershwin, and Groucho Marx. It's true that Neptune in Gemini can support a tendency to be shallow, a strained relationship with the truth, and a capacity for spin. (Edward Bernays, known as the father of public relations, was born with this placement.) But this can also be a supremely creative position. Example in chief: William Shakespeare, who knew how to spin a story like no one else.

>> **Neptune in Cancer (1902 to 1915; 2065 to 2078):** "What a wonderful world," sang the gravel-voiced Louis Armstrong, who was born with this placement. Those born with Neptune in Cancer would probably agree. They are observant, receptive, and sentimental, with a hunger for security and safety. They prize the old-fashioned virtues of home and family, and they tend to romanticize the past — which is not to suggest that their politics are necessarily conservative: Ronald Reagan had this placement, but so did Supreme Court Justice Thurgood Marshall and feminist theorist Simon de Beauvoir. Neptune is never about anything so commonplace as politics. It is about vision, imagination, and enlightenment.

>> **Neptune in Leo (1915 to 1929):** You're extravagant, artistic, entertaining, and romantic — or at least you'd like to be. You idealize love, children, friendship, and the creative process. You take big risks and often win those outrageous bets. But you're prone to infatuation and may prefer the glitter of your ideals to the gritty imperfections of reality. I hate to say it, but you can become so enamored of an ideal that you fail to see how moth-eaten it is. And it's true that sometimes you mistake surface for substance. But say this for Neptune in Leo: You've got style.

>> **Neptune in Virgo (1929 to 1942):** Neptune, the planet of murk and mist, isn't happy in meticulous Virgo. With this placement, you can't always tell which details matter and which ones don't, so you can become anxious about all the wrong things. That which is nebulous makes you nervous, and it's hard for you to let your imagination float. "Freefall" doesn't sound appealing to you. But finding work that taps into your imagination — and yet still operates within identifiable parameters — brings you satisfaction, and spiritual activities that focus on service will bring you joy.

>> **Neptune in Libra (1942 to 1957):** Idealistic and compassionate, you crave tranquility, stability, love, and beauty. You respond strongly to art, music, and film, and you idealize notions of sharing and cooperation. But romance can be mystifying to you. Much as you may wish for love, your high ideals about human interaction (and marriage) are always bumping up against reality. If you were born with this placement, you can expect to see major shifts in the patterns of human relationships over the course of your life.

>> **Neptune in Scorpio (1957 to 1970):** Dream interpretation, occult studies, and mystery novels of the most sinister sort pique your curiosity, but nothing enthralls you more than the workings of the psyche. Secrets fascinate you. You project an aura of magnetic intensity and instinctively understand the concept of sexual healing. But you're also prone to sexual extremes and self-destructive behavior, and you may be unwilling to recognize the sources of your own pain. At your intuitive best, you have remarkable powers of discernment and understanding. Your task is to apply them to yourself.

>> **Neptune in Sagittarius (1970 to 1984):** The big questions of philosophy and religious values intrigue you but you have no taste for dogma because your belief system is constantly in flux. You have a thirst for personal freedom and travel, ideally to sacred spots. But you tend to be gullible, and you're easily misled. Be wary about dealing with anyone who wants to be thought a guru. You prefer to forge your own way.

>> **Neptune in Capricorn (1984 to 1998):** You're ambitious, pragmatic, and willing to shoulder responsibility. You aspire to success and respect. But you have high expectations of the world of the establishment, and you may have trouble acknowledging the disappointments you find there. Uncertainty and aimlessness make you uneasy, and you sometimes react by becoming controlling and inflexible. Your spiritual hunger is best satisfied within the comforting boundaries of a structured organization.

>> **Neptune in Aquarius (1998 to 2012):** As one of the enlightenment-seeking, technologically gifted, altruistic souls born since 1998, you have a progressive approach to social reform and an intuitive understanding of the common good. But you may idealize your friends, and your ideals could be pie-in-the-sky. Be aware that your desire to live in a utopian community with a simpatico group of ecologically aware, peace-loving vegans may be more difficult to achieve than you imagine.

>> **Neptune in Pisces (2012 to 2026):** You have the typical traits of Pisces – squared. You're a daydream believer: psychic, generous, artistic, empathetic, mystical, gullible, possibly self-destructive, a lover of fantasy and film, and an aficionado of music that baffles your elders. You're also a candidate for all manner of addictions. And yet, this is where Neptune is most at home. This is where its highest potential can be reached. Sigmund Freud, Johann Sebastian Bach, Vincent van Gogh, and Nikola Tesla share this placement. And now we have a new Neptune in Pisces generation. This could be exhilarating.

Pluto: The Power of Transformation

Pluto was discovered in 1930. It soon gained a mighty reputation as the planet of death, rebirth, regeneration, secrets, and nuclear energy. It destroys, purifies, purges, and renews, bestowing consciousness on that which has been hidden and ultimately bringing about transformation. The metamorphosis can be tedious — and terrifying — because while Pluto moves at a glacial speed, it moves relentlessly. But the rewards of grappling with it are profound and permanent.

PLUTO'S DEMOTION

When Pluto was discovered in 1930, it was front page news. "SEE ANOTHER WORLD IN SKY," trumpeted the *Chicago Daily Tribune* in a headline that stretched across the page. In Flagstaff, Arizona, where the planet was discovered, *The Coconino Sun* called it the "Scientific Discovery of Century." Pluto mania was so infectious that a few months after the discovery, Walt Disney named Mickey Mouse's hound after the planet.

But as the decades rolled by, questions began to surface. There were odd things about Pluto, including its size (smaller than the Moon), its peculiar orbit, and its location in the far-away Kuiper Belt, a donut-shaped area populated by thousands of icy, Pluto-sized bodies. Pluto was the first of these objects to be discovered. It was followed in 1992 by another and in 2005 by Eris, which is even larger than Pluto. Was Eris the tenth planet? And what is a planet anyway? In 2006 members of the International Astronomical Union convened to decide that question. They decreed that to be recognized as a planet, a celestial body had to satisfy three requirements:

- It had to orbit the Sun, as Pluto does.

- It had to be round, like Pluto, not shaped liked a peanut or a biomorphic blob of neon-colored play dough.

- And it had to "clear the neighborhood," meaning it had to be so massive, so gravitationally powerful, that nothing of similar size could exist in its orbit. But Pluto doesn't do that. It lives in the Kuiper Belt, and it does not live alone.

So Pluto was downgraded to "dwarf planet." An avalanche of publicity followed. There were headlines. There were protest marches. Astronomers were asked to explain the demotion, and astrologers were asked, generally with a smirk, what they planned to do about this outrage. The answer was simple: Astrologers did nothing. We have thrown our lot in with Pluto and we will continue to do so. Astrology is a symbolic language, a language of the soul, and Pluto represents a facet of that evolving code. It doesn't matter what the learned astronomers think.

Pluto is small, rocky, and mysterious, with an elongated orbit that is noticeably tilted to the rest of the solar system. Of Pluto's five moons, the largest, Charon, is so close to Pluto in size and so near it physically that after its discovery in 1978, astronomers classified Pluto as a double planet. Nowadays, it's considered a double dwarf.

The myth behind the Planet

In classical mythology, Pluto (Hades to the Greeks) was the god of the dead, the king of the underworld, and the lord of wealth, reflecting the fact that gold, silver, and precious gems are hidden in the earth, which is also where seeds germinate and the dead are buried. Virtually every major character in mythology visits the underworld, and frequently that journey is round-trip. In mythology as in real life, no one visits the underworld and returns unchanged. A notable example is Persephone, who divides her time between the underworld, where she lives with Pluto for a third of the year, and our world, which she re-enters at the beginning of Spring, and where she spends time with her mother.

Pluto's largest moon, Charon, is named after the ferryman who transported the dead across the River Styx and into the underworld. The second largest moon, maintaining the theme, is called Styx.

Pluto has two symbols. One is a snazzy-looking metaphysical design: a circle held within a crescent and balanced on a cross. I try to avoid this symbol because it's so easy to confuse it with the glyphs of other planets (Mercury and Neptune in particular). But many astrologers prefer it.

I'm partial to the second, more mundane image, which has its origins in the world of science. That symbol (see Figure 10-3) represents both the first two letters of Pluto's name and the initials of the aristocratic astronomer Percival Lowell, who was so convinced that there was life on Mars that he built an observatory for the purpose of observing it. He also hoped to find the hypothetical Planet X, which he believed was in orbit somewhere past Neptune. He never found it. But 14 years after Lowell's death, Clyde Tombaugh, a farmer's son without a college education, got a job at the Lowell Observatory taking photographs of the night sky and doggedly comparing pairs of them taken a few days apart to see if, among all those stationary stars, he might discern a bit of planetary movement. A year into this dreary chore, he found what he was looking for. This symbol acknowledges Lowell's contributions. (As for Tombaugh's contributions, he became an acclaimed professional with a multitude of discoveries to his credit. His name is attached to a comet, a crater on Mars, some cliffs in Antarctica, and a heart-shaped region of Pluto. After he died in 1997, his ashes were sent, at his request, into space.)

Pinpointing Pluto's influence

REMEMBER

Like Uranus and Neptune, Pluto primarily influences generations. Its influence in an individual's birth chart is usually subtle — unless Pluto occupies a prominent spot in your chart. Pluto is prominent if

>> It occupies an angle — that is, it's in the first, fourth, seventh, or tenth house of your chart. It is especially strong if it's close to your Ascendant or Midheaven. (See Chapter 11 for more on that topic.)

>> It makes a number of close aspects to other planets and, in particular, to the Sun, the Moon, or the planet that rules your Ascendant.

>> You have one or more planets in Scorpio.

Pluto in the signs

Pluto's placement by sign describes the deepest passions of your generation and shapes the way you grapple with transforming life events.

>> **Pluto in Aries (1823 to 1852):** This generation was willful, headstrong, impulsive, and obsessed with power and independence.

>> **Pluto in Taurus (1852 to 1884):** Security brought power for these hard-working folks, but their values, particularly regarding possessions, were in flux. With Pluto in an earth sign, ownership was an issue. The American Civil War was fought during those years over that horrible compulsion.

>> **Pluto in Gemini (1884 to 1914):** Wit rules. Novelty delights you. Unconsciously, you seek to transform yourself through gathering information, traveling, and communicating. Your mind is ever young. People born in the second half of this transit, starting around 1900, belong to the so-called greatest generation, which fought in World War II.

>> **Pluto in Cancer (1914 to 1939):** If you were born during these years when Pluto was discovered, you belong to a generation for whom security is paramount. You were taught to hold on to what you've got, and that's what you do — even when you should know better. It's no wonder that you feel this way: The Great Depression of the 1930s was a significant event in your life or in the experiences of your parents.

>> **Pluto in Leo (1939 to 1957):** Your desire to express yourself dramatically, creatively, and expansively can become an obsession. This placement is the trademark of the baby boomers, who look with disdain upon the previous generation's search for security — and who are looked upon with scorn by the generations that follow because, in true Leo style, you can't help showing off.

>> **Pluto in Virgo (1957 to 1972):** The excesses of the baby boomers drive you to distraction, and you react against them. You seek personal control, obsess about details, and have every intention of becoming perfect. If you were born between 1962 and 1969, you also have Uranus in Virgo, so unexpected upsets may throw you off track. But these impediments won't stop you from striving for the perfect Plutonian/Uranian pivot — the one that redirects everything.

>> **Pluto in Libra (1972 to 1984):** Justice, balance, beauty, social relations, and equality: these are lifelong concerns for you and your generation. In your personal life and in society, you seek a marriage of equals. You are also attracted to the arts, both as a consumer and as a creator. One caveat, if you have artistic ambitions: Though yours is the generation that elevated the term "slackers," Pluto won't let you get away with idleness. Pluto demands commitment — and bravery.

>> **Pluto in Scorpio (1984 to 1995):** Yours is the millennial generation. You're passionate, resolute, deeply sexual, and intent on drinking in every last drop of whatever life has to offer. Driven by a sense of purpose, you intuitively recognize the link between money and power, and you're interested in accumulating both. Scorpio is the sign where Pluto is most at home, making this a formidable placement.

>> **Pluto in Sagittarius (1995 to 2008):** Freedom in all its manifestations is essential to you. Meaning is equally important. You long to find a philosophy or religion that deepens your understanding of life and encourages you to explore wider vistas of thought or experiene. Education and travel are more than diversionary; they can be life-changing. In your search for a belief system, you may notice (or maybe someone will tell you) that you are becoming pompous or fanatical. Try not to let that happen.

>> **Pluto in Capricorn (2008 to 2024):** People born with Pluto in buttoned-down Capricorn are goal-oriented, persistent, and pragmatic, with an inborn sense of how the world works. You think you've seen savvy politicians? Wait 'til these babies come along. Pluto's last sojourn in the sign of the goat was between 1762 and 1778, years that covered the American Revolution. (The United States will experience its first Pluto return in 2022.)

>> **Pluto in Aquarius (2024 to 2044):** This do-your-own-thing, woke generation is likely to foster change through unconventional associations, shared aspirations, and group membership, albeit not in the ethnocentric, binary ways of the past. This is the generation that could put Aquarian ideals into practice.

>> **Pluto in Pisces (2044 to 2068):** This will be interesting. Expect to see a self-sacrificing, mystical generation that can align itself with the collective unconscious. In the face of chaos, they maintain reserves of empathy, strength and flexibility. William Shakespeare, Abraham Lincoln, and Harriet Tubman are examples of this placement at its finest.

Chiron: The Wounded Healer

Is it an asteroid? A comet? A type of asteroid called a *Centaur*? Ever since November 1, 1977, when astronomer Charles Kowal discovered Chiron careering around the Sun between the orbits of Saturn and Uranus, scientists have been trying to make up their minds. At the moment, Chiron answers to all those classifications and is also identified as a "small solar system body." It represents healing in all its complexity.

TECHNICAL STUFF

Smaller by far than any planet (less than 150 miles across), Chiron has an eccentric, unstable orbit that causes it to linger in some signs (Pisces, Aries, and Taurus) and race through others (Virgo, Libra, and Scorpio). It makes a complete sweep through the zodiac in 51 years.

The myth behind the . . . uh . . . small solar system body

In mythology, Chiron is a centaur, half man and half horse. Unlike other centaurs, who were crass and bellicose, Chiron was wise and compassionate, a tutor whose students included the warrior Achilles and the hero Hercules. One day, Chiron was accidentally scratched by one of Hercules's poison arrows. The pain was so excruciating, he wanted to die. But Chiron was immortal. Unable to die, he delved into the arts of healing. Yet despite his knowledge, his pain never lessened, and he never developed a tolerance for it. He did, however, find a way out. After negotiating with Zeus, he bequeathed his immortality to Prometheus, who had stolen fire from the gods and given it to the human race, a transgression for which he was chained to a rock and tortured on a nightly basis. Thanks to Chiron, Prometheus was freed from his ordeal and permitted to join the society of gods on Mount Olympus, while Chiron, relieved of his agony, took up residence in the underworld.

Chiron embodies the full spectrum of healing: The wound, the pain, the ongoing suffering, the knowledge of medicine, the search for a cure, and the acceptance of death.

REMEMBER

The symbol for Chiron (see Figure 10-4) designed in honor of Charles Kowal, the astronomer who discovered it, shows a letter K balanced atop a circle or oval. It resembles a vintage skeleton key.

FIGURE 10-4:
The symbol of
Chiron.

Chiron's influence

In the years following its discovery, few practitioners were brave enough to insert Chiron into birth charts. It seemed too soon, and astrologers didn't know enough about it. That has changed. Today, Chiron, referred to as the Wounded Healer, is often (but not always) included in interpretations. Astrologers see Chiron as both a point of pain and a wellspring of healing — an area where you have suffered or been disappointed and where you must find resolution. Astrologers also associate Chiron with the holistic health movement.

Note that the astrological Chiron is more than a victim and a healer. As a tutor, Chiron was also known for his quest for knowledge and his teaching ability.

REMEMBER

Chiron is small, distant, and not usually emphasized in horoscopes. It is prominent in your chart if

>> It occupies an angle (and especially if it conjuncts or opposes your Ascendant or Midheaven).

>> It closely aspects the Sun, the Moon, or the planet that rules your Ascendant.

Chiron in the signs

Chiron spends, on average, a little over four years in each sign. It indicates an area of vulnerability for you and for members of your immediate generation.

>> **Chiron in Aries:** Your efforts to express your personality have been thwarted. You suffer from a bad case of fear of failure, and taking the initiative isn't easy for you. Mustering the courage to do so — and you've got courage aplenty — is the only way to shore up your lack of confidence and conquer your fears.

>> **Chiron in Taurus:** Stability and security are key. You dread the thought of poverty, and financial restraint is part of your DNA. But consider the cautionary tale of Hetty Green, whose Chiron in Taurus directly opposed

her Scorpio Sun. When she died in 1916, she was the wealthiest woman in America (and possibly the world) and the most notorious miser. No matter how rich she was, she never shed her fear-based, penny-pinching ways. To avoid her fate, pursue your noblest value, build something tangible, and don't worry so much.

» **Chiron in Gemini:** Communicating your ideas with clarity and conviction is a trial for you. You feel misunderstood, inarticulate, too introverted, or too brash. Seeking knowledge and acting as an educator enable you to heal this feeling of inadequacy. (Also beneficial: keeping a journal.) And here's another phenomenon that may envelop you from time to time: gossip. It's one way people learn about each other, and yet it can be toxic.

» **Chiron in Cancer:** Your domestic life and/or your childhood may be tinged with sorrow or shadowed by alienation. You may feel that your family didn't love you: a grave wound, but not a lethal one. Recovery comes through consciously seeking to fashion a supportive environment for yourself and through recognizing that we all have to find a way to nurture ourselves.

» **Chiron in Leo:** In childhood, your efforts to get attention may have been ignored, and you may question your own talents as a result. This self-doubt can be overcome. Creative expression of any sort helps heal the hurt. Acting, teaching, and public speaking are also valuable because, putting aside the torments of the past, everyone needs to be center stage once in a while.

» **Chiron in Virgo:** You grew up in an authoritarian atmosphere — or at least that's how it felt. Now you are bedeviled by anxiety. Seek relief by focusing on wellness, by serving others without sacrificing yourself, and by refusing to be a martyr. Or try another approach entirely by taking up a craft wherein your perfectionism, which can be a liability in other situations, is rewarded.

» **Chiron in Libra:** Partnerships are vital to your well-being, but they're also disappointing. You're sure that a healthy relationship could heal you, if only you could find one. Defusing the fear of rejection is your challenge. Balancing romance with common sense is your triumph. And yes, it is an achievable goal.

» **Chiron in Scorpio:** You ache for love, passion, and phenomenal sex. But your cautious ways and deep-seated fear of revealing yourself (and hence of being known) make it difficult to fulfill your desires. Healing comes by digging into your buried secrets and working your way through them. Becoming comfortable with power dynamics is part of the process.

» **Chiron in Sagittarius:** What's the purpose of life? The usual answers, like traditional religions, may leave you feeling frustrated and unheard. A personal search lessens the anguish. Strange as it may seem, lifelong education, designed to fit your individual requirements, can be therapeutic and even fun. And in your case, knowledge really is power.

>> **Chiron in Capricorn:** You value success and feel proud of your work ethic and integrity. But although you follow the rules, they let you down. Doubling down is not the solution. Only by coming up with your own definition of success will you be able to galvanize your deepest authority.

>> **Chiron in Aquarius:** What's wrong with people anyway? You're aware of the resoundingly negative impact of inequality and injustice, and you would like to correct those wrongs. But you can't seem to find a cohort of like-minded individuals, and a sense of solidarity may elude you. Even so, working for the greater good, even under conditions that are less than ideal, can enhance your confidence and heal your wounds.

>> **Chiron in Pisces:** Pisces is the sign of compassion, sensitivity, and sacrifice. But you can't help observing that many people who give lip service to those qualities don't practice them. Your mission: To be conscious of the trauma of others and to react to it appropriately and sympathetically, without feeling overwhelmed or sacrificing your own wellbeing. Finding a spiritual base can ease your angst. Also helpful: not caring whether others appreciate your kindness.

And More . . .

In the decades after the discovery of Chiron, many astrologers welcomed it into their charts. Others hesitated, worried that if you let in one small solar system body, others might soon follow. And that's just what happened. The inclusion of Chiron has flung open the doors to all manner of small celestial bodies that are now routinely featured in birth charts. There are Ceres, Pallas, Juno, and Vesta, the first four asteroids to be discovered; centaur asteroids such as Chiron, Nessus, Pholus, and Chariklo; dwarf planets such as Eris, Makemake, and Haumea; Kuiper belt objects such as Sedna. And that's not counting imaginary bodies. All are interesting and worth investigating. But all are secondary to the planets.

Chapter **11**

What You See versus What You Get: The Rising Sign (And More)

once worked at a bookstore with a woman who was so well-organized and in control that everyone relied on her. She knew what was on the shelves, what was on order or out of print, what was in the back room, and what was behind the counter. She was good with the cash register, glad to alphabetize inventory cards, and an affable presence. On top of that, she had read everything, including the classics that most people don't even know are classics, and she could advise the most hard-to-please customer. So I wasn't surprised when I did her chart and discovered that she had Virgo rising. She was as intelligent, organized, and meticulous as any Virgo I ever met.

But rising signs can be deceptive. Sure, on the surface she was detail-oriented and in control like a Virgo. But her Sun was not in Virgo. It was in sensitive, charitable Pisces, the most impressionable sign in the zodiac. And indeed, that sign described her more fully. She was kind, compassionate, and imaginative (that's why she was such an avid reader — she lost herself in books). She had many devoted friends, a husband she adored, a city loft filled with original artwork, and a second home — a tiny cottage — on a windswept island in a distant sea. Her life was suffused with romance, creativity, and water. But if she had experienced the poetry of Pisces, she also knew the pain of it. In one form or another, she had coped with everything from a relative in jail to alcoholism. She was a Pisces down to her toes.

Nonetheless, she looked like a Virgo. That's because Virgo was her *rising sign,* or *Ascendant.* The Ascendant describes the surface level of your personality. It is who you appear to be — the facade you present to the world. In the past, many astrologers considered the Ascendant the most essential part of the birth chart, even more crucial than the Sun. Today, most astrologers rank the Sun, the Moon, and the Ascendant as the three most important parts of a chart, in that order.

In this chapter, I tell you how to identify the four major angles of your chart: the Ascendant; its opposite, the seldom-discussed Descendant; the Midheaven; and its opposite, the I.C. (which stands for the Latin *Imum Coeli,* the lower part of the heavens). And I tell you what they all mean. These spots on your chart are not as well known as the Sun and the Moon, but they are a fundamental part of who you are.

Identifying Your Ascendant

Anyone who ever figured out an Ascendant the pre-digital way knows how arduous it was — and how easy it was to make a mistake. Today, if you have access to the Internet, you can get an accurate copy of your natal chart in a nanosecond. (If you haven't already done that, please do it now. Chapter 2 tells you how.)

REMEMBER

As the Earth spins on its axis, the zodiac seems to revolve around it like a gigantic ring. At any given moment, one sign is climbing over the eastern horizon and another is sinking in the west; one sign is riding high above you and another is on the opposite side of the planet. Each of these points represents one of the four main angles of your birth chart, as shown in Figure 11-1.

About every four minutes, a new degree of the zodiac rises over the horizon. So it's important to get an accurate copy of your chart. Once you have that, you can find your rising sign easily by superimposing an imaginary clock face over your chart. Your Ascendant is at 9:00 o'clock. That spot represents the eastern horizon. (On a land-based map, east is on the right, west is on the left. With a natal chart, which is basically a stylized a map of the cosmos, it's the other way around.)

The point opposite your Ascendant on the western horizon is the *Descendant,* or *setting sign,* which is always 180° away from the Ascendant. At the top of your horoscope is the *Midheaven, or M.C.,* an abbreviation for the Latin *Medium Coeli,* middle of the skies. Opposite that, 180° away from the Midheaven, is the I.C., short for the Latin *Imum Coeli,* the lower part of the heavens.

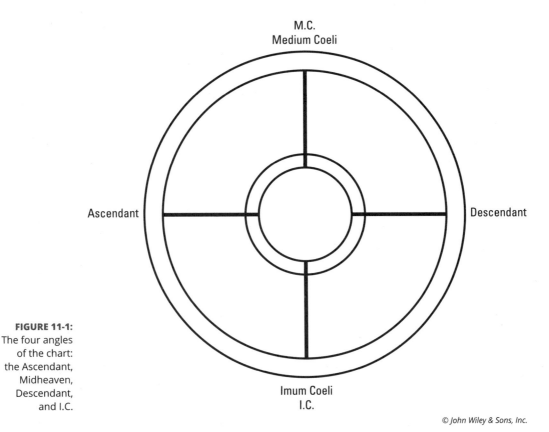

M.C.
Medium Coeli

Ascendant

Descendant

Imum Coeli
I.C.

FIGURE 11-1:
The four angles
of the chart:
the Ascendant,
Midheaven,
Descendant,
and I.C.

© *John Wiley & Sons, Inc.*

What Your Ascendant Says about You

The Ascendant is the surface of your personality. It's your image, your persona, your mask, your vibe, your veneer. Or think of it this way: Your rising sign is like the clothes you wear; those outfits aren't exactly *you*, but they aren't irrelevant either. They convey an unspoken message to others — and even *you* may come to associate them with your deeper self.

>> **Aries rising:** You're active, assertive, adventurous, headstrong, and possibly accident-prone. Reckless and extroverted, with an abundance of energy, you invigorate everyone around you. You take pride — for good reason — in your ability to get things moving. When you know what you want, you go after it boldly. But you can also be competitive and insensitive, with a propensity for taking over. And when obstacles block your path, your patience (never your high card) may evaporate. You love to be there at the start of an enterprise when the excitement is building. Later on is another story. Numbering among

those with Aries Ascendant are Rihanna, Penelope Cruz, Bette Midler, Joan Rivers, Che Guevara, John Lennon, Yo-Yo Ma, and Lin-Manuel Miranda.

Regardless of your Sun sign, your ruler is Mars, the warrior planet. Its location by sign, house, and aspects describes your energy level and the nature of your desires.

>> **Taurus rising:** You're warm, generous, loyal, and likeable, even if you're slow to open up and resistant to change. There's something reassuring and calming about your steady presence. You're pragmatic and patient — a reasonable person who doesn't let the small stuff get to you. You're also affectionate and hedonistic, with a sincere appreciation of food, drink, art, and the delights of the body. You care about appearances, and you aren't indifferent to money either. It brings you the security you need. Bonnie Raitt, Amy Tan, R. Buckminster Funller, Gabriel García Márquez, Ursula K. Le Guin, and Serena Williams share this placement.

REAL LIFE EXAMPLE

THE WIFE OF BATH

When astrologers analyze literary characters, they're usually forced to intuit what their birth dates might be. Once in a while, an author imparts the essential information. Geoffrey Chaucer, for example, clearly knew his astrology. In his *Canterbury Tales,* he explained the Wife of Bath's bawdy behavior as the natural consequence of having a Taurus Ascendant with Mars, the planet of desire, in the same lusty sign. Don't let the 14th-century English stop you from enjoying her own explanation of her lascivious ways:

Myn ascendent was Taur and Mars therinne —

Allas, allas, the evere love was sinne!

I folwed ay my inclinacioun

By vertu of my constellacioun;

That made my I coude nought withdrawe

My chambre of Venus from a good felawe.

So who are the real-life people with Taurus rising and Mars therein? Queen Latifah, Salmon Rushdie, and Linda Blair of *The Exorcist* are among them. So is Barbara La Marr. An actress from the days of silent films, La Marr married six times before her death from drug abuse at age 29.

Regardless of your Sun sign, your ruler is Venus, the planet of love and attraction. Its location by sign, house, and aspect affect the role of love, art, and beauty in your life.

>> **Gemini rising:** You're talkative, excitable, funny, possibly an insomniac, and ever youthful. You pick up information (and trivia) in a flash, and you swiftly adapt to changing circumstances, even if you also complain about them. You have a curious mind and may have writing ability. But you're nervous and easily bored, with a tendency to scatter your energy. It soothes your anxiety to have two of everything: two best friends, two jobs, two phones, a couple of books on your night stand. Orson Welles, Margaret Atwood, E. E. Cummings, Regina Spektor, Kristen Stewart, Mindy Kaling, Matthew McConaughey, and Amy Winehouse can all claim Gemini Ascendants.

No matter what your Sun sign is, the ruler of your chart is fleet-footed Mercury, the lord of communication. It shapes the way you communicate, the way you learn, and the way your mind operates.

>> **Cancer rising:** Moody, sensitive, and imaginative, you live at a high emotional pitch, caught up in the flood of your feelings. You're attuned to other people and gifted at nurturing them, yet you may feel drained by their needs and resentful of their requests. You're shrewd and ambitious, though your plans may crumble in the face of your emotional reactions. When you feel besieged by the demands or criticism of others, you withdraw into the solitude of your shell. Home, food, family, and financial well-being are key to your peace of mind. Arnold Schwarzenegger, Cher, Angelina Jolie, Tyra Banks, Joni Mitchell, Julia Roberts, Hasan Minhaj, and Adele all have Cancer rising.

The Moon is your ruling planet, regardless of your Sun sign. By house, sign, and aspect, it reveals the ebb and flow of your emotions and instincts.

>> **Leo rising:** You're flashy, fun-loving, charismatic, and friendly. The very opposite of a wallflower, you can't stand not being noticed. Because you have great pride, you do your best to look confident, and you usually succeed. You have leadership ability with opinions on everything — and you're not disposed to alter your views. But your certainty is persuasive, and people follow your lead. You want to make life better for them — and you wouldn't mind basking in the glow of their appreciation. Among those ebullient folks with Leo rising are Richard Branson, Meryl Streep, Selena Gomez, Anthony Bourdain, Marilyn Monroe, Drake, and Catherine, Duchess of Cambridge. Also Bernie Madoff and Donald J. Trump.

The Sun is your ruling planet, no matter what sign of the zodiac you were born under. It represents your essential self and your vitality, which is enhanced by having a Leo Ascendant.

» **Virgo rising:** A skilled conversationalist, you have a clever, incisive mind and a thoughtful, controlled demeanor. Methodical and articulate, with an astounding ability to juggle details, you communicate effectively, pick up knowledge effortlessly, and have a sharp, observant intelligence (which is one reason you're so much fun to talk to). You make a concerted effort to engage with the world on a mental level, but emotional displays make you want to hide. You're a worrier, especially about your health. And despite what you may think, your efforts to conceal your feelings aren't always successful. Among those with Virgo rising are Leonard Cohen, Paul Simon, Steve Jobs, Jay-Z, Charlize Theron, Keanu Reeves, kd lang, Kris Jenner, Louisa May Alcott, and Jane Austen.

Regardless of your Sun sign, your ruler is Mercury. Its position in your chart describes your thinking process and the way you communicate.

» **Libra rising:** You're charming, tactful, refined, attractive, and easy to be around. Your social graces will take you far. But you can't bear to be in a hostile environment, and you may disengage if you find yourself in such a spot. You're also artistic and intellectually engaged, with a commitment to justice, equality, and balance (that's what those scales are about). Partnerships, romantic and otherwise, are your lifeblood. Some examples: Yoko Ono, Denzel Washington, Jennifer Aniston, Eric Clapton, Adrienne Rich, Bernard Kouchner, Rock Hudson, Frank Sinatra, Leonardo di Caprio, and Stevie Wonder.

No matter what your Sun sign is, your ruler is Venus, the planet of love, art, and attraction. Its position in your chart by house, sign, and aspect is central to who you are.

» **Scorpio rising:** Traditional astrology claims that the Ascendant determines appearance. To my eye, that influence is generally a subtle one — with one big exception: Scorpio rising. Your magnetism is unmistakable, and your intense eyes, be they dark or light, are compelling and seductive. (Real-life example: Bette Davis.) You're mysterious, sexy, and private, with a reservoir of pain that can cause you to lash out or withdraw. Despite whatever heartaches you may have suffered in the past, you're a survivor who takes control in periods of crisis. You have courage, willpower, and the ability to transform yourself, internally and externally. Admittedly, Scorpio placements are not easy. But Scorpio is a potent sign. Do you occasionally intimidate people without intending to? Of course you do. As do the following, Scorpio rising all: Clint Eastwood, Tom Cruise, Robin Williams, Keith Richards, Paul Auster, Justin Bieber, Victor Hugo, Julio Cortázar, Nicole Kidman, Jacqueline Kennedy Onassis, and yes, the Marquis de Sade.

SCORPIO RISING ALIASES

Some people born with Scorpio rising can't help playing around with their own identity. Examples include writer Mary Anne Evans, who published under the name George Eliot; Samuel Clemens, who wrote as Mark Twain; Washington Irving (of Rip van Winkle fame), who went by Dietrich Knickerbocker and Geoffrey Crayon; Prince Rogers Nelson, who changed his name to a symbol and became The Artist Formerly Known as Prince; Margaretha Zelle MacLeod, who changed her name to Mata Hari and became a spy; David Berkowitz, the murderer who dubbed himself "Son of Sam" (although he was not); the chameleon-like comedian Tracey Ullman, whose alter egos are of all races, genders, ages, and opinions; and Olympic decathlete Bruce Jenner, who changed his name to Caitlyn and became a woman. Why do they do it? Ask Sigmund Freud. Like others with Scorpio rising, he too was fascinated by the mystery of identity — and the power of secrets.

Scorpio has two rulers, and therefore, so do you, no matter what your month of birth happens to be. The modern ruler of your chart is Pluto. And don't let anyone blather on about Pluto being a dwarf planet. Pluto rules destruction, transformation, and nuclear power. It doesn't have to be big. Your traditional ruler is Mars, the planet of action. By sign, house, and aspect, both planets play leading roles in your chart.

>> **Sagittarius rising:** You're outgoing, restless, and reckless. In your optimistic search for variety and vision, you cultivate friends and acquaintances from many backgrounds and travel as widely as possible. In your quest for understanding, you can get wound up over ideas. Witty and excitable, you're a fortunate person with a breezy personality, scores of friends, and an independent attitude. When opportunities come your way, you grab them instinctively. But it's difficult for you to sacrifice your freedom, and you suffer when constrained. Against all advice, you insist on going your own way. Your friends are wasting their breath. Those with Sagittarius rising include Leonardo da Vinci, Brad Pitt, Marlon Brando, Patti Smith, Chaz Bono, Elvis Presley, Sarah Silverman, Kim Kardashian, and Alexandria Ocasio-Cortez.

It makes no difference where your Sun is; Jupiter, the planet of expansion, is the ruler of your chart. Its position by house, sign, and aspect, indicates areas of luck and opportunity.

>> **Capricorn rising:** Chaos makes you crazy. You're serious, reserved, reliable, and determined, with a method for everything. Ambitious and competitive, you prefer to work within an established system. You wield authority effectively and with a firm sense of ethics. But your childhood may have been tightly controlled, and learning to relax can be a challenge. Though you may be rigid and prone to depression, your outlook improves as you age (and thanks to your healthy habits, you maintain a youthful appearance). People with Capricorn Ascendants include Queen Elizabeth II, Harry, Duke of Sussex, Ava DuVernay, America Ferrera, Jane Fonda, Sophia Loren, Kylie Jenner, James Joyce, and Ariana Grande.

Saturn, the planet of discipline, is your ruler, regardless of your Sun sign. Its position by house, sign, and aspect points to areas where you have to pay your dues, face down your fears, and create structures in order to achieve your potential.

CAN'T TELL A BOOK

Spend a few hours tracking down celebrity birthdays, and sooner or later you will be flabbergasted. That happened to me with David Bowie, *Rolling Stone*'s "greatest rock star ever." He was flamboyant, innovative, androgynous, cool, and campy, the alien maestro of Space Age music. When I learned that Ziggy Stardust was an earthbound Capricorn, it shook my faith in astrology. Capricorn is serious, practical, steady, dependable, dignified, mature, a lover of tradition — conservative not necessarily in thought but in style. Whereas David Bowie was such an oddity that his eyes didn't even match.

Then I saw Bowie's chart, and my faith came zooming back. He is undeniably a Capricorn. But his Capricorn Sun and Mars are hidden in the 12th house. What's not hidden is his Ascendant in Aquarius, the sign of innovation, eccentricity, rebellion, and the avant-garde. He looks like — and in many ways is — a taboo-breaking, future-oriented Aquarian.

But open the book of Bowie, and you will find an ambitious, hardworking family man who collaborated with an insurance company to create a royalty-backed, financial tool called the Bowie Bond. You can't get more Capricorn than that. You will also find his Moon in Leo, proof that he loved the limelight, and Venus at the apex of his chart, showing that he had no trouble holding our attention. But the first thing that comes to mind when you think about David Bowie is likely to be his unforgettable façade, which is to say, his rising sign or Ascendant.

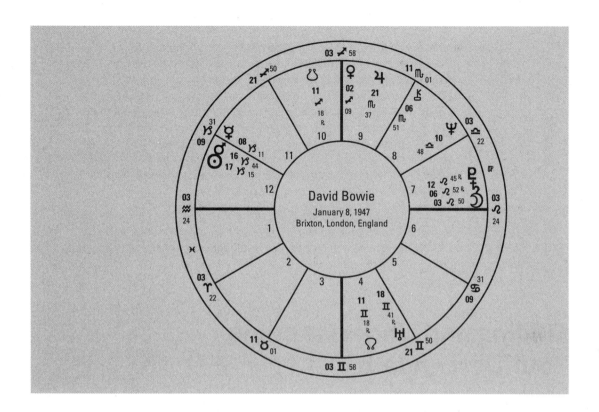

>> **Aquarius rising:** You have dozens of interests, legions of friends, and a cool, amiable personality. But you maintain a certain aloofness that can make you seem disinterested or remote, and you're unwilling to limit your options for the comfort of others. If you strike them as willful or eccentric, well, that's their problem. Unanticipated events, especially in childhood, made you conscious of the necessity of protecting yourself. More than that, you resist authority. Why should anyone else have power over you? You can't think of a single reason. People with Aquarius ascendants include Barack Obama, Whoopi Goldberg, Michael J. Fox, Audrey Hepburn, Roseanne Barr, William S. Burroughs. and J. K. Rowling.

Regardless of your Sun sign, you have two rulers: rebellious Uranus and Saturn, the planet of self-discipline. Together, they have dominion over your chart.

>> **Pisces rising:** You're romantic, impressionable, sentimental, kind, and so empathetic that just being around unhappy people can be tormenting. Moody and idealistic, you have powerful artistic and psychic abilities. At your most self-actualizing, you can mobilize your inner forces and turn fantasies into realities. But your boundaries are permeable. You are strongly affected by your surroundings, and you can become gullible, passive, and submissive. Your yearning for creative and spiritual fulfillment can keep you on track. Here are some people with Pisces rising: Whitney Houston, Johnny Cash, John Coltrane, Allen Ginsberg, Pablo Neruda, Deepak Chopra, Laura Dern, Gwyneth Paltrow, Richard Pryor, and John McCain.

Elusive Neptune, the planet of inspiration, is your ruler, no matter the season of your birth. Its position in your chart illuminates an area of creative and spiritual involvement. You also have a co-ruler: auspicious Jupiter, bringer of expansion and opportunity.

Finding and Understanding Your Descendant

Once you've identified your rising sign, you automatically know your Descendant, no calculation required. By definition, the Descendant is always exactly opposite your Ascendant.

REMEMBER

A less powerful point than your Ascendant, the Descendant determines the approach you take toward marriage and partnerships. It describes the nature of those relationships in your life, and it discloses the kind of person you're likely to fall for. What's your type? Your Descendant provides the answer:

>> **If you have Aries rising:** Your Descendant is in Libra. You flourish in an egalitarian alliance, and your perfect partner, unlike yourself, is poised and balanced, a force for peace and harmony — the very quality you need the most.

>> **If you have Taurus rising:** Your Descendant is Scorpio. Your best possible partner is sexually passionate, emotionally intense, and eager to engage in intimate conversation. You probably don't think you want someone who's secretive or manipulative. The evidence suggests otherwise.

>> **If you have Gemini rising:** Your Descendant is Sagittarius, which suggests that the best partner for you is an independent, upbeat person who can expand your world. You romanticize relationships and may marry more than once. But since when is that a crime?

>> **If you have Cancer rising:** Your Descendant is Capricorn, which means that you seek a solid relationship with a partner who's responsible, protective, and possibly older than you or more established. Being with a person of maturity — a grown-up — will help you feel secure.

>> **If you have Leo rising:** Your Descendant is Aquarius. So although you may think that you want a dazzling, swashbuckling companion, your ideal mate is actually a stimulating freethinker with whom you feel a lively mental connection.

>> **If you have Virgo rising:** Your Descendant is Pisces, which suggests that your ideal partner is a sympathetic, easygoing person who can help you stop that crazy worrying thing you do. You may dream of someone as organized and efficient as yourself. Notice how you keep not getting it? There's a reason: It's not what you need.

>> **If you have Libra rising:** Your Descendant is Aries, which suggests that the ideal mate for you is someone with an independent streak and a fiery personality who can stir up your enthusiasms, energize you, and help you deal with conflict, even if that means providing it in the first place.

>> **If you have Scorpio rising:** Your Descendant is Taurus. The most natural partner for you is down-to-earth, trustworthy, and stubborn enough to withstand your considerable blandishments. You may think you want someone who's spicy and complicated (like yourself). Actually, you'd be better off with someone who's as straightforward and nourishing as a loaf of bread.

>> **If you have Sagittarius rising:** Your Descendant is Gemini, so you may postpone commitment out of a fear of being tied down. When you do find the courage, the proper partner for you is an active, multifaceted person whose conversation is so stimulating that you're never bored.

>> **If you have Capricorn rising:** Your Descendant is Cancer, which means that a supportive mate can give you the warmth you hunger for (and the home-cooked meals). A traditional relationship — even if you don't call it that — brings you comfort and security.

>> **If you have Aquarius rising:** Your Descendant is Leo, suggesting that a liaison offering Leo's passion, vivacity, and personal devotion would counter your airy objectivity and bring you satisfaction. A little pizazz on your partner's side goes a long way to keeping you interested.

>> **If you have Pisces rising:** Your Descendant is Virgo, which suggests that a mate who's practical, analytical, and attentive to details would balance your intuitive, dreamy approach to life and help reduce the chaos that you create — or attract — without even half trying.

Looking into Your Midheaven and I.C.

How come some people grow up in ordinary circumstances and yet end up becoming incredibly famous or accomplishing extraordinary things? The Midheaven, also known as the M.C. (from the Latin *medium coeli,* meaning "middle of the heavens"), frequently explains it.

The Midheaven is the highest point in your chart. It doesn't determine your talents, but it influences your public persona, your profession, and the way you feel about authority, status, and reputation. The M.C. also says a lot about one of your parents. Which one? Some astrologers think it refers to the mother, others to the opposite-sex parent, still others to the more dominant parent. In short, it's definitely one or the other. You choose.

Directly opposite the Midheaven is the I.C., or *imum coeli* (from the Latin *imum coeli,* meaning "lowest part of the heavens"). The I.C. influences your attitude toward home and family, and, like the M.C., is associated with one of your parents. It affects the circumstances at the end of your life and is said to represent the "base of the personality," which tells you that its importance is greater than it appears.

REMEMBER

If you have an accurate copy of your birth chart, you can find your Midheaven or M.C. on or near the cusp of the tenth house around the twelve o'clock spot. Your I.C. is opposite the Midheaven, at or near the lowest point of your chart.

TIP

Still don't have a copy of your chart? Turn to Chapter 2 for recommendations about how to get one for free, right now.

The Midheaven affects your career and public image. The I.C. speaks to your experience of home and family.

>> **Aries Midheaven:** You have a daring attitude toward your career. You respond to a challenge and are most jazzed when you're launching a new endeavor. You're a leader, and you don't mind taking a risk. What you do mind is being powerless. Being your own boss is your best move.

The planet ruling your Midheaven is Mars.

Your I.C. is in Libra, indicating that while you may be unfazed by conflict in a professional setting, at home you seek harmony and serenity. Take the advice of William Morris, a nineteenth-century Aries known for his textile and wallpaper designs: "Have nothing in your houses that you do not know to be useful, or believe to be beautiful." And if in doubt as to which matters more — utility or beauty — opt for the latter.

>> **Taurus Midheaven:** Security matters, and you have the stamina to make it happen. You need to do something tangible in your profession — and whatever it is, you need to receive substantial rewards.

The planet ruling your Midheaven is Venus. The arts may appeal to you, along with anything connected to pleasure or beauty.

Your I.C. is in Scorpio, signifying that your home is a hideaway where you can express your deepest passions and enjoy the privacy you crave.

>> **Gemini Midheaven:** In your career, you require diversity, intellectual stimulation, and the ability to fulfill your curiosity. Writing and other forms of communication are favored. You also benefit from the chance to take spontaneous jaunts out of the office. You don't have to go far — you just need to go *out*.

The planet ruling your Midheaven is Mercury.

Your I.C. is in Sagittarius, which suggests that you move frequently (or would like to), that religious principles may form the foundation of your family life, or that you secretly long to be an expatriate. You agree with the Gemini writer G. K. Chesterton: "The home is not the one tame place in a world of adventure; it is the one wild place in a world of rules and set tasks."

>> **Cancer Midheaven:** A profession that encourages you to activate your intuition and make emotional connections has long-term appeal, especially if it focuses on real estate, interior decoration, family relations, food, a family business, or anything connected to children. No matter what you do, your unstated purpose may be to provide for your loved ones. You also need to be involved in the wider community and to receive recognition from authority figures there.

The planet ruling your Midheaven is the changeable Moon.

Your I.C. is in Capricorn, which implies that you would prefer a house of classic, time-tested design, and that you take a conservative attitude toward family, an arena in which you shoulder enormous responsibility.

>> **Leo Midheaven:** You need a career that provides room for creative expression as well as opportunities for leadership and recognition. Your considerable pride is on the line, so the more acknowledgment you receive for your efforts, the happier you will be.

The planet ruling your Midheaven is the Sun.

Your I.C. is in Aquarius, which implies that you grew up in circumstances that were atypical in some way. One of your parents is also unusual. As a result, you have an idiosyncratic attitude toward home and family, and there's something curious about your domestic life as well.

BJÖRK

Is it fair to say that the Icelandic singer/composer/performer Björk, a wildly experimental artist who has been in the public eye since childhood, presents a strange and riveting image? I think it is, and not just because of her infamous swan dress, which looked like a cross between a dead bird and a pouf skirt. She's had pearls sewn into her skin, otherworldly appendages sprouting out of her pixie-ish head. But her appearance is secondary to her songs, which are emotional and abstract, raw and refined; her startling, bell-like voice; her haunting performances; and her ability to conjure worlds. She even invents musical instruments. If genius means anything, she's got it.

Her brilliance begins with her Sun, Moon, and Ascendant in Scorpio, making her a triple Scorpio — a creature of depth and determination.

But it's the angles that give her so much presence and power. Her rising sign and Midheaven are both conjunct weighty outer planets. Her Scorpio Ascendant is conjunct dreamy Neptune, planet of the imagination, while her Midheaven is precisely conjunct Pluto and inventive Uranus. There are other important aspects in her chart, but it's the line-up at the angles that sets it all in motion.

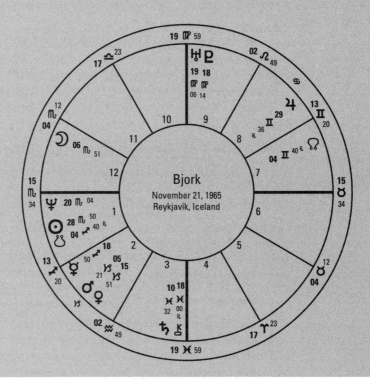

>> **Virgo Midheaven:** Whatever your vocation or community involvement, you succeed because you do your due diligence and pay attention to the details. People learn to rely on you. Still, you may feel that you don't receive the recognition you deserve. Keep in mind that Virgo is the sign of the martyr, and resist the temptation to torture yourself.

The planet ruling your Midheaven is Mercury.

Your I.C. is Pisces, which indicates that feelings of abandonment in childhood make you long for a home filled with spiritual solace. (In Björk's case — see sidebar — her parents split up when she born, which may explain the position of Chiron, the Wounder Healer, conjunct her I.C.) Your attitude might be that of the French philosopher Gaston Bachelard: "If I were asked to name the chief benefit of the house, I should say: The house shelters day-dreaming, the house protects the dreamer, the house allows one to dream in peace."

>> **Libra Midheaven:** You want a pleasant, rational career that enables you to balance your public and private lives. Ideally, you'd enjoy a career in the arts or one that features plenty of socializing. You easily attract people who can help you reach your goals.

The planet ruling your Midheaven is Venus.

Your I.C. is Aries, which means that you can renew your energy and express your individuality at home. But you can also be rebellious and quick-tempered with members of your family.

>> **Scorpio Midheaven:** You gravitate toward a career that offers you the opportunity to feel intensely and to exercise authority. Once you set your mind on a goal, you're determined to achieve it. But you can tie yourself in knots over the emotional complexity of your world, and you're always aware of the political undercurrents.

The planets ruling your Midheaven are Pluto and Mars.

Your I.C. is in Taurus, so financial security and the comforts of family are important to you. Owning a comfortable, well-designed home and having access to nature brings you satisfaction.

>> **Sagittarius Midheaven:** You're happiest with a career that offers independence, the opportunity to broaden your mental horizons, and plenty of frequent-flyer miles. Within your profession or community, you're known for your ideals and powerfully held beliefs. You are likely to idealize your colleagues. And although you benefit from encounters with authority figures, they may rub you the wrong way anyway.

The planet ruling your Midheaven is Jupiter.

Your I.C. is in Gemini, suggesting that your natural environment is a busy place filled with books, magazines, communication devices, and endless talk. You'd like to shuttle back and forth between two residences, and you may move from time to time, just to keep things interesting.

>> **Capricorn Midheaven:** Reliable and ambitious, you're willing to do whatever is necessary to achieve success. Major responsibilities regularly — and at times unfairly — end up on your salad plate. You're complimented by the responsibility. To maintain confidence, you need clear signs of progress — like promotions, raises, and a corner office with a ficus tree. You do well in a corporate setting.

The planet presiding over your Midheaven is Saturn.

Your I.C. is in Cancer, suggesting that your ties to family, and to your mother in particular, are enduring (even if they're also disappointing). Living near water soothes you.

>> **Aquarius Midheaven:** Your attitude toward career and community is unconventional, as is your ideal career. Because your talents are unique and you're less adaptable than you may think, the best job for you is shaped to you personally. You shine in forward-looking, progressive areas that benefit the public.

The planets governing your Midheaven are Uranus and Saturn.

Your I.C. is in Leo. You take pride in your home, which doubles as a stage where you can express your emotions and creative talents. Even if you're shy elsewhere, you're the star on your own turf.

>> **Pisces Midheaven:** Compassion and/or imagination determine your career choices. You may be drawn to the helping professions or to an expressive field, such as music or dance. Either way, your intuition and psychic abilities guide you.

The planets ruling your Midheaven are Neptune and Jupiter.

Your I.C. is in Virgo, suggesting that a clean, neat, intelligently organized home gives you the security you need.

IN THIS CHAPTER

» Checking out the houses of your birth chart

» Contemplating the Sun and Moon in the houses

» Ruminating on the planets in the houses

» Pondering those empty houses in your chart

Chapter **12**

The Sun, the Moon, and the Planets in the Houses

onsider two babies born on July 6, 1935, one around 4 a.m. local time and one, in another part of the world, around 6 a.m. Their planets are in identical signs of the zodiac. But their rising signs (see Chapter 11) aren't the same, and neither are their house placements. How much difference would that make?

It would make a world of difference. One child, born with Gemini rising and the Sun in the first house, is Candy Barr, the platinum-haired Texas stripper who died in 2005 (and received an appreciative obituary in the *New York Times*). The other, born the same day with Cancer rising and the Sun in the twelfth house, is the Dalai Lama. This glaring difference suggests how pivotal the Ascendant and house placements can be. They're as consequential as signs.

It's easy to confuse the signs with the houses. Though they overlap and often share meaning, they are not the same. The signs are divisions of the celestial ecliptic, that ribbon of stars where the Sun, the Moon, and the planets can be found.

The signs tell us how those planets express themselves. The houses name the arena where that expression takes place. Read on to discover how each planet operates in each house.

REMEMBER

The planets represent types of energy, the signs represent ways of expressing those energies, and the houses represent areas of experience where those energies are likely to operate.

HOUSING CRISIS?

Every field of study has unresolved questions. In astrology, one of the most contentious focuses on houses. Everyone agrees that there are twelve of them. But how should we determine their boundaries? There are dozens of methods to choose from. I'm going to discuss only two.

The first is Placidus. Long the most popular system of house division, Placidus is a time-based formula planted so deeply in the weeds that I won't even try to explain it. It was named after Placidus de Tito, a seventeenth-century Italian monk, but invented by a tenth-century Arabic astrologer named Mohammed ben Gebir al Batani, who in turn based his system on the foundational manuscripts of Claudius Ptolemy, a second-century century geographer, astronomer, and astrologer known throughout the Roman Empire. So this system has been around for ages. But Placidus has its drawbacks, chief of which is that the Earth revolves around the Sun at a tilt and, as a result, the houses are unequal in size — and the farther north or south you go, the worse the distortion gets. Nonetheless, this is the system I learned when I was initiated into astrology, and with rare exceptions, it's the system I use in this book. It's also the system preferred by most online astrological services. Until recently, I'd have said that it's the most popular system, hands down.

But recently, a competing system has popped up. Whole Sign is the oldest system of house division and by far the easiest. It assumes that all the houses are equal in size and congruent with the signs. And, unlike Placidus and other systems, there's no trigonometry involved.

So let's say you have Gemini rising. It doesn't matter if your Ascendant is 0° Gemini or 29° Gemini. Under the rules of Whole Sign, the entire first house will be the domain of Gemini, with the Ascendant merely a point within it. The second house would belong to Cancer. The third house is Leo's. And so on, around the zodiac. Simple. Appealing.

But is it accurate? Does it reflect the granular reality of life better than Placidus? It's hard to say. Still, many astrologers have converted to Whole Sign and are zealously advocating on its behalf. As for me, I'm sticking with Placidus. But I could be persuaded.

House placements are based on the time of your birth, not on your sign. Thus, if you were born right before dawn, your Sun is in the first house — no matter whether you were born in January or in June. If you were born around noon, your Sun will be at the apex of your chart, in the ninth or tenth house. Born at dusk? Summer or winter, your Sun will be in the sixth or seventh house. And if you were born around midnight, your Sun will be in the third or fourth house, rolling around at the bottom of your chart.

If you have an accurate copy of your chart based on your time of birth, you can see right away which houses are occupied and which are not. If you don't have a copy of your chart, go to Chapter 2 and get one now.

I'm sorry to report that if you don't have a birth time that's at least fairly accurate (within an hour or so), you might as well skip this chapter. Houses depend on time of birth, so if you don't know when you were born, you cannot know what houses your planets occupy. It's too bad, but don't let it bother you for a moment. Even without houses, astrology is vast.

Thinking about the Houses

Every birth chart embraces all twelve houses — no more, no less. But some houses are more important than others. The more planets you see squeezed into a house, the more central the matters of that house are likely to be. Table 12-1 lists the twelve houses along with the areas of life that they cover.

The following sections show how the Sun, Moon, and planets operate in each of the twelve houses.

TABLE 12-1

Houses and Their Significance

House	Areas of Concern
First house	Your appearance, apparent disposition, and sense of self
Second house	Money, income, possessions, values
Third house	Communication, writing, short journeys, brothers and sisters
Fourth house	Home, roots, one parent, circumstances at the end of life
Fifth house	Romance, children, creativity, entertainment
Sixth house	Work, service, routines, health and wellbeing
Seventh house	Marriage and other partnerships, open enemies

(continued)

TABLE 12-1 *(continued)*

House	Areas of Concern
Eighth house	Sex, death, regeneration, other people's money
Ninth house	Higher education, long journeys, religion, philosophy, law
Tenth house	Career, status, reputation, the other parent
Eleventh house	Friends, groups, goals and aspirations
Twelfth house	Seclusion, the unconscious, secrets, self-undoing, transcendence

The Sun in the Houses

The Sun symbolizes your will, your purpose, and your most essential self. Its house position describes the area in which you can most effectively express those aspects of your being.

>> **Sun in the first house:** You're active, enterprising, and proud of your accomplishments. Your strong personality enables you to assert yourself in a natural, dignified way. This placement indicates leadership potential and success that comes about through your own efforts.

>> **Sun in the second house:** You're practical, persistent, security-minded, and skilled at judging the value of things, material and immaterial. Your possessions reflect your deeper values. Financial stability is a worthy goal; achieving it makes you feel on track and is something you can be proud of.

>> **Sun in the third house:** Articulate and observant, you collect information and communicate with ease. Learning absorbs you. Short trips — even jaunts around the neighborhood — bring you cheer and keep you engaged. Sibling rivalry — or any form of communicating with a sibling — could play a major role in your life.

>> **Sun in the fourth house:** You're intuitive and introverted, with a strong sense of self, a close tie to your ancestors, and an interest in the past. Home and family are of primary importance. Whether your experience of family is positive or negative, knowing something about your roots reinforces your sense of self.

>> **Sun in the fifth house:** Pleasure-seeking and dynamic, you find happiness through romance, children, and activities that give you the opportunity to express your creativity.

>> **Sun in the sixth house:** Finding fulfilling employment is crucial. As a perfectionist who is susceptible to becoming workaholic, you define yourself through your vocation, and productivity lifts your spirits. You also tend to worry about your health but respond positively to the healing arts. Examples: Serena Williams, Barack Obama.

>> **Sun in the seventh house:** Marriage and other partnerships are essential to your identity, though you may bounce back and forth between fear of isolation and fear of commitment. Balancing power is an issue in both personal and professional relationships.

>> **Sun in the eighth house:** You're a profoundly emotional person whose need to explore your own psyche brings liberation and motivates you to seek union with someone or something outside of yourself. Sex, joint resources, and legacies of all types captivate you.

>> **Sun in the ninth house:** You're a lifelong seeker who looks to find meaning and to expand your awareness through education, religion, and travel. Everyone talks about having a philosophy of life. You really mean it.

>> **Sun in the tenth house:** Your determination to succeed and your desire for public recognition make you a born leader. This position is an excellent indicator of professional success.

>> **Sun in the eleventh house:** You have high ideals and aspirations, a wide circle of friends and acquaintances, and the ability to collaborate. Becoming part of a group that expresses your most cherished values enables you to fulfill your deepest goals. Friends can be the most important people in your life.

>> **Sun in the twelfth house:** Even if you have an outgoing personality, you are ultimately a sort of hermit. Intuitive, reclusive, and secretive, you find nourishment in solitude and spiritual activity. Helping others through institutions such as hospitals or prisons brings fulfillment.

The Moon in the Houses

Night after night, the Moon is never the same shape and never in the same location. The house it occupies in your chart shows where you can expect circumstances to change and feelings to fluctuate. Your emotional well-being depends on the matters described by that house.

>> **Moon in the first house:** Don't imagine that your emotions are hidden or disguised. Thanks to your unconscious need to express your feelings and be accepted, they're obvious to all. Your well-being is oddly dependent on how

you look and how people perceive you. Your appearance and your moods are linked.

>> **Moon in the second house:** Although you experience financial ups and downs throughout your life, you also become increasingly persistent about holding on to the green stuff — which is fortunate because material security is vital for your well-being. Although you may not think of yourself as materialistic, your possessions mean more than you might care to admit.

>> **Moon in the third house:** You're a skilled communicator in speech and in writing. You have an adaptable intellect, an attachment to brothers and sisters, and a gift for establishing connections and linking people together. Short journeys bring emotional sustenance.

>> **Moon in the fourth house:** Your parents and family heritage are profoundly important, and the past has an irresistible allure. Security improves your peace of mind, and having a home that feels right is fundamental. In your search for the perfect nest, you're likely to experience many changes of residence.

>> **Moon in the fifth house:** You're romantic, dramatic, and creative. A risk-taker in the realm of love, you are entertaining and emotional but erratic in your affections. You connect easily with children and are talented in a multitude of ways.

>> **Moon in the sixth house:** Until you find satisfying work, you're likely to change jobs repeatedly. Toiling for a paycheck isn't enough; you need to feel productive and fulfilled, possibly in service or health professions. You also worry about your body. It may help to know that the more contented you are at work, the healthier you will feel.

>> **Moon in the seventh house:** Marriage and other partnerships loom large for you — sometimes too large. Fearful of being alone, you feel indecisive and anxious about relationships, and may run through many. Because you feel as if your stability depends entirely on others, you may become too dependent. But people are drawn to you. Example: Marilyn Monroe.

WALT WHITMAN

The poet Walt Whitman, born May 31, 1819, had the Moon in Leo in the sixth house. As a Gemini, he's known for his literary accomplishments. As someone with the Moon in the house of work and health, he's also recognized for regular jobs he held during his lifetime. Among other professions, he was a journeyman printer, a journalist, a teacher, a government clerk, and a Civil War nurse, a job that was both dramatic, in keeping with Leo, and service-oriented, as the sixth house demands.

» **Moon in the eighth house:** You experience emotional ups and downs through romantic or business relationships. You have strongly fluctuating moods, passionate sexual urges, and the ability to heal emotional wounds for yourself and possibly for others. Though you may occasionally overdramatize your emotions, you're both sensitive and brave. Not everyone can say that.

» **Moon in the ninth house:** The more you push beyond the boundaries of everyday life and seek out fresh experiences, the happier you are. You have an active imagination and a desire for knowledge. You may explore many religions and philosophies before you find one that satisfies you. Travel lifts your spirits, and you take many journeys.

» **Moon in the tenth house:** Your peace of mind goes hand in hand with your ambition and professional accomplishments. Once you identify the right career, you pour yourself into it and may receive public acclaim. Although the ordinary slings and arrows of criticism wound you more than you might care to admit, success can be yours.

» **Moon in the eleventh house:** Popular and easygoing, you have an instinctive understanding of other people and a rare ability to connect. Friends and acquaintances play a major role in your life, and you are strongly influenced by them. Your goals are likely to mutate many times, and as they do, your circle of friends will shift.

» **Moon in the twelfth house:** Digging out your secrets is no easy task. You're intrigued by the hidden side of life, but you're moody and sensitive. Withdrawal is your mode. You prefer to conceal your emotions. Clandestine relationships offer a form of sustenance that you don't find elsewhere. And yet, even there, getting to know you is a challenge.

The Nodes of the Moon in the House

Unlike the other celestial bodies discussed in this chapter, the Nodes of the Moon don't exactly exist, at least not in physical form. They're simply the points in space where the path of the Moon crosses the ecliptic. Nonetheless, there they are in your chart: The North Node and the South Node, two sensitive spots carrying a message that some astrologers consider the most vital part of your horoscope.

Though western astrologers have long debated the meaning of the Nodes, they basically agree that the North Node represents growth, while the South Node symbolizes patterns established in previous lifetimes and thus stands for the path of least resistance. To interpret the Nodes, consider their position by sign, by aspect, and most of all, by house.

» **North Node in the first house/South Node in the seventh:** Expressing your personality and pursuing your ambitions puts you in motion. You stand still by surrendering your power to others and becoming dependent (particularly on a spouse).

» **North Node in the second house/South Node in the eighth:** Pursuing financial security through your own efforts and in accordance with your core values brings fulfillment. Relying on others to take care of you, even through inheritance, brings disappointment, as do relationships that are entirely about sex.

» **North Node in the third house/South Node in the ninth:** Gathering information and using it for concrete purposes brings fulfillment; setting up a permanent residence in the airy realms of philosophical thought brings frustration. Teaching school, pursuing journalism, getting involved in neighborhood activities, and spending time with siblings bring benefits; religious and academic reveries, and world-wide ramblings, though enjoyable, do not.

» **North Node in the fourth house/South Node in the tenth:** Look to family, tradition, and inner life for fulfillment. Don't expect it from the outside world. Like Serena Williams or director George Lucas, you may find success in a career. But your greatest joy comes from home, family, and getting in touch with your roots.

» **North Node in the fifth house/South Node in the eleventh:** Beware of pointless socializing. Group activities, although diverting, lead nowhere. Romance, children, and creative expression expand your awareness and bring fulfillment.

» **North Node in the sixth house/South Node in the twelfth:** Satisfying work is essential to your personal development, as is a positive approach to health. Solitude and escapism may feel soothing because they are familiar. But they limit you. Don't be a hermit.

» **North Node in the seventh house/South Node in the first:** Accepting the challenge of relationship and becoming an equal partner benefit you. Cooperation with others, personally as well as professionally, speeds your progress. Concentrating on your individual concerns slows you down.

» **North Node in the eighth house/South Node in the second:** Beware of overemphasizing the importance of material security. Instead, look for opportunities to collaborate and form intimate ties with others.

» **North Node in the ninth house/South Node in the third:** Rather than running around in a frenzy, broaden your horizons. Higher education and world travel benefit you. Playing on your phone doesn't. Expand your mind.

- » **North Node in the tenth house/South Node in the fourth:** Though it may scare you, you long for public recognition. Pushing past obstacles and pursuing your career bring personal growth. Devoting yourself solely to home and family, though tempting in certain ways, does not.

- » **North Node in the eleventh house/South Node in the fifth:** Focusing on love affairs, personal pleasures, recreation, and children limits your development. Take a larger view. Align yourself with others in pursuit of a cause. Become political. Develop a social conscience and become an active member of your community.

- » **North Node in the twelfth house/South Node in the sixth:** Your job needs your attention, but so does your soul. You're a bit of a perfectionist, so going overboard comes naturally to you, and office politics can sap your energy. The quest for spiritual transcendence in whatever form it may take strengthens and sustains you. Serving others, perhaps in a prison, hospital, or nursing home, is also gratifying.

Mercury in the Houses

Mercury is the planet of communication. Its position by house suggests those areas that fill your thoughts and shape the way you communicate.

- » **Mercury in the first house:** You're a talker — on the ball, loquacious, and eager to share your views. You may be a gregarious storyteller, the sort of person who becomes the heart and soul of any dinner party. Even if you're not outgoing, you rise to the occasion when giving a speech. Your ability to communicate draws people to you.

- » **Mercury in the second house:** You understand the importance of facts and figures, and have the capacity to understand business and finance. By thinking in practical terms, you can turn an idea to concrete advantage. You can also earn money by writing.

- » **Mercury in the third house:** You're fortunate to possess this much-admired placement, for it gives you an alert and vibrant mind, intellectual curiosity, and a way with words. You're an effective public speaker, a clever conversationalist, and a gifted writer.

- » **Mercury in the fourth house:** There's much to discuss because your family heritage is complicated, and you have to deal with its repercussions. Fortunately, you're tuned in and acutely conscious. Unlike many, you enjoy delving into your history — and you're capable of change.

» **Mercury in the fifth house:** A fun-loving person with a variety of interests, you're a creative thinker with a tendency to speculate and a liking for fiction. In love, you look for someone who gets you going mentally. As a parent, you derive enormous pleasure from your children (and you chat about them endlessly).

» **Mercury in the sixth house:** Skillful, efficient, and good with your hands, you tend to immerse yourself in work, either managing the details with ease or becoming obsessed with them. In the absence of something else to do, you're the master of make-work — so it's essential that you find worthwhile employment. The more satisfying your work, the less likely you are to fret about your health.

» **Mercury in the seventh house:** You're a sociable person who adores banter and craves relationships with lots of talk. Although you're outgoing and connect easily with others, you quickly become bored and may shy away from commitment. When you find the relationship you're seeking, the conversation never ends.

» **Mercury in the eighth house:** This placement gives you intuition, the ability to ferret out secrets, amazing researching skills, and a profound engagement with the mysteries of life, including sex, death, money (which you resent having to worry about), and the metaphysical arts.

» **Mercury in the ninth house:** You're fortified by ideas, invigorated by the forces of the intellect, and glad to explore the world, though you have little patience for mundane errands and other details. You enjoy grappling with ideas and meeting people, which makes education a natural field for you. Other smart choices include law, publishing, and religion.

» **Mercury in the tenth house:** With this high-profile placement, you're likely to develop a career in communications. You require continued mental stimulation, so your ideal job has variety built into it. In the absence of that, you experience frequent job changes. You prefer to be in charge and are most successful when you can pursue your own ideas.

» **Mercury in the eleventh house:** People want to talk with you, online and off, and you make friends easily. But there can be a revolving-door quality to your friendships. Professionally you benefit from being in a group setting and from actively networking with people who support your ideals and aspirations.

» **Mercury in the twelfth house:** You're mysterious, intuitive, contemplative, and guarded — a private person who doesn't share your secrets easily. But you can interpret dreams, break codes, and do all kinds of other mental tasks that require creative thinking. Solitude refreshes you.

Venus in the Houses

The house occupied by Venus, the planet of love, indicates those areas in life that bring you pleasure and enhance your ability to connect with others.

>> **Venus in the first house:** Whatever appears in the first house is obvious to all. With Venus rising, you're warm, sociable, and undeniably attractive, a quality you also admire in others.

>> **Venus in the second house:** You've heard that money can't buy you love. You just don't believe it. You derive sensuous pleasure from beautiful things — those that money can't buy, and those that it can. The material world sings to you, which is probably why astrologers associate this particular Venus with shopping. Fortunately, you're adept at pulling in the green.

>> **Venus in the third house:** You love to talk, travel, and gather information. You express yourself eloquently and attract many admirers with your charm. You also interact well with your neighbors and siblings. This is an excellent position for a teacher, journalist, or public speaker.

>> **Venus in the fourth house:** In the absence of other factors, this fortunate placement bestows a happy childhood, a close tie to your mother, a talent for decorating, and a beautiful home.

>> **Venus in the fifth house:** You attract love and interact beautifully with children (being somewhat of a child yourself). You're naturally talented in fields such as fashion, design, music, art, theater, and the sundry aspects of play. A delight to be around, you relish the pleasures of life, and you get along with everyone. You'll never lack for admirers or invitations.

>> **Venus in the sixth house:** Work and love: what else is there? When the one prospers, so does the other. Fulfilling employment pulls friends and potential partners into your orbit. If the physical environment is pleasant, all the better. Venus responds to beauty, even at the office. If you can avoid the peril of over-indulgence, Venus here will improve your health.

>> **Venus in the seventh house:** Affectionate and well-liked, you're a congenial person who's happiest in a committed relationship. Thanks to your innate charm, you attract a wide selection of potential mates and have the ability to create a loving relationship, maybe with someone in the arts. You benefit from forming business partnerships.

>> **Venus in the eighth house:** You're seductive, manipulative, obsessive, passionate, and often under the sway of a raging storm of feelings and appetites. Your love life could be a maze of complications. You're also shrewd with money, which comes your way through marriage, inheritance, or savvy investments.

>> **Venus in the ninth house:** Anything that expands your horizons can bring happiness and love. Philosophical and idealistic, you can find success in travel, education, law, religion, and publishing. Or you might marry a foreigner (or someone you meet far from home), a professor, a writer, a lawyer, a member of the clergy, an editor, or a publisher.

>> **Venus in the tenth house:** You're beguiling, outgoing, and socially ambitious. Your career, perhaps in diplomacy or the arts, means a lot to you. Because your reputation is sterling, people want to be around you, and you will always find potential partners through professional activities. Just remember: People are naturally attracted to you. You don't have to push.

>> **Venus in the eleventh house:** You're open-minded, affectionate, tactful, and cooperative. The hub of your social circle, a boon to every group, and a devoted pal, you know how to make people feel comfortable. Your charm easily attracts admirers.

>> **Venus in the twelfth house:** Highly attuned to the feelings of others, you're a sensitive person with a tendency to be secretive and a gift for unconditional love. But this can be undone by your lack of boundaries or your willingness to sacrifice. Many people with this placement tumble into clandestine love affairs, while others, shy and vulnerable, retreat into the shadows. Spiritual pursuits can bring you peace and courage.

Mars in the Houses

The position of Mars by house tells you where you're most likely to act on impulse, take risks, and pursue your personal desires.

>> **Mars in the first house:** Vigorous and passionate, you initiate activities, sometimes impulsively. Your vitality draws people to you, but your desires (and anger) are obvious to all. This position gives you an assertive personality and can be a sign of the warrior.

>> **Mars in the second house:** You are competitive, acquisitive, and practical. When you want something, you go after it with gusto. Most content when you can focus on a concrete goal, you also want to be rewarded for your efforts — and not solely with praise. Money and material objects do the trick more effectively than mere words.

>> **Mars in the third house:** You have an independent, argumentative attitude, and you call things as you see them — even if that means jumping to conclusions or being less than diplomatic. With your razor-sharp wit, you're impatient and easily distracted, and you can be aggressive in conversation.

>> **Mars in the fourth house:** You're independent and restless with a sturdy constitution and innate verve. When you were a child, an angry parent may have made your home an unpredictable and upsetting place. As an adult, your attempt to create a serene, harmonious home may fail. Instead, you may unconsciously create a discordant environment characterized by fighting and dissension.

>> **Mars in the fifth house:** You're impulsive, excitable, fun-loving, and highly sexed. You take pleasure in initiating love affairs and creative projects. You're also involved with your offspring, whether they're literal flesh-and-blood babies or children of your imagination. Although you can be impatient, you enjoy play and are energized by risk-taking.

>> **Mars in the sixth house:** Work excites you (even if it exhausts you). You're independent and hardy, with a genuine affection for the tools of your trade. A challenge perks you up, but a dull job makes you impatient, and constricting organizational rules frustrate and irritate you. Guard against overwork and get plenty of exercise — the kind that makes you sweat. And don't take foolish chances. Bicycle helmets were invented for a reason.

>> **Mars in the seventh house:** Partnerships energize you, but that doesn't mean you have an easy time with them. You either attract an aggressive partner or become one, and you have a temper. The truth is, a calm, peaceful relationship isn't what you want. You'd prefer passion and fireworks, and you're willing to pay the price. When a relationship isn't going well, you bravely seek resolution, making Mars in the seventh house the position of kiss-and-make-up.

>> **Mars in the eighth house:** You have powerful desires with plenty of sexual charisma. A skilled researcher, you may be attracted to healing arts, occult subjects, and high-stakes finance. Because you yearn for intense experience, you fearlessly take steps that more sensible souls avoid. That touch of wildness makes you irresistible to others — and an occasional danger to yourself.

>> **Mars in the ninth house:** You're an independent thinker, a fearsome debater, and an intrepid traveler with an itch to see the world. You're at home in the realms of religion, education, publishing, and law — especially the adversarial kind. You're a fighter, not a mediator. Your convictions are strong. But you can slip into fanaticism and must guard against becoming intolerant.

>> **Mars in the tenth house:** A demanding, exciting career invigorates you and fills you with resolve. You'd like to be famous, but more than that, you'd like to be part of some grand effort, something that takes strategy and wits — like a revolution, a social movement, or the making of an epic film. Competitive and aggressive, you want to make an impact on the world.

THE MARS EFFECT

It has long been an embarrassment to astrologers that so little research has been done in the discipline. One significant piece of astrological research was conducted in the 1950s, by Michel Gauquelin, a French statistician who explored astrology in his youth, and his wife, Françoise. They set out to prove that astrology had no basis in scientific fact. They examined the birth charts of over 20,000 people, and what they found was astrology at its finest. They didn't announce that Sagittarians were better horseback riders or that Capricorns were better CEOs — nothing that obvious. Instead, they unearthed a link between professional success and planets located near the Ascendant, Descendant, Midheaven, or I.C.

Specifically, they found that angular Jupiter appeared more often than statistically probable in the charts of successful actors; angular Moon showed up in writers' charts; angular Venus turned up in the charts of painters and musicians; angular Saturn appeared in the charts of doctors and scientists; and angular Mars showed up in the charts of champion athletes. Two positions were the most powerful: Those close to the Midheaven (in either the ninth house or the first ten degrees of the tenth house) and those close to the Ascendant (in either the twelfth house or the first ten degrees of the first house).

Many people tried to disprove this association, and controversy raged over statistical methods. Ultimately, the phenomenon held up and became known as the *Mars effect*. Athletes who have an angular Mars include Tiger Woods, Muhammad Ali, Arnold Schwarzenegger, Derek Jeter, and Neil Armstrong, the first man to walk on the moon (and yes, in my opinion, he counts as an athlete).

Not every successful professional has one of these placements. The absence of an angular planet doesn't in any way doom you to failure. But if, perchance, Mars (or another planet) happens to occupy the angular Gauquelin zones in your chart, that planet should be considered especially robust. In the case of Mars, it may not endow you with the ability to whirl like a top in midair, like Olympic gymnast Simone Biles, or outshoot Lebron James. They both have Mars conjunct the Midheaven. If you do too, it should at least lend you a certain swagger.

>> **Mars in the eleventh house:** Your friends stimulate you, go the gym with you, and help you achieve your aspirations. In a group, you rise to a leadership position because you can energize the troops. But you can also be unreasonably demanding and may unconsciously create conflicts or be drawn to quarrelsome individuals.

>> **Mars in the twelfth house:** Other people may not understand who you are because much of your energy and anger is repressed or hidden. You're hesitant to reveal these aspects of yourself, and as a result, you may feel unrecognized. Finding an outlet for your aggression, perhaps through a martial art, is restorative, a way to compensate for your tendency to retreat. In collaborating with others, you're a motivating force for action behind the scenes.

Jupiter in the Houses

Jupiter's position by house determines the areas of life that are most bountiful for you — the places where blessings come most effortlessly and also the areas where you may become too complacent.

>> **Jupiter in the first house:** You have an expansive, charismatic personality that naturally draws people to you. You may also have a tendency to gain weight.

>> **Jupiter in the second house:** Prosperity comes your way, often in the form of windfalls. You're a lucky person. But your desire to spend and your generosity to others may outweigh your ability to earn, so be prudent — if you can.

>> **Jupiter in the third house:** Talkative and hungry for information, you're intelligent and well-informed, though you run the risk of spending way too much time on social media. You benefit from travel, reading, and the company of your siblings.

>> **Jupiter in the fourth house:** You're a generous person who opens your home to others. Comfortable, even luxurious, housing comes your way, and you have a knack for making your home an agreeable place to be. Life improves as you grow older, and in old age, you're surrounded by comfort.

>> **Jupiter in the fifth house:** Having fun yet? If you have Jupiter here, the answer is probably yes. It brings a profusion of romantic affairs, a love of play, the ability to have fun in trying circumstances, and a joyous creativity. Although not everyone with this placement becomes a parent, those who do enjoy it thoroughly.

>> **Jupiter in the sixth house:** Finding the right work is essential to your happiness, and you like to be of service. You're a happy entrepreneur or a devoted employee who gets along famously with colleagues. But you suffer from a tendency to neglect the details, and you may become a workaholic. In work and in health, you need to avoid excesses.

>> **Jupiter in the seventh house:** You're sociable and easy to be around. Marriage and business partnerships are favored by this placement, and you have multiple opportunities to form alliances. Even in an age of divorce, people with this placement marry for life.

>> **Jupiter in the eighth house:** Financially, you stand to gain from insurance, inheritances, business agreements with other people, and the stock market. Partnership arrangements generally work out to your advantage. You also have a strong sex drive and excellent powers of recuperation.

>> **Jupiter in the ninth house:** You're an explorer with an expansive, optimistic attitude toward life. A natural teacher with a philosophical bent, you want to see it all and understand it all. You benefit from travel, education, religion, publishing, and anything that expands your horizons. As the ruler of the ninth sign, Jupiter is at home in the ninth house, making this an enviable component of your natal chart.

>> **Jupiter in the tenth house:** With a little effort, you can fulfill your desire for recognition. You have natural leadership ability; people want to assist you, and you thrive in the public eye. This position brings success, prominence, and possibly fame. Lady Gaga and Kim Kardashian are prime examples.

>> **Jupiter in the eleventh house:** You're open-minded, congenial, helpful, and fair. You work effectively with others, you know a zillion people, and your friends are crazy about you. Large ambitions bring out the best in you. Success comes through group enterprises.

>> **Jupiter in the twelfth house:** You're sympathetic, introspective, and generous, though you may suffer from a tendency to overextend yourself. Solitude and spiritual pursuits calm you down and prepare you for your forays into the world.

Saturn in the Houses

Saturn's position by house determines those areas of life in which you feel the pinch of limitation and will benefit from establishing boundaries, creating structures, and practicing self-discipline.

>> **Saturn in the first house:** You're self-conscious and afraid of being hurt. You worry what people think of you, and as a result you may cloak your personality in defensive armor. Beneath your cautious exterior, you're complicated, serious, and well worth the effort of getting to know. But you don't make it easy.

>> **Saturn in the second house:** You worry about the practical side of life, and money is an issue, whether you're frugal or a spendthrift. Even when dealing with emotional situations, you're aware of the pragmatic implications. You'd like to win the lottery, but if you did — and it's highly unlikely — it could stir up tons of trouble. Instead, you manifest the security you require the old-fashioned way: through hard work.

>> **Saturn in the third house:** You are conscientious and contemplative, with the ability to explore a subject in depth. Communication issues, whether in speech or in writing, are paramount. You have complicated relationships with your brothers and sisters, and sibling rivalry may be an issue for you.

>> **Saturn in the fourth house:** Although your family is extremely important to you, you feel alienated from them (and perhaps from one parent in particular). Understanding family members and interacting with them in a constructive way requires effort. Owning your own home is a gratifying source of identity and security.

>> **Saturn in the fifth house:** You take a serious approach to playful things, and it's difficult for you to lighten up. You don't flirt easily and are more comfortable dating people who are older than you. Creativity is important to you, but because you may fear that you aren't talented, you may suppress your artistic urges. Or, you may rise to the challenge of Saturn and bring structure to your creative life. As a parent, you're responsible and committed.

>> **Saturn in the sixth house:** In your work, you're reliable and exacting. If you have the courage to insist on doing something you consider valuable, you find fulfillment through your work. In daily life, you pay close attention to your responsibilities, but you're a big-time worrier, especially regarding your health. Reassure yourself by getting regular checkups.

>> **Saturn in the seventh house:** You take a serious approach to marriage, but you may also shy away from it. If you overcome your fears of intimacy, you can create a long-lived, solid relationship. You'll be most comfortable with an older partner who's responsible and sober-minded.

>> **Saturn in the eighth house:** You have deep psychological insight. Your challenge is to overcome your fear of death and to face your sexual issues. You're both cautious and skilled in making money — which is fortunate, because there's a good chance that you'll team up with someone who has financial issues.

>> **Saturn in the ninth house:** You're a thoughtful person with wide-ranging intelligence and an interest in large ideas, but you struggle with doubts and uncertainties. Although obstacles may arise in education and religion, taking a disciplined, serious approach makes your search for meaning a satisfying adventure.

>> **Saturn in the tenth house:** You're responsible, organized, and persevering in your effort to achieve your ambitions. But you can also be arrogant, and you have to pay your dues before you achieve the recognition that's ultimately yours. Although one of your parents may have been demanding or distant, your own professional quest is likely to be successful.

>> **Saturn in the eleventh house:** You set impressive goals, and although you may fear that you aren't up to them, you forge ahead anyway. You can turn a vague aspiration into a plan, and a plan into an accomplishment. Your organizational ability and tenacity enable you to mobilize the help you need. Friendship may be tougher. You don't make friends lightly, but the bonds you do form are long-lasting and solid.

>> **Saturn in the twelfth house:** Many people would be astonished to know that beneath the surface, you wrestle with fear, pessimism, insecurity, loneliness, and guilt. Although you're accustomed to working by yourself or behind the scenes, solitude can exaggerate your anxieties. That's a problem you need to conquer. Finding the courage to face your fears is essential to your welfare.

Uranus in the Houses

The position that Uranus occupies by house determines the area in life in which you can expect the unexpected.

>> **Uranus in the first house:** There's something about you — your appearance, your demeanor, your voice — that causes people to see you as a true original. No matter how hard you try to seem conventional, your attempts to pass for ordinary are doomed. (Examples: Mia Farrow, Keanu Reeves, Kurt Cobain, and Douglas Adams, author of *The Hitchhiker's Guide to the Galaxy*.) Out-of-left-field events can turn your world upside down.

>> **Uranus in the second house:** The things of this world — money, belongings, technology — come and go, arriving and departing with equal speed. You may strike oil or go bankrupt or come up with an invention so brilliant that it changes everything. Your finances are volatile and, like your values, can undergo a sudden turnaround.

>> **Uranus in the third house:** You have an innovative mind and a clever way of expressing yourself. You could be a brilliant thinker or writer, known for your revolutionary, idiosyncratic ideas. You have interesting siblings, but your relationships with them have their ups and downs.

>> **Uranus in the fourth house:** You come from or create an unconventional family. An erratic relationship with one of your parents has a strong impact on you. You find it hard to settle down, and when you do, you set up housekeeping in a thoroughly individual way. Professional changes affect your domestic life.

>> **Uranus in the fifth house:** You have a wild creative streak and an intriguing amorous life. You're prone to love at first sight, preferably with rebellious types. But sudden breakups are also part of the picture. Your children may be remarkable people, though you may feel that they hamper your freedom.

>> **Uranus in the sixth house:** You don't resent working, but you oppose the concept of nine-to-five. You manage to find offbeat, peculiar jobs, and you do things in a unique way both at work and in your private life. Your nerves affect your health, and you benefit from unorthodox healing techniques.

>> **Uranus in the seventh house:** You may marry an unconventional person, a rebel of some sort, or you may create a free-wheeling relationship that acknowledges, in its radical format, your need for independence. You're liable to marry with lightning speed, but be aware — you could divorce the same way.

>> **Uranus in the eighth house:** Your sex life has a remarkable, sometimes outrageous, aspect to it, and the same is true for your finances (and those of your spouse). You benefit from unusual investments and unexpected legacies. You're also drawn to metaphysical and occult subjects, including reincarnation and life after death.

>> **Uranus in the ninth house:** Unusual experiences come to you through travel, education, and the law. You could study an unconventional subject or attend an unconventional school. In religion and other areas, you rebel against dogma and received opinion. Your philosophy of life is your own invention.

>> **Uranus in the tenth house:** You insist on maintaining your independence, especially regarding your career. You have an original viewpoint, which people notice. Professional opportunities spring up out of nowhere. But you have trouble adapting to authority or working in a hierarchical organization. You're a natural entrepreneur or freelancer. Fulfilling areas include social activism, technology, science, and astrology.

>> **Uranus in the eleventh house:** You're a tolerant person with unusual aspirations and equally oddball companions. Groups can motivate you, but you rebel against rules and regulations. People enter your life on a moment's notice, especially when you're involved with a cause, but you can lose contact with them just as quickly. Your diverse friends reflect your widely scattered interests

>> **Uranus in the twelfth house:** Your love of independence and distrust of doctrine may cause you to explore various forms of spirituality. Your deepest individuality emerges when you're alone or behind the scenes in a protected environment. Flashes of intuition and insight arise from your core. Learn to pay attention to them.

Neptune in the Houses

The house that Neptune inhabits in your horoscope tells you where you can access the most profound level of intuition — and where you're prone to deception.

>> **Neptune in the first house:** You're dreamy, glamorous, easily influenced, and hard to pin down. Your intuition is acute, but you can fall into dependency. You mystify and mesmerize people; they aren't sure who you are or what you're up to because your identity seems fluid. There's a strong chance that you have musical or artistic ability.

>> **Neptune in the second house:** You have an intuitive sense of how to earn money, or at least you think you do. But the mechanics of the whole business may escape you, and as a result, your financial affairs may slip into chaos. Hire a responsible earth sign to help. You can profit from artistic or spiritual pursuits.

>> **Neptune in the third house:** You're imaginative, visionary, and highly responsive to the nuances of language. Persuasive but easily distracted, you soak up knowledge and have poetic ability. You're also gullible — and no one knows how to fool you better than your brothers and sisters.

>> **Neptune in the fourth house:** The members of your family are a talented, bewildering lot, and you find it difficult to separate from them. You may have inherited psychic ability. But sensitivity to drugs and alcohol could also be part of your heritage. Although your home could be an area of confusion and doubt, it could also be your sanctuary. It's up to you.

>> **Neptune in the fifth house:** Although you may find it difficult to direct your free-flowing creative impulses, this placement is a compelling indicator of artistic imagination. Learning how to use its amorphous energy is part of your challenge. More than a touch of dreaminess may characterize your romantic life, which features secret affairs, platonic relationships and a fog of confusion. Your children (should you conquer your ambivalence about that subject and decide to become a parent) are gentle and creative, and you have a psychic tie with them.

- » **Neptune in the sixth house:** You tend to get caught in the web of office politics, and the physical aspects of regular jobs — the fluorescent lights, the hideous décor — make you long for escape. Job possibilities exist in film, pharmacology, music, fashion, and anything connected to the sea. Because doctors may struggle to diagnose you properly, your health complaints are often solved through alternative healing practices or non-Western-style medicine.

- » **Neptune in the seventh house:** Moody people and artistic souls attract you. You seek your spiritual soul mate, but in your confusion about relationships, you may sacrifice yourself to an image or ideal that has nothing to do with your actual partner. When people use the phrase "smoke and mirrors," they're talking about Neptune. Idealism about relationships is wonderful, but only when it's tempered with clarity.

- » **Neptune in the eighth house:** Séances, Ouija boards, Tarot cards. extrasensory perception, and all forms of communication with the psyche and the unseen world attract you. You consider sex a spiritual exercise. But when it comes to joint bank accounts and other shared assets, you may trust your instincts too much. Be cautious in business associations.

- » **Neptune in the ninth house:** Mystical religions and spiritual journeys are your cup of chai. You would like to identify a spiritual path, but it may not happen as easily as you hope, for visionary Neptune will take you in many directions. You may meander in the wilderness for a while, searching for a teacher or mentor. Or you could become one.

- » **Neptune in the tenth house:** Tap into your intuition and you can find the success you covet. Following a profession just because you think it's practical (as if you would know) is a waste of time. Though you tend to drift and find it hard to assert yourself, you can be both inspired and inspiring. You flourish in Neptunian occupations such as art, poetry, music, film, photography, pharmacology, and any profession that involves liquids.

- » **Neptune in the eleventh house:** You have fluctuating ideals, vague aspirations, and a variable collection of talented friends who may have drug and alcohol problems. Compassionate but gullible, you tend to see what you want to see in them. To expand your horizons, consider joining a film club, a political campaign, a community theatre, a poetry workshop, an environmental organization, a drum circle — you name it. It could alter your perception in an entirely positive way.

- » **Neptune in the twelfth house:** You're empathetic, contemplative, reclusive, and possibly clairvoyant. You receive a continual flow of messages from your unconscious. Dreams fascinate you. Helping people in need, perhaps because they have been shunted away or isolated in some way, satisfies your need to be of service and actually makes you happier. Finally, your creative efforts flourish when you can address them in private. A little solitude promotes your peace of mind.

Pluto in the Houses

The house that tiny Pluto occupies in your natal chart determines the area in life where you're most likely to experience obsession and renewal, to sink into darkness and to emerge, revitalized.

>> **Pluto in the first house:** Much as you try to repress them, the emotions roiling about within you make you feel frighteningly vulnerable. You have a magnetic personality but your need to protect yourself may cause you to be compulsive and controlling. You make a tremendous impact on people — but you may also alienate them.

>> **Pluto in the second house:** You find concrete outlets for your abilities, but you can also become obsessed with material possessions. Your fear of loss can cause money to become a battlefield. You may struggle to control other people with economic sanctions: a losing endeavor, needless to say.

>> **Pluto in the third house:** You have a reflective, thoughtful mind, pinpoint perceptions, a longing to understand the mysteries of life, and a complicated relationship with a sibling. Obsessive thoughts may plague you, and you have a deep need to communicate. You also have a strong sense of privacy. Surely the inventor of the locked diary had Pluto in the third house.

>> **Pluto in the fourth house:** One of your parents was a force to be reckoned with; dealing with the psychological fallout of childhood is your Plutonian task. Home and family may be perilous, but the domestic mess holds the key to your evolution. Change revitalizes you.

>> **Pluto in the fifth house:** Romantic entanglements can turn into fixations and power struggles that never get resolved. You can't win and you can't lose. No matter how hard you try to manipulate your lover (or child), the person most altered by the liaison is you. Learning to access your power without making a hash of things is a lifelong process. Creative endeavors bring renewal. One warning: gambling can be addictive.

>> **Pluto in the sixth house:** You have more power than you think, especially on the job. No matter what your work may look like to others, if it has merit and purpose for you, it can be transformative. One pitfall to avoid: laboring past the point of exhaustion. One skill you may not know you have: healing ability.

>> **Pluto in the seventh house:** Trust and secrecy cannot co-exist for long if a relationship is to be a healthy one, either in your personal life or in business. That is the test you face. You attract a commanding partner whose influence causes you to change in profound ways. Maintaining your sense of self in the presence of this magnetic being isn't easy, but you are equipped for the challenge.

- **Pluto in the eighth house:** You're intuitive, perceptive, and deeply serious. You grapple with the big issues in life, including sex, death, and clashes over savings and investments. Your bravery in tackling these issues pays off. In hard times, these metaphoric journeys to the underworld bring you face to face with your fears, but they also strengthen your resolve and rejuvenate your spirit.

- **Pluto in the ninth house:** Knowledge attracts and fortifies you. By immersing yourself in serious study or becoming involved with people from a culture other than your own, you deepen your understanding. Education and travel are your tickets to transformation. Seek wisdom. See the world.

- **Pluto in the tenth house:** You're an irresistible force in the political or professional arena. You resent authority figures (starting with one of your parents), and yet you wish to wield authority. When you decide to seek power, you can be a serious player. There are perils as well as opportunities here, but on the whole, this position favors success.

- **Pluto in the eleventh house:** Friendship is thorny. You may stumble into relationships tinged by conflict or rivalry. Friends can disappear but they can also help mold your aspirations and act as catalysts to change. Becoming involved with a group can be intense and rewarding, even if it does lead to a power struggle.

- **Pluto in the twelfth house:** You're a private person with a secret life. You shy away from expressing your power, and yet you're fascinated by whatever is going on beneath the surface and in your own psyche. Delving into your unconscious can be frightening but that's where the power of transformation can be found.

Interpreting Empty Houses

Do the math: Your chart has twelve houses, but only ten planets. This means that you're bound to have empty houses somewhere in your chart. They're unavoidable and nothing to worry about.

Having an empty house of marriage, for example, doesn't mean that you're fated to be single. Consider Zsa Zsa Gabor, bombshell Hollywood socialite of the mid-twentieth century, and one of the first to be famous for being famous. She was married nine times, although her house of marriage is without a planet. So what accounts for all this amorous activity? Her house of marriage may be vacant but her fifth house of romance and flirtation is packed.

REMEMBER

Often, an unoccupied house signifies that the affairs of that house are simply not a major concern. But you can't make that determination with a casual glance. Just because a house is uninhabited doesn't mean it's unimportant. The truth is that there's so much to think about in a natal chart that even an empty house can keep you busy. To investigate an empty house, I suggest the following three-step method:

1. **Look at the sign on the cusp of the house.**

The sign at the beginning of each house determines your approach to the concerns of that house. For example, turn to Andy Warhol's chart in Chapter 19. Notice that his second house of money is empty, with Virgo on the cusp. (The cusp of the second house is at eight o'clock, the cusp of the third house is at seven o'clock, and so on.) Thus his approach to financial matters was Virgoan: meticulous and detail-oriented. And, indeed, he made a habit of recording his daily activities and expenses — just like a Virgo. When he spent $1.50 on a cab ride, he wrote it down.

Table 12-1 at the beginning of this chapter summarizes the concerns of each house. Table 12-2 at the end of the chapter suggests ways to interpret the sign on the cusp.

TABLE 12-2 **House Rulership**

If the Sign on the Cusp Is	Your Approach to the Concerns of That House Is	And the House Ruler Is
Aries	Spontaneous, energetic	Mars
Taurus	Productive, deliberate	Venus
Gemini	Flexible, communicative	Mercury
Cancer	Intuitive, defensive	Moon
Leo	Dignified, expressive	Sun
Virgo	Discriminating, detail-oriented	Mercury
Libra	Diplomatic, artistic	Venus
Scorpio	Intense, penetrating	Pluto
Sagittarius	Independent, expansive	Jupiter
Capricorn	Responsible, traditional	Saturn
Aquarius	Unconventional, detached	Uranus
Pisces	Receptive, vulnerable	Neptune

2. Check out the planet that rules the sign on the cusp.

The position of that planet conveys a lot of information. In Andy Warhol's case, Virgo, the sign on the cusp of his empty second house, is ruled by Mercury. It can be found in flamboyant Leo — perfect for an artist who literally painted pictures of the dollar sign.

Or look at Beyoncé's chart in Chapter 5. Her seventh house of marriage and partnership is empty. Since Aries is on the cusp of that house, she's drawn to aggressive, fiery types. And since the ruler of Aries, warlike Mars, is in her tenth house of fame and public life, she is likely to marry someone who is ambitious and prominent and possibly has anger issues.

3. Look at the aspects made by the ruling planet.

If the ruling planet of the empty house is close to the Sun, the Moon, or one of the angles of a chart, its relevance increases. If it is conjunct Jupiter, the concerns of that house are blessed with good fortune. If it opposes Saturn, difficulties may abound. And so on. For more about aspects, turn to Chapter 13.

Every year, as the Sun makes its annual pilgrimage through the zodiac, it travels through your entire chart, illuminating every sign and every house. The Moon and the other planets visit as well, each at its own speed and according to its own schedule. Over time, those transiting planets spin through each and every house, infusing them with energy. Sooner or later, every house, the empty ones included, will have its day.

Chapter **13**

Amazing Aspects: The Secrets of Cosmic Geometry

Knowing the position of the planets by sign and by house isn't enough. To comprehend the true complexity of an astrological chart, you need to know how the planets interact with each other. That information is revealed by the mathematical angles, or *aspects*, between the planets.

Consider the case of a woman whose Venus, the planet of love, is located within a few short degrees of expansive Jupiter. That combination gives her a certain charm and makes expressing affection and finding love easy for her — theoretically. But what if both planets are 90° from Saturn? With that harsh right angle, disappointment enters the picture. Now you have an individual who struggles with rejection or attracts others who fail to meet her standards — a person who, like Groucho Marx, doesn't want to be in a club that would have her as a member.

TIP

To detect that kind of internal process in your own chart, you need to know the degree of the zodiac that each planet occupies. And for that, you need an accurate copy of your chart. If you don't already have one, go to Chapter 2 and following the instructions there for getting your chart online.

Once you have a copy of your chart, you're ready to pick out the major aspects in it. It's not nearly as complicated as you might think.

Identifying the Major Aspects

An astrological chart, like any circle, has 360°, with each sign of the zodiac covering exactly 30°, or one-twelfth of the whole. Within that circle, each pair of planets is separated by a specific number of degrees. Planets at certain significant distances from each other form an aspect. Table 13-1 lists the *major aspects,* along with their symbols.

TABLE 13-1

Major Aspects

Distance	Name of Aspect	Symbol	Effect
0°	Conjunction	☌	Unifies or blends
60°	Sextile	✶	Supports
90°	Square	□	Creates friction
120°	Trine	△	Assists and brings opportunities
180°	Opposition	☍	Opposes

Roughly speaking, there are three types of aspects. If two planets are within a few degrees of each other, they're *conjunct,* which means that they operate in unison. If two planets are 60° or 120° apart, they support and assist each other. These aspects — sextiles and trines — are considered *harmonious.* And if two planets are at right angles (90°) or opposite each other (180°), they're basically at war. These aspects — squares and oppositions — are considered *hard.*

REAL LIFE EXAMPLE

The chart in Figure 13-1 belongs to Alexandria Ocasio-Cortez, a former bartender who is also the youngest woman ever elected to the U.S. House of Representatives. Her vivid, insistent personality, progressive politics, and mastery of social media propelled her into the kingdom of celebrity, where she is both hated and adored. She has the Sun in Libra, an audacious Moon in Aries, Sagittarius rising and, like everyone else on Earth, a mix of aspects. They include:

>> A high-profile conjunction between Mercury and the Midheaven in Libra.

>> A beneficial trine between the Moon in Aries and Venus in Sagittarius.

>> A dramatic set of interlocking squares and oppositions that ropes in most of the planets in her chart, forming what is known as a "Grand Cross" — the dominating feature of her chart. (See Chapter 14 for more information on interpreting a birth chart.)

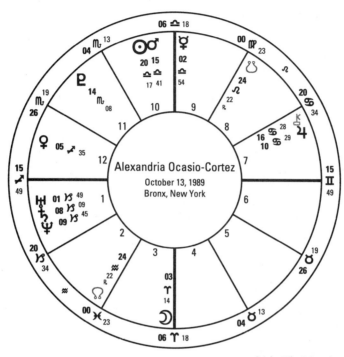

FIGURE 13-1:
Birth chart of a
firebrand:
Alexandria
Ocasio-Cortez.

REMEMBER

An "easy" chart festooned with sextiles and trines isn't better than a "hard" chart crisscrossed with squares and opposition. Astrologers have long noted that people with harmonious charts risk becoming lazy and self-satisfied, while accomplished achievers frequently have high-stress charts.

The most powerful aspects occur when the distances between the planets are close to those listed in Table 13-1. A 90° square, for example, is stronger than an 82° square, regardless of the planets involved. But observation indicates that an aspect doesn't have to be precise to have an influence. So astrologers allow a little leeway on either side. How much depends on the person. A few practitioners use an orb as wide as 14°. Stricter seers permit no more than a 5° orb. Most astrologers, myself included, fall somewhere in the middle.

TIP

In general, I recommend using an 8° orb for the conjunction, square, trine, and opposition and a 6° orb for the sextile, which is a slightly weaker aspect. (Minor aspects, which I discuss later in this chapter, can handle only a 2° orb.) In each case, you can tack on an additional 2° if the Sun or Moon is involved. This means that if your Sun is at 14°, any planet between 4° and 24° of your Sun sign is considered conjunct, a planet 82° to 98° away is square, and so on. Remember: The tighter the orb, the more potent the aspect.

Figuring Out Your Aspects

Here's how to locate the five major aspects in your chart:

>> **Conjunctions:** Most of the time, you can detect conjunctions just by looking. Planets that are conjunct are huddled together in the same area of the chart, within 8° of each other (10° if one of those planets is the Sun or the Moon). Most planets that are conjunct are in the same sign, but there are exceptions. For instance, if Venus is at 28° Capricorn and the Moon is at 1° Aquarius, they're only 3° apart and hence are conjunct, despite inhabiting different signs.

>> **Oppositions:** To identify oppositions, look for planets on opposite sides of the chart. (See Chart 13-2 below). Then check whether they're within orb. If Mars is at 18° Sagittarius, any planet between 10° and 26° Gemini is in opposition. (In western astrology, a planet at 4° Gemini isn't considered in opposition. Vedic astrology is different; it recognizes two planets in opposing signs as being in opposition, regardless of their specific degrees. But Vedic astrology is not the subject of this book.)

>> **Squares:** Squares are harder to spot. Look for planets in signs of the same quality or modality (cardinal, fixed, or mutable). Then check that they're about 90° apart, plus or minus 8°. If they are, you've found the source of your deepest frustrations.

>> **Trines:** You can find trines between planets in signs of the same element — that is, both planets are in fire, earth, air, or water signs. Maybe you have Mercury in Gemini and Uranus in Libra? If they're within 8° of each other, they're trine — in which case, congratulations: You have a quick, original mind.

>> **Sextiles:** The weakest of the major aspects, sextiles arise between planets that are two signs apart.

Table 13-2 gives you squares and oppositions at a glance, and Table 13-3 does the same for the harmonious aspects. Most of the time, aspects are in the sign combinations delineated below. But other sign combinations can appear, a situation described in the next paragraph.

TABLE 13-2

The Hard Aspects

If a Planet is in . . .	It Squares Planets in . . .	And Opposes Those in . . .
Aries	Cancer and Capricorn	Libra
Taurus	Leo and Aquarius	Scorpio
Gemini	Virgo and Pisces	Sagittarius
Cancer	Aries and Libra	Capricorn
Leo	Taurus and Scorpio	Aquarius
Virgo	Gemini and Sagittarius	Pisces
Libra	Cancer and Capricorn	Aries
Scorpio	Leo and Aquarius	Taurus
Sagittarius	Virgo and Pisces	Gemini
Capricorn	Aries and Libra	Cancer
Aquarius	Taurus and Scorpio	Leo
Pisces	Gemini and Sagittarius	Virgo

TABLE 13-3

The Harmonious Aspects

If a Planet is in . . .	It Sextiles Planets in . . .	And Trines Those in . . .
Aries	Aquarius and Gemini	Leo and Sagittarius
Taurus	Pisces and Cancer	Virgo and Capricorn
Gemini	Aries and Leo	Libra and Aquarius
Cancer	Taurus and Virgo	Scorpio and Pisces
Leo	Gemini and Libra	Sagittarius and Aries
Virgo	Cancer and Scorpio	Taurus and Capricorn
Libra	Leo and Sagittarius	Gemini and Aquarius
Scorpio	Virgo and Capricorn	Cancer and Pisces
Sagittarius	Libra and Aquarius	Aries and Leo
Capricorn	Scorpio and Pisces	Taurus and Virgo
Aquarius	Sagittarius and Aries	Gemini and Libra
Pisces	Capricorn and Taurus	Cancer and Scorpio

REMEMBER

Of course there are exceptions. Most aspects occur between planets in the signs listed above, but out-of-sign aspects also happen, and they are notoriously difficult to spot. If you're looking at a chart with, say, the Sun at 28° Gemini and Saturn at 1° Libra, it's easy to assume that because both planets are in air signs, they must be trine. In fact, they're separated by 93° and are therefore square. This is yet another reason for getting a computer-generated chart. It'll probably come with an aspect grid like the one in the next section. Even an experienced astrologer can fail to notice an out-of-sign aspect, but those computer-generated aspect grids never miss a trick.

Reading an Aspect Grid

The aspect grid shown in Figure 13-2 is simpler than it looks. It shows the major aspects — and only the major aspects — in Alexandria Ocasio-Cortez's chart. Start on the left-hand side with the symbol of the Sun. As you move across the top row, you can see that the Sun sextiles the Ascendant, squares Jupiter, and forms a conjunction with Mars. Her Aries Moon, showcased on the next row down, forms many more aspects than the Sun — and most of them are squares and oppositions. No wonder she's riled up. Anybody would be.

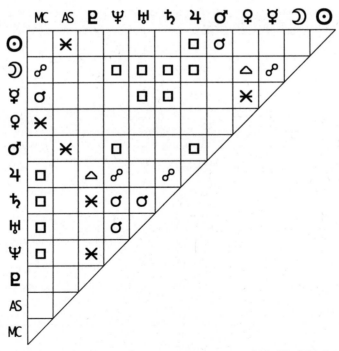

FIGURE 13-2:
Alexandria's aspect grid.

© *John Wiley & Sons, Inc.*

A Note about Minor Aspects

The major aspects discussed in this chapter aren't the only geometrical connections that astrologers consider significant. Other aspects, typically described as *minor aspects,* also connect two planets. Because minor aspects are relatively weak, the orb allotted to them is small — only 2°.

Two minor aspects I refer to in this chapter are the *semi-sextile,* a 30° aspect that's mildly positive, and the *semi-square,* a 45° aspect whose influence is somewhat stressful. These minor aspects rise in importance if the chart has a scarcity of major aspects, as can happen. But remember, they call them minor for a reason.

Table 13-4 lists the most important of the minor aspects.

TABLE 13-4

Minor Aspects

Distance	Name of Aspect	Symbol	Effect
30°	Semi-sextile	⊻	Mildly supportive
45°	Semi-square	∠	Mildly irritating
72°	Quintile	Q	Promotes creativity
135°	Sesquiquadrate	⊡	Stressful and active
144°	Bi-quintile	bQ	Supports creativity
150°	Quincunx or inconjunct	⊼	On again/off again

Are there other minor aspects? You bet. There's the *septile,* the *novile,* and more. I've seen symbols for aspects I've never even heard of. You can reach a point when adding more aspects to a chart only obliterates the big picture. That's why I recommend sticking with the majors.

A Word about Mutual Reception

There are a few situations in which two planets have a special tie regardless of whether they form an aspect. One such circumstance is known as *mutual reception.* It happens when each planet is in a sign ruled by the other planet.

For example, in Albert Einstein's natal chart, which you can see in Chapter 7, Saturn and Mars do not form an aspect. But because Saturn is in Aries, which is ruled by Mars, and Mars is in Capricorn, which is ruled by Saturn, the two planets are said to be in mutual reception. It's as if they understand each other on some level. Both planets are strengthened by the arrangement.

TIP

To find a mutual reception, you have to know which planet rules which sign. If you're not sure, go to Chapter 1, where you can find a Table of Essential Planetary Dignities.

Interpreting the Aspects

In this section, I interpret the main aspects for each of the planets. I bundle sextiles and trines together as harmonious aspects. Their actions are similar, though trines are more powerful. Similarly, I categorize squares and oppositions as hard aspects, though they aren't identical either. In general, a square generates internal conflicts, while oppositions are more likely to create external obstructions.

REMEMBER

There is a system to looking up aspects. Aspects of the Sun always come first, followed by lunar aspects. After that, planetary aspects are listed in order of their distance from the Sun: Mercury, Venus, Mars, Jupiter, Saturn, Uranus, Neptune, and Pluto. So if your chart shows 3° between Mercury and Uranus, astrologers would say that Mercury is conjunct Uranus — not the other way around. You can read about that aspect under the heading "Aspects to Mercury."

Aspects to the Sun

Your Sun sign represents the most essential part of your nature. Some of the aspects it makes with other planets help you shape and express your potential, while other set obstacles in your way.

Sun/Moon

The Sun represents your conscious identity, while the Moon governs your feelings and subconscious self. The Sun/Moon aspect shows how comfortably these two cooperate.

>> **Conjunction:** If your Sun and Moon are conjunct, you were born around a new Moon, with all the vitality and promise that implies. You have clear intentions, eagerness, and the will to initiate; thought completion may be harder to achieve. Examples include Fiona Apple, Mindy Kaling, and Georgia O'Keeffe.

>> **Harmonious aspects:** With your Sun sextile or trine the Moon, you're genial and energetic. Opportunities come your way. All things being equal, you're basically at peace with yourself. Consider yourself blessed.

>> **Hard aspects:** If your Sun and Moon are square, your conscious self desires one thing, and your subconscious yearns for something else. So you're never truly satisfied, and you may unconsciously sabotage yourself. Yet this discomfort turns out to be highly motivating. Legions of accomplished people in every field have this aspect — so many that I'm not even sure it's a disadvantage.

If your Sun and Moon are in opposition, you were born under a full Moon, a time when emotions run high. Restless and conflicted, you find it difficult to match your desires to your abilities. You attract stressful relationships and may overreact to problems. Although a few people with Sun/Moon oppositions screw up in astonishing ways, the opposition also motivates them to conquer the internal divide, crush the external barriers, and become successful. Examples include Samantha Bee, Michael Jackson, and Susan Boyle.

Sun/Mercury

The fiery Sun governs your ego while Mercury rules communication. This aspect reveals the ease with which you express your thoughts.

>> **Conjunction:** These two bodies can never be more than 28° apart, so plenty of people have this aspect. It indicates a nervous disposition. When the conjunction is exceptionally close, within a degree or less, it may indicate an over-the-top level of self-involvement.

>> **Harmonious aspects:** Mercury and the Sun are never far enough apart to form a sextile (60°) or trine (120°). But they can occasionally be separated by 28°, making them semi-sextile, a mildly helpful aspect that strengthens your ability to communicate.

>> **Hard aspects:** Mercury and the Sun are always so close that they never form a hard aspect.

Sun/Venus

How these two planets interact influences your artistic talents, your sociability, and your knack for attracting relationships, money, and beautiful things.

>> **Conjunction:** You're appealing and affectionate. You have a craving for intimacy, a love of pleasure, an inborn aesthetic sensibility, and an abiding

need to be in relationships. Because Venus can never be farther than 48° from the Sun, this is the only major aspect that these two bodies can form.

» **Harmonious aspects:** Venus and the Sun are never far enough apart to form a sextile or a trine. But if they're 30° apart, they're semi-sextile, a friendly minor aspect that supports artistic talents and the expression of affection.

» **Hard aspects:** The Sun and Venus are never in opposition and never square. When they're close to their maximum distance, they're semi-square, a 45° minor aspect that can lead to sexual issues. Think of Hugh Hefner, Bill Clinton, Woody Allen, Bill Cosby, and the Marquis de Sade.

Sun/Mars

This aspect describes the way you mobilize your energy and put your intentions into action.

» **Conjunction:** You're an adventurer with stamina and courage. You're enterprising, competitive, passionate, and willing to take the initiative — a contender in every way. Examples: Idris Elba, Gloria Steinem, poet Natasha Trethewey, and Alexandria Ocasio-Cortez.

» **Harmonious aspects:** Energy is there when you want it. You're assertive without being combative and energetic without being manic.

» **Hard aspects:** Controlling the river of energy that flows through you isn't easy. You tend to overdo it, often by becoming a workaholic. Your temper can spin out of control. You can be contentious and accident-prone, and you have a tendency to act rashly. Examples: Mark Zuckerberg. Also — I know this isn't fair — Lizzie Borden.

Sun/Jupiter

Combine the Sun, which represents your potential, with Jupiter, the bringer of opportunities, and you have an enviable aspect. The challenge is to make use of the link between the two planets — not to waste it.

» **Conjunction:** You're blessed with good fortune, a sense of humor, high intelligence, generosity, a cheerful spirit, and a hopeful attitude. You can also be careless and overconfident, relying on the indisputable fact that luck is with you. Examples: Kanye West, Mick Jagger, Sonia Sotomayor.

» **Harmonious aspects:** This aspect augurs health, success, a pleasing and optimistic approach to life, and a generous nature. Possible downside: Laziness. You love to kick back.

>> **Hard aspects:** You're inclined to exaggerate, to become self-important, to misjudge, and to lack a sense of moderation. Overindulgence may plague you. Even so, this aspect, because it features Jupiter, can deliver lucky breaks. Examples: Fidel Castro, Hunter S. Thompson.

Sun/Saturn

The Sun wants to dazzle. Somber Saturn advocates caution. When these two planets form a major aspect, you will often feel judged or boxed in. This aspect shows the way you handle that trial.

>> **Conjunction:** Restrained but relentless, you're conscientious and introspective. You take yourself seriously. This is a taxing aspect but one that brings direction, determination, and the capacity to overcome your early sense of inadequacy through solid accomplishments.

>> **Harmonious aspects:** You're industrious, goal-oriented, and willing to accept responsibility for your own situation. Purposeful and pragmatic, you look before you leap, and your restraint pays off.

>> **Hard aspects:** In childhood, disappointments and frustrations battered your sense of self-worth. If your Sun and Saturn are square, the resulting woes, among them melancholy, pessimism, and rigidity, can ground you down. If your Sun and Saturn are opposed, external obstructions or enemies may block your path. In each case, advantage comes from harnessing the Saturnian virtues of structure and persistence. Examples: Malala Yousafzai, Virginia Woolf, Bradley Cooper, Zadie Smith.

Sun/Uranus

The Sun represents the shining core of your identity. Uranus represents your most individualistic side. If they form a major aspect, you can be sure of this: You aren't like anybody else.

>> **Conjunction:** An independent denizen of the cosmos, you cleave to your distinctive vision and insist on writing your own script. You're spontaneous, inimitable, part genius and part rebel, a singular personality. Examples: Sacha Baron Cohen, Keanu Reeves, Richard Albert (Baba Ram Dass), Laurie Anderson, Ronan Farrow, Marianne Williamson, Donald J. Trump and, finally, Meryl Streep and Elizabeth Warren, who were born on the same day with the Sun and Uranus at 0° Cancer.

>> **Harmonious aspects:** A free-spirited adventurer, you possess originality, independence, resilience, and a tendency to stumble into unexpectedly fertile patches of luck.

>> **Hard aspects:** You're a provocative, independent, possibly brilliant person who can make rash decisions and very much likes to think of yourself as unique. Rebellious and easily bored, you're likely to head off in unknown directions, especially when you feel ambushed by events. Examples: Victoria Beckham, Elon Musk.

Sun/Neptune

The Sun bestows vitality, while dreamy Neptune brings inspiration . . . or indolence. This combination promotes creative expression at its most rarified.

>> **Conjunction:** You're a dreamer, intuitive and inspired, with a taste for mystical and artistic endeavors but little interest in day-to-day matters. A possible downside: seeing only what you want to see. A possible upside; embracing the world whole, in all its nuance and beauty. Examples: Thomas Alva Edison, M.C. Escher, poet Mary Oliver, astrologer Caroline Casey.

>> **Harmonious aspects:** You have a well-developed sense of intuition and the ability to use your imagination in constructive ways.

>> **Hard aspects:** You have an active imagination combined with a discouraging penchant for deluding yourself. As with all Neptune aspects, deception can be a problem, either because you choose to deceive others or because you're so gullible that anyone — yourself included — can pull the wool over your spectacles.

Sun/Pluto

If these two planets form a major aspect, control is a matter of importance for you. This aspect reveals the way you balance your core identity with your need to express personal power and to deal with authority.

>> **Conjunction:** A vigorous, charismatic person, you have courage, commitment, and willpower. You may struggle with a tendency to dominate or be dominated, and the demon of obsession may infiltrate your thoughts. But you also know how to summon the gods of change and are capable of metamorphosis. Examples include Natalie Wood, Gwyneth Paltrow, and Meghan McCain.

>> **Harmonious aspects:** Strong-willed, persevering, and at ease with power and its uses, you have insight combined with the ability to adapt to circumstances and create positive change.

>> **Hard aspects:** Competition eggs you on. Acutely aware of the uses of personal power, you're manipulative, resourceful, and sometimes intimidating. The challenge, whether you're competing with others or simply trying to fulfill your own considerable ambition, is to avoid becoming overly aggressive or power-crazy. Friedrich Nietzche (Sun in Libra, Pluto in Aries).

Aspects to the Moon

The Moon represents your emotions, instincts, habits, and subconscious.

Moon/Mercury

Do you have a persistent need to tell people how you feel? If Mercury and the Moon form a major aspect, the answer is yes.

>> **Conjunction:** You're intelligent, responsive, and in touch with your emotions. You know how to communicate confidently and with grace.

>> **Harmonious aspects:** You think clearly, communicate effectively, have an excellent memory, and can even claim a sense of humor.

>> **Hard aspects:** You respond quickly but your thoughts and your feelings may not be aligned. You often feel that people misunderstand you, and criticism makes you apprehensive and fretful.

Moon/Venus

If the Moon and Venus form a major aspect, your emotional needs and your need for love (and beauty) are intertwined.

>> **Conjunction:** A connoisseur of comfort, you're responsive, appealing, kind, and pleasant to be around. Your mood depends on your relationships, and you can get all wrapped up in the game of love.

>> **Harmonious aspects:** You express your affections easily. You're a likable person with finely honed sensibilities, even if you do occasionally drop into the pit of self-indulgence.

>> **Hard aspects:** Affairs of the heart travel a bumpy road, and you can't help feeling that love is a struggle. That doesn't mean you won't find the intimate bond you're seeking. It just means that, on the way, you'll accumulate stories.

Moon/Mars

If you have a major aspect between the Moon and Mars, you're assertive about the way you express your emotions.

» **Conjunction:** You're emotionally impatient and quick to anger. You let people know how you feel, and you aren't necessarily diplomatic about it.

» **Harmonious aspects:** Courageous, energetic, confident, and direct, you're a risk-taker who's always ready to jump into new situations.

» **Hard aspects:** Rash, defensive, and impulsive, you're competitive and combative. You don't hold back from voicing your opinions, and your fluctuating moods can provoke conflict. No matter what face you show the world, sooner or later you have to come to terms with your anger.

Moon/Jupiter

The Moon wants to pour out her feelings, while extravagant Jupiter says "More is more" — which makes for a cascade of emotions.

» **Conjunction:** You're warm, optimistic, considerate, and empathetic, a person of huge feeling even if you do occasionally promise more than you can deliver. You have faith in your own abilities. You feel best when your options are multiplying and your universe expanding.

» **Harmonious aspects:** You're responsive, gentle, and supportive: a genuine human being.

» **Hard aspects:** It's all or nothing with you. You're ecstatic or grief-stricken, blissed out or on the verge of collapse. You have trouble controlling your feelings and tend to go overboard.

Moon/Saturn

Saturn is the planet of restraint, and the Moon is all about unbridled emotions. This pair might be called "Sense and Sensibility."

» **Conjunction:** The past has a hold on you. You may suffer from self-doubt and despondency as a result of a less-than-warm relationship with your mother but you also possess admirable self-control. Common sense helps you direct your feelings in a more rewarding direction. Example: Jane Austen.

» **Harmonious aspects:** Disciplined and sensible, you make a prodigious effort to manage your emotions. This explains how daredevil Evel Knievel and horror writer Stephen King do what they do.

>> **Hard aspects:** A history of emotional deprivation makes you hesitant and self-conscious. Though pessimism, repressed emotions, self-doubt, and difficulties with women may distress you, your understanding grows with maturity, as does your ability to find contentment.

Moon/Uranus

Why settle for dull predictability when you don't have to? And you don't — not if the ever-changing Moon in your chart pairs up with wayward Uranus, the planet of defiance.

>> **Conjunction:** Impetuous and reckless, you attract and pursue quirky people and odd experiences, and you may wrestle with mood swings. This can be a volatile combination.

>> **Harmonious aspects:** A rebel against restriction and convention, you value your autonomy, even within relationships. You're attracted to stimulating people and uncommon situations.

>> **Hard aspects:** Talented and distractible, you can't tolerate restrictions. You can get worked up, and occasionally you generate (or attract) a crisis. To maintain your independence, you may unconsciously distance yourself from others.

Moon/Neptune

The Moon harbors your tender private side, while Neptune cloaks everything in mystery. Together this pair can sensitize and extend your empathy and imagination — or trap you in an emotional fog.

>> **Conjunction:** You pick up on the slightest emotional clues and often feel overwhelmed, drained, or self-pitying. You're vulnerable and kind, with spiritual leanings, psychic potential, an active dream life, and a keen imagination. It can also promote escapism and substance abuse.

>> **Harmonious aspects:** Compassionate and intuitive, you find it difficult to say no. You're easily inspired, but inclined to float off on a daydream. Turning fantasy into reality involves work — and that can be a problem.

>> **Hard aspects:** Although you struggle with wishful thinking, delicate feelings, and irrational fears (such as hypochondria), you're creative and receptive, with psychic sensitivities.

Moon/Pluto

Pluto lends intensity and drama to the emotional issues overseen by the Moon. A major aspect between these two means that your feelings are deep and your perceptions are laser sharp.

>> **Conjunction:** You're magnetic, controlling, possessive, intense, and compulsive. You resist changes. But when it's unavoidable, you acknowledge the need and do just fine.

>> **Harmonious aspects:** You handle changes well. You also experience a compelling need, from time to time, to purge yourself of old feelings and rejuvenate yourself.

>> **Hard aspects:** You're emotionally inhibited. Fearful of trusting other people or failing to maintain control, you manipulate situations in an effort to gain control and overcome your fears. Domestic upheavals and power struggles are painful but can clear the way.

Aspects to Mercury

Mercury represents the way you think, your curiosity, the way you express yourself, and your intellect.

Mercury/Venus

Lovely Venus, the muse of the zodiac, bestows grace and charm on Mercury's mental gymnastics.

>> **Conjunction:** You express yourself with elegance, humor, and possibly literary aptitude. An attentive listener, you delight in juicy conversation and information exchange.

>> **Harmonious aspects:** You're alert, diplomatic, and a skilled communicator.

>> **Hard aspect (sort of):** Mercury and Venus are never farther than 76° apart, so they can't form a square or opposition. But they can be semi-square — a 45° angle that may enhance your creative abilities but can also stimulate you to be critical of those you love.

Mercury/Mars

When Mercury, the nimble ruler of the intellect, teams up with the planet of aggression, you get a sharp, lawyerlike intelligence.

- » **Conjunction:** You have a lively, argumentative mind and the intellectual authority to win most of your debates, whether you know anything about the topic or not.

- » **Harmonious aspects:** You're forthright and mentally astute, with a decisive intelligence and the power of persuasion.

- » **Hard aspects:** You respond immediately and sometimes recklessly. You have a quick tongue and a tendency to be combative. Examples: Sandra Oh, Randy Newman.

Mercury/Jupiter

When the guardian of the intellect connects with the planet of expansion, thoughts and theories percolate through the ether. This pair can inspire solid ideas or degenerate into distracted trivia.

- » **Conjunction:** You're smart, philosophical, open-minded, and aware. You ask the important questions and can influence others. Gathering information absorbs you; mastering new skills makes you happy.

- » **Harmonious aspects:** You're a persuasive speaker, affable, optimistic, and clear-eyed, with a multitude of interests.

- » **Hard aspects:** You're filled with exciting ideas and the best of intentions. But you tend to exaggerate and leap to conclusions, your judgment can be offbase, and sometimes you talk too much.

Mercury/Saturn

Fleet–footed Mercury rules the thinking process while stern Saturn is the zodiac's proponent of control, discipline, and getting things done. Together, they put thoughts into action.

- » **Conjunction:** You're cautious and reserved, with a rational mind, a dry sense of humor, and an appreciation for useful knowledge.

- » **Harmonious aspects:** You're methodical and intelligent, with a gift for concentration. You absorb information quickly and can put it to good use.

- » **Hard aspects:** You don't take things lightly, even when you should. Though you're an effective planner, you can be inflexible, melancholy, and uncomfortable with new ideas.

Mercury/Uranus

Mercury represents the way you think; Uranus symbolizes the lightning strike of insight. Together, these two encourage the farseeing inventor, the literary pioneer, the brilliant scientist, or the talkative eccentric down the street.

>> **Conjunction:** The Eureka! aspect. You're a progressive thinker given to sudden insights and electrifying ideas. You have a novel way of communicating and even a touch of genius.

>> **Harmonious aspects:** New ideas excite you. Your mind is unconstrained and bright, and you express yourself with style and effervescence.

>> **Hard aspects:** Your spontaneous, idiosyncratic intellect can take you far. Sometimes brilliant, sometimes irritable and impatient, you rebel against authority, routine, and convention, and in so doing you may trigger the forces of tension and conflict. Still, no one thinks the way you do. Examples: Benjamin Franklin, Jane Austen, Jimi Hendrix, Howard Stern, Ursula Le Guin, Wanda Sykes.

Mercury/Neptune

Mercury thinks and talks; Neptune floats and fantasizes. When they collaborate, Mercury can manifest Neptune's murkiest vision, while Neptune can lift and illuminate Mercury's thoughts. When they are at odds, Neptune can dissolve Mercury's aspirational To Do list with little more than a sigh.

>> **Conjunction:** You're a visionary with an inspired imagination, a multitalented artist capable of conjuring worlds, a dreamer sensitive to mood and skilled with language. But when you're in the grip of an idée fixe, you can lose touch with reality. Examples: Taylor Swift, Neil Gaiman, Stephen King.

>> **Harmonious aspects:** You have a discriminating mind, an artistic imagination, and a graceful way of phrasing your thoughts and conveying your ideas.

>> **Hard aspects:** Fantasy and reality vie for your attention, and it isn't always clear which one is winning. At your best, you're intuitive and visionary. At your worst, you are disorganized and oblivious, with a tenuous grasp of the truth.

Mercury/Pluto

When Pluto, the zodiac's alchemist, connects with quick-thinking Mercury, the combination gives you a commanding intelligence and shrewdness to peer past the obvious.

>> **Conjunction:** You're analytical, incisive, and skilled at digging up secrets. With your penetrating intelligence, you can be a gifted researcher, investigative reporter, or detective. This aspect brings depth, writing aptitude, and willpower, along with the capacity to conquer fearful or obsessive thoughts.

>> **Harmonious aspects:** You're a shrewd, observant thinker who can dig beneath the surface, grapple with whatever you find there, and emerge, transformed.

>> **Hard aspects:** You're thoughtful, resources, curious, and determined, as well as tense and combative, with an inclination to brood.

Aspects to Venus

Venus symbolizes love, relationships, art, pleasure, possessions, and money.

Venus/Mars

In classical mythology, Venus and Mars — the goddess of love and the god of war — were lovers. In your chart, they kindle the forces of desire and sensuality.

>> **Conjunction:** Demonstrative and magnetic, you radiate pure life force. You have no trouble attracting others because people want to be near you. Your warmth entices, as does your sexuality. But you like to see sparks fly and may unconsciously create tumultuous relationships.

>> **Harmonious aspects:** Your loving manner and overall attractiveness bring romantic fulfillment. Mars lends vitality to Venus, enhancing your liaison with all things Venusian, including music, dance, art, fashion, interior design, and money.

>> **Hard aspects:** You aren't sure what you want, especially in romantic liaisons. As a result, your love life may be troubled by arguments, unhappiness, and tension. Examples: Demi Moore, Hillary Clinton, Katharine Hepburn.

Venus/Jupiter

When amorous Venus meets generous Jupiter in a birth chart, the result is an out-pouring of affection and a love of luxury, art, and beauty.

>> **Conjunction:** This is a lucky aspect. Because you're affectionate and giving, you attract love, friendship, and even money — which is amazing, considering how reckless and self-indulgent you can be. This aspect also confers artistic ability and a keen awareness of beauty.

>> **Harmonious aspects:** This fortunate aspect increases the ease with which you attract attention, make money, and choose the right mate.

>> **Hard aspects:** You go overboard. You eat or drink or spend to excess, you're unreasonably demanding, or you blow your feelings out of proportion. One way or another, excess is an issue.

Venus/Saturn

Restrictive Saturn inhibits affectionate Venus. This aspect grounds and strengthens your feelings but can bring suffering and delays in love.

>> **Conjunction:** Emotionally reserved and afraid of being hurt, you take yourself too seriously to treat romance in a lighthearted, casual way. You're most comfortable in a relationship with someone older or more established than yourself. Love is something you approach with caution. This aspect also builds your artistic talents.

>> **Harmonious aspects:** Emotionally and financially, you value security over excitement. Responsible and loyal, you seek an enduring, loving, mature partnership — and a well-stocked portfolio.

>> **Hard aspects:** Romance can be a struggle. Defensive and afraid of rejection, you hide behind a wall of your own creation. Even when you find a fulfilling partnership (and plenty of people with this aspect are happily married), you may feel isolated or deprived. Something similar happens with money. In both cases, fear of loss is a feeling you live with.

Venus/Uranus

If Venus, the divinity of love, and unconventional Uranus cavort in your birth chart, you're the impetuous star of your own soap opera.

>> **Conjunction:** This is the lightning-bolt aspect, the one that offers you a buoyant personality and a dramatic, unstable love life. Like Elizabeth Taylor (married eight times),'60s It-Girl Edie Sedgwick, or Miley Cyrus, you want instant attraction and fireworks.

>> **Harmonious aspects:** In friendship as in romance, you're drawn to people who are exciting and offbeat. You're original, artistically talented, and lucky in love. Plus, you have the enviable — but entirely unpredictable — ability to attract windfalls of cash.

>> **Hard aspects:** Looking for a steady relationship with an appropriate person? I doubt it. You seek the thrill of the forbidden. Out-of-the-blue love is part of your story; sudden betrayal may be another. Among the people in my files with a hard aspect between Venus and Uranus, I find one who had an affair with her sister's spouse, one who ran off with her best friend's husband, one who married her first cousin, and several who defied expectation by marrying someone of another race or nationality. Another example: Diana, Princess of Wales.

Venus/Neptune

Venus lives for romance and beauty. Glamorous Neptune encourages mystery and magic. When they're in sync, you walk on air, but events can bring you back down to earth in a hurry.

>> **Conjunction:** Your compassion and vivid imagination can make you an inspired artist, or they can get you into hot water, especially in romance. You're an idealist and a spiritual seeker who may let your desire for love cloud your vision. Examples: Leonard Cohen, Amelia Earhart, Alice B. Toklas.

>> **Harmonious aspects:** You can be gentle, mystical, musical, refined, poetic — or lazy and self-indulgent.

>> **Hard aspects:** Illusion enters your life in a positive way through art, music, and film. But you're prone to starry-eyed infatuation. Being realistic about romance isn't your strength. You fall for Heathcliff every time — until, at last, you don't. Examples: Tina Turner, Mia Farrow, Kim Kardashian.

Venus/Pluto

Love meets obsession. You can guess what happens. Intrigue and passion are watchwords for this pair.

>> **Conjunction:** You're jealous, possessive, profoundly sexual, and controlling. This aspect also confers artistic depth and financial aptitude.

>> **Harmonious aspects:** Intense but not destructive, you attract powerful people, both in love and in business.

>> **Hard aspects:** This aspect brings passion and can make you magnetically appealing, which doesn't stop you from becoming fixated on someone who isn't right for you. The good news is that Pluto doesn't stand still. You evolve, like it or not.

Aspects to Mars

Mars represents your will, desires, drive, vitality, and aggression.

Mars/Jupiter

A robust, enthusiastic pair: Daring, undaunted Mars and upbeat Jupiter, avatar of abundance.

>> **Conjunction:** Why does the most famous astrological song ever written ("Age of Aquarius" by the Fifth Dimension) suggest that we will experience peace and love "when the Moon is in the seventh house and Jupiter aligns with Mars"? Frankly, I have no idea. I will say this: If Jupiter aligns with Mars in your chart, you have initiative, good timing, vigor, and confidence. Queen Elizabeth II, the longest-reigning monarch in British history, has this aspect — plus, her Moon is in the seventh house.

>> **Harmonious aspects:** Setting ambitious goals comes naturally to you. You're adventurous, untiring, self-assured, and stalwart — a magnificent combination.

>> **Hard aspects:** You have stamina and drive along with a fondness for the extravagant gesture. Moderation, though oft recommended by warier souls, is not your way.

Mars/Saturn

Hot-blooded Mars is the planet of action; somber Saturn is the lord of caution. They don't much like each other, but they can work it out.

>> **Conjunction:** At its best, this aspect brings self-discipline, endurance, and courage. At its worst, it leads to shyness, inhibition, resentment, and destructive behavior.

>> **Harmonious aspects:** You're ambitious, decisive, industrious, and sensible. You get things done.

>> **Hard aspects:** Impatience does you in. You feel blocked and frustrated. Plus, you may feel that you have enemies, and run-ins with authority could be all too common in your life. This is a challenging aspect. Just ask Anderson Cooper, Tim Cook, Dennis Rodman, Daryl Hannah, Richard Pryor, RuPaul, and Robert Downey, Jr.

Mars/Uranus

Impatient Mars and unpredictable Uranus: the original bad-boy combination of the zodiac. These two just can't help stirring up trouble.

» **Conjunction:** You're unrestrained and determined, with unconventional sexual attitudes, unusual desires, and tremendous dynamism. But your energy is erratic, and you may be accident-prone.

» **Harmonious aspects:** Jumpy and outspoken, you pursue unusual goals, seek the new, and react to threatening situations with alacrity. But do you use your considerable vitality in constructive ways, or do you fritter it away? Your choice.

» **Hard aspects:** You're a risk-taker and a free spirit whose rebellious ways can disrupt everything around you. At its worst, this aspect stimulates truly ridiculous acting-out behavior and accidents. At its best, it encourages independence and adventure.

Mars/Neptune

Two scenarios: Mystical Neptune lolls around in a foggy reverie, while heedless Mars charges into battle. Sparks shoot off in all directions. Or: Mars fuels Neptune's creativity, setting it on a trajectory that runs from airy nothing straight into the manifested world.

» **Conjunction:** Despite your talent, you are insecure and find it difficult to marshal your energy, perhaps because your goals are impractical and vague. Or the opposite may occur: Your Neptunian vision could be so inspiring that it allows you to overcome your doubts and actually accomplish something.

» **Harmonious aspects:** You're romantic, artistic, and able to direct your dreams and inspirations into action.

» **Hard aspects:** You're idealistic but readily discouraged, with a tendency to drift off course or indulge in escapist behavior.

Mars/Pluto

You draw from a deep well of energy and purpose. This aspect brings fierce ambition and extraordinary endurance.

» **Conjunction:** Endowed with enormous reserves of energy, you're aggressive and hardworking. You go after what you want with stunning determination. This is a formidable aspect. Examples: Hillary Clinton, Malcolm X, Paul McCartney.

>> **Harmonious aspects:** You have clear-cut likes and dislikes, confidence, and the rare ability to end a relationship or a job without collapsing. Your fearlessness may not apply in every area of life, but it enables you to go after your deepest desires with fervor and commitment.

>> **Hard aspects:** You fight to contain your passions and to avoid unnecessary skirmishes and confrontations. Though you may undermine yourself, you have impressive stamina and the willingness to eradicate damaging behaviors in pursuit of what you want. The struggle may be monumental, but you're up to it. Examples: Shonda Rhimes, Angelina Jolie, Justin Trudeau.

Aspects to Jupiter

Jupiter represents prosperity, wisdom, abundance, and growth. Its placement in your horoscope tells you where you can look for luck and opportunity.

Jupiter/Saturn

Expansive Jupiter and restrictive Saturn aren't natural allies. Mix them together, and you get tension — and determination.

>> **Conjunction:** When gloomy Saturn encounters optimistic Jupiter, idealism gets squashed by practicality, and frustration is rampant. Your path is littered with impediments, but your capacity for hard work is breathtaking. This demanding aspect comes around about every 20 years. Look for it in the charts of those born in 1901, 1921, 1940 to 1941, 1960 to 1961, 1981, 2000, and 2020. Examples: John Lennon, Jennifer Hudson, Michael J. Fox.

>> **Harmonious aspects:** You're sensible and cool-headed enough to recognize your limitations and compensate with your strengths. Saturn prods you to develop a strategy and apply self-discipline. Jupiter opens doors, enabling you to turn daydreams into realities. Examples: Jane Goodall, Gloria Steinem, Steve Jobs.

>> **Hard aspects:** Discontent, bad timing, and tension plague you. A tug of war between the forces of expansion and the guardians of restriction keeps you off balance. On some deep level, you fear that your judgment is unreliable, and your confidence suffers accordingly. Examples: Reese Witherspoon, Winono Ryder, Guillermo del Toro.

Jupiter/Uranus

Surprises abound when benevolent Jupiter joins Uranus, the planet of the unexpected. Uranus adds a maverick twist to Jupiter's big-hearted ability to unlatch doors you didn't know were there.

>> **Conjunction:** You're a risk-taker who often succeeds in being in the right place at the right time, sometimes through sheer happenstance. This is the aspect of sudden good fortune and rare opportunities — but, as with everything Uranus touches, those blessings may not come in the form you would expect.

>> **Harmonious aspects:** You are alert, conscious, and generous. When unimagined possibilities come your way — and they will — you rise to the challenge.

>> **Hard aspects:** The predetermined path is distasteful to you. You make startling choices and may suffer when your impulsive decisions turn out to be less than prudent. But better that the well-trod path to mediocrity. You're a natural rebel.

Jupiter/Neptune

Bountiful Jupiter encourages impressionable Neptune to dream big. This aspect heightens imagination, idealism, and spiritual longings.

>> **Conjunction:** Your idealism, financial well-being, artistic efforts, and spiritual life benefit from this aspect. You're friendly and sympathetic but predisposed to zoning out or becoming preoccupied. Nonetheless, you're blessed with a certain amount of luck. Be careful that it doesn't blind you to the truth.

>> **Harmonious aspects:** You're compassionate, gentle, insightful, and lucky, with an innate attraction to artistic and spiritual pursuits.

>> **Hard aspects:** You can be way too gullible, and your refusal to face facts can drive your friends to distraction. This aspect can bring money and talent, especially of the musical variety. You may also be naïve and scattered, and pie-in-the-sky thinking can be your downfall.

Jupiter/Pluto

Jupiter brings opportunities and expands whatever it touches — the good and the bad. Pluto represents the journey inward and the power of transformation.

>> **Conjunction:** When these two planets are joined, you have strong convictions and can become a powerful agent of change. Examples: Peter Dinklage, Cory Booker, Jennifer Lopez, and Bill Gates.

>> **Harmonious aspects:** When times of change roll around, you benefit from the upheaval. A compelling leader, you combine foresight and vision with tactics that actually work. Example: Ruth Bader Ginsberg,

>> **Hard aspects:** You want to change the world. At your best, you bravely confront the most fearsome of Goliaths — and win. But you harbor a desire for power, and you can be self-destructive, and fanatical. This is a powerful aspect that appears in the charts of powerful people. Examples: Eminem, Bruce Lee, Jon Stewart.

Aspects to Saturn

Saturn symbolizes limitation, contraction, restriction, responsibility, authority, and the need for structure and stability. Its placement tells you where you have to face facts, establish boundaries, and get to work.

Saturn/Uranus

Tradition (Saturn) meets innovation (Uranus). Cautious Saturn wants to follow the rules. Defiant Uranus wants to break them. With this combo, something's gotta give.

>> **Conjunction:** You have drive, determination, and leadership potential. You also have a certain amount of inner turmoil because it's hard to play it safe and rebel at the same time. But there is a middle way. By combining the brilliance of Uranus with the pragmatism of Saturn, you can bring your ideas to life and find your place in the world.

>> **Harmonious aspects:** You're determined and decisive, able to blend the attainable goals and objectives of Saturn with the experimental, freewheeling approach of Uranus. This is an aspect of accomplishment.

>> **Hard aspects:** Compromise is difficult. You may feel hampered by circumstances, controlled by others, denied the recognition or material assistance you deserve. All too often, you may feel that your most idiosyncratic and extraordinary qualities somehow don't find an outlet. Either that, or you may feel that your need for stability remains unmet. Either way, applying fresh (Uranian) solutions to old (Saturnian) problems is one approach to this dilemma.

Saturn/Neptune

Saturn follows directions and builds systems. Dreamy Neptune soaks up impressions and dissolves boundaries. Together, they either strengthen the forces of perception or cause you to wander aimlessly, in search of something you cannot name.

>> **Conjunction:** If the two planets are well-matched, you will be both disciplined and imaginative in the pursuit of your dreams. If stern Saturn dominates, you distrust your intuition and muzzle your creative impulses. If woozy Neptune prevails, it undercuts your efforts to be in control.

>> **Harmonious aspects:** Neptunian idealism combines with Saturn's level-headedness, allowing you to direct your flights of fancy in concrete ways.

>> **Hard aspects:** You don't trust people easily, you tend to hold back, and you may be reclusive. You also have trouble getting organized. The placement of Saturn in your chart indicates where you need structure. Chances are you know exactly what you should do to provide that for yourself. The problem is that, thanks to mysterious Neptune, you may have trouble doing it.

Saturn/Pluto

In mythology, Pluto reigns over the underworld. In your chart, Pluto is a portent of evolutionary change, while Saturn, the taskmaster, forces you to set boundaries and do what needs to be done. Neither planet is a lot of fun. But when they link up in your chart, they fuel your sense of purpose and put you on the road to deep, permanent metamorphosis.

>> **Conjunction:** Pluto is all about transformation, but wary Saturn restricts its action with hard-to-break habits and a mother lode of resistance. To get around this, you need a systematic approach to problem solving, a healthy dose of resolve, and a rueful — or joyous — acceptance of the fact that although change may be glacial in its speed, glaciers nonetheless reshaped the world.

>> **Harmonious aspects:** A trine or sextile connecting Saturn and Pluto fortifies your willpower, sense of control, confidence, and endurance.

>> **Hard aspects:** Obsessive thoughts or compulsive behaviors can keep you in their grip until you find a way to diminish their power. Although obstacles of various sorts, internal and external, may slow you down, you have exceptional tenacity and can overcome them. Examples: Nancy Pelosi, Toni Morrison, Tony Kushner.

Aspects to Uranus, Neptune, and Pluto

Uranus represents individuality, disruption, revolution, and the unpredictable. Neptune symbolizes spiritual strivings, dreams, visions, and the imagination. Pluto represents obsession, compulsion, death, rebirth, and regeneration.

REMEMBER

Uranus, Neptune, and Pluto, the three outer planets, travel across the zodiac so slowly that the aspects that they form are in orb for a long time, and their greatest influence is on generations, not on individuals. Neptune and Pluto, for example, have been sextile — about 60° apart — since the 1940s, and they will continue to be sextile through much of the 2030s. So the mere fact of having such an aspect in your chart doesn't distinguish you. It merely makes you a member of your generation, with all the pluses and minuses that implies.

There are, however, certain circumstances that can elevate the importance of an aspect. An aspect involving the outer planets can rise to prominence in the chart of an individual when:

>> Either of the planets occupies an angle or is conjunct your Ascendant or Midheaven.

>> Either body makes several close aspects to other planets and in particular to the Sun, the Moon, or the ruler of your Ascendant.

>> Either planet rules your Sun sign, Moon sign, or rising sign.

Uranus governs Aquarius, Neptune presides over Pisces, and Pluto rules Scorpio.

REMEMBER

Uranus/Neptune

Uranus, the planet of revolution, and mystical Neptune, the planet of dreams and visions, inspire you, bring you insight, and shake things up.

>> **Conjunction:** In 1993, Uranus and Neptune were exactly conjunct for the first time since 1821 — a trick they won't repeat until around 2165. Anyone born with this aspect is likely to have an innovative approach to social change. Examples: Susan B. Anthony, Clara Barton, Frederick Douglass, George Eliot, and Alexandria Ocasio-Cortez.

>> **Harmonious aspects:** If you have a trine or a sextile between Neptune and Uranus, you belong to a generation that's compassionate, utopian, and spiritually inclined.

>> **Hard aspects:** You're one of a kind, edgy and original, especially in times of unrest. This aspect is emphasized if either planet closely aspects a third. Examples: Spike Lee, Bill Maher, Sonia Sotomayor.

Uranus/Pluto

Unconventional Uranus and heavy-duty Pluto collaborate to promote crucial, sometimes earth-shattering, changes.

>> **Conjunction:** Ever wonder why the 1960s were so turbulent? Here's why: For the first time in 115 years, unruly Uranus was conjunct Pluto, the planet of transformation. Transiting planets affect everyone — not just babies born under their influence. If you were born during that decade — if you're a true child of the '60s — you're independent and willful, and you carry that Woodstockian spark of wild abandon within you.

>> **Harmonious aspects:** Trines and sextiles between freedom-loving Uranus and Pluto usher in disruptive changes but allow you to direct the energy that's released in creative ways.

>> **Hard aspects:** When catastrophe strikes, you suppress your natural reactions, thus inadvertently producing, on top of everything else, an extra measure of anxiety. You're not alone in this: This aspect has generational influence. Like everyone else in your generation, you were born during America's Great Depression, and you've seen it all.

Neptune/Pluto

Neptune, emissary of the imagination, responds to dreams, music, poetry, mysticism, and the unseen. Pluto, lord of the underworld, plumbs the caverns of the forbidden. Together, they make a mighty duo and inspire a heroic quest.

>> **Conjunction:** This rare conjunction, which rolled around most recently in 1892 and will not reappear until the 24th century, combines Neptunian spirituality with the Plutonian drive for power and renewal. Examples: Paramahansa Yogananda, author of *Autobiography of a Yogi,* and J. R. R. Tolkien, author of *The Lord of the Rings.*

>> **Harmonious aspects:** For almost a century, Neptune and Pluto have been roughly sextile, an aspect that links the mystical yearnings of Neptune with the transformative mojo of Pluto, creating an upsurge of interest in spirituality and the occult.

>> **Hard aspects:** Energy tinged with sexuality or the supernatural can bubble up through the cracks of this charged aspect, but the direction it takes depends on the individual. Two examples, born a week apart: Queen Victoria, who lent her name to an era known for its repressive ways, and Walt Whitman, whose poetry is suffused with joyous sexuality and uninhibited love.

Chapter **14**

Interpreting Your Birth Chart: A Guide

ost astrologers agree that Sun sign astrology, which describes types rather than individuals, is only a starting point. But Sun sign astrology can claim one advantage: It's simple. A full astrological chart, on the other hand, with its web of planets, signs, houses, and aspects, is as complex and confounding as an actual human being — and just as hard to understand.

Fortunately, you don't have to be psychic to be an astrologer. But you do need a system. This chapter provides just that.

Step One: Identifying Overall Patterns

Leaf through a pile of birth charts, and you may notice that in some the planets are huddled together in one part of the circle, while in others they're scattered around the wheel like numbers on a clock. These groupings can be revealing regardless of the signs and planets involved. Astrologers have developed two main ways of assessing the configurations of an astrological chart:

>> **Hemisphere analysis:** This one is easy. All you have to do is divide the chart circle in half, once horizontally and once vertically, and count the number of planets on each side.

>> **Pattern analysis:** This method, pioneered by astrologer Marc Edmund Jones in his *Guide to Horoscope Interpretation,* analyzes the way the planets are strewn around the wheel of the horoscope.

Both methods rely only on patterns, not on signs and planets.

Hemisphere analysis

A quick glance at your horoscope provides an easy entry into interpretation — and all you have to do is count. First locate the *horizon line* in your chart — the line running from the Ascendant to the Descendant, as shown in Figure 14-1. (Turn to Chapter 11 for more on your Ascendant and Descendant.) If seven or more planets are above the horizon, you're an extrovert who looks to the external world for recognition and endorsement. If most of your planets populate the area below the line, you're an introvert who needs privacy, seeks personal fulfillment, and may be uncomfortable in the limelight.

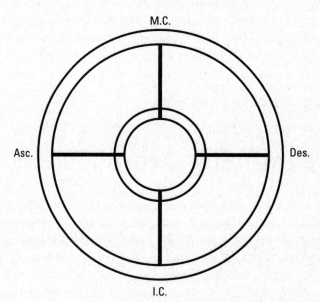

FIGURE 14-1:
Dividing your chart by the horizon and the meridian.

© *John Wiley & Sons, Inc.*

Now divide your chart in half vertically or along the *meridian,* which runs from your Midheaven, or M.C., at the twelve o'clock spot on your chart to your I.C. at the six o'clock spot (refer to Figure 14-1). That line splits the horoscope into two sectors: the eastern hemisphere on the left and the western hemisphere on the right. If most of your planets lie on the eastern or left side of the horoscope, you have the enviable ability to make things happen, to pave your own way. You're highly independent, but you may also be intolerant of people who can't seem to call the shots the way you can.

If your chart leans to the right, so to speak, with seven or more planets on the western or right side of the circle, you're more dependent on circumstances than you may appear to be. You need to seize the moment when it arrives, and you may feel that you must bend to the demands of others in order to succeed.

Most of us have planets on both sides of divide, no matter which way you bisect the circle. But there are some people, including the greatest of the great, whose planets occupy only one hemisphere. Serena Williams, the most gifted female athlete on Earth, has all her planets on the right side of her chart. That doesn't in any way belittle her accomplishments. It merely suggests that she responds to circumstances and is adaptable. Not so Beyoncé. With every one of her planets on the left side of her chart, she is self-reliant and independent, a self-starter with a will of iron.

REMEMBER

The Ascendant symbolizes your surface personality. The Descendant represents your approach to marriage and partnerships. The Midheaven or M.C. — the apex of your chart — describes your ambition and public image. At the bottom of your chart, the Imum Coeli, or I.C. indicates your attitude toward home and family.

Pattern analysis

In 1941, astrologer Marc Edmund Jones (a Libran) identified seven planetary patterns which, like hemispheric division, operate without regard to specific signs and planets. Ever since then, students of astrology have been exploring the meaning of those patterns. Here they are:

>> **The bundle:** If all your planets are concentrated within four signs or about 120° (a *trine*), you have a bundle chart, regardless of which signs are involved or where on the wheel that bundle of planets happens to fall. This pattern, shown in Figure 14-2, grants you a clear focus, firm interests, confidence, and personal strength. It also limits you: You're strong where you're strong and thoroughly unconscious (or uninterested) where you aren't. Examples: George W. Bush, Sylvester Stallone, Paul McCartney, and Scarlett Johansson.

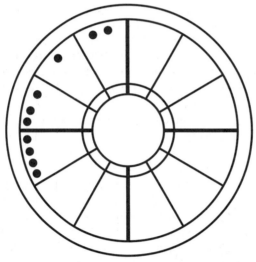

FIGURE 14-2:
The bundle
pattern.

>> **The bowl:** If your planets cover more than 120° but no more than 180° (or half the zodiac), you have a bowl chart, as shown in Figure 14-3. This highly motivating pattern can create a frustrating feeling that something is missing, combined with a determination to fill that void. These people don't sit around waiting. They're activists, and they get things done, like it or not. Examples: Abraham Lincoln, Vincent van Gogh, Amelia Earhart, Billie Jean King, Ella Fitzgerald, and Donald J. Trump.

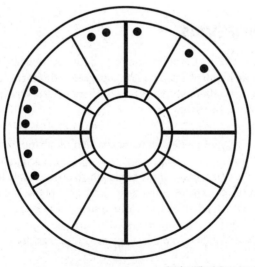

FIGURE 14-3:
The bowl pattern.

>> **The bucket:** A bucket chart (sometimes called a funnel) is like a bowl except that one planet (or two in close conjunction) is separated from the rest, as in Figure 14-4. That singleton planet, the handle of the bucket, becomes the focus of the chart. Because its needs are always paramount, Marc Edmund Jones compared that lone planet to a toothache. It commands attention — and it hurts. By sign and by house, it acts as a counterweight to the rest of the chart. Four people with bucket charts: Taylor Swift; Harry, Duke of Sussex; Harry's sister-in-law, Catherine, Duchess of Cambridge; and Alexandria Ocasio-Cortez.

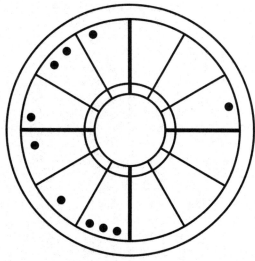

FIGURE 14-4:
The bucket pattern.

>> **The locomotive:** If the ten planets in your chart line up neatly over two-thirds of the zodiac, as shown in Figure 14-5, you've got drive, stamina, and practicality. The two most important planets are the first and the last: the locomotive, which leads the starry parade when the chart is rotated in a clockwise direction, and the caboose, which picks up the rear. Isaac Newton, George Washington, Jennifer Lawrence, and Oprah Winfrey share this pattern.

>> **The splash:** Just as it sounds, the planets in this relatively rare pattern are sprinkled more or less evenly around the celestial wheel, as in Figure 14-6. With a splash chart, a profusion of experience is yours for the taking. The drawback? Much as you enjoy splashing around in that bright blue pool, your energy can be scattered and diffuse. Examples of the splash at its finest: George Harrison, Steve Jobs, and the French politician and physician Bernard Kouchner, co-founder of Doctors without Borders.

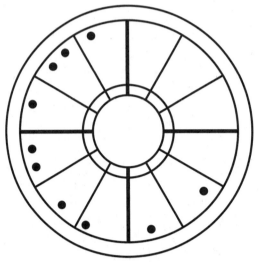

FIGURE 14-5:
The locomotive pattern.

© John Wiley & Sons, Inc.

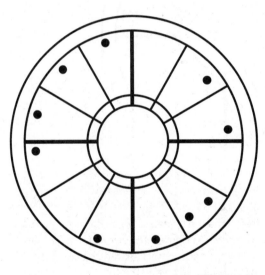

FIGURE 14-6:
The splash pattern.

© John Wiley & Sons, Inc.

>> **The splay:** This pattern, shown in Figure 14-7, is similar to the splash except that here, the planets are distributed unevenly over the chart, with as many as three clumps of three or more planets. People with this pattern have a multitude of talents but it takes them a while to find themselves as they ricochet from one activity to another. When at last they settle into something, they are strongly dedicated, refusing to bow to popular opinion or to be pushed. Example: W. B. Yeats.

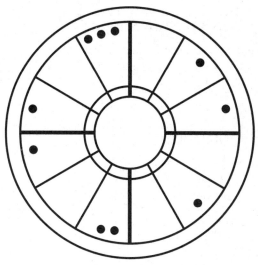

FIGURE 14-7:
The splay pattern.

>> **The seesaw:** If you have two groups of opposing planets separated by a couple of empty houses on each side, as shown in Figure 14-8, you're always bouncing up and down on the seesaw of circumstance. An excellent mediator, judge, and administrator, you can view things objectively because you're supremely aware of the two sides of your own nature. But you may feel internally split because you have two sets of needs and talents, and you may find it a challenge to satisfy both. Examples include Whitney Houston, Ted Kennedy, Frank Sinatra, Malcolm Gladwell, Alexander McQueen, and Barack Obama.

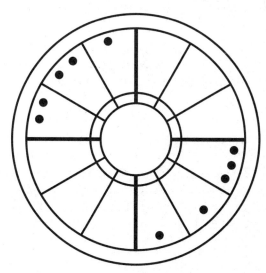

FIGURE 14-8:
The seesaw
pattern.

TWO SINGLETON SENSATIONS

Whenever you find a birth chart with a true singleton — that is, a bucket chart with one planet sitting apart from all the others — you have found a key to the person. Here are two examples from my files:

- **Lulu (not her real name), the hostess with the mostest.** With three planets in charismatic Leo, she attracts people wherever she goes, throws the best dinner parties I've ever been invited to, and looks like the queen of confidence. She's also one of the kindest, most successful women I know. But she has been married and divorced several times, has had more boyfriends than the rest of my friends combined, and is obsessed with relationships. Why? She has a bucket chart with nine planets on the eastern side balanced by the security-seeking Moon on the other. Thanks to the nine planets, she's active and autonomous, a real doer. But with the Moon smack in the middle of her seventh house of partnership, her emotional well-being revolves around relationships. That's what the location of the singleton indicates: The focus of a life.

- **Dr. X (not his real name), the most entertaining psychiatrist I know.** His warm personality comes from his Leo Ascendant. His interest in psychiatry clearly comes from his singleton Moon which, like Dr. Freud's Moon, is in the eighth house of intimacy, secrets, psychoanalysis, regeneration (or healing), and occult knowledge. In his work as a psychotherapist, Dr. X is a master at creating an easy intimacy with his patients that enables him to unearth their secrets. In his private life, the Moon spurs him on to investigate topics most doctors won't admit even thinking about — areas such as palmistry (his palm was read for the first time when he was 5 years old), astrology (that's how we became friends), and all manner of spiritual techniques. Once again, the singleton planet is the key.

TIP

Be advised: These patterns are valuable aids to interpretation, but sometimes it's hard to detect any pattern at all. When that happens, forget about finding the perfect label. Don't think, don't judge. Just take in the chart as the visual symbol of a soul. Just look.

Considering the signs

After mulling over the patterns of hemispheric division and overall design in your chart, you're ready to assess your chart according to element and mode. Begin by counting the planets in each *element* (fire, earth, air, and water) and in each *mode* (cardinal, fixed, and mutable). Table 14-1 shows you which is which. If you know the time of your birth, add your Ascendant and Midheaven for a total of 12 distinct components. Want to include Chiron? Be my guest. But keep in mind that we're still learning about it.

TABLE 14-1

Elements and Modes

	Fire	Earth	Air	Water
Cardinal	Aries	Capricorn	Libra	Cancer
Fixed	Leo	Taurus	Aquarius	Scorpio
Mutable	Sagittarius	Virgo	Gemini	Pisces

REMEMBER

Most charts are more or less balanced, with two to four planets in each element. If you have five or more planets in signs of one element, the traits associated with that element are emphasized. See Table 14-2 for explanations of what such an abundance may mean for you.

TABLE 14-2

Emphasis by Element

With a Preponderance of Planets in . . .	You Are . . .
Fire signs	Active, spirited, assertive, a natural leader
Earth signs	Realistic, sensual, stable, prudent, hard-working, security-minded
Air signs	Communicative, intellectual, sociable, fueled by ideas and social interaction
Water signs	Sensitive, impassioned, impressionable, compassionate, and insightful

TIP

When classifying the components of a chart, remember that the Sun, Moon, and Ascendant are more influential than other placements and therefore deserve extra weight. Some astrologers even count them twice, just to make sure they get their due.

The modes (or qualities) work the same way as the elements. Most people have an approximate balance. But if you have a pileup of planets in one particular mode, those traits are accentuated. Table 14-3 tells you more.

TABLE 14-3

Emphasis by Mode

With a Majority of Planets in . . .	You Are . . .
Cardinal signs	Action-oriented, brave, geared up to take the initiative
Fixed signs	Unyielding, determined, focused, opposed to change
Mutable signs	Versatile, resourceful, open to change

There is one other possibility. What if you have nothing in one of the elements or modes? Here's what it means when an element or a mode is missing.

Missing in Action: Elements gone AWOL

Elemental voids can affect entire generations. For instance, between 1943 and 1955, Pluto was in Leo, a fire sign, and Neptune was in airy Libra. So no one born during that those years has a void in either fire or air — which may be why baby boomers, say what you will about them, can't be faulted for lack of energy (fire) or ideas (air). But among members of that generation, voids in water (emotional awareness) and earth (practicality) are common. Which makes a certain amount of sense.

During the 1960s, Neptune was in Scorpio and Pluto was in Virgo, so it was not possible to have a void in water or earth. But a baby born in those years could easily come up short in fire or air — or both, as was the case for Kurt Cobain. He had an astonishing eight planets in water signs plus two voids, one in fire and one in air: an emotional avalanche for anyone.

If you have an elemental void, here's how it could affect you:

>> **No fire:** It's hard for you to assert yourself, to maintain a consistent level of enthusiasm, and to mobilize the energy you need.

>> **No earth:** The material side of life eludes and possibly distresses you. Paying the bills on time, keeping track of your keys — these ordinary chores can do you in.

>> **No air:** You react emotionally and personally. It's hard for you to assess a situation objectively. Dealing with abstractions fills you with apprehension.

>> **No water:** Feelings baffle you. At times you don't even recognize your own reactions, and you have limited understanding of the emotions of others.

Missing in Action: Modes in retreat

Missing modes are less common than elemental voids. But they do occur. If you happen to have one, here's how to interpret it:

>> **No cardinal planets:** Taking the initiative isn't easy for you. When times of change descend upon you, you adjust. But you'd rather stick with the miserable known than risk getting lost in the unknown.

>> **No fixed planets:** You bend with the wind, happily charging off in new directions as the situation calls for it. You might even take pride in your flexibility. The truth is, you lack persistence. That's your weakness.

>> **No mutable planets.** Bend with the wind? Why would you want to do that? You have the ability to get a new endeavor off the ground and the tenacity to stick with it to the end. But adapting to circumstances? Compromising? Not your high card.

Finding mitigating factors

Here's the thing: Planets are not the only players. You might have a planetary void in, let's say, water. But if the Ascendant, Midheaven, the nodes of the Moon, or even Chiron is in a water sign, then that void is not total.

House placements can also be a mitigating factor. In the alphabet of astrology, the first house corresponds to Aries, the second house to Taurus, and so on. So the first house has a hint of fire to it, no matter what sign is on its cusp. The second house has a touch of earth. And so on. See Table 14-4.

So maybe you have a void in water. But if you have planets in the fourth, eighth, or twelfth house — the houses that correspond to water signs — that alleviates the situation. Those house placements direct your attention in ways that can help balance a slightly out-of-whack chart. This is a subtle influence. But that doesn't mean it's not real.

To see this effect in action, turn to Chapter 7 and take another look at Oprah Winfrey's chart. She has very little earth in her chart — only Chiron and the north node of the Moon. None of her planets inhabit earth signs. But she has three planets in the second house of money and possessions, one in the sixth house of work, and two in the tenth house of career and reputation. So most of her planets are in the houses associated with earth signs, also known as the houses of substance (see Table 14-4) — which might explain how an idealistic Aquarian got to be one of the richest women in the galaxy.

Voids in cardinal, fixed, or mutable signs operate the same way. Let's say you have nothing in Aries, Cancer, Libra, and Capricorn — not a planet, not an Ascendant, not even a node. This cardinal void makes it hard to get a new enterprise into motion. But wait a second. . . take a look at your chart. Is there anything in the angular houses, that is, houses one, four, seven, and ten? If so, you're in better shape than you thought. Taking the initiative will never be your most outstanding quality. But when you need to step up, you will find the wherewithal you need. (See Table 14-5.)

TABLE 14-4   **Houses and Elements**

Houses	Group Name	Characteristics
1, 5, and 9	Houses of Life (fire houses)	Fiery; vigorous; ready to enjoy life
2, 6, and 10	Houses of Substance (earth houses)	fond of systems and methods; motivated to seek security and recognition
3, 7, and 11	Houses of Relationship (air houses)	Communicative; intent on creating fulfilling relationships
4, 8, and 12	Houses of Emotion (water houses)	Emotional; discerning; interested in delving into family connections, the psyche, and the past

TABLE 14-5   **Houses and Qualities**

Houses	Group Name	Characteristics
1, 4, 7, and 10	Cardinal Houses	Enterprising, active
2, 5, 8, and 11	Fixed Houses	Stable, unwavering
3, 6, 9, and 12	Mutable Houses	Thoughtful, adaptable

Step Two: Six Components of a Birth Chart

Now you're prepared to look at the signs and planets. To get a sense of your chart without drowning in detail, concentrate on these factors:

» **The Sun:** The Sun reflects your basic identity — your motivations, needs, will, and individuality. Its sign describes the way you express these aspects of yourself. Its house determines the arena in which you can most effectively be yourself.

» **The Moon:** The Moon describes your feelings, subconscious, instincts, habits, and memory. Its sign determines the way you experience emotions. Its house placement points to the area of life that is most essential to your wellbeing.

» **The rising sign or Ascendant:** The Ascendant describes the surface level of your personality — the face you show the world. (See Chapter 11.)

» **The ruling planet:** The planet that governs your Ascendant is the ruler of your chart, regardless of its location or of anything else in your horoscope. As the ruler, it contributes both to your sense of self and to the impression you give others. Table 14-6 shows you the rising signs and their ruling planets. Turn to Chapter 9 or 10 for insight into your ruling planet.

TABLE 14-6   **Rising Signs and Rulerships**

If Your Rising Sign Is . . .	You Strike People as . . .	And Your Ruling Planet Is . . .
Aries	Impetuous, strong-willed	Mars
Taurus	Stable, sensuous	Venus
Gemini	Verbal, high-strung	Mercury
Cancer	Emotional, responsive	Moon
Leo	Confident, exuberant	Sun
Virgo	Methodical, discerning	Mercury
Libra	Charming, appealing	Venus
Scorpio	Controlled, reserved	Pluto and/or Mars
Sagittarius	Cosmopolitan, irrepressible	Jupiter
Capricorn	Respectable, proud	Saturn
Aquarius	Friendly, individualistic	Uranus and/or Saturn
Pisces	Idealistic, receptive	Neptune and/or Jupiter

One of the most illuminating qualities of the ruling planet is its position by house. Take the actor Peter Dinklage, who played Tyrion Lannister in *Game of Thrones*. A Gemini and a dwarf, he has Pisces rising with Neptune, the co-ruler of Pisces, in Scorpio in the eighth house of sex. Plus, his Neptune is conjunct Mars, albeit widely. You can't get any sexier than that.

Or glance at Rachel Maddow's chart. An Aries, she has Cancer rising with the Moon, her ruler, conjunct Mercury in Pisces in the ninth house of publication (she is the author of a #1 *New York Times* bestseller,) education (she has a doctorate from Oxford), and broadcast journalism. Whatever you may think of her political views, I think it's fair to say that she has answered the calling of her chart.

Table 14-7 tells how the ruler of your Ascendant affects you.

>> **Stelliums:** A cluster of three or more planets in the same sign and preferably in the same house is known as a stellium. Such a grouping is automatically noteworthy. When it appears in the same sign as the Sun, as commonly happens, it reinforces the message of that sign. When it shows up elsewhere, it can rival the Sun in importance. Either way, a stellium offers an intense concentration of passions and interests. It is always a focal point in a chart. If it includes four planets, and if one of those is Uranus, Neptune, or Pluto, it can take over the entire chart.

TABLE 14-7 **Ruling Planet by House Position**

If Your Ruling Planet Is in the . . .	You Are . . .
First house	Self-conscious, motivated, a personality, and a self-starter
Second house	Security-mined; stubborn; someone for whom material values are primary
Third house	Busy, restless, a communicator and a master of small talk
Fourth house	A family member who appreciates the arts of domesticity
Fifth house	What's wrong with having fun? You are a romantic, an entertainer, a devoted parent, a creative soul
Sixth house	Health-conscious, hardworking, someone who finds identity in vocation
Seventh house	A confidante and a companion. Partnership is central to your being
Eighth house	A sharp-eyed observer, a questioner, a magician
Ninth house	An explorer and a thinker, adventurous and opinionated
Tenth house	An achiever, a leader, a person of prominence
Eleventh house	A friend, a joiner, a person with hopes and aspirations
Twelfth house	A spiritual seeker and a hermit

To see a stellium in action, consider the chart of the Nobel-Prize-winning Chilean poet Pablo Neruda. His chart shows six planets in Cancer, including the Sun, the Moon, and Neptune, the ruler of his Ascendant. Most of those planets are in his fifth house of romance, which was one of his frequent subjects — but far from his only subject. In addition to love sonnets, he wrote odes to, among other household objects, a spoon, a plate, a bar of soap, an artichoke, and a box of tea. He was the poet of domesticity.

Or ponder Mick Jagger's chart. The world's oldest, most indefatigable rock star has a stellium in Leo: the Sun, Jupiter, Pluto, Mercury (his ruling planet), North Node of the Moon, and — not conjunct any of the above but still in Leo — Chiron. So of course he's still performing. He will always want to be on stage. That's the nature of Leo.

>> **An Elevated Planet:** Finally, there may (or may not) be a planet in your chart that receives no other honors — it's not your chart ruler, it's not part of a Grand Cross — and yet it stands out for a simple reason: It's a flag, a weather vane, a flashing beacon at the top of your chart. That's all — and that's enough. Just by virtue of being at the apex, it gains in importance.

Step Three: Looking for Aspect Patterns

A birth chart can easily have dozens of aspects in it. The aspects that deserve the closest attention are those that are the tightest, those that involve the Sun or the Moon, and those that weave three or more planets into a single pattern, as in these configurations:

>> **The Grand Trine:** Three planets, each at a 120° angle to the other two, form a giant good-luck triangle called a *Grand Trine,* shown in Figure 14-9.

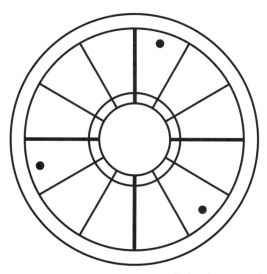

FIGURE 14-9:
A Grand Trine.

© John Wiley & Sons, Inc.

A perfect Grand Trine includes at least one planet in each sign of a given element. In those areas of life, things seem to click into place — you don't have to do much — and opportunities abound. Horror writers Shirley Jackson and Stephen King have Grand Trines in fire signs. Babe Ruth and Ruth Bader Ginsburg have Grand Trines in water. Stephen Hawking had one in earth, F. Scott Fitzgerald in air. But not everyone fortunate enough to have this harmonious aspect uses it effectively. The Grand Trine, a symbol of the slacker, is notorious for bringing just enough good fortune to keep you from feeling that you have to exert yourself.

» **The Grand Cross:** If two sets of planets in your chart oppose and *square* each other, as shown in Figure 14-10, you have your hands full because there are many moving pieces with this pattern. The perfect *Grand Cross* is a relatively rare but insistent aspect that brings conflicting motivations, uncomfortable clashes, and a boatload of tension, obstruction, and frustration. The Grand Cross can be a source of commitment and courage. Examples are Miles Davis, Mia Farrow, Conan O'Brien, and Jan Morris, the Welsh historian and writer of renown who became one of the first prominent people to have sex reassignment surgery and to write openly about her transition.

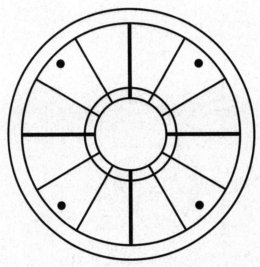

FIGURE 14-10:
A Grand Cross.

© John Wiley & Sons, Inc.

» **The T-square:** When two planets oppose each other with a third planet square to both, as shown in Figure 14-11, they form a *T-square* — a dynamic, troublesome but commonplace pattern. A T-square, inevitably creates tension, discontent, and the feeling of being besieged. It also spurs you to alter your situation, which may be why so many successful people have T-squares in their charts. Among them: Prince, Ronald Reagan, Diane Arbus, Stephen Hawking, Elon Musk, Steve Jobs, and Cher.

» **The Yod, Finger of Fate, or Hand of God:** Sounds serious, doesn't it? Actually, this challenge-to-spot configuration, shown in Figure 14-12, is subtler than the other aspect patterns. It looks like a long, narrow triangle, with two planets at its base forming a *sextile* (a 60° angle) and a third at the *apex,* or peak, forming 150° angles to the other two.

That 150° aspect, also called a *quincunx* or *inconjunct,* has a stop-and-go energy that creates false starts, backslides, uncertainties, and frustrations. It demands continual adjustment and impairs your decision-making abilities, notably in the areas affected by the planet at the tip of the triangle. This aspect sets up complex dynamics within a chart. But is it lethal? No. Is it a sign of special favor from God? No. Do plenty of people have this aspect? Yes. (Try Leonardo da Vinci, Winston Churchill, Meryl Streep, Bonnie Raitt, Margaret Atwood, Amal Clooney, and Barack Obama.) Don't let the name of this aspect unhinge you.

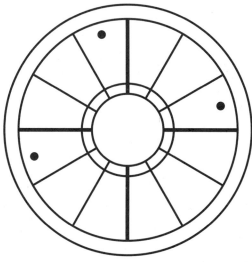

FIGURE 14-11:
A T-Square.

© *John Wiley & Sons, Inc.*

Astrologers have invented all kinds of additional aspects, most of them variations on those described above. There are kites, castles, cradles, mystic rectangles, pentagrams, trees, wedges, trapezoids, and a series of 60° angles called a Grand Sextile, Star of David, or Seal of Solomon. There's a hammer, a butterfly, a warrior, a variation of the Yod called a boomerang, and more. But it's not necessary to know every possible combination. Start with the Grand Trine, the Grand Cross, the T-square, and the Yod. For quite a long time — maybe forever — that should be sufficient.

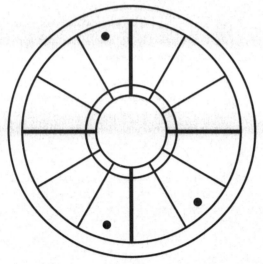

FIGURE 14-12:
A Yod, or Hand
of God.

Step Four: Putting the Puzzle Together

REMEMBER

Before you reach any wild conclusions about a chart (especially your own), look at everything: the planets, the aspects, the Ascendant and Midheaven, the houses, and anything else you can think of. If asteroids intrigue you, by all means check them out. Looking at something new in a chart could give you a new perspective.

And yet you may discover that the more you delve into your chart, the more the information repeats itself. You'll unearth a few contradictions: Everyone has them in their charts, just as everyone has them in their psyches. You'll also find the occasional placement or aspect that doesn't gel with the rest of the horoscope or that simply doesn't fit the person you think you are. Don't toss it out too quickly. Your discomfort could be an indication that you haven't understood yourself as fully as you might.

After you evaluate all these factors, you'll notice that certain characteristics seem to pop up everywhere. It's amazing how in every case, a few themes wind their way through the entire chart. No matter where you begin — with the hemisphere balance or the element countdown, with the Sun sign or with that peculiar stellium in the third house — the same theme keeps coming around again and again. Once you see that, the entire chart will click into place. That's when you know you're becoming an astrologer.

4

Using Astrology Right Now

IN THIS PART . . .

Scrutinize your relationships, sign by sign.

Plug into the cosmos and see how the moving planets affect you.

Live day to day by the light of the moon.

Get a grip on retrograde motion.

Celebrate the creativity of every sign of the zodiac.

Chapter **15**

The Sun Sign Combinations

Astrology does not judge. All 12 signs are equally worthy. That's the official line. In reality, everyone has preferences. Peering out from within the confines of your own horoscope, you can't help feeling that some signs are easier to get along with than others. In this chapter, I talk about the Sun sign combinations — the ones that feel natural from day one, and the ones that make you crazy. "How do I love thee?" There are 78 ways — one for each pair of Sun signs.

In the pages that follow, I talk about each combination under the sign that comes first in the zodiac. If you're a fiery Aries and your beloved is a peace-loving Libra, turn to Aries for a description of the dynamics of your relationship. As the first sign of the zodiac, Aries comes first in every pair. But if you're a sentimental Pisces involved with a warm-hearted Cancer, look up your relationship under the sign of the crab. Since Pisces is the last sign, every relationship you have (except for one with a fellow fish) is classified under the other sign. Pisces always comes last. It may not be fair. But that's the way it is.

Aries in Love

Lusty and exuberant, you're passionate, idealistic, and devoted, especially when you're in love. You're also impatient and rash, and you don't like to feel hemmed in. Lovers who try to control your behavior lose favor with you, as do friends who text too often or demand too much intimacy. Here's how you do with other signs of the zodiac:

>> **Aries + Aries:** Think of chili peppers, saxophones, and volcanoes — everything hot. This fast-moving, action-oriented, competitive combo leads to fireworks — when you want them and when you don't. Example: Matthew Broderick and Sarah Jessica Parker.

>> **Aries + Taurus:** The impetuous Ram is feisty, impatient, and hot-to-trot; the steady, stubborn, seductive Bull is unhurried and immovable. As with all next-door-neighbor combinations, the differences in style and tempo can drive you crazy. Examples: Spencer Tracy (Sun in Aries with Venus in Taurus) and Katharine Hepburn (Sun in Taurus with Venus in Aries); Victoria Beckham (Aries) and David Beckham (Taurus).

>> **Aries + Gemini:** You're both high-spirited and lively, with a million interests and a love for activities of all sorts. Aries is a forceful presence, straightforward and physical, while inconstant, curious Gemini lives in the head. Nonetheless, this is a terrific combo. Example: Warren Beatty (Aries) and Annette Bening (Gemini).

>> **Aries + Cancer:** You're both dynamic and expressive but the resemblance ends there. Cancer is sensitive, devoted, and often shy, while hot-tempered Aries is dominating and courageous. But Aries isn't tuned in emotionally — to the continual frustration of the Crab. Example: Steve McQueen (Aries) and Neile Adams (Cancer); Betty Ford (Aries) and Gerald Ford (Cancer).

>> **Aries + Leo:** Two fire signs generate a lot of heat. Except for occasional power struggles and outbursts of ego on either part, it doesn't get any better than this merry, vigorous match. When it's good, it's great. Example: Debbie Reynolds (Aries) and Eddie Fisher (Leo); Jennifer Garner (Aries) and Ben Affleck (Leo); Reese Witherspoon (Aries) and Jim Toth (Leo).

>> **Aries + Virgo:** The rambunctious Ram prefers to leap first and look later; the inhibited Virgin wants to mull over the pros and cons. Impulsive Aries says it like it is, blunt and to the point; analytical Virgo thinks before speaking and tries — not always successfully — to be aware of the impact words can make. Both signs have legitimate complaints about the other. Examples: Reese Witherspoon (Aries) and Ryan Phillippe (Virgo); Heath Ledger (Aries) and Michelle Williams (Virgo).

» **Aries + Libra:** Opposites attract in this combo. Aries brings impassioned energy, curiosity, and enthusiasm to the mix; Libra adds intelligence, courtesy, and charm. Even though the differences between you aren't to be dismissed — Aries is spontaneous and direct while Libra is thoughtful and restrained — this is nonetheless a recipe for romance. Examples: Kelly Ripa (Libra) and Mark Consuelos (Aries); Bonnie Parker (Libra) and Clyde Barrow (Aries).

» **Aries + Scorpio:** Sexually, this combo is off the charts. Both are strong willed, but dashing Aries is straightforward, while jealous Scorpio is anything but. In general, this pairing is asking for trouble. Examples: Ethel Kennedy (Aries) and Robert F. Kennedy (Scorpio); Meg Ryan (Scorpio) and Dennis Quaid (Aries).

» **Aries + Sagittarius:** Two fire signs egging each other on makes for a classic high-energy, good-time combo, assuming that you don't burn yourselves out. Even though the fights may be fierce, laughter gets you through — unless it doesn't, in which case neither of you has the patience to patch things up. Examples: Emma Thompson (Aries) and Kenneth Branagh (Sagittarius).

» **Aries + Capricorn:** The Goat initially gets off on the adventure of being with such a reckless, blustery creature. But Capricorns are strivers, grown-up and driven, while Rams can be perpetual adolescents overflowing with gusto and half-baked plans. In time, the thrill fades. Example: Patricia Arquette (Aries) and Nicholas Cage (Capricorn); MacKenzie Bezos (Aries) and Jeff Bezos (Capricorn).

» **Aries + Aquarius:** Although these two signs are sextile, this isn't as contented a duo as you might expect. Airy Aquarius is envisioning the future; Aries is brash, bold, and be-here-now. A Venus/Mars tie can help. Example: Andre Previn (Aries) and Mia Farrow (Aquarius).

» **Aries + Pisces:** The fluid, sympathetic Fish can tame the dominating Ram for a while. But what happens at the inevitable moment when Pisces needs a little nurturing? The Ram is on the lam. Protect yourself, Pisces. Look elsewhere — though Sarah Michelle Gellar (Aries) and Freddie Prinze, Jr. (Pisces) seem to be doing fine. Here's the reason: she has the Moon and Mars in Pisces, conjunct his Sun, and he has Jupiter in Aries, conjunct her Sun. They complement each other.

TIP

If you're in love with an Aries, don't be hesitant or subtle. Flirt boldly. Suggest something casual and spur-of-the-moment. Leave no doubt in Aries' mind that you're interested. If your efforts fall flat, pull back instantly and become unavailable. Above all, don't beg, plead, or whine. Aries has no patience for small-time behavior or any form of neediness.

Taurus in Love

Possessive, faithful, and not always as mellow as you'd like to be, you require physical contact, emotional and financial security, and domestic comfort. Once you find someone who shares your basic values and is equally sensual, you're content. You can cheerfully while away the hours just being together, doing nothing much. Clouds roll in when your partner wants a change of pace. Inevitably, you resist. You're the immovable object. Learn to bend.

>> **Taurus + Taurus:** Assuming one of you has the gumption to make the first move, this could be a long-term love-in. But when disagreements emerge, you lock horns. Although you'll encounter big passion and big fights, this combo could be a lasting one, despite the unfortunate first example: Bernie Madoff and Ruth Madoff; also, Rosario Dawson and Cory Booker.

>> **Taurus + Gemini:** Effervescent Gemini tries to loosen up the stolid Bull, but the effort may be wasted. Gemini appreciates change and jumps into it gleefully, while cautious Taurus prefers stability. As always, neighboring signs can be problematic. Examples: Queen Elizabeth II (Taurus) and Prince Philip (Gemini); Melania Trump (Taurus) and Donald J. Trump (Gemini). Also, tennis champion Andre Agassi (Taurus with Venus in Gemini) and Steffi Graf (Gemini with Venus in Taurus); or Andre Agassi and his first wife, Brooke Shields (Gemini).

>> **Taurus + Cancer:** Welcome home. Taurus is sensual, loving, and security-minded; Cancer is tuned-in, nurturing, and security-minded. A perfect, harmonious match. Example: Barbra Streisand (Taurus) and James Brolin (Cancer); Daniel Day Lewis (Taurus) and Isabelle Adjani (Cancer).

>> **Taurus + Leo:** Reliable Taurus wants to have a normal life, a regular bedtime, and a growing bank account. Demanding Leo wants to live large. And neither of you give an inch. Two fixed signs may strike sparks, but both are immovable. Example: Bianca Jagger (Taurus) and Mick Jagger (Leo); Kylie Jenner (Leo) and Travis Scott (Taurus).

>> **Taurus + Virgo:** You both value practical solutions, even if sensible, sensuous Taurus takes longer to get there than efficient Virgo. In addition to sharing values, comfort-loving Taurus calms Virgo's frazzled nerves, while goal-oriented Virgo prods Taurus into action. A fine combination. Examples: Leonard Cohen (Virgo) and Marianne Ihlen (Taurus); Faith Hill (Virgo) and Tim McGraw (Taurus).

>> **Taurus + Libra:** You're both ruled by sexy Venus, yet what a difference there is between you. Libra values refinement, music, soft lighting; earthy Taurus wants to skip the preliminaries and get to it. When the thrill of the moment

fades, you may have little to say to each other. As always, other planetary contacts can ease the pain. Example: Serena Williams (Libra, with Taurus rising) and Alexis Ohanian (Taurus).

» **Taurus + Scorpio:** Passion's playground. Scorpio simmers with erotic ideas; Taurus goes along. But Scorpio's love of secrecy, melodrama, and control receives a chilly welcome from the Bull, who moves slowly and is considerably more upfront. When troubles arise, you're equally stubborn. Example: Pierre Curie (Taurus) and Marie Curie (Scorpio); Jessica Lange (Taurus) and Sam Shepard (Scorpio); Uma Thurman (Taurus) and Ethan Hawke (Scorpio).

» **Taurus + Sagittarius:** Sexually, you're a match, at least for a while. Otherwise, you're so different it's astonishing that you ever got together at all. Sagittarius collects frequent-flyer miles, needs more than the usual amount of personal space, and hungers for stimulation; Taurus needs cuddling (and a cozy den), and loves to relax at home, making this a balky combination. Example: Channing Tatum (Taurus) and Jenna Dewan (Sagittarius).

» **Taurus + Capricorn:** A fine match you've got here. You have similar values, an appreciation for physical comfort, a desire for financial prosperity, a shared work ethic, and a frequently reinforced belief in the healing power of sex. Example: Coretta Scott King (Taurus) and Martin Luther King, Jr. (Capricorn); Gigi Hadid (Taurus) and Zayn Malik (Capricorn).

» **Taurus + Aquarius:** Airy, eccentric Aquarius is all about ideas; conservative, stable Taurus is rooted in the real world. Both are rigid. This isn't a good long-term prospect, despite the notable example of Alice B. Toklas (Taurus) and Gertrude Stein (Aquarius). (For more about this couple, read the nearby sidebar, "Incompatible? You be the judge.") Other examples: Sonny Bono (Aquarius) and Cher (Taurus); George Clooney (Taurus) and Amal Clooney (Aquarius).

» **Taurus + Pisces:** Earthy Taurus is essentially physical; dreamy Pisces is metaphysical. Yet these two share similar rhythms, tastes, and romantic notions. Examples: Robert Browning (Taurus) and Elizabeth Barrett Browning (Pisces); Penelope Cruz (Taurus) and Javier Bardem (Pisces); Behati Prinsloo (Taurus) and Adam Levine (Pisces); Mark Zuckerberg (Taurus) and Priscilla Chan (Pisces).

TIP

Head over heels for a Taurus? Hang in there. Be patient. Avoid arguments. Reveal no deep-seated neuroses. And give Taurus a chance to feel comfortable. Security is essential for Taurus. To give your Bull a haven, provide rich food, soft touches, lazy afternoons, good wine, leisurely walks in the woods, and every reason to feel relaxed. Taurus responds to scent and texture, so wear silk, velvet, cashmere, tweed — anything touchable. That's where Taurus lives.

Gemini in Love

Wanton Gemini, the last living proponent of casual sex, flirts outrageously, connects easily, and moves on at warp speed when things disintegrate. Because you relish intellectual challenges, you seek out witty, up-to-date people who share your delight in easy banter and constant stimulation. You're enchanting, flighty, and hard to pin down — yet another victim of the grass-is-always-greener myth.

» **Gemini + Gemini:** Despite the overall level of nervous energy that you generate together, you amuse and engage one another. And you never have to contend with those bleak silences that descend on the relationships of others. A definite talkfest. Example: George H. Bush and Barbara Bush.

» **Gemini + Cancer:** Distractible Twins are emotional lightweights, capable of denying their feelings for years on end; sensitive Crabs, Olympic gold-medal champions of the weeping event, want to connect on a deep level. Gemini, abuzz with natural energy, wants to be out and about; Crabs want to stay home. Look for solid planetary ties because this is ordinarily not a match made in heaven. Example: Wallis Simpson (Gemini) and the Duke of Windsor (Cancer); Nicole Kidman (Gemini) and Tom Cruise (Cancer).

» **Gemini + Leo:** This pair gets good marks, but with an asterisk. These two playful revelers truly enjoy each other. But they may unconsciously compete for center stage, which Leo requires and Gemini, an incessant talker, hates to relinquish. Also, Leo is loyal to a fault, while Gemini . . . well, consider this example: John F. Kennedy (Gemini) and Jacqueline Kennedy Onassis (Leo).

» **Gemini + Virgo:** Smart and tart, you click immediately and you can't stop talking. But Gemini believes in free association and serendipity, while Virgo relies on logical analysis and the benefits of reframing. Ultimately, you get on each other's nerves. Examples: Elizabeth Hurley (Gemini) and Hugh Grant (Virgo); Courtenay Cox (Gemini) and David Arquette (Virgo).

» **Gemini + Libra:** This wonderful combination promotes affectionate flirting and easy connection. Although it may not be the most fervent liaison, you get along swimmingly. Examples: Marilyn Monroe (Gemini) and Arthur Miller (Libra); Blake Shelton (Gemini) and Gwen Stefani (Libra); Paul McCartney (Gemini) and Linda McCartney (Libra); Kanye West (Gemini with Moon in Pisces) and Kim Kardashian (Libra with Moon in Pisces).

» **Gemini + Scorpio:** Scorpio counts sex as the central mystery of life. Gemini, a lustier sign than is often acknowledged, enjoys it without getting all emotional about it. Soon jealous Scorpio is feeling wounded, while flighty Gemini, who is lost in the labyrinth of the smart phone, can't help wondering what the problem is. Example: Donald J. Trump (Gemini) and Marla Maples (Scorpio); Nicole Kidman (Gemini) and Keith Urban (Scorpio).

» **Gemini + Sagittarius:** Despite an occasional bout of head-butting, this freedom-loving, loquacious pair is on the same wavelength. So fill your schedules with varied activities and plenty of travel; pile reading matter and notebooks on the bedside tables; and don't get hung up on togetherness, because that's not where this independent couple lives. Examples: Marilyn Monroe (Gemini) and Joe DiMaggio (Sagittarius); Angelina Jolie (Gemini) and Brad Pitt (Sagittarius).

» **Gemini + Capricorn:** Somber Capricorns take themselves seriously; easygoing Geminis, though self-absorbed, take things lightly and are always trotting off in new directions. Not a tranquil combination. Examples: Jean-Paul Sartre (Gemini) and Simone de Beauvoir (Capricorn); Priscilla Presley (Gemini) and Elvis Presley (Capricorn); Johnny Depp (Gemini) and Kate Moss (Capricorn).

» **Gemini + Aquarius:** You may be soul mates. You're sociable and playful, and you both have hyperactive minds, though Aquarius wants to delve into contemporary issues, while Gemini, who likes to hop around and be entertained, has innumerable opinions about pretty much everything. Neither of you is in touch emotionally, so when times are tough, the glue that holds you together may weaken. Example: Anderson Cooper (Gemini) and Benjamin Maisani (Aquarius).

» **Gemini + Pisces:** Laid-back Pisces wishes to sleep in; Gemini likes to grab an early coffee. Mystical Pisces wants to interpret your dreams; Gemini is mesmerized by the tiny screen. You hail from different planets. Clashes are inevitable, but this relationship is not impossible because you're both willing and able to bend. Examples: Laurie Anderson (Gemini) and Lou Reed (Pisces); Ruth Bader Ginsburg (Pisces) and Martin Ginsburg (Gemini).

TIP

If a Gemini is on your mind, be upbeat, up to date, and available. Gemini is inquisitive and game for anything. To capture Gemini's attention, exhibit those same qualities. Don't be morose. Don't bemoan the sad state of affairs in the world today. Don't complain. Don't demand that your assignations be scheduled weeks in advance. Above all, remember that Gemini values stimulating conversation. Ever wonder why Geminis have a reputation for infidelity? It's because they're easily bored. Consider yourself warned.

Cancer in Love

Cancer has a talent for intimacy and caring. When you're in love, you blithely ignore the most glaring flaws while homing in on your beloved's hidden potential. Compassionate and generous, you need to be with someone who shares your drive and mirrors your willingness to explore complex emotional issues. When you find such a person, you're totally supportive — even when the reverse isn't true. Some Cancers have a tendency to cling. The smothering mother is a Cancerian archetype for a reason: Sometimes you can't let go, not even a teensy bit. But let's also recall the positive, more representative mother archetype. Cancer knows how to love — deeply, supportively, and for life.

» **Cancer + Cancer:** You're aware and responsive, with plenty of energy and drive. Give it a go. This could be a productive, loving partnership. But remember: Emotions run high during full Moons, and you both feel the pull. Examples: Rodgers and Hammerstein; Barnum and Bailey; literary critics Diana and Lionel Trilling.

» **Cancer + Leo:** The domineering Lion loves passion, adventure, and five-star hotels; the moody Crab imagines a quieter existence in a vine-covered cottage. If Leo is willing to downsize glamorous expectations and Cancer is ready to stroke the Lion's fragile ego and take a chance, you can find common ground. Examples: Josephine, Empress of France (Cancer) and Napoleon Bonaparte (Leo); Kevin Bacon (Cancer) and Kyra Sedgwick (Leo); Gisele Bündchen (Cancer) and Tom Brady (Leo).

» **Cancer + Virgo:** After you establish trust, Cancer helps Virgo relax, and Virgo helps Cancer feel more secure. Problems arise with emotional issues. Supersensitive Cancer wants to deconstruct feelings, while critical Virgo would rather skip the emotional stuff (unless it can be approached in a calm and systematic way) and make practical plans. Examples: Ringo Starr (Cancer) and Barbara Bach (Virgo); Priyanka Chopra (Cancer) and Nick Jonas (Virgo).

» **Cancer + Libra:** Domestic Cancer and artistic Libra have a fabulous time decorating a house together. But Cancer's emotional make-up and shifting moods can cause logical Libra to retreat. Like other signs that square each other, these two aren't a natural fit, though Libra's desire to be mated — combined with Cancer's need to nest — can be a mitigating factor. Examples: Pamela Anderson (Cancer) and Tommy Lee (Libra).

» **Cancer + Scorpio:** You're both in touch with your feelings and in love with love. Problems crop up if Scorpio can't cope with the ebb and flow of Cancerian emotions. Scorpio feelings, while deep, mutate slowly (and, at times, invisibly); Cancer feelings are always in flux. Though you process emotions differently, you are compatible. Examples: Tom Hanks (Cancer) and Rita Wilson (Scorpio); George W. Bush (Cancer) and Laura Bush (Scorpio); Princess Diana (Cancer) and Prince Charles (Scorpio); also Camilla Parker-Bowles (Cancer) and Prince Charles (Scorpio).

» **Cancer + Sagittarius:** Cancer wants to love, nourish, and possess; Sagittarius can't be possessed. Though you may love each other dearly, you're completely different. Think twice. Examples: Frida Kahlo (Cancer) and Diego Rivera (Sagittarius); Tom Cruise (Cancer) and Katie Holmes (Sagittarius).

>> **Cancer + Capricorn:** Like every set of opposites, this one has plusses and minuses. Moody Cancer has an instinctive sense for how things ought to be done and an unshakeable faith in the power of intuition; sensible Capricorn prefers to go by the established rules. But Capricorn helps Cancer feel protected, Cancer helps Capricorn feel loved, and you share a reverence for tradition and family. Examples: Egon von Furstenberg (Cancer) and Diane von Furstenberg (Capricorn); William, Duke of Cambridge (Cancer) and Catherine, Duchess of Cambridge (Capricorn).

>> **Cancer + Aquarius:** Warm, vulnerable Cancer with cool, detached Aquarius? Not recommended. Example: Natalie Wood (Cancer) and Robert Wagner (Aquarius). But some couples have defied the odds. Example: Nancy Reagan (Cancer) and Ronald Reagan (Aquarius).

>> **Cancer + Pisces:** You're equally sensitive. Great feeling flows between you, your rhythms are similar, and you may even share a rare psychic bond. This is a perfect match, though Cancer, who loves to rescue, may find it difficult to overcome the famed Piscean ability to self-destruct. Examples: Johnny Cash (Pisces) and June Carter Cash (Cancer); Courtney Love (Cancer) and Kurt Cobain (Pisces).

TIP

If you fall for a Cancer, think chocolate, candlelight, white flowers. A monogamist at heart, Cancer is tender and amorous — the real deal. To woo a Moonchild (as they are sometimes called), go to the ocean. Dance under the stars. Cancer yearns for intimacy and responds to these traditional symbols. Three suggestions: Ask about your Crab's entire family tree; prove that you can cook; and be willing to analyze your emotions — in detail.

Leo in Love

Uninhibited and fun, you're romantic, generous, manipulative, and, despite your confident appearance, desperately in need of love. When someone wins your heart, you want that person in your life forever. But you want to be wooed in just the right way and insist on holding the reins of power. Despite your controlling behavior, you're so radiant and likable that you get away with everything.

>> **Leo + Leo:** You have big, theatrical personalities, and your house is filled with laughter. But you also have big, thirsty egos in need of constant infusions of applause and praise. Sexually, you're dynamite. Still, the question remains: Who's the king of this castle? A tough call. Example: Jennifer Lopez and Alex Rodriguez.

>> **Leo + Virgo:** Glamorous Leo makes grand gestures; uptight Virgo focuses on the details that Leo let slide. This isn't an easy duo. Ideally, one or both of you has at least one planet in the other's sign to bridge the distance between you. Examples: Percy Bysshe Shelley (Leo) and Mary Shelley (Virgo); Jacqueline Kennedy (Leo) and Aristotle Onassis (Virgo); Meghan, Duchess of Sussex (Leo with Venus in Virgo and Moon in Libra) and Harry, Duke of Sussex (Virgo with Venus in Libra).

>> **Leo + Libra:** Libra is a flirt; Leo likes to play games. Both take pleasure in romance. Though Leo is more flamboyant than even-tempered Libra, these two stimulate and delight each other. Examples: Zelda Fitzgerald (Leo) and F. Scott Fitzgerald (Libra); Jimmy Carter (Libra) and Rosalyn Carter (Leo).

>> **Leo + Scorpio:** Leo blazes, Scorpio burns; both are drama queens, passionate and proud. The heights! The depths! This spellbinding alliance generates good times and fierce battles — fire and ice. Examples: Ted Hughes (Leo) and Sylvia Plath (Scorpio); Arnold Schwarzenegger (Leo) and Maria Shriver (Scorpio); Bill Clinton (Leo) and Hillary Rodham Clinton (Scorpio); Mary Matalin (Leo) and James Carville (Scorpio).

>> **Leo + Sagittarius:** This exuberant duo offers laughter, passion, and shared adventures. But loyal Leo, who wants to do everything together, should remember that free-wheeling Sagittarius needs to be off the leash once in a while, and upfront Sagittarius has to get used to the fact that melodramatic Leo can be surprisingly manipulative. (Note: This is a simpatico, buoyant blend of two fire signs. I've seen it work in real life. But I cannot find a celebrity example.)

>> **Leo + Capricorn:** Leos love grand gestures, overstated emotions, and dramatic scenarios. Conservative Capricorns prefer to underplay their reactions and may feel the need to keep Leo in check, which isn't easy. But Capricorn benefits from Leo's extroverted warmth; Leo respects Capricorn's sturdy sense of responsibility; and they both appreciate luxurious surroundings and the finer things in life. This combination can work. Examples: Barack Obama (Leo) and Michelle Obama (Capricorn); David Bowie (Capricorn) and Iman (Leo).

>> **Leo + Aquarius:** If expressive Leo can accept the Water Bearer's eccentric ways (and oddball friends), and if freedom-loving Aquarius has no problem showering the needy Lion with adoration, this can be a match. Leo must also give up some control though, because Aquarius resists being marshaled into someone else's plan. Example: Roman Polanski (Leo) and Sharon Tate (Aquarius); Mila Kunis (Leo) and Ashton Kutcher (Aquarius).

>> **Leo + Pisces:** Pisces is bewitched by the over-the-top confidence of the audacious Lion, who in turn is bowled over by the expressive, impractical, aware Fish. Initially, quixotic Pisces feels protected by Leo, who wants to make everything okay. But in the end, the Fish, who has screwed things up in ways that incredulous Leo can scarcely believe, feels criticized and judged. Approach with care. Examples: David Duchovny (Leo) and Téa Leoni (Pisces); Lucille Ball (Leo) and Desi Arnez (Pisces).

TIP

To capture the heart of a Leo, look your best, exude confidence, and open your wallet. Leo expects flowers after the first date, and after that the stakes rise. It's not a matter of greed; Leo just wants to be sure of your feelings. So don't think that you can get away with second-class goods — Leo knows the difference. Plus, Leo is a glutton for affection, attention, and compliments. You can't be too brazen — Leo frogs think they're princes; Leo princes think they're kings; Leo kings think they're gods. You can't lay it on too thick.

Virgo in Love

You're understanding, easy to talk to, and far sexier than your virginal symbol suggests. But your idealistic standards are impossibly high, and mere mortals have trouble making the cut. When someone does prove worthy, you're devoted and full of praise. But you may have to learn the hard way that well-meaning suggestions and advice, no matter how gently delivered, can pack a terrible punch.

>> **Virgo + Virgo:** Your minds work in similar ways. Assuming your perfectionist compulsions can coexist, this should be a happy, healthy union. Example: Claudia Schiffer and David Copperfield.

>> **Virgo + Libra:** Analytical, industrious Virgo and thoughtful Libra connect mentally. But Virgo aims for efficiency and perfection, while Libra needs more down time and hungers for romance even if there's laundry to be done. As always with neighboring signs, look for planets in the other person's sign. Example: Jada Pinkett Smith (Virgo with Venus in Libra) and Will Smith (Libra with Mars in Virgo).

>> **Virgo + Scorpio:** This is an admirable match. Virgo is earthy enough to satisfy Scorpio's lustier moments, while Scorpio, a skilled detective who likes to dig into the meanings of things, can meet Virgo on their shared intellectual ground. Example: Blake Lively (Virgo) and Ryan Reynolds (Scorpio).

>> **Virgo + Sagittarius:** An erotic charge runs between you, and you connect mentally. But extravagant Sagittarius likes to speculate into the night and deal with the small stuff later (if at all), while prudent Virgo prefers to get to bed on time. After the initial fascination fades, the differences may be too much to overcome, as is often the case with two signs that square each other. Still, it can work. Examples: Beyoncé (Virgo) and Jay-Z (Sagittarius); Sophia Loren (Virgo) and Carlo Ponti (Sagittarius), together for more than 50 years.

>> **Virgo + Capricorn:** Two signs of the same element understand each other. You have great rapport, no effort required. You're both practical, methodical, accomplished, and ardent: prime material for a durable, congenial relationship. Example: Lyndon Johnson (Virgo) and Lady Bird Johnson (Capricorn).

>> **Virgo + Aquarius:** Virgo's unique, well-stocked mind excites brilliant Aquarius, whose rebellious ways help virtuous Virgo loosen up. You have fun together, and you click intellectually. But neither of you is at home in the gooey realm of emotions, meaning that when problems come up in that sphere, you both feel ill-equipped to handle the blowback. Examples: Lauren Bacall (Virgo) and Humphrey Bogart (Aquarius); Michael Jackson (Virgo) and Lisa Marie Presley (Aquarius).

>> **Virgo + Pisces:** You intrigue each other because you're polar opposites. Virgo needs order, schedules, and rational explanations. Sensitive Pisces trusts its intuition, reacts instinctively, and has a deep and abiding attraction to chaos. Naturally, Virgo wins the arguments. But easygoing Pisces has ways of not going along at all. It's a contest of equals: Anal-compulsive meets passive-aggressive.

TIP

To entice Virgos, admire their astute intelligence; engage in word play and banter; and don't be needy. Between the sheets, Virgo can be red-hot, but Virgo is also a control freak, which is no fun at all. So avoid messy emotions. In fact, avoid messes of all kinds. And remember: Virgo is concerned about appropriate behavior and proper appearance, so no affection in public, please.

Libra in Love

You're gregarious and attractive, a natural flirt. Born to be mated, you're restrained in public, amorous in private, and thoroughly identified with the object of your affection. As a single person, you're charming and popular. But being part of a duo brings you equilibrium and is essential to your fulfillment, and ultimately you're glad to leave the single life behind.

>> **Libra + Libra:** A harmonious partnership of equals, this is an easy, natural match. You're both creative, diplomatic, logical, and likable. The downside is that if you both feel unsure, you can flounder forever in a sea of indecision. Examples: Michael Douglas and Catherine Zeta-Jones; Naomi Watts and Liev Schreiber.

>> **Libra + Scorpio:** Although these two signs share a longing for romance, Scorpio craves intensity and melodrama, while even-handed Libra yearns for serenity. Unless Libra has planets in Scorpio, the initial attraction is strong, but the long-term connection isn't. Example: John Mellencamp (Libra) and Meg Ryan (Scorpio).

>> **Libra + Sagittarius:** Though the independent Archer's need for adventure may cause Libra a few jealous moments, Libra's charm reels the wandering gypsy back in. A fine pairing despite the creepiness of this example: Soon-yi Previn (Libra) and Woody Allen (Sagittarius).

>> **Libra + Capricorn:** Old-fashioned romance appeals to you both, and you adore being part of a couple. But you both tend to repress emotions. When issues arise, as they inevitably do, the challenge is to admit that there's a problem and to deal with it. Example: Howard Hughes (Libra) and Ava Gardner (Capricorn); Dita van Tees (Libra) and Marilyn Manson (Capricorn).

>> **Libra + Aquarius:** Your mental connection fuels your relationship. Other aspects of love may leave something to be desired. Examples: Eleanor Roosevelt (Libra) and Franklin D. Roosevelt (Aquarius); John Lennon (Libra) and Yoko Ono (Aquarius). Yoko's Libra Ascendant in John's Sun sign and his Aquarian Moon in her Sun sign helped knit the two of them together.

>> **Libra + Pisces:** You seem to be soul mates, but you aren't. Mysterious Pisces is a seething mass of soul, and Libra, though temptingly romantic on the surface, is uncomfortable with emotions. After a while, the gentle Fish feels ignored, while Libra, never the energy capital of the zodiac, feels exhausted. Examples: Abbott (Libra) and Costello (Pisces); Gwyneth Paltrow (Libra) and Chris Martin (Pisces); John Krasinski (Libra) and Emily Blunt (Pisces).

TIP

In love with a Libra? Be smart, stylish, cultured, and good-looking. Take Libra to scenic places — Libra melts in the presence of natural beauty. Don't be demanding or needy; Libra responds only when it matters, so don't cry wolf. Don't be jealous; Libra attracts admirers everywhere, so you might as well get used to it. And don't be loud or lewd or angry; Libra can't stand it. Librans can stand healthy disagreement, though. In fact, they often thrive on it. That's because Libra is actually looking for a relationship, not a clone.

Scorpio in Love

You're captivated by the game of love. You think of romance in heroic terms, demand grand passion, and often fall into the quicksand of obsession. Because you radiate sex appeal, other people often become fixated on you. Note, however, that though Scorpio has a well-deserved reputation as the sexiest sign in the zodiac, many Scorpios struggle with sexual complications that range from sexoholic excess to impotence to the full range of uncertainties concerning identity and orientation. Still, the bottom line is this: You expect love (and sex) to transform you — and that's exactly what happens.

>> **Scorpio + Scorpio:** Communication is eerily easy, and sex is deliciously erotic. But should there be even a hint of suspicion or jockeying for power, the psychic warfare is unbearable. This can be a union for the ages, or an exercise in tortured excess. Examples: Roy Rogers and Dale Evans; Ryan Gosling and Rachel McAdams; Kris Jenner and Bruce (later Caitlyn) Jenner.

>> **Scorpio + Sagittarius:** Scorpio is complicated and covert; Sagittarius is straightforward and honest. Scorpio seeks total immersion; Sagittarius wants independence. The Sun signs are stunningly different. But when at least one partner has planets in the other's sign, the attraction is compelling. Examples: John Adams (Scorpio) and Abigail Adams (Sagittarius with Mercury in Scorpio); Pablo Picasso (Scorpio with Moon in Sagittarius) and Françoise Gilot (Sagittarius); Ike Turner (Scorpio) and Tina Turner (Sagittarius); Neil Young (Scorpio with Mercury in Sagittarius) and Daryl Hannah (Sagittarius with Mercury in Scorpio).

>> **Scorpio + Capricorn:** These serious, lusty signs seem different because Scorpio dives into the tropical sea of emotion, while Capricorn skates on the frozen surface. The trade-off is that Scorpio gives Capricorn permission to have feelings, Capricorn protects the ever-emotive Scorpio, and you both feel safe and supported. Examples: Georgia O'Keeffe (Scorpio) and Alfred Stieglitz (Capricorn); Mike Nichols (Scorpio) and Diane Sawyer (Capricorn); Robert Maplethorpe (Scorpio with Moon in Pisces) and Patti Smith (Capricorn with Moon in Pisces).

>> **Scorpio + Aquarius:** Scorpio seeks attachment, is absorbed by emotional complexity, and leads from the heart, while Aquarius, however mentally vibrant, prefers a little distance, making this a volatile mix. Both signs are fixed, and neither submits willingly. Examples: Lee Krassner (Scorpio) and Jackson Pollock (Aquarius); Demi Moore (Scorpio) and Ashton Kutcher (Aquarius); Ben Harper (Scorpio) and Laura Dern (Aquarius).

>> **Scorpio + Pisces:** Although both of you are sensual and emotionally aware, possessive Scorpio is more at ease with the ways of the world than the out-of-this-world Fish. But Scorpio longs for magic, and imaginative Pisces can make it happen. Examples: Richard Burton (Scorpio) and Elizabeth Taylor (Pisces); Goldie Hawn (Scorpio) and Kurt Russell (Pisces); Kris Jenner (Scorpio) and Robert Kardashian (Pisces).

TIP

If you're fixated on a Scorpio, be passionate and expressive, and look for experiences to share. Watch an eclipse together. Go scuba diving. And when the object of your affections enters your domain, exploit your home-court advantage. Feel free to flirt, to imply and to pull back. Scorpio loves that stuff. Be guarded — Scorpions can sting — and at the same time, be brave. Let Scorpions know how fascinating they are. Really, no one compares.

Sagittarius in Love

You cherish your freedom, long for adventure, and take "Don't fence me in" as your personal credo, consciously or not. It goes without saying that romance can be a challenge. When a relationship excites you or introduces you to a wider world, you're enthralled and eager. Unpredictability attracts you. But "settling down" sounds a lot like "settling" to you. Too many rules and too much domesticity drive you to despair.

>> **Sagittarius + Sagittarius:** Like two Don Quixotes, you understand each other well. Eternally young at heart, you share adventures, aspirations, and the ability to amuse each other. But you tend to dream the impossible dream and may fail to address concrete concerns when they arise. Make frequent reality checks, please. Example: Katie Holmes and Jamie Foxx.

>> **Sagittarius + Capricorn:** Capricorn is charmed by the Archer's madcap ways, while jaunty Sagittarius is amazed at how organized and grown-up the Goat is. Like two neighboring countries, you can either go to war or establish a cultural exchange. It helps if one of you has a planet or two in the other's sign. Examples: John F. Kennedy, Jr. (Sagittarius) and Carolyn Bessette Kennedy (Capricorn); Chrissy Teigen (Sagittarius) and John Legend (Capricorn).

>> **Sagittarius + Aquarius:** You're both lively and exceptionally broad-minded. You're also unregimented, and neither of you has much talent for domesticity — or togetherness. Prepare for a life of takeout dinners, late-night streaming, and all-night chatter with offbeat friends. It could be fun. Whether it's more than that is another matter. Example: Mary Todd Lincoln (Sagittarius) and Abraham Lincoln (Aquarius); Frank Sinatra (Sagittarius) and Mia Farrow (Aquarius); Woody Allen (Sagittarius) and Mia Farrow (Aquarius); Brad Pitt (Sagittarius) and Jennifer Aniston (Aquarius).

>> **Sagittarius + Pisces:** You are two seekers, each with an inclination to dream. But Sagittarius deflates the fragile Piscean ego, while sensitive Pisces, though bewitching, can become strangely passive, which action-oriented Sagittarius can't abide. A questionable couple at best. Examples: Mileva Einstein (Sagittarius) and Albert Einstein (Pisces); Felicity Huffman (Sagittarius) and William H. Macy (Pisces); Hailey Baldwin (Sagittarius) and Justin Bieber (Pisces).

TIP

To snag a Sagittarius, don't come on too strong. Clichéd courting gestures make the Archer squirm. Instead, be casual, witty, lighthearted, and spontaneous. Spur-of-the-moment outings work in your favor; laying down requirements works against you. Don't forget that Sagittarius wants to be a free spirit and delights in the unexpected. So keep your passport up-to-date. Be willing to be daring. And don't rush Sagittarians: No matter what they say, most of them are commitment-phobic. They need to relax into relationships.

Capricorn in Love

Conservative and classy, you want a traditional relationship with all the trappings. You aren't particularly interested in wild flings, which is not to say that you're uninterested in sex. On the contrary, as an earth sign, you're a highly hormonal, high-stamina lover. But random sex seems meaningless to you. You're a devoted spouse, an attentive parent, a true friend, a loyal son or daughter — the whole shebang. You seek ever-after commitment and nothing less.

>> **Capricorn + Capricorn:** You're ambitious, committed, and lusty. But you run the danger of leading a life so upright and scheduled that, aside from sex, you never have any fun. Plus, if either one of you gets depressed, you're in trouble. You need a little levity. But who will provide it if both of you are brooding? Example: Tiger Woods and Elin Nordegren.

>> **Capricorn + Aquarius:** Capricorn is a traditionalist who believes in systems; progressive Aquarius is a maverick who likes to overturn them. Capricorn worries and feels despondent; Aquarius is sure that the future is bright. Chances are you irritate each other. This can be a disaster — unless one of you has a planet or two in the other's sign. Example: Gayle King, a Capricorn whose Moon in Aquarius is conjunct her best friend Oprah Winfrey's Sun in Aquarius. Plus, Gayle's Venus in Scorpio and Oprah's Mars are exactly conjunct — to the degree. They will never run out of things to talk about.

>> **Capricorn + Pisces:** Enterprising Capricorn knows how to handle the workaday world but can get bogged down in it; compassionate Pisces, who has other values, specializes in escaping from (or ignoring) the dull strictures of

ordinary life. But Pisces can lift Capricorn's spirits, and Capricorn can help Pisces get a toe or two on the ground. You inspire and support each other. Example: Richard Nixon (Capricorn) and Pat Nixon (Pisces); Henry Miller (Capricorn) and Anaïs Nin (Pisces).

TIP

Fixated on a Capricorn? Cool and contained, Capricorn understands the system and follows the rules. You should, too. Dress with class. Be polite and admiring. Offer up high-class activities — concerts, art exhibits, lectures. Don't jump into bed right away. Don't be aggressive. Don't be vulgar. Don't nag. Let things unfold naturally. And be patient: Capricorn represses emotions and takes things slowly. But Capricorn plays for keeps.

Aquarius in Love

A friendly, unconventional sort who's intrigued by everyone, you connect quickly but superficially, and you value your freedom. Despite your reputation for bohemian behavior, when you find someone you respect, you happily make the commitment — which doesn't mean that you intend to give up your independence or your eccentric ways. Those are forever. You can be as passionate as anyone else (and kinkier than most), but much as you enjoy it, you aren't a slave to sex. You live in your head.

>> **Aquarius + Aquarius:** Ah, the people you meet, the causes you support, and the parties you throw. Not to mention the way you decorate your house. You're unfettered, unorthodox, opinionated, and visionary — a couple unlike any other. Mentally, you connect. Romantically, it's more ambiguous. But maybe that doesn't matter. As air signs, you can both be carried away on the jet stream of out-there ideas. Example: Ellen DeGeneres and Portia de Rossi.

>> **Aquarius + Pisces:** This match is initially enticing but disappointing in the long run. Pisces is too easily hurt to be with someone as detached and cerebral as the Water Bearer; Aquarius is too independent to put up with Pisces' insecurities. Still, some couples make it work. Examples: Oprah Winfrey (Aquarius) and Stedman Graham (Pisces); Paul Newman (Aquarius) and Joanne Woodward (Pisces); Justin Timberlake (Aquarius) and Jessica Biel (Pisces); Anaïs Nin (Pisces) and Hugh Parker Guiler, her tolerant, devoted, forgiving husband (Aquarius).

TIP

If you're beguiled by an Aquarius, prepare to meet more eccentrics than you thought existed outside of Oz. Aquarius collects them. Your mission is to strike the Water Bearer as irreplaceable and fascinating enough to add to the collection. There's no need to present yourself falsely or to iron out the kinks. On the

contrary. Be independent but available. Express your opinions. And be yourself —
the more unorthodox, the better. A dozen roses? No, no, no. An invitation to a
midnight ramble through the meat-packing district? A master class in flamenco?
That could work.

Pisces in Love

Gestures — the moonlit stroll, the mariachi singers — mean the world to you.
You're a romantic who wants a cosmically connected, karmically generated,
some-enchanted-evening union with a soul mate. Though your intuition is pinpoint accurate at other times, when you're in love you can be amazingly gullible
and more demanding than you may realize. Ruled by your emotions, you're also
generous, erotic, affectionate, supportive, and kind.

> » **Pisces + Pisces:** Same-sign mergers are a mixed blessing because they
> magnify both the strengths and the weaknesses of the sign. Two dreamy
> Pisceans can communicate in ways that other signs can't conceive. But
> practicality eludes you. Does that matter? In the end, it probably does.
> Examples: Daniel Craig and Rachel Weisz; George Harrison and Patti Boyd
> (after their marriage crumbled, she wed his Aries friend, Eric Clapton.); or
> Supreme Court Justices Ruth Bader Ginsburg and Antonin Scalia, both Pisces
> with Moon in Scorpio. Although opposed politically, these colleagues joked
> together, shared a love of opera, vacationed together with their spouses, and
> considered themselves "best buddies."

TIP

If you fall for a Pisces, be romantic. Pisces wants to be swept away, but not á la
Tarzan and Jane. Being too aggressive may work short term (Pisces can be pas-
sive), but over the long run, it won't sit well. Pisces wants love to mean a coming
together of twin souls, two companions against the slings and insults of everyday
life. Pisces also wants sentimental gifts, breakfast in bed, Valentine's remem-
brances, the whole bit. What Pisces doesn't want is advice. No matter how you
phrase it, Pisces hears it as criticism, so lay off.

Finding Other Ties

What if your sign and your beloved's aren't compatible? Should your next stop be
Match.com? Not necessarily. Conjunctions or other close aspects between the
Moon in one chart and the Sun in another — or between the two Moons — breed

emotional understanding. Close aspects (up to and including oppositions) that link Venus in one chart with Mars in another kindle sexual attraction. Aspects to Mercury encourage clear communication. Ascendants of agreeable signs make for personalities that mesh. This is true not only for partners but also for everyone else you will ever meet. All relationships can be looked at through the lens of astrology.

INCOMPATIBLE? YOU BE THE JUDGE

REAL LIFE EXAMPLE

Some Sun signs just don't seem to go together. But it all depends on what else is happening in the two charts. Take the actors and civil rights activists Ruby Dee (Scorpio) and Ossie Davis (Sagittarius). They were born under neighboring — and hence incompatible — signs. But her Ascendant and Venus were in his Sun sign, Sagittarius; her Moon and his Venus were conjunct; and they both were born with the Moon in Aquarius. Even though their Sun signs weren't an ideal pairing, the marriage, which was also a working partnership, lasted 57 years — until his death.

Or consider Gertrude Stein, the avant-garde Aquarian writer, and her companion, Alice B. Toklas, a Taurus. They met in 1907 in Paris, where Gertrude entertained everyone from Picasso to Hemingway in her famous salon, and they stayed together until Gertrude's death in 1946. Although the earthy Bull and the airy Water Bearer don't usually mix, the connection between them was immediate. As Gertrude wrote when she described their meeting in *The Autobiography of Alice B. Toklas* (which she composed in Alice's voice, as if Alice herself had penned it), "I have met several great people but I have only known three first class geniuses and in each case on sight within me something rang."

I know what that something was. It was Alice's Mars, closely conjunct Gertrude's Venus and exactly opposite her Uranus. In the dominion of the heart, that bolt-from-the-blue connection — along with a series of harmonious trines linking the two charts — quickly prevailed over the warring Sun signs.

The other two geniuses that Alice met, by the way, were Pablo Picasso and the philosopher Alfred North Whitehead. Personally, I never doubted that Alice might have responded to Picasso, who clearly had a way with women, and who shared Alice's Moon sign. But Alfred North Whitehead? I wasn't so sure. So I tracked down his birthday, and guess what? Whitehead's Venus in Aquarius was conjunct Alice's Mars, and his Pluto in Taurus was exactly conjunct her Venus. I'm confident that when they met, within her something rang. And maybe within him too.

In general, sextiles and trines make things easier, oppositions and squares stir up differences, and conjunctions can go either way, depending on the planets involved. The only planetary aspects that scarcely matter are conjunctions of slow-moving outer planets such as Uranus and Uranus, Neptune and Neptune, or Pluto and Pluto. These planets orbit the Sun so sluggishly that they define generations, not individuals. The fact that your Neptune is conjunct someone else's doesn't mean that you're destined to be together. It means that you're about the same age — which isn't much of a tie. But it isn't nothing either, as anyone who has ever attended a high school reunion can attest.

Chapter **16**

The Times of Our Lives: Transits

O nce upon a time, astrology was the province of the privileged. Kings and pharaohs consulted astrologers, not because they were fascinated by the intricacies of personality but because they wanted to know when to wage war, when to stockpile grain, when to build a temple, and when to marry. They wanted to know, in short, how to lead their lives. Astrology provided some answers.

Today, anyone can take advantage of the wisdom astrology has to offer. You can glean some of that understanding from your birth chart and some of it from the current position of the planets, which are always on the move. *Transiting planets* are the planets as they appear in the sky right now. As they wheel across the zodiac, they trigger your birth planets, influencing your moods and presenting you with challenges and opportunities. Transiting Saturn is conjunct your Moon? Be prepared to combat the blues. Uranus is crossing your Midheaven? Get ready for a possible upheaval, good or bad, in your career. Every time a planet in the sky forms an aspect to a planet or an angle in your birth chart, it stirs up a different part of your psyche.

Sad to say, this book isn't long enough to consider every transit. I'm leaving out the transits through the houses. I ignore transiting squares (they're stressful) as well as sextiles and trines (they're helpful). And I entirely omit aspects made by transiting Venus, Mercury, and the Sun because they move so fast that their influence is fleeting. (The Moon whizzes through the signs at an even faster clip. But it's so close that it exerts an influence anyway, which is why I devote Chapter 17 to lunar transits.)

In this chapter, I focus on the slower-moving planets, beginning with Mars and ending with Pluto. I consider the conjunctions and oppositions that those planets make to your natal chart. And I try, as best I can, to highlight the possibilities that they open up for you. Transits don't change your natal chart. Like it or not, your birth chart is eternal. But the transits can help you achieve the potential contained within it.

Investigating Transits

There are several ways to identify the transits. The easiest way is to look them up in an old-fashioned astrological calendar. Using such a calendar, you can see the precise position of the planets at a glance, and you can also look ahead to find out where they're headed and when they're going to get there. Apps are great for discovering what's happening right now. At this very moment, for example, a quick look at my app reminds me that Mercury is retrograde. (That's okay; I'm revising.) But when will it go direct? The easiest way to find out is to consult a calendar. Flip through the pages and you can find out.

TIP

The calendars I like the most are *Jim Maynard's Celestial Guide* and *Pocket Astrologer* and any of the numerous calendars available from Llewellyn Publications. Of these, my favorite is *Llewellyn's Daily Planetary Guide*, a spiral-bound datebook filled with useful information including weekly forecasts, daily aspects, and enough space left over so you can jot down your appointments. Or you might prefer the smaller *Astrological Pocket Planner* or the illustrated wall calendar. Any of them will tell you what aspects the planets are forming and when. When will there be a New Moon? When will Venus enter your sign? Get the calendar and you'll know.

TIP

You can also get an app. There are many. My favorite is TimePassages, which is free, and TimePassages Pro, which charges a fee (a totally reasonable amount) and gives you more, and is the one I use. (Turn back to Chapter 2 for more about TimePassages.)

But here's the trouble: any app you pick can provide an endless — one might say infinite — supply of data that includes dozens of aspects a day — the long-term ones, the ones that scarcely matter, the ones that can slam you to the ground, and the ones that make your dreams come true. That's why I like TimePassages. It does you the favor of separating "Today's Astrological Influences," which are fleeting, from "Long-term Influences," which are the ones you want to pay attention to.

Visualizing transits

To get a handle on the transits that are affecting you now, I recommend the following steps:

1. **Get an accurate copy of your birth chart, as per the instructions in Chapter 2.**

2. **Find out where the planets are right now.**

   You can do that with a paper calendar, with an electronic app, with astrological software, or by Googling, which will show you any number of options including these:

   - `https://astro-charts.com/chart-of-moment/` This gives you everything you need: the actual chart of the cosmos as it is now, and, below that, a convenient list of every planet with its position in the zodiac.

   - `https://www.astro.com/h/pl_e.htm`. Or do it the easy way. Google Current Planets – Astrodienst, and you will find a neat little list, just what you need. You can also click on "Chart of the moment" and see it displayed as a round chart, not a list.

3. **Jot down the positions of the planets, omitting the Ascendant and the Midheaven, which change every four minutes.**

4. **Inscribe those transits around the rim of your chart.**

Writing in the transiting planets this way isn't complicated, and it will give you a concrete sense of where they are and what parts of your chart they are activating. The following section shows an example of transits in action.

Showing the importance of transits

REAL LIFE EXAMPLE

Serena Williams has been called the greatest athlete of all time. The inner wheel in Figure 16-1 shows her natal horoscope, dominated by six planets in the sixth house including the Sun, the Moon, Jupiter, and Saturn (so you know she works hard and probably worries about her health). The outer wheel shows the transits on May 12, 2015 — not a random day, as you will see. The narrow border filled with symbols for the signs of the zodiac shows the house cusps for her natal chart.

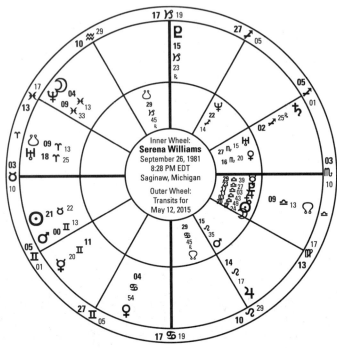

FIGURE 16-1:
Serena Williams's
birth chart iwith
transits on the
outer wheel.

© John Wiley & Sons, Inc.

Looking at her transits on the outer wheel, the first thing you might notice is Pluto, riding high at the top of her chart. Pluto is the slow-moving outer planet that symbolizes transformation. It is conjunct her Capricorn Midheaven (which in this case is the same as the cusp of her tenth house). This transit suggests a big shift in her public image. Pluto hasn't reached her Midheaven quite yet — that moment is less than a year away — but the aspect is close enough to count. And since Pluto is the ruler of her seventh house of partnership — and since it is also sextile to her natal Venus in the seventh house — this transit could augur a change in relationship status.

The next step is to examine the other slow-moving, transiting outer planets. Neptune, transiting through her eleventh house, doesn't make a close aspect to any of her natal planets, so it's just not the most influential planet at the moment. I'm going to skip it.

Saturn is transiting close to the cusp of the eighth house, its long transit of her seventh house almost over. It is sextile her natal Sun, which is a positive influence but not a powerful one. Saturn is also conjunct Uranus in the seventh house, but that conjunction is wide – more than five degrees — and the planets are in different signs. So I'll skip over Saturn too.

That leaves Uranus, the lord of surprise — always a player worth watching. It is in the twelfth house, closely opposing Serena's natal Jupiter, the guardian of good fortune, and squaring her Midheaven, which represents her public image and reputation. This is an indication of unexpected change — and there's more.

Located in the outer wheel is transiting Jupiter, spinning through her fifth house of romance for the first time in a dozen years. It is conjunct her natal Mars, the planet of action and desire. It is also squaring — which is to say, activating — her natal Venus in the seventh house. So here is a tasty cocktail: transiting Jupiter, Pluto, and Uranus mixing it up with natal Venus, Mars, and Jupiter. Could be good.

Added to that is a bit of garnish: transiting Mars in the first house. It's at zero degrees Gemini, so it has just entered a new sign. Mars spins into a new sign about every two months, so I can't emphasize this particular transit. Frankly, it's not important. Still, it trines her natal Sun — and a new sign could be a sign of something new. And so it was: these were transits on the day Serena Williams met Alexis Ohanian, her future husband.

REMEMBER

The inner chart is the birth chart. The planets in the outer circle represent the transits.

To follow your transits, make a copy of your chart. Then position the transiting planets around the outer rim. You'll see right away that there's a lot going on. So how can you tell which transits to concentrate on?

REMEMBER

Here's the rule: The transits that pack the biggest wallop are those made by the slow, more distant planets — Saturn, Uranus, Neptune, and Pluto — to the Sun, the Moon, the Ascendant, the Midheaven, and the fast, inner planets.

Contacts made by the faster planets are usually short-lived and therefore less important. Contacts made by the slower planets to the slower planets (such as Uranus opposite your Pluto or Neptune conjunct your Saturn) have a generational impact but may be too subtle to detect in an individual chart (unless the natal planet happens to occupy a prominent position in your birth chart, in which case all bets are off).

But contacts made by a slow outer planet to the faster-moving inner planets and the angles of your chart — Pluto conjunct your Midheaven, Uranus opposite your Sun, and so on — signify the chapters of your life.

Tracking Mars

Mars is associated with vitality, initiative, passion, force, anger, and aggression. Mars stirs your desires and prods you to take action. As a rule, Mars spends about two months in a sign, taking about two years to travel through the zodiac and return to the position that it occupied at your birth. But those figures are only averages because, like the other planets, Mars sometimes slows down, turns retrograde, and lingers in one sign (see Chapter 18 for more on retrograde planets). To show you how varied its schedule can be, in the summer of 2012, Mars sped through Libra in about seven weeks. But when it returned to that sign in December of 2013, it remained there for eight months. Naturally, the more time it spends in a sign, the more it energizes the planets it contacts there.

The major transits of Mars are as follows:

>> **Mars conjunct the Sun:** You feel determined, aggressive, and brave. But try to avoid lashing out. Mars boosts your initiative but also jabs at your anger. The transit of Mars conjunct your natal Sun usually lasts only a few days, although occasionally, when Mars goes retrograde, it can carry a longer, hardier charge. But it will also spend about two months, on average, in your Sun sign, bringing an increase in energy you haven't had for two years.

>> **Mars opposite the Sun:** You're energetic but ready to do battle at a moment's notice. This is a don't-mess-with-me transit.

>> **Mars conjunct the Moon:** You're feisty, spontaneous, and in no mood to repress your powerful emotions or peevish irritations. Directed in a purposeful way, this transit helps you combat a wrong or accept a challenge. Undirected, it can lead to animosity. A little self-awareness goes a long way.

>> **Mars opposite the Moon:** Take care. Your emotional outpourings — which feel externally caused, whether they are or not — can escalate into confrontation.

>> **Mars conjunct Mercury:** You feel impatient, excited, and filled with ideas. You express your opinions with confidence but a hint of hostility or sarcasm could sneak into your communications. Verbally, you're all fired up.

>> **Mars opposite Mercury:** You argue, you debate, you take no prisoners. You're quick to respond, but you may also feel besieged and hostile. Be careful what you say. You may decimate your opponent, but you won't win any friends.

>> **Mars conjunct Venus:** Your sex drive, ability to love, and artistic impulses are working overtime. You're at your most irresistible.

>> **Mars opposite Venus:** Socially and sexually, you're in the mood for love. But don't push too hard. You run the risk of being too assertive or of attracting people who are behaving in a similarly out-of-balance fashion.

>> **Mars conjunct natal Mars:** Mars returns. The hero's journey begins anew as a bright wave of energy and desire washes over you. Your challenge is to harness that energy. This important transit, which occurs about every two years, marks the end of one energy cycle and the beginning of another. This is the moment to pursue a new interest, invent a project, begin a new physical fitness program, get a new job, and stay open to possibilities that arrive unbidden. Transiting Mars can generate hostility, so watch your temper. But it also clears the path for something new.

>> **Mars opposite natal Mars:** Though your stamina is high, you may not find it easy to channel your energy in a constructive, consistent manner. Something you've been involved in for about a year has reached a critical stage. Much effort is required at this turning point. Action is called for.

>> **Mars conjunct Jupiter:** The universe supports your visions by prompting you to get off the couch and do something to actualize them. You're ready to take action. Under this expansive transit, you benefit from travel and education.

>> **Mars opposite Jupiter:** This can be a fortunate transit. You have plenty of energy, and you're buoyant and optimistic. But you run the risk of promising too much, overestimating your capabilities, and overreacting.

>> **Mars conjunct Saturn:** Whatever is holding you back or blocking your way, whether it is internal or external, can be addressed now. Because you bristle at the obstructions you face, this tends to be a challenging transit. It can also be a time of accomplishment, thanks to your increased ability to focus on the very thing that needs to be done.

>> **Mars opposite Saturn:** This transit calls for caution, diligence, and responsible behavior. Alas, you're likely to act rashly, resist the dictates of others, and express your authority awkwardly. In this time of tension, being irritable or feeling sorry for yourself won't help. At the very least, go the gym.

>> **Mars conjunct Uranus:** You act impulsively and rebelliously, sometimes taking off in a direct that may shock everyone, yourself included. During the few days when Mars is conjunct your natal Uranus, buckle your seat belt, shun the skateboard, and look both ways. With Uranus, the rule is simple: Expect the unexpected.

>> **Mars opposite Uranus:** Tension, strain, accidents, and unpredictable events can interrupt your plans and mess with your technology. Don't take reckless chances during this agitating transit. And be sure to back up your computer files.

>> **Mars conjunct Neptune:** Your dream life picks up, and you seek inspiration. Artistic, spiritual, or healing activities excite you. But be careful about drugs and alcohol, and avoid making big decisions — your judgment may be skewed.

>> **Mars opposite Neptune:** Vivid dreams and artistic inspiration characterize this transit. But your efforts to get something done in the workaday world could go awry. You may feel confused or out of the loop. Yoga, swimming, or other forms of physical exercise may help disperse the fog.

>> **Mars conjunct Pluto:** Pursue your ambitions and don't hesitate to take charge. You may be stunned by how powerful you can become.

>> **Mars opposite Pluto:** You feel competitive and determined. But in your desire to establish yourself, you run the risk of churning up conflicts and power struggles. Maintain your courage — and your standards.

>> **Mars conjunct the Ascendant:** You are overflowing with vitality and fully prepared to take steps on your own behalf, but you may also be feeling impatient or quarrelsome. Following the conjunction to the Ascendant, Mars travels through your first house, boosting your energy and lending you a boldness that you may not normally experience. Take advantage.

>> **Mars opposite the Ascendant:** About a year after Mars conjuncts your Ascendant, it opposes it. You are unwilling to be passive, especially regarding marriage or business partnerships. But the ambient tensions upset you, and you may take out your frustration on those to whom you feel the closest. Your challenge is to act decisively and positively.

>> **Mars conjunct the Midheaven:** This transit, along with the two-month-long sojourn of Mars in your tenth house, motivates you to chase after your professional desires. It increases your professional visibility and your desire to be involved. Volunteer for anything that interests you and let your eagerness show.

>> **Mars opposite the Midheaven:** Your professional efforts fizzle out or are rebuffed, and your attention goes elsewhere. As Mars conjuncts the nadir of your chart, which is directly opposite your Midheaven, and travels through your fourth house, it awakens your interest in home and family and enlivens your domestic life. Hidden conflicts may emerge. But this is also a good time to fix up your domicile.

REMEMBER

Mars transits are dynamic and motivating. When Mars is traveling through a house, you find the energy to take action in that area. You benefit from being assertive. You suffer from doing nothing. Be not afraid.

Activating Jupiter

Jupiter spins through the zodiac in slightly fewer than 12 years, spending about a year in each sign. Its transits are among the most eagerly anticipated — and the most disappointing. As the planet of expansion, opportunity, generosity, and prosperity, Jupiter can bring happiness, growth, and success. As the planet of philosophy, religion, and education, it can stimulate an exploration of belief and the pursuit of knowledge. But despite its reputation as the lord of abundance and the bringer of good fortune, Jupiter doesn't always deliver, and people who sit around passively waiting for their wishes to come true under its influence are bound to be dissatisfied. The problem is that while genial Jupiter may lead you right up to the doors of opportunity, it also prompts feelings of contentment and self-indulgence. Instead of trying to kick those doors open, many people lean back to enjoy the transit and thereby miss it.

In my experience, a Jupiter transit is a distant trumpet call to arms. When you see Jupiter poised on the brink of your Sun sign, about to contact your career-oriented Midheaven, or entering your seventh house of partnership, you know that opportunities are available in those arenas. But you have to hold up your end of the bargain. To get the most out of Jupiter, make a legitimate effort to learn something, to tackle an old dilemma in a novel way, or to find time for the things you always say you want to do. When you take action under a Jupiter transit, your efforts will be recompensed. But first, you have to do your share.

Jupiter is about expansion and opportunity. It brings benefits. But a transit can only activate the potential that already exists in your chart.

>> **Jupiter conjunct the Sun:** Seize the opportunity to branch out during this year of growth, but be warned: If life is going well, you may be tempted to do nothing. If life isn't going your way, you may become disheartened or cynical. Don't let Jupiter lull you into complacency. This is the time to reach out, be generous, and take risks.

>> **Jupiter opposite the Sun:** Opportunities are available, but you run the risk of overextending yourself, overdramatizing your situation, or simply promising too much.

>> **Jupiter conjunct the Moon:** This transit brings expanded sensitivity and a greater flow of emotions — which is pleasant if your birth Moon makes mostly harmonious aspects to other planets but exhausting if your Moon is afflicted by squares and oppositions.

>> **Jupiter opposite the Moon:** Why does every emotional blip — every minor snub, every disappointment, every passing compliment, and every little boost — feel utterly seismic? The answer is that, thanks to Jupiter, you're supersensitive, with a tendency to inflate your feelings.

>> **Jupiter conjunct Mercury:** Jupiter enlivens your intellect and expands your ability to express yourself. You speak up freely, travel happily, and easily absorb information, making this an ideal time to learn a language or tackle that literary classic you've always meant to read.

>> **Jupiter opposite Mercury:** Seek knowledge. Read voraciously. Write. Travel widely, soak up ideas, seek advice. Communicate but don't pontificate. Jupiter can be overconfident, but under its influence, your intellect will flourish.

>> **Jupiter conjunct Venus:** Your social life blossoms, your inner beauty shines forth, and you attract love and affection. This fortunate transit even improves your earning ability.

>> **Jupiter opposite Venus:** You're attractive to others, and your social life expands accordingly. If you want to grow your social circle, you can easily do it now. But excessive self-indulgence may tempt you. Venus is the planet of money, so beware: Jupiter's inherent optimism could lure you into spending too much.

>> **Jupiter conjunct Mars:** You're eager, active, generous, and filled with enterprise. Being assertive produces desired results.

>> **Jupiter opposite Mars:** You feel energetic but you may find it difficult to direct that energy effectively. Overestimating your ability to get something done leads to self-recrimination and problems with other people. Demands and disagreements are numerous. Exercise helps.

>> **Jupiter conjunct natal Jupiter:** Jupiter circles back to its birth position every 12 years, renewing your optimism. This can be a lucky, adventurous time during which you can find fulfillment through travel, education, philosophical or spiritual explorations, and a concerted push into areas that have long tempted you. Your efforts to brush past old boundaries pay off, and you have some fun along the way. But Jupiter can also promote self-satisfaction, laziness, and smug indifference. Don't waste this transit.

>> **Jupiter opposite natal Jupiter:** You're in a generous, exuberant mood, but you may be merrier than the situation merits. Watch out for overindulgence and excessive optimism.

>> **Jupiter conjunct Saturn:** You may become supremely conscious of your fears and limitations, but they have less of a charge than once they did. You find the help you need, or you figure out a way to get around a problem, or you finally buckle down and address the lingering issues that have held you back.

>> **Jupiter opposite Saturn:** As much as you want to break out of your old patterns, circumstances may not permit it. However tempted you may be by new acquaintances and fresh opportunities, your responsibilities are ongoing or even increasing. Your best move is to accept your obligations.

- >> **Jupiter conjunct Uranus:** Unusual opportunities present themselves to you, lending you the courage to take a leap and try something outside your usual experience. There's no point in hiding your idiosyncrasies because it can't be done! Your uniqueness shines forth. This is the time to embrace your individuality.

- >> **Jupiter opposite Uranus:** Remarkable opportunities may bring a longed-for chance to break away from confining circumstances. Overconfidence leads nowhere, but there's something to be said for taking a calculated risk.

- >> **Jupiter conjunct Neptune:** Your mystical side, spiritual interests, supernatural ability, and imagination are enlarged. Possible problems include excessive daydreaming, substance abuse, and the refusal to accept reality. But if you ever wanted to write poetry, try a new meditation technique, sign up for a dream workshop, or learn to sing, now's the time.

- >> **Jupiter opposite Neptune:** Accepting reality isn't easy — and you probably aren't even trying. Your imagination may be soaring, but your judgment is poor. You're impractical and easily deceived. If you've ever struggled with substance abuse, you must be vigilant now.

- >> **Jupiter conjunct Pluto:** Your ambition and personal power are enlarged, and your labors bear fruit. In the past, you may have journeyed through the underworld of sorrow, fear, or isolation. If so, you now return to the light.

- >> **Jupiter opposite Pluto:** Your desire for power can get out of hand, and obstacles may block your way. At this moment of transition, you may feel as if you have little control or that you're caught in a power struggle.

- >> **Jupiter conjunct the Ascendant:** You're open, ebullient, and even lucky. During the year or so when Jupiter contacts your Ascendant and travels through your first house, you're outgoing and receptive, and people respond to you positively. The bad news: Gaining weight is easy. Be advised.

- >> **Jupiter opposite the Ascendant:** You readily connect with others, and your relationships with individuals as well as with the general public flourish. During the year or so when Jupiter opposes the Ascendant and inhabits the seventh house, you could attract a business partner or a companion for life.

- >> **Jupiter conjunct the Midheaven:** Jupiter's conjunction with the Midheaven, followed by a yearlong passage through your tenth house, can bring success, an enlarged role in the world, and career options galore. Take advantage of them.

- >> **Jupiter opposite the Midheaven:** Family relationships improve. This is a fine year to move, invest in real estate, focus on domestic pursuits, and heal family wounds.

REMEMBER

Jupiter transits bring growth and opportunity but also the danger of indolence.

Coping with Saturn

People who know something about astrology tend to look forward to Jupiter's transits with joyous anticipation and to view Saturn's transits with alarm and even dread. Saturn takes almost 30 years to wheel through the zodiac. It spends about two and a half years in each sign, and it's associated with duty, discipline, effort, obstructions, limitations, boundaries, and lessons learned. Gloomy Saturn can bring despair, apathy, and a dangerous case of the blues. But just as Jupiter doesn't necessarily deliver matchless love or winning lottery tickets, Saturn doesn't necessarily beget misery. It can bring responsibility in the form of a more high-profile job, limitation in the form of a committed relationship, and the enhanced self-esteem that accompanies self-discipline. To benefit from a Saturn transit, you need to create structure, get organized, and figure out how to manage your time.

REMEMBER

Transits, by definition, are transitory. They don't last long, so you must act promptly to take advantage of them.

>> **Saturn conjunct the Sun:** You reap what you sow: That's the message of this serious and sometimes dispiriting transit. Saturn can slow things down and create obstacles. Saturn stimulates your ambitions and increases your need for security. It also forces you to confront your weaknesses and battle negative thinking. Remember that Saturn also brings security, fulfillment, recognition, and achievement. Behind every great accomplishment is Saturn. Nothing important happens without him. But Saturn demands hard work.

>> **Saturn opposite the Sun:** Pessimism and low vitality characterize this difficult transit, which takes place approximately 14 years after Saturn conjuncts the Sun. Other people may oppose your efforts. Be patient.

   Note: The squares of Saturn to the Sun, which occur about seven years before and after the opposition, are also trying.

>> **Saturn conjunct the Moon:** Worries afflict you. You may feel melancholy, misunderstood, unloved, or unlucky — not to mention filled with doubt and self-pity. You're imprisoned momentarily in the abyss, where the time is always right for confiding in a journal, talking to a therapist, and reminding yourself that this too shall pass.

>> **Saturn opposite the Moon:** Insecurity, bitterness, and demanding relationships may cause you to withdraw during this isolating time. Though you may wish for sympathy from others, you aren't likely to get it. Take practical steps and read the paragraph immediately before this one. It applies to you.

>> **Saturn conjunct Mercury:** You're in a thoughtful and possibly pessimistic mood that favors study, concentration, withdrawal, and careful communication. Perhaps you've been too rigid or disjointed or rambling in the way you've

presented your thoughts. This is the ideal time to improve your communication skills and clean up your act.

» **Saturn opposite Mercury:** Circumstances may cause you to clash with someone over ideas or to question your own assumptions. Negative thinking could seep into everything. Find a way to contain it.

» **Saturn conjunct Venus:** Weak relationships may crumble. You may feel lonely, inhibited, unloved, and underfunded. And yet a new, more serious relationship can begin, possibly with an older or more established person. This is also a fine time to launch an artistic project.

» **Saturn opposite Venus:** Breaking up is hard to do, even if it's the only move to make. Healthy relationships survive this stressful transit. But even then the blinders come off as you face the truth.

» **Saturn conjunct Mars:** Your efforts are frustrated, provoking you to feel resentful and overburdened. If anger is an issue for you, learn to manage it now. You're being challenged to learn control. If you act methodically, you can accomplish a lot.

» **Saturn opposite Mars:** This transit can be rough, especially if you're the sort of person who collects enemies. Obstacles impede your progress as Saturn, the lord of discipline, forces you to take appropriate action and — worse — to be patient.

» **Saturn conjunct Jupiter:** Even though the opportunities that arise during this tedious time may not be flashy, they're nonetheless real. During a Saturn transit, you may need to streamline your goals or trim your expectations. But you've got plenty of stamina, and Saturn rewards your efforts.

» **Saturn opposite Jupiter:** Luck isn't with you, but it isn't against you, either. Instead, this is a time of restricted growth, dampened enthusiasm, industriousness, and acceptance of the status quo.

» **Saturn conjunct Saturn:** Saturn returns. This is a watershed moment, a time to come to terms with reality. Saturn returns to the position it occupied in your birth chart when you're between the ages of 28 to 30, 58 to 60, and 88 to 90. The first Saturn return represents the true onset of adulthood. During this typically trying time, you're forced to face the truth about yourself, stop messing around, and grow up. Many people fear this transit. But it is here, during the first Saturn return, that you clear away the underbrush and find your true path. The second and third Saturn returns represent further pivots, each of which motivates you to admit to your dissatisfactions and prepare for a new phase in your life. In each case, Saturn emboldens you to confront your fears, acknowledge the boundaries of the possible, identify and possibly alter your direction, and fine-tune your habits. Meanwhile, the path keeps winding.

>> **Saturn opposite Saturn:** This transit, which forces you to see yourself in relation to the larger world, can be upsetting, especially the first time around, when you're about 14 years old. Subsequent experiences occur roughly at ages 44 and 74. In each instance, you may feel lonely and insecure. Focusing on specific tasks and practical efforts can increase your sense of security. The message is: persevere.

>> **Saturn conjunct Uranus:** Though you may feel hemmed in, rebelling just to make a statement will get you nowhere. Radical resistance won't work. But you can't do nothing either. Instead, seek controlled ways of expressing your individuality and breaking free of — or loosening — some of the restrictions that make you feel imprisoned. That will allow you to sail through this transit with aplomb.

>> **Saturn opposite Uranus:** Born free? That's not the way it feels. Events conspire to make you feel as if your options are shrinking, but don't underestimate the positive power of Saturn. Saturn supports organization and self-discipline. Together with Uranus, it allows you to develop the most original aspects of your unique self.

>> **Saturn conjunct Neptune:** You may feel steadier and more in control during this introspective phase — or you may be pessimistic and creatively stymied. Saturn transits are seldom fun. But if you've been troubled by alcohol or drug abuse, this is a brilliant time to come to terms with it. And if you are a songwriter or a poet, there could be no better time for learning the fundamentals of craft and applying them to the products of your imagination.

>> **Saturn opposite Neptune:** You may feel beset by confusion, doubt, and despondency. You feel tested, disappointed. This transit presents yet another chance to accept responsibility and face down your fears without being too hard on yourself. A structured approach works best.

>> **Saturn conjunct Pluto:** Issues of control and manipulation arise during this long-term, transformative transit. Despite restrictive and frustrating circumstances, you can find a way to acknowledge your mistakes or obsessions and rethink your purpose. As always with Saturn, reaching these goals requires you to acknowledge the realities of your situation. It may help to know that everyone who is close to you in age is experiencing this transit. All Saturn transits to Neptune, Uranus, and Pluto have a generational aspect. You are not alone.

>> **Saturn opposite Pluto:** Your desire to control your circumstances and pursue your goals collides with external pressures, which may be more powerful than you are. A compulsion or habit that may have you in its grip needs to be broken, and you may feel incapable of doing so. When Saturn is involved, the solution is always to build a structure, brick by brick. Saturn rewards discipline, persistence, and willpower.

>> **Saturn conjunct the Ascendant:** You strike people as dependable and trustworthy, and greater responsibility may come to you as a result. Though you may feel restrained and overworked, this difficult transit brings some benefits. It improves your ability to concentrate, stimulates you to regulate your behavior, and encourages you to rethink your ambitions. In the cycle of Saturn, you're beginning a seven-year stretch known as the *obscurity cycle,* which is characterized by introspection and a search for personal growth. This is the season for looking inward.

>> **Saturn opposite the Ascendant:** This transit marks a turning point in the way you relate to the world. It may bring dissatisfactions to the surface and disrupt relationships, both personal and professional. New alliances are likely to be with people who are older or more authoritative. Though relationships are likely to be a challenge during the next two and a half years, the good news is that you're beginning a seven-year period of opportunity and accomplishment known as the *activity cycle.* For 14 years, your focus has been primarily internal; now you're opening up to the world.

>> **Saturn conjunct the Midheaven:** With this transit, the seven-year *influence cycle* begins. If you've been paying your dues, you can expect to reach a peak of recognition and responsibility. This is a time of success and prominence during which you establish your place in the world. But remember that with Saturn, effort is always required. If you haven't found your footing in a profession or community, this transit could trigger a wave of discontent. If that's your situation, remember that Saturn responds positively to organization, structure, and the conscious allotment of time.

>> **Saturn opposite the Midheaven:** Home and family beg for attention. Perhaps a parent or grandparent needs your assistance, your dwelling place needs to be refurbished, or you will have to move. Whatever the issue is, you may feel weighed down by family needs or burdened by the problems of the past. Although this isn't an easy transit, it marks the beginning of another component of the Saturn cycle. Having just completed the seven-year obscurity cycle, described earlier in this section, you're now entering the *emergence cycle,* a more creative and exciting time.

REMEMBER

As the planet of limitation and loss, Saturn brings responsibility and requires a clear-eyed assessment of your situation. It also rewards discipline, willpower, organization, and hard work.

Unpredictable Uranus

When Uranus rides into town, life gets interesting. As the planet of revolution, technology, invention, electricity, individuality, and eccentricity, Uranus disrupts the usual flow of events and is associated with unforeseen occurrences and unusual people. Uranus takes 84 years — about a lifetime — to traverse the zodiac. (Turn to Chapter 10 for more information about the outer planets.)

>> **Uranus conjunct the Sun:** If you've been in a holding pattern, you aren't going to be there long. Your need to express your individuality propels you toward once-in-a-lifetime change. If you're on track, this transit shouldn't be traumatic. But if you're drifting or otherwise off your path, this transit could augur disruptive change. If you don't initiate alterations on your own, you can expect it to arrive unbidden from external sources. Act now. As the great poet Rilke said, "Want the change."

>> **Uranus opposite the Sun:** A change is gonna come — there's no getting around that. This disruptive transit supports innovative thinking and could herald an explosive era of instability. Digging in your heels against it won't work. Flexibility is required.

>> **Uranus conjunct the Moon:** Intuitive flashes bring insight during this moody, unstable transit. Look for emotional storms, shifts in family dynamics, or a sudden urge for independence.

>> **Uranus opposite the Moon:** Feelings of restriction and a need to break from the past make this a time of emotional fluctuations and revolutionary changes. Jogging in place is no longer an option. You need to move, to see things in a new way or to break free of an emotional constraint that has held you back.

>> **Uranus conjunct Mercury:** Though you may feel overscheduled and frantic, rigid thinking holds you back. You benefit from — and find pleasure in — learning something new. Fresh insights and facts compel you to abolish tired ideas and patterns of communication. Uranus triggers your ability to think in an original way. Record your thoughts.

>> **Uranus opposite Mercury:** You're mentally active and physically nervous, and you may have trouble sleeping. Tackling your problems in the same old way leads to the same old result. Willingly or not, you must try a new approach.

>> **Uranus conjunct Venus:** If the sizzle has gone out of a relationship you value, you can no longer be passive about it. Reinvigorate it or look elsewhere. If you're alone, you could meet someone in an unexpected way, and that person won't be like anyone else you know. Relationships that carry a hint of unpredictability appeal to you. Boring old alliances, no matter how worthy or rooted in history, don't.

>> **Uranus opposite Venus:** You feel restless and in need of stimulation. In your desire to escape boredom, you — or your partner — may be tempted by a relationship that seems to offer more pizazz. But will this new union last? It depends on what else is happening in your chart.

>> **Uranus conjunct Mars:** You're agitated, anxious for change and ready to take the initiative: that's the positive part. You're also accident-prone, angrier than usual, and likely to act rashly and make impulsive decisions. If your energy feels erratic, channel it via a martial arts class. That's one way to manage the aggression that this transit can deliver.

>> **Uranus opposite Mars:** Something needs to change during this volatile period, but you aren't sure what you want. Controlling your animosity and competitive feelings can be tricky, and you may provoke the opposition of others. Yet those outer influences may provide just the kick you need.

>> **Uranus conjunct Jupiter:** Rare opportunities and startling changes in circumstances distinguish this conjunction. In one chart from my files, this transit coincided with the loss of a family member and an unplanned pregnancy. In another case, it brought a disruptive but positive cross-country move. In a third instance, a woman rocketed to professional prominence when Uranus conjoined her tenth-house Jupiter — and plunged to Earth a year later when Saturn contacted her Sun and she received the dreaded pink slip, which launched her on a journey she never wanted to a place that — as it turned out — she loved.

>> **Uranus opposite Jupiter:** A need for independence and an urge to take a risk characterize this unruly influence. Fresh possibilities may tantalize (or frustrate) you. In your desire to lead a bigger life, you make some astonishing choices. Amaze your friends by all means — but don't let your optimism (or grandiosity) run away with your common sense.

>> **Uranus conjunct Saturn:** You feel boxed in and tense and no longer able to tolerate the limitations you put on yourself. Uranus acts as a catalyst, forcing you to shed old fears, limitations, and even jobs in search of a less confining sense of self.

>> **Uranus opposite Saturn:** You feel uneasy and anxious. Old habits die, and outworn patterns crumble under the onslaught of forces beyond your control.

>> **Uranus conjunct natal Uranus:** The Uranus return occurs when you're 84 years old. It symbolizes a complete cycle of individuality and can stimulate you to seek a new expression of your most essential self.

- >> **Uranus opposite natal Uranus:** This unsettling, anxiety-provoking, midlife-crisis transit, which happens around age 42, prods you to take risks and to rebel against the status quo.

- >> **Uranus conjunct Neptune:** If you were born in the late 1990s or afterwards, you will not experience this perplexing, mind-bending transit until you are old. It's a mystical and radical influence, and it will be accompanied by all sorts of novel ideas. But that isn't going to happen until late in this century.

- >> **Uranus opposite Neptune:** If you're feeling the effects of this transit, you're old enough to get into the movies at a discount, smart enough to avoid get-rich-quick schemes, and wise enough to care less about what other people think and more about what matters to you. Uranus stirs up your dreams, and nontraditional spiritual pursuits have a fresh appeal.

- >> **Uranus conjunct Pluto:** This heavy-duty transit can bring transitions that are unforeseen and momentous. However, unless you're over 100 years old, you aren't going to experience it any time soon.

- >> **Uranus opposite Pluto:** Old patterns and obsessions fall by the wayside with this transit, especially if Pluto is prominent in your horoscope.

- >> **Uranus conjunct the Ascendant:** Altering your appearance, acting in an abrupt or unpredictable manner, and emphasizing your greatest eccentricities are methods of expressing your insistent need for personal freedom. This transit can also coincide with unexpected recognition.

- >> **Uranus opposite the Ascendant:** Whether you initiate these changes or someone else does, unexpected shake-ups in relationships clear the way for greater freedom and individuality. The people who attract you now are markedly different from your usual type.

- >> **Uranus conjunct the Midheaven:** Career disturbances can open a dramatic chapter in your life. When an unusual opportunity presents itself, be courageous and grab it. Don't let unresolved feelings of inferiority stop you from fulfilling your destiny.

- >> **Uranus opposite the Midheaven:** Unexpected events and problems within the family can turn your domestic life upside down and alter your social status or professional relationships. A sudden change of residence is not out of the question.

REMEMBER

Uranus, the planet of upheaval, brings surprising changes and is associated with chaos, disorientation, and liberation.

Nebulous Neptune

Magical, mysterious Neptune bewilders and inspires. It dissolves boundaries, spawns illusions, encourages compassion, and stimulates the imagination. Unlike Uranus, Neptune's influence can be hard to detect, because it comes wrapped in a mystifying fog of vagueness and misapprehension. When something's happening and you don't know what it is, look to Neptune.

» **Neptune conjunct the Sun:** Self-pity, a diminished sense of self-esteem, and a tendency to drift are the downsides of this lengthy transit. It's a time of wondering, but also of visionary awareness and psychic sensitivity. The greatest benefit is that creative projects, hitherto only daydreams, can gradually be made manifest in the world. If you happen to be a Pisces, you might take up swimming. It will clear away the fog.

» **Neptune opposite the Sun:** Your ability to deceive yourself (or to allow yourself to be deceived) is at a peak during this confusing transit. Though your confidence may waver, sometimes wandering in the wilderness is all you can do. You're looking for a larger, more compassionate sense of self.

» **Neptune conjunct the Moon:** You're empathetic, forgiving, and highly attuned to the emotional environment around you. Pay attention to your dreams and intuition. And defend yourself against illusion by checking in from time to time with your most grounded confidant.

» **Neptune opposite the Moon:** Waves of emotional uncertainty and the urge to escape wash over you. You're easily misled, so be cautious about falling in with an untrustworthy lover or a spiritual advisor with an answer for everything. Don't let others erode your faith in yourself.

» **Neptune conjunct Mercury:** If you're a poet, artist, or musician, you're going to love this transit. But be prepared: The imaginative boost occurs at the expense of the ordinary things you count on Mercury for — like making intelligent decisions or remembering to pay your bills.

» **Neptune opposite Mercury:** Think you're communicating clearly? Think you've come up with a foolproof plan to save the environment? I wish. Neptune stimulates your artistic impulses, but it also weakens your concentration and foments an atmosphere in which misguided thinking can thrive.

» **Neptune conjunct Venus:** This could be a magical time. You're acutely sensitive and primed to fall in love. It could certainly happen. But does the object of your devotion return your affection? Is the relationship as perfect as you imagine? Remember that Neptune is the planet of delusion. Similarly, if you become convinced that you'll always be alone, dismiss that feeling and put your trust in things of the spirit.

>> **Neptune opposite Venus:** You feel riled up, especially (but not solely) about your love life. Romantic — or financial — visions dance in your head, yet you're unwilling or unable to fulfill those dreams. Be aware that this transit, like the conjunction of Neptune and Venus, stimulates wishful thinking.

>> **Neptune conjunct Mars:** Anger or envy can cause you to dissipate your energy. By acting intuitively and marshaling your talents, you lay the groundwork for success, especially in creative endeavors. Pay attention to coincidence and luck, good or bad. The outer world mirrors your inner reality and tells you whether you're on the right path.

>> **Neptune opposite Mars:** Confused about what you want? Observe as your suppressed desires float into awareness and express themselves in your actions. And watch, too, if you find yourself responding negatively to other people. Those reactions reflect your shadow, the dark side of your personality.

>> **Neptune conjunct Jupiter:** You fantasize about scores of possibilities. And so, without even realizing it, you open yourself up to new experiences. Your idealism, compassion, and faith in life grow.

>> **Neptune opposite Jupiter:** You're sympathetic, idealistic, and open to experience — but you're out of touch with reality. Travel. See the world. Don't buy that bridge.

>> **Neptune conjunct Saturn:** The rigid rules and regulations you live by aren't working anymore, and you need to update them with a less fearful set of bylaws. Remind yourself that everyone who was born within a few months of you is experiencing this transit. Let your idealism conquer your fear.

>> **Neptune opposite Saturn:** Old fears and blockages appear, and you have to face them squarely. This is a challenging but not necessarily negative time, for Neptune can dispel the limitations of the past.

>> **Neptune conjunct Uranus:** This generational transit is likely to produce altered states of consciousness, a vision of freedom, and an outbreak of eccentricity.

>> **Neptune opposite Uranus:** Vague dissatisfaction of the midlife-crisis kind afflicts you. If you've been in a rut, even if it's one you dug yourself, you may try to redefine yourself through exciting experiences.

>> **Neptune conjunct natal Neptune:** If you're experiencing this transit, you're too young (still an infant) or too ancient (164 years old) to bother about it.

>> **Neptune opposite natal Neptune:** This transit happens at age 82, about two years before Uranus returns. It can coincide with increased confusion, but it can also strengthen your imagination and spiritual awareness.

>> **Neptune conjunct Pluto:** This conjunction isn't going to happen in your lifetime.

>> **Neptune opposite Pluto:** This transit exerts a subtle influence that increases awareness and encourages you to rethink various aspects of your life, including psychological issues you've tried to repress.

>> **Neptune conjunct the Ascendant:** Neptune dissolves the boundaries of the external personality, leaving you unfocused or lost in a reverie. Consciously or not, you may alter your image. At worst, you're self-destructive. At best, you're intuitive and creative. Acting, painting, making music, and spiritual exploration are healthy outlets. Pay attention to your dreams — and daydreams. They're trying to tell you something.

>> **Neptune opposite the Ascendant:** If you're in a satisfying relationship, the two of you develop a form of communication that's virtually clairvoyant. But if your relationship is shaky, secrecy and deception can bring the house down. Pay attention to nuance.

>> **Neptune conjunct the Midheaven:** The boundaries of your career are dissolving. You may find it increasingly difficult to focus on the most tedious parts of what you do. Or mysterious goings-on in the office may cause you to ruminate on other, more inspiring options. Film, photography, music, art, oceanography, anything that involves healing, and all the Neptunian professions are options worth pursuing.

>> **Neptune opposite the Midheaven:** Confusion or dissatisfaction with your career, parents, or home life clouds your decision-making ability. To find purpose and resolution, listen to your inner voice. Or talk to your grandparents. As always with Neptune, help can be found through art, music, spiritual pursuits, and long walks on the beach.

REMEMBER

Neptune dissolves boundaries, creates confusion, invites illusion, and sensitizes the imagination.

Power-Hungry Pluto

In 2006, astronomers reclassified Pluto as a dwarf planet. This may make a difference to astrophysicists (though I can't see why it should). Astrologers essentially don't care. In our interpretation of the universe, Pluto is associated with power, regeneration, and the underworld of the psyche — a place where alchemy is the operative metaphor and size is deeply, truly meaningless. Plutonian transits, which last for two or three years, coincide with periods of profound transformation.

>> **Pluto conjunct the Sun:** Your awareness increases. You become increasingly conscious of your potential and unwilling to be anyone other than your most powerful self. Inappropriate relationships and jobs can drop away, and you can summon up the courage to resolve issues regarding your father or other authority figures. None of this may be easy. Pluto is heavy lifting. But the benefits are vast. Over the next couple of years, a new phase of your life begins. Between 2020 and 2050, only Capricorn, Aquarius, and Pisces will experience this transit.

>> **Pluto opposite the Sun:** Circumstances force you to take control of your destiny. Although you may feel blocked or frustrated, you're determined to act in the most powerful possible way. Above all, you seek recognition. Constructive action leads to success; vengeful, fear-based, or egotistical behavior backfires. This transit, like the conjunction, isn't easy but it can lead to permanent change, as Cancer, Leo, and Virgo will discover between 2020 and 2050.

>> **Pluto conjunct the Moon:** Powerful emotional forces are swirling around you. Concerns that you may have ignored since childhood reemerge, including issues regarding your mother. Confronting matters of dependency and inferiority brings healing and catharsis.

>> **Pluto opposite the Moon:** Emotional turmoil and changing family circumstances provoke shifts in your domestic life. Facing the truth is the only option, painful though it may be.

>> **Pluto conjunct Mercury:** Take yourself seriously. Your mental capacity is developing, and your insights are more penetrating than ever before. You're able to influence others through the spoken or written word.

>> **Pluto opposite Mercury:** Differences in opinion, problems in communication, and obsessive or depressive thoughts may distress you. Secrets may be revealed. You also have a chance to communicate in a more forceful way.

>> **Pluto conjunct Venus:** Crazy in love? Jealousy, resentment, or unstoppable obsession may have you in its grip. Unconsciously you seek a profound connection. You can probably find it during this intense — if occasionally melodramatic — period.

>> **Pluto opposite Venus:** An emotional crisis can cause a relationship either to crumble or to deepen. A clash of values or a sexual mismatch may need attention, and financial problems could hound you.

- **Pluto conjunct Mars:** Increased determination and ambition open many doors. Although you may need to manage your anger, your heightened ability to focus enables you to act with tremendous effect.

- **Pluto opposite Mars:** Upsetting events or circumstances beyond your control urge you to take action and to channel your anger in constructive ways.

- **Pluto conjunct Jupiter:** Expand the boundaries of your life, and you can totally transform it. Opportunities arrive through education, travel, religion, or the law.

- **Pluto opposite Jupiter:** Your desire for success and power motivates you to seek change, but you may feel stymied in your quest. Be careful not to overestimate your ability or promise more than you can do. Also, if you're religious, you could experience a crisis of faith.

- **Pluto conjunct Saturn:** Shedding your self-imposed chains is far from easy. This conjunction ushers in a period of intense self-examination that results in concrete change.

- **Pluto opposite Saturn:** Outside forces thwart your efforts and force you to alter your plans during this trying time. As always with Saturn, you benefit from self-discipline and diligence.

- **Pluto conjunct Uranus:** If you've repressed your individuality, it now reemerges. Rather than hiding your idiosyncrasies, embrace them. You'll find it most gratifying.

- **Pluto opposite Uranus:** Surprising circumstances propel you into the future, forcing you to come to terms with who you are and who you want to be.

- **Pluto conjunct Neptune:** Your dreams, beliefs, and ideals are slowly shifting.

- **Pluto opposite Neptune:** Unless you're over 100, this transit isn't one that will affect you any time soon.

- **Pluto conjunct natal Pluto:** Not possible.

- **Pluto opposite natal Pluto:** If you're experiencing this transit, you're in your 90s. It's not easy — Pluto transits never are — but you've seen worse. Don't be alarmed.

- **Pluto conjunct the Ascendant:** You're no longer willing to deny or suppress your personal power. A strong self-image fortifies your resolution and spurs you to initiate change.

- **Pluto opposite the Ascendant:** You demand to be recognized for the powerful person you are, and you want to make an impact on the world. If a toxic relationship is holding you down, it must go. If some habit of timidity or self-denigration has limited you, it too must go. Claim your authority.

>> **Pluto conjunct the Midheaven:** Your career or role in the community enters a new era. Your public image changes.

>> **Pluto opposite the Midheaven:** Over the next few years, your circumstances at home and perhaps your relationship with your parents or heritage will undergo a shift. Power flows in your direction.

REMEMBER

Pluto brings disintegration, regeneration, and metamorphosis. Conflicts with other people and internal rumbles characterize these transformative transits.

Warning: The Astrologer's Curse

If you're anything like me, you may discover that knowing the rudiments of transits can fill you with fear. Sooner or later, you'll notice a troublesome transit approaching and you'll start to panic as worst-case scenarios haunt your imagination. Will someone die? Is calamity imminent? Weeks or months later, you may be relieved to realize that not one of the disasters you pictured has occurred. Major events, whether positive or negative, require a confluence of influences, which is why the longer you follow the transits, the more restrained you're likely to become in your predictions.

The rules of transit interpretation are simple:

>> **If the configurations in your birth chart don't make a certain event possible, it won't happen, no matter what the transits.** Unpredictable Uranus waltzing through your second house of finances with bountiful Jupiter brings a lottery bonanza if and only if your birth chart is littered with aspects for making easy money. The predisposition has to be there.

>> **Even with a birth predisposition, a single transit seldom correlates with a life-altering event.** Those dramatic situations arise from multiple influences, all pointing in a similar direction.

>> **Any transit has several possible interpretations.** Nothing is predestined. But the energy of the transit must be expressed. The way that occurs depends on circumstances and on the choices you make.

REAL LIFE EXAMPLE

Here's a case where foreseeing catastrophe would have been so easy — and so wrong. Imagine a person whose Sun, Ascendant, and several planets are being pummeled not only by Saturn but also by Uranus, Neptune, and Pluto. Even individually, those distant worlds have been known to make astrologers twitch. When they all act up at once, it's hard not to worry.

So I wonder what I would have said in 1993 if Toni Morrison, whose chart is reproduced in Figure 16-2, had come to me for a consultation. Her birth chart is in the interior part of the wheel. The transiting planets are in the outer part. Looking at that chart, I would have noticed that transiting Saturn — the planet of karma, of lessons, of reaping what you have sown — was reeling back and forth over her Sun (and had twice made an exact conjunction with it earlier that year); that transiting Uranus and Neptune, traveling in tandem through the ninth house, were conjunct her natal Saturn and opposed to her natal Pluto; and that transiting Pluto had been dueling with her Ascendant for about a year and was approaching an exact opposition.

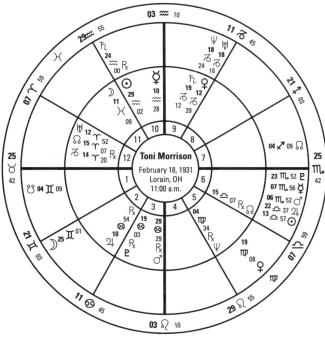

© John Wiley & Sons, Inc.

FIGURE 16-2:
Toni Morrison's natal chart. Her birth chart is on the inner part of the wheel. The planets scattered around the outer rim represent the transits for 1993.

Observing all of this, I might have uttered hopeful words about transformation (Pluto) and responsibility (Saturn). I certainly would have told her that Saturn transiting through the tenth house often correlates with professional success. But secretly, I would have been worried. Like a lot of people, I find it easy to imagine catastrophe.

So what actually happened to Toni Morrison in 1993? She won the Nobel Prize for Literature. With Saturn in her Sun sign, she had indeed reaped what she had sown.

REMEMBER

The most self-destructive mistake you can make as an astrologer is to allow your knowledge of transits to become a source of anxiety. Take it from me: Most of the terrifying things that astrologers agonize over (particularly in their own charts) never come to pass. Don't waste your time fretting over the worst possible damage that transits might do.

IN THIS CHAPTER

» Benefiting from the phases of the Moon

» Tuning into the Moon in the signs

» Watching the Moon in the houses

» Surveying the top five lunar influences

» Wondering about the Moon void-of-course

Chapter **17**

The Lunar Advantage: Using Astrology in Daily Life

D o you know where the Moon is right now? Without looking out the window, do you remember its phase? Can you name the sign of the zodiac that it inhabits? Do you know whether it's waxing or waning?

Don't feel bad if you can't answer these questions. Except when the Moon is full (and often even then), most people don't have a clue about where it is or what it's up to. But thousands of years ago, men and women on every continent worshipped the Moon and were attentive to all its phases. In ancient Greece, for example, storytellers invented a full cast of lunar deities, a dramatis personae, each of whom reflected a different phase of the moon. Tomboy Artemis, patron of girls and goddess of the hunt, symbolized the New Moon; Hera, queen of the gods, along with Demeter, mother of Persephone and goddess of the harvest, ruled the Full Moon; and Hecate, a goddess of a certain age, reigned over witchcraft and the waning lunar crescent.

Unlike ourselves, the people of long ago who worshipped those goddesses observed the Moon carefully. Over time, they tracked the monthly journey of the Moon as it waxed and waned, and they discovered the 18-year cycle of eclipses. They also came to believe that the Moon, in its monthly orbit around the Earth, reflected and supported the pattern of human activity.

That ancient knowledge is within your grasp. When you understand the Moon and its fundamental changes, you can choose dates that strengthen your intentions, avoid dates that could lead to frustration or failure, and live your life according to the rhythms of the stars. This chapter tells you how — and when — to seize the day.

Timing Your Actions by the Phases of the Moon

How many phases of the Moon are there? It depends on whom you ask. In India, astrologers identify 27 "lunar mansions." The 20th century astrologer (and composer) Dane Rudhyar counted eight phases: New, Crescent, First Quarter, Disseminating, Full, Gibbous, Last Quarter, and Balsamic (no relation to the vinegar). Ancient goddess worshippers, like their contemporary Pagan and Wiccan equivalents, generally acknowledged three phases: waxing, full, and waning. Today, most people recognize the following four phases of the Moon.

>> **New:** A time of increasing energy and new beginnings. New Moons that coincide with solar eclipses are especially powerful. Solar eclipses occur about twice a year and can affect you even if they're not visible from your part of the world.

>> **First Quarter:** A time of growth, friction, and activity.

>> **Full:** Ongoing situations come to a head, emotions are heightened, and major events take place. Full Moons are especially revealing when they're also lunar eclipses.

>> **Last Quarter:** A time of completion, release, and fading vitality.

REMEMBER

By taking note of these natural rhythms, you can time your activities to maximum advantage — and you don't need an astrological calendar either. Just glance at the Moon whenever you're out at night, and soon, knowing its phase will become second nature to you. Table 17-1 describes the approximate appearance and orientation of the Moon along with the actions best suited to that phase. Each phase lasts for about a week.

TABLE 17-1

What To Do by the Light of the Moon

Phase of the Moon	Appearance	Recommended Activities
New Moon	Invisible at first; then it appears as a sliver with the tips of the crescent pointing east. Rises at dawn, sets at sunset.	A time of beginnings. Set goals; make wishes; start projects; plant seeds; initiate endeavors.
First Quarter Moon	A semicircle with the flat side facing east (on the left) and the curved side facing west. Rises at noon. High in the sky after sunset. Sets around midnight.	A time of activity. Take action; develop projects; take essential steps; make decisions; deal with conflict.
Full Moon	A glowing orb. Rises at sunset. High in the sky at midnight. Sets around dawn.	A time of culmination when emotions run high and things come to fruition. Assess progress; make adjustments; deal with the fallout.
Last Quarter Moon	A semicircle with the flat side facing west (on the right) and the curved side facing east. Rises at midnight. High in the sky before dawn.	Finish up; wind down; reflect; retreat.

TIP

Once a year, there's a New Moon in your sign. Regardless of whether it comes before or after your birthday, the highly charged period between those two days is ideal for setting yearly goals and taking the initial steps toward fulfilling them. If the New Moon happens to fall right on your birthday, congratulations. The coming year promises to be a time of new beginnings.

Watching the Moon

I don't want to overstate this, but knowing the location of the Moon, both by phase and by sign, is more than useful. It is thrilling, and not just because you can amaze your friends. Even in the heart of the heart of the city, where no one has seen the Milky Way in years, you can observe the Moon in all its splendor. You can see that its shape is never the same two nights in a row and that the stars surrounding it change nightly. You'll know when the Moon is waxing, when it is full, and when it is waning. And you will begin to feel in sync with the rhythm of the stars. And this isn't hyperbole. It's what will happen.

Taking Advantage of the Moon in the Signs

Is the Moon full? Then it's in the sign opposite the Sun. So if you happen to see a full Moon in early May, when the Sun is in Taurus, you know for a fact that the Moon is in Scorpio. Two nights later, observing that the Moon is looking distinctly lop-sided, you might conclude that it's probably in Sagittarius. But is it definitely in Sagittarius? To know for sure, you have a choice. You can go online or refer to an app. Or you can use an astrological calendar. Personally, I wouldn't be without one.

TIP

Two of the best are *Jim Maynard's Celestial Guide* and the many calendars published by Llewellyn, including my favorite, *Llewellyn's Daily Planetary Guide*. These calendars, available in a variety of sizes, are filled with information about the signs, the planets, and the astrological activity of each day. Most important, they tell you exactly when the Moon enters each sign and what aspects it makes while it's there.

Knowing the location of the Moon is oddly satisfying. Over the years, I've found that I enjoy certain lunar placements more than others, and I look forward to them. As a writer, I love Moon in Gemini. I always hope to accomplish a lot on those few days — even though experience has taught me that Moon in Gemini pulls in more out-of-town visitors, inconsequential errands, and unavoidable engagements than any other sign. Nonetheless, when I do manage to sit at my desk on those days, the words pour out.

I love Moon in Virgo, too: It's ideal for taking care of business and cleaning the house. I'm not the most efficient person on the planet, but you might not know it on these days.

Most of all, nothing tops the Moon in my sign. I feel invigorated and hopeful. I think you'll feel that way too.

REMEMBER

Here's how to make the most of the Moon's journey through each sign:

>> **Moon in Aries:** Be bold. Assert yourself, start short-term projects, do anything that requires a blast of energy and a spark of courage. Watch out for temper tantrums.

>> **Moon in Taurus:** Be practical. Begin long-term projects, garden, pay your bills. Concentrate on jobs that call for patience. Listen to your body. Walk in the woods. Sing.

>> **Moon in Gemini:** Read, write, call your siblings, have coffee with a friend. Buy books, magazines, writing supplies, anything that comes in duplicate. Run errands, take short trips, change your mind. Don't text and drive.

- >> **Moon in Cancer:** Stay home. Cook, redecorate, call your mother. Spend time with people you love. Shop for antiques. Walk on the beach. Gaze at the stars. The Moon is at home in Cancer, the sign that it rules, making this a time of emotional vulnerability. Buy Kleenex.

- >> **Moon in Leo:** Be romantic, cavort with children, learn to tango, see a play, throw a party. Dare to approach high-status people. Be confident. Be stylish. Let the good times roll.

- >> **Moon in Virgo:** Take care of the mundane. Tidy up. Eliminate clutter, visit the dentist, make appointments, bring the pet to the vet, deal with the nitpicky details you normally try to sidestep. The Moon in Virgo boosts productivity.

- >> **Moon in Libra:** Indulge yourself. Go to a concert or museum, do something artistic, have a beauty treatment, smooth over disagreements. Form a business partnership. Sign a peace treaty. Get married.

- >> **Moon in Scorpio:** Expect intense encounters. Have sex, see your therapist, read a mystery novel, file your taxes, pay your debts, get insurance, write your will. Go scuba diving or spelunking. Explore the depths.

- >> **Moon in Sagittarius:** Go outside. Travel or plan a trip, attend a class, talk to a lawyer, pursue spiritual or philosophical interests, ride a bike, go for a run, alter your routine.

- >> **Moon in Capricorn:** Be businesslike. Update your résumé, prepare a contract, do tasks that involve corporations or other large organizations. Talk to an older person. Investigate the past. Do your duty.

- >> **Moon in Aquarius:** Socialize. Volunteer for a cause. Buy software, get together with friends, see an independent film, visit a planetarium. Participate in a group event. Do something unusual.

- >> **Moon in Pisces:** Relax. Meditate, take a nap, take a bath, space out, listen to music, analyze your dreams. Have an intimate talk or a good cry. Read a poem (or write one). Paint. Swim. Stare at the ocean or the stars.

Tracking the Moon through the Houses

Tracking the Moon through the houses of your birth chart is another way to tap into its power. Start with your Ascendant or rising sign. Let's say that it's Leo — that is, Leo is on the cusp of your first house. So when the Moon is in Leo, it's traveling through your first house. Once it swings into Virgo, it enters your second house. And so on.

At any given moment, the Moon is in one sign of the zodiac and one house of your chart. If you want to get persnickety about it, you could figure out exactly when the Moon will hit the precise degree of each house cusp. But who has time for that? Not me. I suggest that you simply note the sign on the cusp of each house.

When the Moon enters that sign, that's your cue to turn your attention to the matters of that house. For example:

>> **Moon in the first house:** Do something for yourself. Get a haircut or a manicure. Schedule an interview or a date. Give a presentation at work. Your visibility is high, so present yourself with flair. You'll make a positive impression.

>> **Moon in the second house:** Greater security means greater peace of mind. Practical or financial matters demand your notice. Pay bills. Meet with a financial advisor. Have a yard sale. Make important purchases. And if you're involved with construction in any way, get to work.

>> **Moon in the third house:** Feeling restless? Run some errands. Go to the library. Gather information. Answer your email. Talk to the neighbors. Get together with brothers and sisters. Take a short trip. This position favors reading, writing, and anything having to do with school.

>> **Moon in the fourth house:** Focus on home, family, parents, real estate, the past.

>> **Moon in the fifth house:** Romance, recreation, creative pursuits, and anything having to do with children are favored during these few days.

>> **Moon in the sixth house:** The emphasis is on work, health, and the routines of daily life. Clear your desk. Organize your files. Catch up on everything you let slide. Also: Start a diet. Go to the gym. Get a checkup. Take care of yourself.

>> **Moon in the seventh house:** If you're married, set your needs aside and focus on your mate. If you have a business partner or you deal with the public at large, put your attention there. This house is about cooperation, but it also rules your adversaries. When the Moon is in the seventh house, other people are in control. Act accordingly.

>> **Moon in the eighth house:** When the Moon is in the domain of sex, death, regeneration, and other people's money, you could have an affair, rob a bank, visit a mortuary, see your shrink, or talk to a close friend, perhaps about your compulsive behaviors or feelings of dependency. Whatever you do, the emotional charge is likely to be intense. This is the house of transformation.

>> **Moon in the ninth house:** Anything that involves publishing, higher education, religion, or the law moves forward now. Go to a lecture. Go to the movies. Plan a trip to faraway places. It's all about expanding your vision.

>> **Moon in the tenth house:** The emphasis is on career, community affairs, and your public image. Send out your résumé. Give a speech. Be in the world.

>> **Moon in the eleventh house:** See friends who support your aspirations. Form a group. Or join one. Whether it's the Audubon Society or a neighborhood book club, you benefit from the association.

>> **Moon in the twelfth house:** Retreat. Relax. Rejuvenate yourself with solitude and sleep. This is the house of the unconscious but also of secrets and self-undoing. So take care of yourself — and don't do anything rash.

Making the Most of Momentous Lunar Influences

The Moon cruises through the zodiac faster than any other planet, so worrying about its precise location as it spins through one sign after another can drive you crazy. Most transits of the Moon make no difference whatsoever and can be safely ignored. But a few monthly lunar transits offer opportunities that are too valuable to miss.

REMEMBER

Here are the top five monthly influences:

>> **The Moon in your Sun sign:** Your personal power is at its peak. You are your most charismatic self during these few days, making them a fine time to schedule important meetings, first dates, or anything that requires you to be at your outgoing best.

>> **The Moon in the sign opposite your Sun sign:** Your personal power is weak. You're at the beck and call of others, and your plans are likely to be scuttled or interrupted. Expect interference.

>> **The Moon in your Moon sign:** Your emotions flow freely, whether you want them to or not. You're more sensitive and easily hurt than usual, but you're also more attuned to emotional subtleties and unconscious motivations. Listen to your intuition.

>> **Dark of the Moon:** At the end of the lunar cycle, the Moon is so close to the Sun that it's invisible. During this period of decrease, attempts to launch new ventures fizzle, and hopelessness often abounds. Instead of exerting yourself in a fruitless attempt to influence events, put the finishing touches on undertakings that are nearing conclusion. Also, get plenty of sleep, secure in the knowledge that the New Moon means a fresh start.

>> **New Moon:** Make wishes, set goals, and inaugurate new projects.

Finally, there is one other momentous lunar influence: the eclipse. If you've ever watched an eclipse, you know how eerie it can be. A solar eclipse, which takes place during a New Moon, literally turns day to night. A lunar eclipse, which happens during the Full Moon, seems to erase the Moon from the sky. No wonder ancient people told so many myths about them.

REMEMBER

Followers of astrology also have myths, one of which is that eclipses always bring bad news. That's flat out false. But people are afraid of change, and change is what eclipses are about. When an eclipse — or a series of eclipses — hits your chart, it delivers a burst of cosmic energy that can shake things up. I've seen eclipses usher in hideous divorces, and I've seen them bring true love. Eclipses slam some doors shut and open others. And sometimes, they do nothing much at all . . . until later. An eclipse can have a delayed effect.

A good astrological calendar will tell you when — and where — to expect an eclipse. Notice its location by sign, by house, and by the exact degree of the eclipse. The closer it is to an important planet or angle in your chart, the more likely it is to affect you. But whether that change is an external event or a psychological shift is another question.

Avoiding the Void

Picture this: The Moon spins into a new sign — let's say Taurus — and begins to connect with the planets. It conjuncts Jupiter in the evening (a splendid sight), trines Venus a few minutes later, squares the Sun the next morning, opposes Mars at noon, conjuncts Saturn during *All Things Considered,* and then sextiles Mercury. After that . . . nothing: No more major aspects. A few hours later, it enters Gemini, and the process begins anew.

That span, between the Moon's last major aspect in one sign and its entrance into the next, can last anywhere from a few seconds to a day or longer. During that time, the Moon is said to be *void-of-course.* If the word "void" makes you nervous, you sense the problem. When the Moon is void-of-course, things fall apart and judgment goes awry. Though ordinary activities are unaffected, business deals made during that time tend to crumble, and decisions, however carefully made, may turn out to be wrong-headed.

The usual advice for a void-of-course Moon is to avoid jumping into anything new or doing anything important like interviewing for a job or getting married or. But let's get real: You'd have to be unnaturally vigilant to live that way. The Moon goes void-of-course every couple of days, and to worry about it on a regular basis is insane. I used to dismiss it entirely. And then one day a publisher called out of the blue, asked me to write a book on a subject I love, and requested a meeting. I agreed to the suggested time even though the Moon was void-of-course. The meeting couldn't have been more exciting. We hit it off perfectly, saw eye to eye on everything, and enthusiastically agreed to terms. Yet the project died. Would it have made a difference if I'd scheduled the meeting for another time? Maybe not. Nonetheless, after that disappointment I began to pay attention to the void-of-course Moon.

Still, the vast majority of the time, I ignore it. But when I'm scheduling an important meeting, starting a project I care about, or getting together for the first time with someone I hope will become a friend, I check my handy astrological calendar and — if at all possible — I avoid the void.

IN THIS CHAPTER

» **Explaining retrograde motion**

» **Contending with retrograde Mercury**

» **Dealing with retrograde Mars and Venus**

» **Contemplating other retrograde planets**

Chapter **18**

Retrograde Hell? The Truth Revealed

I t's amazing how many people there are who can't cast a horoscope, don't know their rising signs, can barely name their Sun signs, and yet descend into panic over the retrograde movement of Mercury. These supposedly sinister periods, during which that little planet appears to travel backward, arrive regularly three or four times a year. And yes, they often do usher in a volley of minor misunderstandings, irritations, and disruptions. Worse yet, they stir up a storm of fear and anxiety in the hearts of astrology fans everywhere. So is this reaction called for? In a word, no. Retrograde motion isn't a tragedy. It isn't a disaster. It isn't even a cause for alarm. It's a respite and a gift from the cosmos — but only if you understand its purpose and use it appropriately. In this chapter, I tell you how to grapple calmly and rationally with retrograde planets.

Retrograde Revealed

When a planet is *retrograde*, it appears to be reeling backward. In truth, the planets always move forward. On a regular schedule, each of them (excluding the Sun and Moon) seems to slow down, pause (or station), and retrace its path, arcing backward across the same stretch of the zodiac that it just passed through. For weeks or months at a time (depending on the planet), it swims against the planetary tide. Then it slows down, pauses, and resumes its forward movement. Or as astrologers say, it *goes direct*.

When ancient astronomers observed this complicated dance, they invented all kinds of scenarios to account for it. In the second century BCE, for example, Greek observers speculated that retrograde planets had veered away from their regular orbits and were looping around them on spheres carved from the purest crystal. But now we know: the planets revolve around the Sun in one direction only, no matter how it looks. And there are no crystal spheres.

REMEMBER

The apparent backwards motion of the planets is only a visual phenomenon, a disconcerting side effect of the geometry of the solar system and the differing speeds of the planets. You can experience a similar sensation on a train. If two trains pull out of the station together but your train is moving faster, the train on the adjacent track appears to slide backward. That backward motion, like the retrograde motion of the planets, is an optical illusion.

When a planet is retrograde, it is revisiting old ground. Nothing much usually comes of that. Usually there's no drama involved. But when a planet turns retrograde close to one of your natal planets, it alerts you to something that you didn't know, ignored, should have done differently, need to redo.

Successfully Handling Retrograde Mercury

Recently, an ophthalmologist who was having trouble with his million-dollar diagnostic equipment asked for my professional opinion: Was he having this problem because Mars was retrograde? No, I was able to tell him. Mars isn't to blame; it's Mercury. The question didn't surprise me (although the source did) because I hear it all the time from people who have lost patience after suffering through a barrage of minor frustrations. The final indignity might be a Wi-Fi breakdown, a missing text, a missed bus, a cancelled appointment, a broken shoelace, or 27 minutes on hold followed by a help line conversation that doesn't help. When these irritations pile up, even card-carrying astrology-deniers wonder if Mercury retrograde might explain their woes.

Often, it does. Tiny Mercury, the prince of communication, goes into "reverse" every four months for three weeks at a stretch. During those irksome interludes — and particularly at the beginning and end — you can expect minor mishaps and annoyances. When Mercury is retrograde, devices act up, transportation takes the maximum amount of time, and the word-of-the-day is "glitch."

Making the best of it

Why crazy things happen when Mercury is retrograde, I cannot claim to know. Astrology, to my way of thinking, is a system of metaphor, a symbolic language that reflects our lives the way water reflects the sky. So even though the planets never actually spin backward, their apparent turn-arounds mirror our reactions and experiences.

When Mercury is retrograde, the offer is withdrawn, the date cancelled, the teacup cracked. Vexation abounds. Yet despite what you may have heard, retrograde Mercury isn't an evil force out to get you. It's a rain-soaked afternoon, not a hurricane; a delayed flight, not a mid-air collision. It encourages you to slow down (because the Wifi isn't working), to adapt (because the situation isn't what you thought it was), to check on things you might normally ignore (because your package should have arrived by now), to wait (because you have no choice). It encourages you to put things into perspective and to be flexible. It also offers something most of us desperately need: a time-out and a chance to pick up the pieces.

Here's how to cope.

First, prepare. Before the retrograde period begins, you can pay your bills, finish that project at work, clear the decks. If something important is pending, try to complete it before the retrograde period begins or postpone it until afterwards. If neither is possible, so be it. Retrograde Mercury never ruined anybody's life.

Still, there are a few caveats. When Mercury is retrograde, do *not*

>> Launch an important project.

>> Open a business.

>> Get married, unless it's your second time around with the same person.

>> Purchase a computer, smart phone, or any other electronic device.

>> Buy a car, a boat, an airplane, an electric scooter.

>> Purchase a home.

>> Move.

>> Start a job (unless there's no other choice).

>> Sign a contract.

>> Expect things to go smoothly.

>> Try to fight the fates. Forcing things to happen on your schedule only creates further mayhem.

TIP

To get the most out of Mercury retrograde, think of it as a positive, a chance to hop off that treadmill. You've been given a reprieve. All you have to do is

>> Review.

>> Revise. (Mercury retrograde is invaluable for writers.)

>> Reconsider. Change your mind.

>> Revisit the past.

>> Redo something.

>> Remember to back up.

>> Confirm your reservations.

>> Check the facts.

>> Make repairs.

>> Reorganize.

>> Release your anxiety.

>> Relax.

>> Make sure your phone is juiced up, but don't count on it to keep you entertained. It could have problems of its own.

>> Carry a book or magazine. When Mercury is retrograde, your chances of having to wait increase exponentially.

Revealing the rhythm of retrograde

Mercury goes retrograde every four months for about three weeks each time. The first few days tend to be the most disruptive, followed by the last couple of days. Although retrograde Mercury affects everyone, every cycle is different. Sometimes, you hardly notice it. Other times, Mercury generates such a blizzard of delays and irritations that you can't miss its baleful influence. What makes the difference? Location, location, location.

You are most vulnerable to retrograde Mercury when it is located near a planet in your chart. If Mercury is traveling through Aries and you have the Sun, Moon, Mercury, or the Ascendant in that sign, you will feel the slowdown. If Mercury begins or ends its retrograde within a degree or two of a planet or angle in your horoscope, you're even more likely to feel the exasperating effects.

Table 18-1 shows you when (and where) Mercury is retrograde from the first day of 2020 to the last day of 2032. The dates for each retrograde period correspond to the degrees of the zodiac listed in the "Location" column.

For example, you can see that in 2020 Mercury is retrograde from February 17 until March 10. During that time it wheels backward from 12° Pisces — its location on the 17th — to 28° Aquarius, its location on March 10. Then it goes direct. It retraces its path and moves forward. Months pass. Then on June 18, 2020, it goes retrograde once more, this time at 14° Cancer. Three times a year this happens. It's part of the rhythm of our lives.

TABLE 18-1 **Retrograde Mercury**

Year	Dates	Location
2020	Feb. 17–Mar. 10	12° Pisces–28° Aquarius
	June 18–July 12	14° Cancer–5° Cancer
	Oct. 14–Nov. 3	11° Scorpio–25° Libra
2021	Jan. 30–Feb. 21	26° Aquarius–11° Aquarius
	May 29–June 22	24° Gemini–16° Gemini
	Sep. 27–Oct. 18	25° Libra–10° Libra
2022	Jan. 14–Feb. 4	10° Aquarius–24° Capricorn
	May 10–June 3	4° Gemini–26° Taurus
	Sep. 10–Oct. 2	8° Libra–24° Virgo
2022-2023	Dec. 29, 2022–Jan. 18, 2023	24° Capricorn–8° Capricorn
2023	Apr. 21–May 15	15° Taurus–5° Taurus
	Aug. 23–Sep. 15	21° Virgo–8° Virgo
2023-2024	Dec. 13, 2023–Jan. 2, 2024	8° Capricorn–22° Sagittarius
2024	Apr. 1–Apr. 25	25° Aries–15° Aries
	Aug. 5–Aug. 28	4° Virgo–21° Libra
	Nov. 26–Dec. 15	22° Sagittarius–6° Sagittarius
2025	Mar. 15–Apr. 7	9° Aries–26° Pisces
	July 18–Aug. 11	15° Aries–4° Leo
	Nov. 9–Nov. 29	6° Sagittarius–20° Scorpio

(continued)

TABLE 18-1 *(continued)*

Year	Dates	Location
2026	Feb. 26–Mar. 20	22° Pisces–8° Pisces
	June 29–July 23	26° Cancer–16° Cancer
	Oct. 24–Nov. 13	20° Scorpio–5° Scorpio
2027	Feb. 9–Mar. 3	5° Pisces–20° Aquarius
	July 10–July 4	6° Cancer–27° Gemini
	Oct. 7–Oct.28	4° Scorpio–19° Libra
2028	Jan. 24–Feb. 14	19° Aquarius–3° Aquarius
	May 21–June 14	16° Gemini–7° Gemini
	Sep. 19–Oct.11	18° Libra–3° Libra
2029	Jan. 7–Jan. 27	3° Aquarius–17° Capricorn
	May 1–May 25	26° Taurus–17° Taurus
	Sep. 2–Sep. 25	1° Libra–17° Virgo
2029-2030	Dec. 22, 2029–Jan. 11, 2030	17° Capricorn–1° Capricorn
2030	Apr. 13–May 6	7° Taurus–27° Aries
	Aug. 16–Sep. 8	14° Virgo–1° Virgo
	Dec. 6–Dec. 25	1° Capricorn–15° Sagittarius
2031	May 26–Apr. 18	19° Aries–7° Aries
	July 29–Aug. 22	26° Leo–14° Leo
	Nov. 19–Dec. 9	16° Sagittarius–29° Scorpio
2032	Mar. 7–Mar. 30	2° Aries–19° Pisces
	July 10–Aug. 3	7° Leo–26° Cancer
	Nov. 2–Nov. 22	0° Sagittarius–14° Scorpio

This table tells you a lot about the retrograde cycles in those years. But there's one part of the cycle that is omitted here. It's not the most important part. But it's not nothing either. It's the shadow.

The shadow of retrograde, decoded

Some people feel the retrograde effects for a few days before the retrograde has started or after it is over. If that happens to you — if the retrograde doesn't start until Thursday, and here it is Tuesday and you have already shattered the screen on your phone and inadvertently stood up a friend — welcome to the shadow. To see how it works, consider the first retrograde period of 2020.

On February 17 of that year, Mercury turns retrograde at 12° Pisces. It continues in a backward direction until it reaches 28° Aquarius on March 10. That's the dreaded retrograde period.

But actually, when Mercury goes retrograde, it spins through the same part of the zodiac three times.

> On February 2, Mercury reaches 28° Aquarius and continues in the usual fashion until it reaches 12° Pisces on February 17. This is the pre-shadow.
>
> On February 17, Mercury turns retrograde at 12° Pisces. It remains so for about three weeks, reaching 28° Aquarius on March 10. This is the traditional retrograde period.
>
> On March 10, Mercury turns direct at 28° Aquarius. It arrives back at 12° Pisces on March 31 — its third tour of that slice of the sky. This is the post-shadow.

What should you do about all this? Many astrologers suggest caution during shadow periods. I'm not against caution. Au contraire. If you're doing something monumental — buying a house, signing a contract, kicking off your campaign for president — it pays to be cautious. If you want to extend the retrograde period for a few days, do so.

But note: Once you add the full shadow periods, any given retrograde period inflates from three weeks to two months. That's a long time. By all means pay attention to Mercury retrograde. But please don't let it take over your life. And don't let the shadow scare you.

Looking for Retrograde Venus

In Meso-American astrology, Venus ruled. The Aztecs and Mayans kept careful note of its rising and setting, its arrival as the morning star and as the evening star, its regular disappearances, and its intervals of retrograde motion, which occur every year and a half for about six weeks. Aztec astrologers believed those retrograde weeks were dangerous, especially in the political arena. Astrologers today generally see retrograde Venus as a time of uncertainty, distraction, misinterpretation, passivity, and unfulfilled desire in two areas: romance and finance.

It sounds bad, I know. But the effects are usually subtle. And if perchance your love life is less than spectacular — if it's nonexistent — retrograde Venus gives you license to forget about it for a while and turn your mind to other matters. What a relief.

Venus retrograde can also sponsor a rerun, reprising a long-ago financial involvement or love affair, in which case, you could be back in the soup. Retrograde motion always comes with a reminder: enjoy yourself — but don't make the same mistake twice.

TIP

Here are three iron-clad pieces of advice:

>> Don't get married when Venus is retrograde (unless both you and your intended have retrograde Venus in your birth chart).

>> Don't make major financial commitments when Venus is retrograde. Don't get a loan, sign a mortgage, sink your life's savings into a sure-fire investment opportunity, or buy artwork, emeralds, couture clothing or anything associated with Venus other than flowers and chocolates.

>> Don't have cosmetic surgery while Venus is retrograde.

Table 18-2 tells you when (and where) Venus is retrograde from 2020 to 2032. During the unlisted years, Venus remains direct.

TABLE 18-2   **Retrograde Venus**

Year	Dates	Location
2020	May 13–June 25	21° Gemini–5° Gemini
2021–2022	Dec. 19, 2021–Jan. 29, 2022	26° Capricorn–11° Capricorn
2023	July 23–Sep. 4	28° Leo–12° Leo
2025	Mar. 2–Apr. 13	10° Aries–24° Pisces
2026	Oct. 3–Nov. 14	8° Scorpio–22° Libra
2028	May 10–June 22	19 Gemini–3° Gemini
2029–2030	Dec. 16, 2029–Jan. 26, 2030	24° Capricorn–8° Capricorn
2031	July 20–Sep. 1	26° Leo–10° Leo

Watching for Retrograde Mars

I love Mars, the red planet. Easily recognizable in the sky by its pale pink tint, it stimulates activity and prods us to take the initiative, Mars is enterprising, dynamic, determined, and dominating. It lends us courage and drive, boosts our energy, and awakens sexual desire, even if it also stirs up anger and hostility. Admittedly, Mars is the planet of war. But without it, nothing would ever get done.

Moreover, I like to think that in my chart, and in yours, the energy of Mars can be funneled in positive directions. If nothing else, it thrives at the gym — and I'm not talking about yoga, though warrior pose might be the single best Martial exercise ever invented. Mars prefers kickboxing or weightlifting or the martial arts. Let's be honest: Mars wants to fight. That impulse, which lives within us all, needs to be acknowledged.

But when Mars is retrograde, its energy is diverted. Taking action turns out to be harder than expected. Roadblocks pop up, and the drive and assertiveness associated with the warrior planet are pushed aside. So progress slows down, even at the gym, and taking the offensive — or trying to — can lead to unanticipated consequences.

REMEMBER

Aggressive Mars goes retrograde every 22 months for about 11 weeks. During those times, the cardinal rule is simple: Don't launch a crusade or go to war, metaphorically or otherwise.

Table 18-3 tells you when (and where) Mars is retrograde from 2020 to 2031. It doesn't go retrograde at all during the years not included in the list.

TABLE 18-3   **Retrograde Mars**

Year	Dates	Location
2020	Sep. 9–Nov. 14	28° Aries–15° Aries
2022	Oct. 30–Dec. 31	25° Gemini–9° Gemini
2023	Jan. 1–Jan. 12	9° Gemini–8° Gemini
2024	Dec. 6–Dec. 31	6° Leo–1° Leo
2025	Jan. 1–Feb. 24	1° Leo–17° Cancer
2027	Jan. 20–Apr. 1	10° Virgo–20° Leo
2029	Feb. 14–May 5	13° Libra–24° Virgo
2031	Mar. 29–Jun.13	24° Scorpio–4° Scorpio

The Other Planets

Past Mars, the planets go retrograde for months on end, and the whole matter becomes unimportant on an individual level. Most of the time, there's no reason to get bent out of shape about retrograde planets beyond Mars.

RETROGRADE MERCURY, VENUS, AND MARS IN THE BIRTH CHART

Years ago, I was under the misapprehension that when a planet is retrograde, its energy is weakened. I changed my opinion when I noticed that some of the smartest, most well-spoken people I know have Mercury retrograde in their birth charts, as do some of my favorite writers — icons like Margaret Atwood, Robert Frost, Gabriel Garcia Marquez, Henry Miller, Philip Roth, Dylan Thomas, J. R. R. Tolkien, and Jorge Luis Borges. Clearly, Mercury retrograde in a birth chart doesn't negate the ability to communicate. Rather, it bends your intellect inward, deepens it, causes greater concern about exactly how you're communicating, and makes you a more independent thinker. My guess is that writers with Mercury retrograde spend more time mulling things over and revising than other writers.

If you have retrograde Venus in your birth chart, you may be shy, uncertain, and hesitant to express affection, especially around potential partners. Romance isn't a light-hearted romp for you, much as you wish it were. It's complex and problematic, a matter for serious reflection, and as a result, you may hold yourself back in romantic situations. But don't despair. Venus retrograde doesn't deny romance. It merely slows it down. Example: Catherine, Duchess of Cambridge, previously known as Kate Middleton. She dated Prince William for seven years, with at least one major breakup along the way, before they married.

Retrograde Mars bottles up your aggression, competitiveness, hatred, anger. But such things can't really be contained. They seek release. If you were born with retrograde Mars, you will be forced at some point to acknowledge your anger and focus it constructively. Some people with a retrograde Mars — Lizzie Borden comes to mind — never find a way to do this. Others succeed triumphantly. This short list of world-class warriors with Mars retrograde speaks for itself: Franklin Delano Roosevelt, Benjamin Disraeli, Billie Jean King, Theresa May, Bernie Sanders, and Martin Luther King, Jr.

There are, however, two situations in which it's good to know what the planets are doing out there. I recommend paying attention to the retrograde motion of the outer planets under these circumstances:

>> **When five or six planets are retrograde at once.** When this happens, as it occasionally does, things slow down. They don't come crashing to a halt, but they inch forward at glacial speed.

>> **When a planet turns retrograde or direct right on top of (or opposite to) your birth planet.** For instance, if Saturn (or any other planet) goes retrograde at 13° Aquarius and you happen to have a planet right there, you can expect to suffer the consequences. A problem from the past, an old adversary or a situation you thought was totally over, could reappear. You'll have to contend with the same issues all over again. Your best and only move, taking your cue from Saturn, is to face reality.

Chapter **19**

Creativity and the Stars

N o one doubts the creativity of a painter, a sculptor, a novelist, a song-writer, a composer, a choreographer, a filmmaker, or a fashion designer. People who work in the arts are certified creative. You might say they've been anointed. But creativity is not a bejeweled crown bestowed on those lucky enough to land creative jobs, and it is not a frivolous addition to an otherwise ordinary life. It is as essential as love, and it belongs in equal measure to every sign of the zodiac. If you have the urge to express yourself in a creative way, you've come to the right place.

This chapter begins with an excursion through the zodiac, sign by creative sign, and continues with a plunge into the planets, houses, and aspects of creativity. Think you're not creative? Think again.

Circling the Zodiac

Just as every sign has its own psychological makeup, every sign has a distinct approach to creative matters. This has nothing to do with a specific art. After all, Taurus may be the sign most associated with music, but musicians are born under every sign. Gemini may be the sign most associated with writing, but writers are born every day of the year (and maybe every hour of the day). And Leo may be the sign most in need of applause, but Golden Globes and Oscars are regularly given to all kinds of people not born in July or August. The truth is, the arts belong to us all. The approach, however, varies from sign to sign. Each sign has its own obstructions to get around and its own creative style.

TIP

To identify your approach to creativity, read your Sun sign and your Ascendant or rising sign. You may notice contradictions, but both signs are part of who you are. Read both.

Aries the Ram

As the first sign of the zodiac, Aries is the astrological equivalent of the Big Bang — and you can't get more creative than that. Aries is daring, impatient, decisive, a bright red splash in a world of tasteful neutrals. With Mars, the planet of war, as your ruler, you benefit from leaping into the creative fray and acting on your ideas without fretting too much about advance planning. Just forge ahead. You are filled with ideas, incredibly productive, and excited to try new things. At your unfettered best, you are an unstoppable creative warrior.

But who among us is unfettered? Obstacles happen. Hindrances are real. And so too are the feelings of anger and frustration that well up within you when you can't get a project off the ground. Once you do, you are filled with enthusiasm and happy to work round-the-clock. But if a problem arises or things don't progress as quickly as you'd thought, your energy flags and you begin to doubt yourself. Big projects with their inevitable slowdowns are especially intimidating.

That's why it is to your advantage to choose short projects or to break a long one into smaller, digestible bits. Even a short burst of creative activity wedged between responsibilities will move your project along, one small piece at a time — *Bird by Bird*, as Aries writer Anne Lamott explains in her book by that title.

Your job is to tend the fire, knowing that, as the sign of cardinal fire, great quantities of energy — and creativity — are yours. Moreover, says Maya Angelou, the Aries author of *I Know Why the Caged Bird Sings*, "You can't use up creativity. The more you use, the more you have."

CREATIVE ARIES

- Quentin Tarantino
- Francis Ford Coppola
- Aretha Franklin
- Johann Sebastian Bach
- William Wordsworth
- Vincent Van Gogh
- Yayoi Kusama (whose wild, polka-dotted masterpieces have made her one of Japan's most revered artists)

Taurus the Bull

The image of Ferdinand the Bull, the children's book character who liked to smell the flowers, captures a lovely part of who you are. Ruled by Venus, the planet of art and beauty, Taurus possesses many talents, not least of which is the ability to enjoy life. Those born under its influence are creatures of the senses who delight in art, music, and everything connected to objects, including the urge to make them. Among the areas that align with your skills are painting, sculpture, design, photography, ceramics, woodworking, fabric art and any other form of expression that has a physical component. Taurus finds satisfaction in projects that have a concrete aspect. Taurus architects like I.M. Pei and Walter Gropius exemplify that quality.

But the art for which Taurus is most famed is music. Taurus rules the throat and often grants its natives the ability to sing. If this is your special ability or interest, finding a way to play music with other people is essential.

The trouble is, it isn't easy for you to take the initiative. Like Ferdinand, you have a knack for indolence. Starting a band — or a novel — is easier said than done. Charging into the wilderness, the way a pioneering Aries might, isn't your style. You'd rather not take the road not taken — at least not until you've mulled it over. So you hold back. As a result, everything takes time, especially a creative project that may lack external support. For Taurus, the first step is the hardest. But once you commit yourself, you are capable of working to completion in a composed, steady, determined way. Nor are you put off by ambitious projects. You can do them. Sure, it doesn't happen overnight. But you know what they say about slow and steady; that's Taurus at its finest.

Although Taurus is famed for its sensuous nature and physicality, it's worth remembering that some of the most creative thinkers the world has known — conveyers of big, abstract ideas — were born under the sign of the bull. Sigmund Freud, Karl Marx: they changed the world.

CREATIVE TAURUS

- Martha Graham
- James Brown
- Lizzo
- William Shakespeare
- Leonardo Da Vinci

- Honoré de Balzac
- Sofia Coppola
- Duke Ellington
- Charlotte Bronte
- Keith Haring

Gemini the Twins

It would be a false — but since when did that ever stop a Gemini? — to claim that all Geminis are quick-witted wordsmiths bristling with trivia and nervous energy. Surely there are exceptions. Still, the majority of Geminis are clever, informed, inquisitive, versatile, talkative, and amusing. You have a multitude of interests, and many possible activities call to you. You hate to limit yourself. Juggling two projects at once — a nightmare to some people — is your ideal. The right creative environment for you encourages choice.

Like every sign, Gemini can claim its share of talented musicians (Prince), artists (Mary Cassatt), comedians (Amy Schumer), and so on. But Gemini is ruled by Mercury, the planet of communication, and it is above all associated with writing, whether that means writing nonfiction like Rachel Carson; poetry like Allen Ginsberg; songs like Bob Dylan and Kanye West; fiction like Salman Rushdie; or everything — and a lot of it — like Joyce Carol Oates. Writing is one area where Gemini's ability to spin a yarn serves a noble purpose.

And you need a purpose, for Gemini can easily meander off. Restless and distractible, Gemini conceives of numerous projects but completes only a fraction of them. Sticking to a project, even when it's something you care about, is a challenge, and yet you feel terrible when you don't finish something you started. The only way around is through. Like Aries, you have to identify projects you can finish quickly, before you get distracted. You benefit from writing short chapters, working in time-limited bursts of activity, and finding a way to quiet, if only temporarily, the clatter of chatter in your mind. Meditation is one way to do that; writing is another. Even if your main activity is not literary, writing aids your thinking process and helps you plan. Make it a daily practice.

Cancer the Crab

If you're searching for domesticity, Cancer is the place to look, even though you may not find that quality in anything remotely like the way you pictured it. Hunter S. Thompson, the wild man of "gonzo" journalism, was a Cancer who retreated in 1968 to a "fortified compound" — a homestead named Owl Farm, filled with books and ammunition — and lived there for the rest of his life. His domesticity was real, even if it wasn't typical. His creative writing wasn't typical either. It was adventurous and wild. Cancer includes those possibilities too.

As a water sign, Cancer is sensitive, shy, and deeply emotional. But Cancer can get so caught up in attending to the needs of others that your own needs go unmet. Among these is the need to immerse yourself in a creative project that is engaging, meaningful, and emotionally rich.

As a cardinal sign, you are capable of starting a project by taking the initiative, despite your insecurity. You are also capable of finding or inventing a project that touches your heart. One way to do that is by digging into the past. Personal memory offers a natural starting point but delving into the past can be painful — even though, as many writers and artists have discovered, wretched experiences often make superb material. The historical past offers another pathway into creativity. It can be a fertile source of inspiration and emotional truth.

Once you've identified a project, you pour yourself into it. Creative work can be healing for you. But it can also stoke your fears, which are considerable and which include fear of not completing the creative work you yearn to do. To get off the treadmill of fear and avoidance, it helps to align yourself with a supportive friend of mentor with whom to share triumphs and defeats. Join a workshop, a support group, a class — anywhere you can find people vaguely like yourself. And read *The Creative Habit: Learn It and Use It for Life,* by Twyla Tharp (Simon and Schuster), the great Cancer dancer and choreographer. She knows what she's talking about.

Leo the Lion

There's no business like show business, especially if you were born under Leo, the natural sign of creativity. Blessed with gregarious personalities and a love of the spotlight, Leos are natural performers. Even those Leos who don't have the radiant presence of, say, Jennifer Lopez or Jennifer Lawrence or Barack Obama, even those who pretend to feel nothing but disdain for the desire for recognition, even they long for the occasional standing ovation. But although they may look confident, their self-assurance is not as solid as it looks. Beneath its elegant façade, Leo has a fragile ego.

One problem is that creativity is an uncertain game. You don't know how your efforts will turn out. It's possible you will fail to distinguish yourself. That thought can even stop you from pursuing an artistic hobby. I've seen that happen. For years, my Leo neighbor showed not an iota of interest in making art, although she liked going to galleries. She knew she had no talent. So why bother? Then someone (it wasn't me) got her to enroll an art class. Now her kitchen is a painting studio suffused with the aroma of turpentine, and oil paintings are propped up all over the house. They're good too. Otherwise, they would not be on display.

What enabled her to overcome her hesitation? There's something Leo wants more than applause. Leo wants to play, preferably in the company of others. Anything performance-related — an improv class, a community theater — can fulfill that urge. Or join a sketch class, a playwriting circle, a jewelry-making workshop. And bring the party with you; that's Leo's job. Turning work into play lowers the stakes and frees your creativity.

Finally, remember the immortal words of Leo writer J. K. Rowling, author of the *Harry Potter* novels: "Anything's possible if you've got enough nerve." Of course you do.

Virgo the Virgin

Much is made in astrological circles of Virgo's critical abilities and perfectionist tendencies. Not enough is made of Virgo's creative gifts, which are honed, polished, and cerebral. Think of Mary Shelley's *Frankenstein*, which animates a concept we're still wrestling with; Sol LeWitt's geometric wall paintings, which you can buy as a set of fanatically precise DIY instructions; or the compositions of the conceptual composer John Cage, whose infamous piece, *4'33"*, instructs the musicians not to play their instruments for four minutes and 33 seconds — just to sit there in silence. Virgo art makes you think.

Virgo's control over process and detail also allows it to take pleasure in crafts such as pottery, weaving, knitting, or glass-blowing, which was once a way to make goblets and vases and is now a high art thanks to the astonishing work of glass-blower Dale Chihuly, whose Sun/Moon/Neptune conjunction in Virgo turned a craft into an art (and, in the process, wiped out that phony distinction).

Virgo art captivates. It's impossible to look away from Michael Jackson's elastic, angular dance moves. It's impossible to put down a Stephen King novel (even if — speaking for myself — you *want* to put it down). The standards for Virgo art are high.

And therein lies the problem. The blocks you face include impossibly high standards, your discomfort with ambiguity, and a storm of repressed emotions rumbling around in your psyche. The challenge for Virgo is to work despite all that. The usual cures — deep breathing, chamomile tea, therapy — apply. But if they don't work, you have to keep at it anyway. Virgo has the capacity to conceive of a creative project, address it in a methodical, time-managed fashion, and complete it on schedule. Setting deadlines doesn't work for other signs, but it works for Virgo. And I don't need to tell you that it helps to have a clean, well-lighted place in which to create. For Virgo, it's essential.

CREATIVE VIRGO

- George R. R. Martin
- Jorge Luis Borges
- Leonard Cohen
- Hildegard of Bingen
- Romare Bearden
- Leo Tolstoy
- Ava DuVernay
- Elvis Costello

But what if the time doesn't seem right? What if you can't get past your anxiety or your standards or your multiple responsibilities? You don't want years to go by during which you never write a poem or throw a pot. You must do something. Here's one possibility: Carry around a tiny sketch pad or notebook and fill it up. It doesn't matter how silly or inconsequential your sketches or haiku are. You must do it anyway. Think of it as a daily practice. Keep the fire burning.

Libra the Scales

With Venus, the planet of art and beauty, as your sign's ruler, it's not surprising that you have a refined sensibility, an affinity for the arts, many talents, and a desire to make something beautiful. To start with, you find beauty everywhere. As a cultivated consumer of the arts, you appreciate its elements: form, harmony, technique, and balance, the ultimate Libra virtue. But finding that balance for yourself isn't easy.

Two stumbling blocks stand between you and the creative, productive life you envision. First, much as you wish it were otherwise, your energy is not infinite. So you must use it judiciously, adding creative activity to your schedule without overburdening yourself. You also need to chill, and you should do so, guilt free. Relaxing is part of a well-balanced life and not something you should skip.

Second, being creative means making decisions. But despite your powerful intellect, even a simple yes-or-no can slow your momentum, and having to choose from dozens of options can mean a tedious slog through self-doubt. In any case, the real challenge isn't making decisions. It's trusting your intuition, upon which creativity depends. Find the courage to follow your intuition, to make the choice that calls to you (in your heart, you know what it is), and you will free your artistic soul.

And if you truly don't know what to do next? Flip a coin. That may not be a wise way to choose a doctor or buy a car. But in the airy realms of literature, music, and the arts, it's better to bow to the oracle of the coin than to dither endlessly, trying to decide.

CREATIVE LIBRA

- Maya Lin
- Annie Leibovitz
- George Gershwin
- Miguel de Cervantes

- Rumi
- John Lennon
- Rei Kawakubo
- Mark Rothko

Finally: if you're really stuck, try collaborating. Libra is the sign of partnership. Your creative life picks up speed when they're another person in the mix.

Scorpio the Scorpion

Anyone in search of a Scorpio artist whose work reflects the celestial heights and the labyrinthine depths of the sign need look no further than Sylvia Plath, Georgia O'Keeffe, or the under-appreciated Robert Louis Stevenson, author of *The Strange Case of Dr. Jekyll and Mr. Hyde*. That book unforgettably demonstrates something we know to be true: that everyone has a dark side. Scorpio is fascinated by the dark side, by mysteries and secrets, and by its own psyche. Moreover, Scorpio has the courage, at least some of the time, to go there. This is your gift — and your punishment.

Scorpio can stir up emotional melodramas without half trying. It can sink into despair or obsession. It can become overly self-involved. And it has been known to take itself way too seriously. Living life as a Scorpio — or with a Scorpio — is not for the faint-hearted.

But artistically? Creatively? Scorpio has it all. Scorpio can turn the heaviest emotion — anger, vengefulness, lust, jealousy — into something interesting and fresh. At the peak of its powers, Scorpio is alchemy in action. "Every act of creation is first an act of destruction," said Pablo Picasso, the premier artist of the twentieth century. Scorpio understands that and doesn't turn away. Your emotional intensity, funneled in a creative direction, can turn terrors into timeless expressions of universal fears and emotions. Think of Margaret Atwood and *The Handmaid's Tale*. (Or try not to think of it.)

CREATIVE SCORPIO

- Jan Vermeer
- Bram Stoker
- Kathy Griffin
- Fyodor Dostoyevsky

- Dylan Thomas
- René Magritte
- George Eliot
- Bonnie Raitt

But what if you're not feeling courageous? What if you don't want to dive into that bubbling cauldron? You could take yourself to the movies or go to a museum. You can postpone the inevitable. But in the end there's no escape. If you are, or aspire to be, an artist, the subject matter, emotions, or obsession that has occupied your mind will seek expression. You don't really have a choice. Here's Picasso once more: "A great painting — any painting — ought to bristle with razor blades." If that's not permission to put everything into your work, I don't know what is. Be ruthless. It's your birthright.

Sagittarius the Archer

The glyph of Sagittarius — an arrow aimed at the upper right-hand corner of the page — says it all. That tiny symbol represents Sagittarian aspiration, perhaps your finest quality. But notice that arrow is connected to nothing. It's untethered. And therein lies the problem. Sagittarians have vision. They think big and aim high. The excitement you feel at the beginning of a creative venture fills you with joy. The beginning, when possibilities are infinite and you are buoyant with optimism, is a thrilling time.

You bump back down to reality when you recognize that, as splendid as your vision is, achieving it is going to require a fair bit of drudgery. Well, you understand that. You're willing to do whatever it takes. But wait. . . what's that glittering in the shadows? Is it. . . could it be. . . a detour? Another project entirely? Oh, how tempting! And off you go. Meanwhile, your brilliant idea, the creative project that could change your life if only you could bring it to fruition, has been abandoned. That wasn't your intention. But that's what happened.

The cures for Sagittarius are remarkably literal. Travel and education may not be panaceas but they do refresh the mind, as does exercise. If you can't go trekking in Nepal, you can still throw your laptop into your backpack and go to a café or a library or a town half an hour away. You can still sign up for a class or a workshop. You can still plant seeds.

CREATIVE SAGITTARIUS

- Emily Dickinson
- Jane Austen
- Sarah Silverman
- Kathryn Bigelow
- Steven Spielberg
- Jay-Z
- Sinead O'Connor
- Diego Rivera

When you're ready to begin a new project or reinvigorate a stalled one, your best bet is to devote an entire day to it, if possible. Immerse yourself in it. Allow it to blossom in your mind. Later on, when it is fully established in your consciousness and in your schedule, you will be able to keep it alive with smaller doses of attention. Until then, don't dabble. Don't dawdle. Aim carefully and keep your eye on the arrow as it flies.

Capricorn the Goat

It doesn't matter what field you examine. You will find Capricorns at the top. That's where they want to be. So no one is shocked that Jeff Bezos, the founder and CEO of Amazon and the richest person on earth (at least until his divorce), is a Capricorn. Of course he is. We expect nothing less.

What's surprising is that Capricorns, who prefer to play by the rules, also rise to the top in creative fields, where following the rules supposedly just proves you're a follower, and breaking the rules is not only valued but glamorized. The truth is, Capricorn may have a stiff and stuffy image, but its creative capability is wild. Consider, for example, Patti Smith — rock musician, poet, memoirist, painter, photographer, not to mention wife and mother. From an early age she surrounded herself with creative people, but she succeeded in the traditional Capricorn way: through "consistent effort and a measure of sacrifice." If that sounds like a strategy for turning creative activity into a form of punishment, you're probably not a Capricorn. For Capricorns, harnessing the power of discipline is not a terrible struggle. "Don't wait for inspiration," said Capricorn artist Henri Matisse. "It comes while one is working."

But still, the road to creative expression is strewn with obstacles. First, like Virgo, you are a harsh judge of your own efforts. For Capricorn, good enough is seldom good enough. If a project isn't moving in the right direction, you grow dissatisfied and melancholy, incapable of letting it go but equally unable to alter your approach and try something new. With no possible solution in sight, you box yourself in and suffer accordingly.

CREATIVE CAPRICORN

- Paul Cezanne
- Edgar Allen Poe
- Joseph Cornell
- Diane von Furstenberg

- Haruki Murakami
- Annie Lennox
- John Singer Sargent
- Elvis Presley

Second, Capricorn can come up short in the category of play. One way to fill that gap is to dally in another arena. David Bowie may not have looked like a Capricorn — he had Aquarius rising — but he worked like a Capricorn to the very end. He also turned to drawing or painting when he felt stymied musically, not to distract himself but to pursue the same thought in another medium. Thus, he turned painting into problem-solving: Capricorn at its finest.

Aquarius the Water-bearer

Is there a Water-bearer out there who isn't proud of being an Aquarian? You're unconventional, independent, and inventive, a fascinating original whose unorthodox ways of thinking offer a bracing tonic for the rest of us. Look at the evidence: there are pioneering Aquarian writers such as James Joyce and Virginia Woolf; groundbreaking artists like Jackson Pollock; directors like Franco Zeffirelli; minimalist composers like Philip Glass and John Adams; and that list doesn't even mention Darwin, Dickens, and Wolfgang Amadeus Mozart. By oscillating between the liberating independence of Uranus and the sturdy foundation of Saturn, Aquarius joyfully pushes creative boundaries — and the farther you venture into the wilderness of your project, the more it will change. When things are going well, your creative efforts will mutate right in front of your eyes.

But there are times when you just can't make it happen, and the world is to blame. Aquarius has a social conscience. Some Aquarians — Charles Dickens, Yoko Ono — find ways to combine their societal concerns with their creative impulses. But others crumble under the weight of what feels like a moral dilemma. Save the world? Or go to film school? In the face of problems that, perhaps, you could help alleviate, pursuing your creative dreams may feel selfish. . . and so they start to wither.

But you can't turn away from societal concerns, and neither can you give up on your creative efforts. To combine them, consider sharing your creative gifts with a community group, perhaps as a volunteer. It may sound counterintuitive, but this could be the single best way to strength your creativity. Adding purpose to your project could give it the jolt it needs.

CREATIVE AQUARIUS

- Toni Morrison
- Alice Walker
- François Truffaut
- Edith Wharton

- Paul Auster
- Laura Ingalls Wilder
- Christian Dior
- Bob Marley

Pisces the Fish

What is the most creative sign? Personally, I reject the concept. Creativity expresses itself in many ways, and creative geniuses are born under every sign. But if I had to pick, Pisces would be a top contender. You are alert, kind, and nuanced in your understanding with a vivid dream life and a singular imagination. In ordinary life, this doesn't necessarily give you an advantage. But in any kind of creative effort, whether you want to invent a better umbrella (somebody ought to) or write a novel without using the letter e (like the French novelist Georges Perec), imagination unlatches the gate and sets the tigers free. Prime Pisces creators include Gabriel Garcia Marquez, author of *One Hundred Years of Solitude* and one of the founders of magical realism, and Alexander McQueen, whose fashions are downright hallucinatory in their surrealistic specificity. "The Edgar Allen Poe of Fashion," as he was sometimes known, incorporated Scuba diving imagery, masks, chain mail, thousands of feathers, and a cloud of red butterflies surrounding a model's head like hair. The Piscean imagination is without limit. Don't let it scare you. This is your great talent, even if at the moment your imagination feels strangled or narrow. Give it attention, and that will change.

One problem you face is that Pisces tires easily and is prone to inertia. You'd like to get something done. But first, maybe a nap? The problem is that you cannot compartmentalize, cannot shoo away extraneous thoughts and concentrate. Emotions, wishes, dreams, memories, worries, and song lyrics fill your mind. Despite all the coffee in the world (and who knows what else), you grow discouraged and disorganized. There comes a point where working is pointless. When that moment arrives, your best move is to clear your mind through ritual, yoga, meditation, walking near a natural body of water, or anything else along similar lines. This may sound like procrastination, and for many people, that's exactly what it is. For you, it clears the way and refreshes the mind.

You also benefit from working with a mentor, setting concrete goals, and reporting for regular check-ins. If you're serious about completing a creative project and you suspect that you don't have the self-discipline required, this could be your ticket.

Finding the Creative Heart of Every Chart

Creativity is not a solitary trait that you either have or don't have. It's a blend of abilities that can be learned, embellished, fortified, expanded, and enjoyed. It shows itself in a chart in many ways including the following:

Signs

Is it necessary to reiterate that every sign is creative? A few minutes on the internet just now convinced me that it is. There I found numerous sites rating the creativity of the signs. On the half dozen I looked at, Aries and Sagittarius earned the lowest ratings, which got me to wondering. Did Van Gogh and Bach know about this? Did Emily Dickinson and Jimi Hendrix get the memo? Evidently not. Every sign is creative. Period. It is absurd — it is slander — to suggest otherwise.

Planets

Similarly, each planet contributes to creativity. To wit:

>> The Sun illuminates your path, purpose, and fundamental self. It provides the roots of your creativity and the will to express yourself creatively, and it is the source of your greatest authenticity.

>> The Moon represents your unconscious, your emotions, your memory, and more. Research suggests that it is especially prominent in the birth charts of writers.

>> Mercury amplifies language, intellect, curiosity, word play, and the ability to tell a story or make a point. It is essential for writers of every stripe.

>> Venus stimulates your sensitivity to beauty and your artistic talents, with an emphasis on visual art and music.

>> Mars imparts energy, passion, and action.

>> Jupiter contributes growth, good fortune, and the impulse to do something big.

>> Saturn brings structure and persistence. Without it, nothing would ever get accomplished.

>> Uranus generates originality and clap-of-thunder ideas.

>> Neptune fosters imagination and intuition.

>> Pluto delivers transformation, the essence of creativity.

All of those forces are operating within you, but in every chart, some planets are stronger than others. A planet is strong under these conditions:

>> It is in a sign it rules, like Mercury in Gemini or Virgo (see Chapter 1 for a rulership chart).

>> It is in the sign of its exaltation, like Mercury in Aquarius (again, see Chapter 1).

>> It rules your Ascendant or Midheaven. So if you have Virgo rising, your Mercury is strong regardless of the sign or house it happens to occupy.

>> It occupies an angle (that is, the first, fourth, seventh, or tenth house) or is conjunct the Midheaven, Ascendant, IC, or Descendant (see Chapter 11).

>> It closely aspects other planets in your chart and, in particular, the Sun, the Moon, and the planet that rules your Ascendant.

>> Or it makes a major aspect with absolutely nothing. That is, it fails to form a conjunction, sextile, square, trine, or opposition with another planet. It might make a minor aspect — more about those in a minute — but that's it. The planet is a solitary actor, a lone wolf whose tendencies, whatever they may be, are unmoderated by other planets. It could be the most important planet in your chart.

Houses

As with signs and planets, every house can make a contribution to creativity in one way or another. But here are the most influential houses one looks to when searching for creative gifts:

>> The fifth house. This is the primary house of creativity, the first place to look. It rules play, games, performance, and children. Any planet here strengthens the creative impulse. Creativity is also reinforced if the ruler of the fifth house is prominently placed.

>> The third house. Anything here, especially Mercury, galvanizes the ability to communicate and thus supports writing. Ninth house planets offer further support.

>> The second house. Planets here, and Venus in particular, promote visual art, decorative ability, music, and the love of money.

>> The tenth house. Planets here strengthen career. If the ruler of the tenth is in the fifth, a creative career becomes a strong likelihood.

>> The sixth house. Anything here or in Virgo strengthens workmanship and craft.

>> The twelfth house. Planets here animate the life of the spirit.

Aspects

It's nice to see major aspects linking Neptune and Uranus with other planets. Neptune and Uranus tend to define generations rather than individuals, but when they connect with the inner, personal planets, their creative gifts become personal and accessible.

Thanks to the 16th-century astronomer Johannes Kepler (see Chapter 3), a couple of minor aspects can also be included. Following the Greek philosopher Pythagoras, Kepler believed in the music of the spheres and the importance of numbers. He noticed that the major aspects are created by dividing the 360 degrees of the zodiac by two, three, four, and six, which produces the 180-degree opposition, the 120-degree trine, the 90-degree square, and the 60-degree sextile. But what about five? Dividing the circle by five creates a 72-degree angle called the quintile that Kepler argued should be added to the list along with the 144-degree biquintile. Those two aspects bestow an additional bit of creativity or even, as is sometimes said, a hit of creative genius.

For proof that all this really does add up to something, look no farther than the chart of Wolfgang Amadeus Mozart (Figure 19-1), whose music inspires people to talk about God, angels, genius, and perfection.

Here are some of the creative signatures in his chart:

>> Three planets, including the Sun, in the fifth house of creativity.

>> Mercury, the ruler of his Ascendant and Midheaven, also in the fifth house.

>> Saturn, the ruler of the fifth house, in the fifth house in Aquarius.

>> Neptune in Leo forming a close opposition to all three fifth house planets.

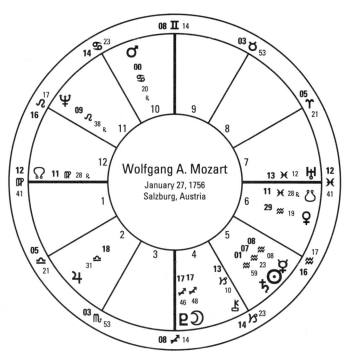

FIGURE 19-1:
Wolfgang
Amadeus Mozart.

© *John Wiley & Sons, Inc.*

>> Uranus in Pisces in a powerful position opposite Mozart's Ascendant and square his Moon and Pluto.

>> Several quintiles and bi-quintiles. Mozart's Moon and Pluto in Sagittarius form quintiles to Venus. Mars forms a quintile with the Ascendant. Mercury and the Sun form bi-quintiles with Mars. And there are more.

He really was a creative genius. It's all over his chart.

5

The Part of Tens

Chapter **20**

Ten Talents You Can Spot in a Chart

Where do extraordinary qualities come from? What goes into the chart of a world-class beauty, a groundbreaking artist, a celebrity, or a billionaire? These people obviously have something special . . . and maybe you do too. In the following sections, I reveal the astrological secrets behind great gifts.

Athletic Prowess

Mighty Mars, the planet of aggression, figures strongly in the charts of athletes, who are statistically more likely than non-athletes to have Mars within striking distance of either the Ascendant or the Midheaven.

A Mars/Midheaven conjunction appears in the charts of Muhammad Ali, a Capricorn with said conjunction in Taurus; Tiger Woods, a Capricorn with the same conjunction in Gemini; and Lebron James, a Capricorn with a Mars/Midheaven conjunction in Pisces. And then there's the astonishing Simone Biles, a Pisces. She has a Mars/Midheaven conjunction in Virgo, the sign of perfection.

Mars can also be prominent in other ways. It could be well-placed by sign — in Aries, the sign it rules, or in Capricorn, the sign of its exaltation. It could be well-placed by aspect. For instance, it might be conjunct the Sun, as in the charts of swimmer Michael Phelps and soccer player Megan Rapinoe. It could be prominent because it connects with almost all the other planets, like Roger Federer's Mars, which aspects every planet except Neptune. Strangely enough, Mars can even be dominant because it makes no aspects whatsoever. Such a solitary body, unhampered by other planets with competing agendas, operates without interference and can consequently be the most powerful planet in a chart.

I don't want to suggest that Mars is the only planet that affects athletic ability. A well-placed Sun gives vitality. Mercury lends quickness. Jupiter, Uranus, and Pluto confer power. Athleticism, like other talents, is an amalgamation of many factors.

Finally, although gifted athletes are born under every sign of the zodiac, fire and earth signs are slightly more common among them than air and water. Athletes, like artists, benefit from a touch of Leo — not because it advances athletic ability but because it stimulates the love of performance. And *that* is definitely part of the game.

Beauty (or the Power of Attraction)

Just as Mars promotes athletic ability, Venus amplifies beauty and the ability to attract, particularly when it is

>> Conjunct the Ascendant, the Sun, the Moon, the Midheaven, or the ruler of the Ascendant.

>> In the first or tenth house.

>> In Taurus or Libra, the signs it rules.

Grace Kelly, Ingrid Bergman, Gregory Peck, and Paul Newman all had Venus conjunct the Ascendant. So do Cameron Diaz, Angelina Jolie, and Beyoncé, who has an unusual triple conjunction of Venus, Pluto, and the Ascendant — an irresistible combination.

Venus also shows up near the Midheaven in the charts of beautiful people. Examples include Marilyn Monroe, James Dean, Nicole Kidman, Kim Kardashian, Victoria Beckham, and David Bowie. Standards of beauty may change. But this is one area whee Venus will always have the last word.

REMEMBER

Not everyone with a prominent Venus boasts a gorgeous face. What they do have is even more valuable, for Venus confers the power of attraction.

"You made me love you," sings Judy Garland to a framed photograph of Clark Gable. "I didn't want to do it." She couldn't help it though, and neither could anyone else. He has Venus right on the Ascendant.

Celebrity Appeal

Pop artist Andy Warhol is known for his paintings of Campbell's soup cans; his silk-screened portraits of Elvis Presley, Jackie Kennedy, and hundreds of other people; his high-profile celebrity life; and his prescient statement, "In the future, everyone will be famous for 15 minutes." Well, that was easy for him to say. Here are the ingredients that celebrity appeal requires (see Figure 20-1):

>> Planets conjunct the Midheaven and/or in the tenth house.

>> Planets conjunct the Ascendant and/or in the first house.

>> A touch of Leo.

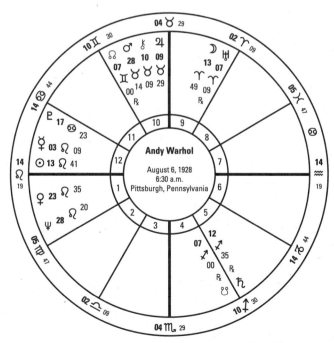

FIGURE 20-1:
Andy Warhol's
birth chart.
He got his
15 minutes and
more.

© John Wiley & Sons, Inc.

So how did his chart stack up to these specifications?

>> He had Jupiter, the planet of expansion and good fortune, conjunct the Midheaven, along with Mars, Chiron, and the North Node in the tenth house.

>> His Sun was closely conjunct the Ascendant, and he had two planets — Venus and Neptune, the guardians of art — in the first house.

>> His Sun, three other planets, and the Ascendant are in Leo. Fame was his birthright.

The same might be said for Kim Kardashian. Is she famous for being famous? Perhaps so, although her celebrity looks less and less ephemeral all the time. Like Andy Warhol, she has all the requirements for fame (see Figure 20-2):

>> Planets conjunct the Midheaven: Jupiter and Saturn in the tenth house, with Venus widely conjunct from the ninth house.

>> Neptune conjunct the Ascendant in the first house.

>> Mars conjunct the Ascendant in the twelfth house.

>> The North Node in Leo.

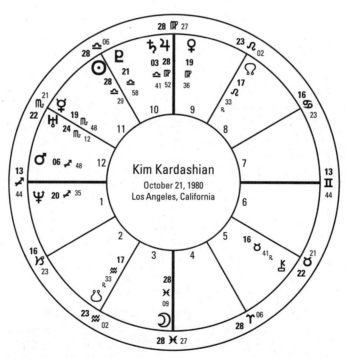

FIGURE 20-2:
Kim Kardashian. She could be famous for more than being famous.

© John Wiley & Sons, Inc.

She also has a formidable Moon in Pisces. Not only does it aspect every other planet in her chart, something that rarely happens, it is also exactly conjunct an angle — the cusp of the fourth house, which represents home and family, two facets of life that are vital to her brand.

Kim also has another kind of strength. With nine planets on the left-hand side of her chart, she has free will, and plenty of it. More than most people, she can choose her own path. When she revealed an interest in following her father's profession by becoming a lawyer even though she doesn't have a college degree, she expected the notion to be greeted "with an eye roll for the ages." But I'm not rolling my eyes. She could be a lawyer.

First, the ruler of her ninth house (of the law) is her Sun. It's in Libra, the sign of justice, in the eleventh house of social awareness. Second, she has two planets and her Ascendant in Sagittarius, the sign of the law. Third, the ruler of her Ascendant is Jupiter, which is in the house of career, exactly conjunct her Midheaven. And I could go on. Really, she could do it.

Healing Hands

Doctors, nurses, acupuncturists, podiatrists, dentists, and others with the desire to heal share certain astrological characteristics:

>> **By sign:** Cancer, Scorpio, and Pisces, the water signs, promote empathy. Virgo encourages an intellectual curiosity about health and healing techniques. Aquarius heightens humanitarian concern.

>> **By planet:** Research has shown that doctors often have Saturn conjunct or opposite the Ascendant or Midheaven. Pluto, the planet of transformation, and Mars also figure heavily in the charts of healers.

>> **By house:** The most crucial placements related to health are the sixth house of health and service; the eighth house of surgery, research, death, and rebirth; and the twelfth house of secrets and hospitals.

REMEMBER

A house is powerful if it holds one or more planets, but even an empty house can be more important than it looks. If the ruler of that house is conjunct the Sun, Moon, Ascendant, or Midheaven, the matters of that house will always be vital.

REAL LIFE EXAMPLE

In the 1950s, Dr. Jonas Salk, who developed the first vaccine against polio, was more than famous. He was revered. In those days, polio was a plague. In 1952 alone, 58,000 people in the United States contracted the disease, many were paralyzed, and over 3,000 died, most of them children. After the Salk vaccine became available, those numbers plummeted. By 1994, there was not a single case of polio in the western hemisphere. The number of lives he saved has been estimated in the millions.

So where does that healing force come from? His chart shows precisely the qualities enumerated earlier in this section (see Figure 20-3):

>> **By sign:** He has planets in all three of the water signs. His Sun is in Scorpio, along with Mars, Mercury, and the Ascendant. His Moon and North Node are in Pisces. And his Saturn and Pluto are in Cancer.

He also has Jupiter and Uranus in Aquarius, showing his enthusiasm for humanitarian causes and his interest in science.

>> **By planet:** He does not have Saturn conjunct or opposite the Ascendant or Midheaven. But his Saturn is prominent anyway as part of a tight Grand Trine linking the Sun, the Moon, Saturn, and Pluto.

>> **By house:** Dr. Salk was not a clinical doctor who saw individual patients in his office. So it's not surprising that he has nothing in the sixth house of service. Instead, as his Sun in the twelfth house suggests, he worked behind the scenes. Three planets plus the Ascendant in Scorpio indicate his interest in research, as do Saturn and Pluto in the eighth house, an inspired placement for investigating matters of life and death.

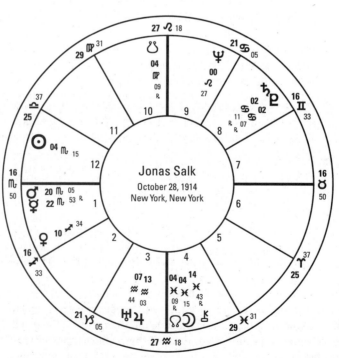

FIGURE 20-3:
Dr. Jonas Salk. His polio vaccine saved millions of lives.

© John Wiley & Sons, Inc.

Business Savvy

How are Fortune 500 CEOs different from you and me? Here's how to spot executive ability:

>> **By sign:** Taurus, Virgo, and Capricorn are the preeminent signs of business. Equally important is Scorpio, the sign of power politics, covert operations, and self-control. In business, as in other areas, you might also expect to see a little Leo. That's because Leos long to be on top, and they'll happily put in hours — make that years — of overtime to achieve that goal.

>> **By planet:** Saturn, well-situated by sign, house, and aspect, grants organizational ability, Mercury provides skill in communication, and Mars fuels the competitive drive.

>> **By house:** Look for planets in the tenth house of reputation, the sixth house of work, the second house of money, and the eighth house of investment. Those houses support executive ability. Also, planets in the first house can bestow charisma, which is often the defining trait of a successful CEO.

REAL LIFE EXAMPLE

Jack Welch, chairman and CEO of General Electric for 20 years, shows many of these traits (see Figure 20-4):

>> **By sign:** With planets in all three earth signs, plus a Capricorn Ascendant, and the Sun in Scorpio, Welch shows clear organizational ability.

>> **By planet:** Saturn rules his Ascendant and is therefore his ruling planet. Mercury is conjunct his Midheaven. But his most notable planet is his commanding Mars. It's angular (in the first house), closely conjunct his Ascendant, well-aspected, and in the sign of its exaltation, all of which makes him exceptionally competitive and aggressive.

>> **By house:** His Sun is in the tenth house of career and public life and is conjunct expansive Jupiter, which is an indication of public prominence and another mark of leadership ability. His Moon is in the eighth house of investments, along with two other planets. His chart ruler, Saturn, is in the second house of money.

Say what you will about the corporate world, that's where Jack Welch belongs. The same might be said for Jeff Bezos, founder of Amazon, and Mark Zuckerberg, co-founder of Facebook. Their birth times, and hence their house placements, are unknown. Their signs say it all. Bezos is a Capricorn, with five planets in earth signs and one in Scorpio. Zuckerberg is a Taurus, with four planets in earth signs and four in Scorpio. Like the rest of us, they're living their charts.

FIGURE 20-4:
Jack Welch's
birth chart.

© John Wiley & Sons, Inc.

REAL LIFE EXAMPLE

Christine Lagarde is the president of the European Central Bank, and before that, she was Managing Director of the International Monetary Fund, and before that. . . let's just say, she has an impressive resumé. In 2018, Forbes named her the third most powerful woman on earth. She is not a CEO, but in terms of business, she has everything going for her (see Figure 20-5):

>> **By sign:** All the earth signs are active in her chart. She has Taurus rising, Jupiter in Virgo, and the Sun, Mercury, and the Midheaven in Capricorn. She also has three planets in Scorpio, including Mars. And the Moon and Pluto are conjunct in Leo.

>> **By planet:** Saturn, Mars, and Mercury are all strong. Saturn rules her Midheaven and is located in an angular house (the seventh) where it is conjunct Mars. Mars is in Scorpio, a sign it rules. Finally, her Mercury, like Jack Welch's, holds court at the top of her chart, conjunct the Midheaven. This is a powerful person, and you can see it all over her chart.

>> **By house:** Lagarde's tenth house holds three planets. Her sixth house holds only Neptune, but the ruler of the sixth house, Mercury, is conjunct the Midheaven, so it's stronger than it looks. Finally, her second and eighth houses contain no planets but they are home to the Nodes of the Moon. With the North Node in the eighth house, working to ensure the security of other people's money is exactly what she ought to be doing.

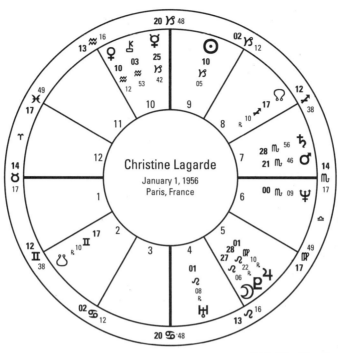

FIGURE 20-5:
Christine
Lagarde's birth
chart.

Making Money

These are the traditional markers that point to the ability to amass money and material goods, whether through your own efforts or through sheer good luck:

>> Planets in the second and eighth houses.

>> Powerful, well-aspected planets ruling the second and eighth houses.

>> A well-placed Jupiter. If you're lucky, it will connect in some way with the second and eighth houses. Maybe it will be placed in one of those houses. It could form a strong aspect with the ruler of one of those houses. It could be rising. Or it could be sitting at the top of the chart like a crown.

A glance at Jack Welch's chart (Figure 20-4) shows just what you might expect:

He has four planets in the second and eighth houses, including Saturn, the ruler of his Ascendant.

The planets ruling his second and eight houses are well-placed. Neptune, the ruler of his second house, is conjunct the Moon in the eighth house. Mercury, the ruler of his eighth house, is conjunct the Midheaven.

As for Jupiter, it's powerful by sign (because it's in Sagittarius, the sign it rules); by house (because it's in the tenth house of reputation); and by aspect (because it's conjunct his Sun).

Something similar is happening in Kim Kardashian's chart. The ruler of her second house is Saturn. It's at the top of her chart conjunct Jupiter and the Midheaven. The ruler of her eighth house is the Moon. It's at the nadir of her chart — a strong position — exactly opposite Jupiter and the Midheaven. And the nodes of the Moon are in the second and eighth houses. Money: it's not her problem.

Activist Capability

In troubled times, it sometimes takes a visionary activist to galvanize public opinion. Activists often pay a steep price for taking a stand. Yet they are unwavering in their commitment and energetic in their actions. Here are a few astrological indications that encourage activism:

>> **Planets in cardinal signs.** If you want to start a movement — or anything else — planets in Aries, Cancer, Libra, or Capricorn are essential, with special emphasis on fiery Aries, the high-energy sign of the warrior, and earthy, ambitious, get-it-done Capricorn, the sign of structure.

>> **Planets in Aquarius,** the freedom-loving, humanitarian sign of the future, or in the eleventh house of friends, community, and society.

>> **A prominent Mars,** the planet of action.

Feminist activist Gloria Steinem has all of these celestial indicators. She is an Aries with four planets in cardinal signs: Pluto in Cancer, Jupiter in Libra, and the Sun and Mars in Aries. She has two planets and the North Node in Aquarius. Finally, her Mars is in Aries, one of the two signs it rules; it is conjunct her Sun in Aries; and it is the ruler of her Scorpio Ascendant. I don't think I've ever seen a stronger Mars.

Or consider the chart of climate activist Greta Thunberg (see Figure 20-6). I don't know what time she was born, so her chart has been calculated arbitrarily for dawn and constructed, for convenience, using "whole sign" houses. But please ignore the houses: without a birthtime, house divisions are meaningless. Signs and aspects, on the other hand, are full of information. Like Gloria Steinem, she has all the markers for activism.

She has four planets, including the Sun and Moon, in pragmatic, goal-oriented Capricorn, a cardinal sign. She was also born under a new moon — a promising indication.

She has two planets in Aquarius, which is a signature of her generation.

And she has Mars in Scorpio — a sign it rules — conjunct Venus, giving her passion and staying power. But Mars also makes a few stressful aspects so it won't always be easy. Watching her is going to be interesting.

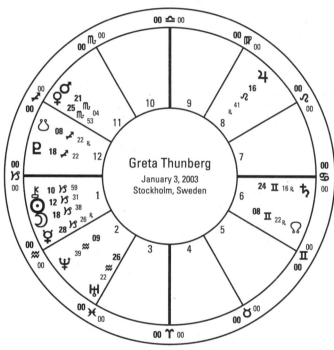

FIGURE 20-6:
Greta Thunberg,
climate activist.

Psychic Ability

Whether you call it extrasensory perception, clairvoyance, a sixth sense, or plain old intuition, psychic ability isn't as rare as you might think. Here's how to find it:

» **By sign:** Pisces, Scorpio, and Cancer bolster psychic ability. Sagittarius can also support a tendency in that direction.

>> **By planet:** Neptune and the Moon keep the channels of reception open, especially if they're conjunct. A prominent Uranus can generate flashes of insight and understanding. Aspects between Pluto and the Sun, Moon, Mercury, or Ascendant boost the powers of perception. None of this is guaranteed to make you psychic. But if your powers of observation are acute enough, no one can tell the difference.

>> **By house:** The twelfth, eighth, and fourth houses carry the most weight.

REAL LIFE EXAMPLE

A classic illustration of psychic ability gone wild is the renowned healer Edgar Cayce, who worked as a "psychic diagnostician" (his term) by entering a trance and suggesting cures for clients he had never even met.

His chart (Figure 20-7) showed all the indications of psychic ability:

>> **By sign:** He had the Sun, three planets, and the North Node in Pisces.

>> **By planet:** He had a Moon/Neptune conjunction in the ninth house, Uranus rising, and a prominent Pluto at the top of his chart.

>> **By house:** His Sun was in the eighth house.

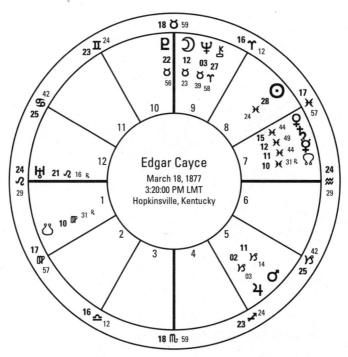

FIGURE 20-7:
Edgar Cayce's birth chart.

© John Wiley & Sons, Inc.

Becoming an Astrologer

Becoming a skilled astrologer has nothing to do with psychic ability. Astrology is an accumulated body of knowledge — not the mystic ability to intercept messages from the spirit world. Anyone can learn it. But you're more likely to be interested if you have some of the following in your chart:

>> A prominent Uranus.

>> Activity in Aquarius and/or an active eleventh house.

>> Activity in Scorpio and/or the eighth house. Scorpio is subtle and incisive. It feels at home with contradictions and hidden motivations, and it loves to ferret out a mystery — and that's what astrology is all about.

REAL LIFE EXAMPLE

Case in point: Isabel M. Hickey, whose 1970 book, *Astrology: A Cosmic Science*, 2nd edition (CRCS Publications, 1992), inspired generations of astrologers. Look what she had going for her (see Figure 20-8): Uranus rising in her first house; Saturn in Aquarius; a Scorpio Ascendant; the Sun in Leo at 25°, one of the so-called astrologer's degrees; and a sensitive Moon/Neptune conjunction in the eighth house.

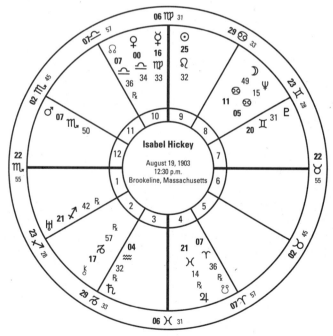

FIGURE 20-8:
Isabel Hickey, astrologer extraordinaire.

© John Wiley & Sons, Inc.

Writing

It's astonishing how many people fantasize about writing. Here's what it takes to be a success:

» **By sign:** Great writers are born under every sign of the zodiac but Gemini is often haunted by the urge to write. Having the Sun, Moon, Mercury, Ascendant, or Midheaven in the sign of the twins stimulates writing ability and facility with language.

» **By planet:** Becoming a successful writer requires a robust Mercury. Mercury is strong if it rules the Ascendant or Midheaven, if it's in Gemini or Virgo, if it's in the third, sixth, ninth, or tenth houses, or if it makes strong aspects to other planets. Don't worry if it doesn't do all of those things. And don't fret if your Mercury is retrograde. That placement is so common among the authors I admire that I've started to wonder whether it's actually an advantage.

Saturn, the planet of self-discipline and structure, is essential for a writer, especially if you're working on your own.

Neptune can be pivotal in writing poetry, fiction, song lyrics, film scripts, or anything that's primarily imaginative.

The Moon is arguably the most important planet, as the researcher Michel Gauquelin discovered. He found that creative writers are more likely than non-writers to have the Moon in one of the so-called zones of power: either overhead (that is, in the ninth house or conjunct the Midheaven in the tenth) or rising (in the first house conjunct the Ascendant or in the twelfth house of secrets and solitude).

» **By house:** Look for activity in the third house of communication, the ninth house of publication, and the fifth house of creativity.

REAL LIFE EXAMPLE

To observe this in real life, take a look at novelist Toni Morrison's chart in Chapter 16. She doesn't have every one of these characteristics. Then again, no one does. But her Mercury is conjunct her Midheaven; Venus, the ruler of her Ascendant, is in the ninth house of publication conjunct Saturn; two planets are in the third house (with one more — Jupiter — knocking at the gate); and Neptune, the planet of the imagination, is located in the fifth house of creativity. By becoming a writer, she fulfilled the potential of her chart.

Chapter **21**

Ten (Plus One) Ways to Use Astrology in Your Life: The Art of Timing

I f timing is everything, then astrology is the key to success — not natal astrology, which has to do with your birth chart, but *electional astrology,* the intricate, high-pressure art of choosing a favorable date in advance. By applying its principles, you can pinpoint auspicious times, avoid problematical ones, align yourself with the cosmos, and magnify your chances of having a happy outcome. In this chapter, I show you how.

TIP

To partake of the wonders of celestial timing, you must have an astrological calendar. I am partial to the spiral-bound *Llewellyn's Daily Planetary Guide* or any of the Jim Maynard calendars, but any sufficiently detailed astrological calendar will do. At minimum, the one you choose should tell you when the Sun, the Moon, and each of the planets enter a new sign, when the Moon is void-of-course, and when major aspects occur. Somewhere in the back of the calendar, there should also be an ephemeris, which allows you to look at the entire month in advance. Check out the Llewellyn offerings at `https://www.llewellyn.com` or (sigh) go to Amazon.

Getting Married

More than any other event, a request to choose a wedding date can cause an astrologer to leaf frantically through the ephemeris in quest of the perfect day and then to throw her arms up in despair. Given the marriage statistics, it won't surprise you to hear that ideal days are hard to come by — and that even astrologers get divorced.

Since a marriage chart can describe the quality of your wedding and of your marriage, you'll want to choose the date with care. Certain celestial events improve your chances of making it past your paper anniversary. One of the most encouraging is a transit of Jupiter through your seventh house of marriage. The problem is that Jupiter only returns to your seventh house every 12 years, and you may not wish to wait that long. But some astrological influences come around fairly often and are worth waiting for. Here's what to look for when you name the day:

» Make certain that Venus, the planet of love, is direct. If it's retrograde, postpone your wedding for a few weeks. (See Chapter 18 for more about retrograde Venus.) If it is orbiting through your Sun sign, your Venus sign, or your seventh house, you're in luck.

» Pick a day when Mercury is direct. When Mercury is retrograde, misunderstandings and problems in communication tend to arise, either immediately or down the line. Also, it's an astrological truism that one should never sign a contract when Mercury is retrograde. Marriage, whatever else it may be, is a legal agreement — and you *will* have to sign on the dotted line.

» Choose the position of the Moon with care. A New Moon, with the Sun and the Moon conjunct, classically signals a new beginning. The best Moon for a wedding is a New Moon in your sign (or your intended's); in your seventh house of marriage; in Libra, the sign of relationship; or in Cancer, the sign of the home.

» If a New Moon isn't in the cards, for whatever reasons, at least get married when the Moon is *waxing* — that is, when it's between New and Full, becoming larger and more luminous every night. A *waning* Moon has passed its peak of luminosity and is on the downward slide, getting smaller and dimmer and finally disappearing. Who needs that symbolism?

» Look for a friendly contract between the Sun and the Moon. A sextile (60°) or trine (120°) creates harmony. A tight 90° square or 180° opposition increases tension and conflict.

>> Look for trines and sextiles involving the Moon, Venus, and Jupiter — the more the better.

>> Make sure the Moon isn't void-of-course. And make sure that your schedule has room for error, just in case the flower girl is late.

REMEMBER

The Moon is *void-of-course* when it has made its last major aspect in one sign but has not yet entered the next. The void-of-course period always comes at the end of the Moon's journey through a sign. To avoid a void-of-course Moon, schedule an event shortly after the Moon enters a new sign. (For more about the void-of-course Moon, turn to Chapter 17.)

Going on a First Date

In the real world, if someone you're interested in asks you out, the last thing you want to do is announce that the Moon is waning, so you'd rather wait for that margarita. On the other hand, maybe you're the one choosing the date. In that case, here's how to schedule a date that might lead to another:

>> Pay attention to the Moon. Look for a *waxing* Moon, meaning a Moon that's somewhere between New and Full. Make sure that the Moon is not void-of-course because relationships begun under a void-of-course Moon are less likely to go the distance. And choose a Moon sign that's either warm and sensitive — like Cancer, Pisces, or Taurus — or fun, like Gemini, Leo, or Sagittarius.

>> Look for harmonious aspects — that is, conjunctions, sextiles, or trines — between the Moon and Venus. Any reasonably thorough astrological calendar will list these. (For more about aspects, turn to Chapter 13.)

>> Watch your planetary transits. Jupiter in your fifth house can ease the pain of dating even for those who hate the whole miserable business. Jupiter spends about a year in your fifth house — but it only comes around every 12 years, so it behooves you to take advantage of it.

>> Look for transits of the Sun, the Moon, Venus, or Mars through your first house and your fifth house.

>> A once-a-year New Moon in your fifth house is definitely a door to romance, as is the once-a-year Full Moon that takes place six months later. Don't be shy.

Opening a Business

Launching a business isn't so different from starting a marriage, and some of the same rules apply. To wit:

>> Make sure that Mercury, the planet that rules contracts, isn't retrograde. The same goes for Venus, the planet of money.

>> Start your enterprise on or right after a New Moon. A New Moon in your second house (or in Taurus) is ideal if the business involves material objects or is primarily financial. (A New Moon in the second house is also the right time to ask for a raise.) A New Moon in your sixth house (or in Virgo) is perfect if your business is service-oriented. And a New Moon in the tenth house (or in Capricorn) supports public awareness of your business and assures that you'll be recognized in your field.

>> Look for beneficial aspects (sextiles and trines) between Saturn and Jupiter. Saturn rules structures and organizations; Jupiter rules luck and expansion. You want them working together. Avoid squares and oppositions involving those two planets.

TIP

An astrological calendar can tell you when an aspect is exact or at its peak. But an aspect between two planets often creates a buzz even before the crucial moment, when the aspect is still in the future. It's like Halloween or Christmas: You can feel it in the air (and see it in the stores) well in advance of the actual day. Afterwards, the energy quickly fades. I suggest that you scan ahead in your calendar to see if any major aspects are approaching. Be aware that if you open your business on a Wednesday, and Thursday there's an opposition between Saturn and Jupiter, you'll feel the tension, even if the aspect is not exact. Also, keep in mind that the slower the planet, the bigger the impact of the aspect. Saturn's going to be conjunct Pluto? I'd reschedule your grand opening to a more advantageous day.

>> To make sure that your brainchild gets noticed, launch your enterprise — by which I mean put up your shingle, cut the ribbon, sign the articles of incorporation, shake hands with your partner — around midday. That way, you can be certain that there are planets near the top of the chart. Win or lose, you won't go unnoticed.

Scheduling a Meeting

The way you schedule a meeting depends entirely on what you wish to accomplish. Follow these rules:

>> If you hope the meeting will enable you to inaugurate a program, introduce a new set of objectives, involve a staff member who hasn't previously participated, or make a case for organizational change, schedule the meeting when the Moon is New or, at minimum, waxing.

>> To encourage brainstorming, look for a conjunction, sextile, or trine between Mercury and Uranus. The Moon in Gemini also promotes an explosion of ideas.

>> If you want the meeting to reach a decision about an issue that's been on the table many times before, schedule it for a day when the Moon is close to Full. Full Moons can be illuminating, emotional times when that which has been hidden is revealed. They are also times when things come to a head and are resolved. If that's what you have in mind, the Full Moon will work in your favor.

>> Make sure the Moon isn't void-of-course and that Mercury isn't retrograde.

On the other hand, if you're planning a meeting to discuss a proposal you thoroughly oppose, here's what to do:

>> Schedule the meeting during a waning Moon, preferably during the last few days of the lunar cycle.

>> Make certain that the Moon is void-of-course. Many ideas may be floated at the meeting. Much discussion may occur. But guess what? Nothing will come of any of it.

Throwing a Party

Once again, it depends on what you have in mind. If you plan to hire a DJ, throw open the doors, and party deep into the night, these are the rules:

>> Let the Moon be in Leo (first choice), Gemini, or Sagittarius, followed by Libra, Aquarius, or Aries. The fire and air signs are boisterous and engaging. They may not generate as much intimacy as other signs, but under their happy authority, the good times roll.

>> Look to Venus and Jupiter. If either planet forms a conjunction, sextile, or trine to another planet, that's a promising indication.

>> To be certain that stern Saturn won't squeeze the fun right out of your fête, make sure that it doesn't make a close conjunction, square, or opposition to the Sun, the Moon, Venus, Mars, or Jupiter.

If you want to host a peaceful family dinner or a champagne brunch for your dearest friends, Moon in Cancer, Taurus, or Pisces will ensure that everyone feels cared for and well-fed.

Purchasing Technology

Follow these three simple rules when buying a computer, a smart phone, or one of those watches that knows what you're thinking:

>> Make sure that Mercury, the planet of communication, isn't retrograde. Okay, I know I keep mentioning this influence. It's always important, but there are times — I admit it — when you can bend the rules. Not in this instance, though. Do not purchase a computer (or a car) when Mercury is spinning backward, not if you can help it.

>> Make sure that Uranus and Mars aren't doing anything malevolent. High-tension squares, oppositions, and conjunctions, especially to Mercury or the Moon, are just the sort of thing you don't want to see.

>> Check that the Moon isn't void-of-course.

TIP

It isn't necessary, but an Aquarian influence — possibly in the form of the Sun or Moon in that sign, or a reassuring trine from Uranus — ensures that your technology is cutting edge.

Buying a House

Considering that buying a house is the largest purchase most people ever make, you might as well get the planets on your side — beginning with Jupiter, the lord of abundance. Once every 12 years, Jupiter travels through your fourth house. That's the single best influence for investing in real estate.

But maybe you can't wait that long. And maybe you can't wait for the right economic market to come along either. If you need to buy or sell a house now, take these suggestions:

>> Begin the process of buying with a New Moon — or at least a waxing Moon — in your fourth house or in Cancer. If you're selling, a Full Moon can be an effective ally.

>> Make sure the Moon is waxing when you buy a house. If it's in Taurus, Cancer, or the sign on the cusp of your fourth house, so much the better. When you sell a house, it's okay if the Moon is waning.

>> Look for trines and sextiles involving the Sun, the Moon, and any planets in your fourth house.

>> To make sure that the sale goes through, never sign a contract when Mercury is retrograde — and make sure that the Moon isn't void-of-course.

Having Surgery

First, let me be clear: If you need an operation immediately, you need it immediately. Listen to your doctor.

But perhaps you're undergoing elective surgery. Or maybe your doctor has given you a choice. That was my situation when I broke my arm in a country where I didn't speak the language. My doctor told me I could have my elbow operated on right away or I could fly home and have the operation there. Either way, I had to have surgery within a week.

In a case like that, how do you decide? These are the rules:

>> Make sure the Moon isn't in the sign that corresponds to the part of your body being operated on. Thus, if you're going to have surgery on your arm, avoid the Moon in Gemini. If you're planning to have knee surgery, make sure the Moon isn't in Capricorn. And so on.

TIP

For a description of the signs and the parts of the bodies associated with them, see Chapter 1.

>> Many astrologers recommend avoiding Moon in Scorpio for any kind of surgery. The astrologer Susan Miller notes that for cosmetic surgery it's smart to avoid Mars in either Aries, which rules the face, or Taurus, which rules the neck.

>> Don't have surgery on a Full Moon.

- >> Avoid retrograde Mercury, Venus, or Mars.

- >> Look for trines and sextiles to the Sun, the Moon, any planets in the eighth house, and the planet that rules the sign its cusp.

- >> Seek out supportive influences, such as Jupiter or Venus in your sixth house of health.

Starting a Diet or an Exercise Program

Going on a diet is a cheerless activity under any circumstances. The least you can do is give yourself a celestial head start. Here's how:

- >> Once a year, there's a New Moon in your sixth house of health. A New Moon helps you usher in a new habit, so that's a perfect time for beginning a diet or exercise program — or looking for a job.

- >> Six months after the New Moon, a Full Moon in your sixth house can help you release an old habit — like compulsive eating or an addiction to 300-calorie chai lattes.

- >> Saturn, the planet of self-discipline, can assist you in sticking to a diet and forging healthier habits. Look for Saturn to form conjunctions, trines, and sextiles with the Sun and the Moon.

- >> Saturn also supports your efforts if it's traveling through your sixth house, your first house, or your Sun sign. It's true that these transits may correspond to difficult times in your life. The silver lining is that they can also bring increased willpower, control, and accomplishment.

- >> Mars in the sixth house gives you a boost of energy — ideal for getting to the gym and making it a habit.

Writing a Novel, a Memoir, or a Screenplay

I often work in the writers' room of a local library, so I know how many people are struggling with novels, screenplays, memoirs, and other writing projects. I see them all the time, marking up their print-outs, jotting down notes, staring disconsolately at their screens, or playing solitaire on their laptops. I sympathize.

Writing projects are like diets: easy to begin, easy to put aside, and harder than they initially sounded. Here's how to better your odds of completing your project:

>> Begin a writing project under a New Moon. It helps if the New Moon is in your third house of communication; in the fourth house of family (especially you're penning a memoir or a cookbook); in the fifth house (if you're writing poems or a screenplay); in the ninth house (of publication); in Gemini or Virgo; or in your own sign.

>> Begin when Mercury is direct. If Mercury is in Gemini, in Virgo, in your Sun sign, or in the same sign as your natal Mercury, that's a plus.

>> Look for an active Uranus if you want to generate original ideas; an active Neptune when you want to stretch your imagination; and an active Pluto when you're ready to dig into emotionally complex material.

>> Take advantage of Mercury's retrograde periods by using them to revise. Mercury retrograde distresses many people, but those people are not writers. For a writer, Mercury retrograde is a gift.

Laying Low

You can only push so hard. Then the universe pushes back, insisting that you need to get some rest:

>> A New Moon or Full Moon in your twelfth house is a clear message that you need to withdraw. The Sun's annual monthly tour through that sector of your chart is a wonderful time to schedule a retreat.

>> It's also wise to withdraw when the Moon is in the sign preceding your own. Thus, if you're a Scorpio, the Moon's journey through Libra is a time to pull back, to meditate, and to catch up on your sleep, content in the knowledge that when the Moon enters Scorpio two or three days hence, you'll feel revitalized.

REMEMBER

That's what astrological timing is about. It isn't about fate. It's about using the stars to maximum advantage.

Index

A

Abbott, Bud (comedian), 299

Abdul-Jabbar, Kareem (athlete), 68

Abrahan ibn Ezra (physician/astrologer), 47

Abū Ma'shar (aka Albumasar) (astrologer), 47

accidental dignities, 24–25

activist capability, spotting of in chart, 384–385

Adams, Abigail (former US first lady), 300

Adams, Douglas (author), 228

Adams, Evangeline (astrologer), 54–55, 171

Adams, John (composer), 366

Adams, John (former US president), 300

Adams, Neile (actress), 288

Adele (singer), 74, 199

Adjani, Isabelle (actress), 290

Affleck, Ben (actor), 94, 288

Agassi, Andre (athlete), 290

Age of Aquarius, 12

"Age of Aquarius" (song), 55, 258

air sign, 17, 275

Albert, Richard (aka Baba Ram Dass), 247

Alcott, Louisa May (author), 200

Aldebaran (star), 72

Ali, Muhammad (boxer), 24, 129, 375

aliases, 201

al-Kindi (philosopher), 47

Allan, William Frederick (aka Alan Leo) (astrologer), 54

Allen, Woody (director/actor), 120, 246, 299, 301

All's Well That Ends Well (Shakespeare), 51

Almagest (Ptolemy), 44

almanacs, astrology as included in, 53

Alpert, Herb (musician), 68

Anderson, Laurie (artist), 247, 293, 359

Anderson, Pamela Lee (actress), 88, 294

Ang Lee (filmmaker), 108

Angelou, Maya (poet), 68, 356

angles, of birth charts, 196, 197

Aniston, Jennifer (actress), 200, 301

Ansari, Aziz (actor), 141

Antares (red star), 111

Anthony, Susan B. (activist), 135, 264

Antoinette, Marie (queen), 114

Apple, Fiona (singer-songwriter), 99, 244

apps, 37–38, 308–309

Aquarius

basic facts of, 16, 17, 18, 122, 133

creativity in, 366–367

dates of, 16, 122, 129

described, 14

examples of people born under sign of, 131, 133–135

health and wellness attributes of, 132

in love, 303–304

mythology of, 132

relationships of, 131

rulers of, 22, 23, 133, 203

sorry side of, 130–131

sunny side of, 130

symbol/glyph of, 16, 129, 133

work attributes of, 131–132

Aquarius Midheaven, 210

Aquarius rising, 203, 205, 279

Arabic astrologers, 46–47

Arbus, Diane (photographer), 141, 282

Archive for the Retrieval of Historical Astrological Texts (ARHAT), 56

Arcturus (star), 97

Aries

basic facts of, 16, 17, 18, 61, 62, 66

creativity in, 356–357

dates of, 15, 61, 62

described, 13

examples of people born under sign of, 67–68

health and wellness attributes of, 65–66

in love, 288–289

mythology of, 66

relationships of, 64

ruler of, 22, 62, 66, 198

sorry side of, 63–64

sunny side of, 63

symbol/glyph of, 15, 62–63, 66

work attributes of, 64–65

Aries Midheaven, 206

Aries rising, 197–198, 204, 279

Aristotle (philosopher), 47

Armstrong, Neil (astronaut), 94

Arnez, Desi (actor), 297

Arquette, David (actor), 292

Arquette, Patricia (actress), 68, 289

Ascendant sign (rising sign), 25–26, 196, 197–204. *See also* rising sign

Asimov, Isaac (author), 129, 271

aspect grid, reading of, 242

aspects, 238–242, 244–265, 304–306, 370

Astaire, Fred (dancer/actor), 74

asteroids, 10, 22–23, 54, 112, 155, 157, 193

Astro Butterfly, 38

Astro-charts (website), 34

Astro-Databank, 35

Astrodienst (website), 34–35

AstroGold (app), 37

Astrolabe (website), 34

astrologer, spotting of talent for becoming of in chart, 387

The Astrologer's Magazine, 54

astrological chart
of Albert Einstein, 139–140
of Alexandria Ocasio-Cortez, 238–239, 242
of Ana Mendieta, 112–113
of Andrew Hamilton, 128
of Andy Warhol, 377–378
of Beyoncé, 98–99
for Björk, 208
of Bruce Springsteen, 106–107
casting yours the old-fashioned way, 30–31
of Christina Lagarde, 382
of David Bowie, 202–203
of Donald J. Trump, 78–79
of Edgar Cayce, 386
of Frida Kahlo, 86–87
gathering information needed for, 31
of George Clooney, 73
getting yours online for free, 33–35

of Greta Thunberg, 384–385

horary astrology, 37, 52

investing in software for, 35–37

of Isabel M. Hickey, 387

of Jack Welch, 381–382

of Jonas Salk, 379–380

of Kim Kardashian, 378–379

of Lady Gaga, 67

of Lin-Manuel Miranda, 126–127

of Ludwig van Beethoven, 118–119

of Meghan Markle, 92–93

of Oprah Winfrey, 133–134

rectification of, 33

as science of the decrees of the stars, 46

of Serena Williams, 309–311

as simple representation of real world, 29

spotting talents in, 375–388

through classical times, 43–47

of Toni Morrison, 331–332

using app for, 37–38

of Wolfgang Amadeus Mozart, 370–371

Astrological Pocket Planner, 308

astrological software, 35–37

astrology. *See also* Vedic astrology
Alan Leo as father of modern astrology, 54
banning of in Nazi Germany, 55
as braided together with astronomy, 52
Chinese astrology, 1, 56
electional astrology, 37, 389
history of, 41–58
medical astrology, 19
Meso-American astrology, 57, 349
mundane astrology, 1, 37

use of, 389–397

use of in daily life, 333–341

Astrology 14 (Schmidt), 14

Astrology: A Cosmic Science (Hickey), 387

Astrology: A History (Whitfield), 58

Astrology for Everyone (Adams), 171

astronomy, as braided together with astrology, 52

AstroTwins, 38

athletic prowess, spotting of in chart, 375–376

Atwood, Margaret (author), 199, 283, 352, 363

Auden, W. H. (author), 141

Augustus (emperor), 10, 44, 45

Aung San Suu Kyi (Myanmar state counsellor), 79

Austen, Jane (author), 120, 200, 250, 254, 365

Auster, Paul (author), 200, 367

The Autobiography of Alice B. Toklas (Stein), 305

autumn, signs of, 101–120

Aznavour, Charles (singer-lyricist), 79

B

Babylonians, 10, 12, 41, 42, 43

Bacall, Lauren (actress), 99, 298

Bach, Barbara (actress), 294

Bach, Johann Sebastian (composer), 357

Bachelard, Gaston (philosopher), 209

Bacon, Kevin (actor), 88, 294

Badu, Erykah (singer-songwriter), 141

Baez, Joan (singer-songwriter), 129

Bailey, James Anthony, 294

Baker, Chet (musician), 129

Baldwin, Hailey (model), 302

Baldwin, James (author), 361

Ball, Lucille (actress), 94, 297

Ballard, Florence (singer), 88

Balzac, Honoré de (author), 358

Banks, Tyra (media personality), 120, 199

Bardem, Javier (actor), 141

Bareilles, Sara (singer-songwriter), 120

Barnum, P. T. (showman), 294

Barr, Candy (stripper), 211

Barr, Roseanne (actress), 114, 203

Barrow, Clyde (criminal), 289

Barrymore, Drew (actress), 141

Barton, Clara (nurse), 129, 264

Barton, Mischa (actress), 135

Baudelaire, Charles (poet), 68

Bearden, Romare (artist), 352

Beatty, Warren (actor), 288

beauty, spotting of in chart, 376–377

Beauvoir, Simone de (author), 293

Beckham, David (athlete), 74, 288

Beckham, Victoria (businesswoman), 288, 376

Bee, Samantha (comedian), 245

Beehive (star cluster), 86

Beethoven, Ludwig van (composer), 118–119

Belafonte, Harry (singer), 141

Bell, Alexander Graham (inventor), 139

Benatar, Pat (singer-songwriter), 129

Bening, Annette (actress), 288

Benioff, David (screenwriter), 108

Bennett, Tony (singer), 94

Benny, Jack (comedian), 135

Berg, Walter (astrologer), 14

Bergman, Ingmar (film director), 360

Berkowtiz, David (aka Son of Sam) (criminal), 201

Bernstein, Leonard (composer), 99

Berossus (astrologer), 44

Berry, Chuck (singer-songwriter), 108

Berry, Halie (actress), 94

Bettleheim, Bruno (author), 99

Beyoncé (singer-songwriter), 96, 98–99, 269, 298

Bezos, Jeff (Amazon CEO), 289, 381

Bezos, MacKenzie (author), 289

Bickerstaff, Isaac, as pseudonym for Jonathan Swift, 53

Biden, Joe (former US vice president), 110, 114

Bieber, Justin (singer-songwriter), 200, 302

Biel, Jessica (actress), 141, 303

Bigelow, Kathryn, 365

Biles, Simone (athlete), 141, 375

bi-quintile, as one of six minor aspects, 243

Bird by Bird (Lamott), 356

Birkin, Jane (actress), 120

birth certificates, 31–33

birth chart. See also astrological chart

   interpretation of, 267–284

   retrograde Mercury, Venus, and Mars in, 352

birth time, houses as depending on, 213

Björk (singer/composer/performer), 207, 209

Black Death, 19, 48

Blair, Linda (actress), 198

Blake, William (poet), 120

Blanchett, Cate (actress), 74

Bloom, Orlando (actor), 129

Blume, Judy (author), 135

Blunt, Emily (actress), 141, 299

Bogart, Humphrey (actor), 298

Bolt, Usain (athlete), 94

Bonatti, Guido (astrologer), 48

Bono (singer), 69, 74

Bono, Chaz (author), 141, 201

Booker, Cory (US senator), 261, 290

Borden, Lizzie (suspected criminal), 246, 352

Borges, Jorge Luis (author), 352

Bourdain, Anthony (chef), 88, 199

Bowie, David (singer-songwriter) (aka Ziggy Stardust), 129, 202–203, 296, 366, 376

bowl, as one of seven planetary patterns, 270

Boyd, Patti (model), 304

Boyle, Susan (singer), 68, 245

Brady, Tom (athlete), 94, 294

Brahe, Tycho (nobleman), 129

Branagh, Kenneth (actor), 120, 289

Brando, Marlon (actor), 68, 201

Branson, Richard (business magnate), 199

Brennan, Chris (astrologer), 38

Brezsny, Rob (astrologer), 39

Bridges, Jeff (actor), 120

Broderick, Matthew (actor), 288

Brolin, James (actor), 290

Brontë, Charlotte (author), 74, 358

Brontë, Emily (author), 94, 361

Brooks, Gwendolyn (author), 79

Brooks, Mel (film director), 88

Brown, James (singer-songwriter), 74, 358

Browning, Elizabeth Barry (poet), 141

Bruce, Lenny (comedian), 108

bubonic plague, cause of, 48

bucket, as one of seven planetary patterns, 271

Buffet, Warren (Berkshire Hathaway CEO), 99

Bullock Sandra (actress), 94

Bündchen, Gisele (model), 88, 294

bundle, as one of seven planetary patterns, 269–270

Buñuel, Luis (filmmaker), 141

Burroughs, William (author), 135, 203

Burton, Richard (actor), 301

Bush, Barbara (former US first lady), 292

Bush, George H. W. (former US president), 79, 292

Bush, George W. (former US president), 269, 294

Bush, Laura (former US first lady), 114, 294

business, timing of opening of, 392

business savvy, spotting of in chart, 380–383

Byatt, A. S. (author), 99

Byrne, David (singer), 74

Byron, George Gordon (Lord Byron) (poet), 135

C

Café Astrology (website), 34

Cage, John (composer), 361

Cage, Nicholas (actor), 289

Campbell, Joseph (professor), 68

Campbell, Naomi (model), 79

Campion, Nicholas (astronomer), 12

Camus, Albert (author), 114

Cancer
basic facts of, 16, 17, 18, 81, 85, 86

creativity in, 359–360

dates of, 15, 81, 82

described, 13

examples of people born under sign of, 86–88

health and wellness attributes of, 84–85

in love, 293–295

mythology of, 85

relationships of, 83–84

ruler of, 22, 86, 199

sorry side of, 83

sunny side of, 82–83

symbol/glyph of, 15, 82, 86

work attributes of, 84

Cancer Midheaven, 207

Cancer rising, 199, 205, 279

Canterbury Tales (Chaucer), 198

Capra, Frank (film director), 74

Capricorn
basic facts of, 11, 16, 17, 18, 121, 122, 126

creativity in, 365–366

dates of, 16, 121, 122

described, 13

examples of people born under sign of, 124, 126–128, 202–203

health and wellness attributes of, 125

in love, 302–303

mythology of, 125–126

relationships of, 124

ruler of, 22, 126, 202

sorry side of, 123

sunny side of, 122–123

symbol/glyph of, 16, 122, 126

work attributes of, 124–125

Capricorn Midheaven, 210

Capricorn rising, 202, 205, 279

Cardi B (rapper), 108

cardinal signs, 17, 275

Carlisle, Belinda (singer), 94

Carrey, Jim (actor), 129

Carroll, Lewis (author), 135

Carson, Rachel (author), 358

Carter, Jimmy (former US president), 108, 296

Carter, Rosalyn (former US first lady), 296

Carver, Raymond (author), 79

Carville, James (commentator), 296

Casey, Caroline (astrologer), 248

Cash, Johnny (singer-songwriter), 141, 204, 295

Cash, June Carter (singer-songwriter), 295

Cash, Roseanne (singer-songwriter), 79

Cassatt (artist), 358

Casteneda, Carlos (author), 129

Castor (star), 77–78

Castro, Fidel (former Cuban president), 94, 247

Catherine (Duchess of Cambridge), 129, 199, 271, 295, 352

Cayce, Edgar (healer), 141, 386

Ceres (asteroid), 54, 193

Cervantes, Miguel de (author), 363

Cetus the Whale, 14

Cezanne, Paul (artist), 366

Chaldean, 43

Chamberlain, Neville (former British prime minister), 183

Chan, Jackie (martial artist), 68

Chanel, Coco (fashion designer), 94

Chang, Iris (journalist), 68

Chapelle, Dave (comedian), 99

Character Is Destiny (Leo), 54

Chariklo (asteroid), 193

Charlemagne (king), 10

Charles (prince), 114, 294

Charles, Ray (musician), 99

Charon (moon of Pluto), 187

chart, astrological. *See* astrological chart

chart, birth. *See* birth chart

chart, marriage. *See* marriage chart

chart, natal. *See* natal chart

Chaucer, Geoffrey (author), 198

Chávez, César (activist), 68

Cheat Sheet, 2, 4

Cheiro (aka William John Warner) (astrologer), 55

Chekhov, Anton (playwright), 135

Cher (singer/actress), 74, 199, 282

Chesterton, G. K. (author), 79, 207

Chihuly, Dale (glassblower), 361

Child, Julia (chef), 94

China, earliest astronomical activity in, 42

Chinese astrology, 1, 56

Chiron, 20–21, 23, 156, 157, 190, 191–193

Chopin, Frederic (composer), 141

Chopra, Deepak (author), 204

Chopra, Priyanka (actress), 88, 294

Christian Astrology (Lilly), 52

Christie, Agatha (author), 99

Churchill, Winston (former British prime minister), 120, 183, 283

Cicero (orator), 10

Clapton, Eric (musician), 68, 200, 304

Clarkson, Kelly (singer-songwriter), 74

Clemens, Samuel (author), 201

Clinton, Bill (former US president), 94, 246, 296

Clinton, Hillary (former US senator and first lady), 110, 114, 256, 259, 296

Clooney, Amal (barrister), 283

Clooney, George (actor/director), 73

Close, Glenn (actress), 141

Cobain, Kurt (singer-songwriter), 141, 228, 295

Cohen, Leonard (singer-songwriter), 99, 200, 290, 352

Cohen, Sacha Baron (actor), 247

Colbert, Stephen (media personality), 74

Cole, Nat King (singer-songwriter), 141

Cole, Natalie (singer), 135

Coltrane, John (musician), 204

Combs, Sean (rapper), 114

conjunct aspects, 238

conjunction, 238, 240

Connery, Sean (actor), 96, 99

constellations, 11–13, 86. *See also specific zodiac signs*

Consuelos, Mark (actor), 289

Conway, Kellyanne (counselor to Donald J. Trump), 129

Cook, Tim (Apple CEO), 258

Cooper, Anderson (media personality), 79, 258, 293

Cooper, Bradley (actor), 129, 247

Copernicus, Nicolaus (polymath), 53, 54, 141, 167

Copperfield, David (magician), 297

Coppola, Francis Ford (film director), 65, 68, 357

Coppola, Sofia (screenwriter), 358

Cornell, Joseph (artist), 366

Cortázar, Julio (author), 99, 200

Cosby, Bill (comedian), 246

cosmic malevolence, 48

Costello, Lou (comedian), 299

Costello, Priscilla (author)
Shakespeare and the Stars, 51, 52

Cox, Courtenay (actress), 292

Craig, Daniel (actor), 141, 304

Cranston, Bryan (actor), 141

Crayon, Geoffrey (author) (pen name for Washington Irving), 201

The Creative Habit: Learn It and Use It for Life (Tharp), 359

creativity, circling the zodiac for, 355–368

Crow, Sheryl (musician), 135

Cruise, Tom (actor), 200, 292, 294

Cruz, Penelope (actress), 74, 198

Cumberbatch, Benedict (actor), 88

Cummings, E. E. (poet), 108, 199

Curie, Marie (physicist), 114

Curtis, Jamie Lee (actress), 114

cusp, use of term, 27. *See also* "on the cusp"

cyberspace, astrological information in, 38–39

Cyrus, Miley (singer-songwriter), 120, 256

D

da Vinci, Leonardo (polymath), 201, 283, 358

Dalai Lama (religious leader), 88, 172, 211

Dali, Salvador (artist), 74

Damon, Matt (actor), 108

Dante Alighieri, 48

Darwin, Charles (naturalist), 131, 135, 366

d'Ascoli, Cecco (astrologer), 48

dating, going on first date, using astrology to decide when, 391

Davis, Angela (activist), 135

Davis, Bette (actress), 200

Davis, Miles (musician), 79, 282, 359

Davis, Ossie (actor), 305

Davis, Viola (actress), 94

Dawson, Rosario (actress), 74, 290

De Niro, Robert (actor), 94, 361

de Palma, Brian (film director), 99

Dean, James (actor), 135, 376

Debussy, Claude (composer), 361

Dee, John (astrologer), 10, 49–50

Dee, Ruby (actress), 305

Degas, Edgar (artist), 88

DeGeneres, Ellen (comedian), 135, 303

Delavigne, Cara (model), 94

Depp, Johnny (actor), 79, 293

Dern, Laura (actress), 135, 204, 300

Descendant sign (setting sign), 196, 204–205

Deschanel, Zooey (actress), 129

detriment (of planets), 23

DeWitt, Sol (artist), 361

Diana (Princess of Wales), 88, 294

DiCaprio, Leonardo (actor), 114, 200

Dickens, Charles (author), 366

Dickinson, Emily (poet), 120, 365

Didion, Joan (author), 120

diet, timing of start of, 396

dignities (of planets), 23–25

DiMaggio, Joe (athlete), 120, 293

Dinklage, Peter (actor), 79, 261, 279

Dior, Christian (fashion designer), 367

disasters, predictions of, 52, 55

Disraeli, Benjamin (former British prime minister), 352

Dorotheus of Sidon (astrologer/poet), 47

Dostoyevsky, Fyodor (author), 114, 364

007, 50

Douglas, Michael (actor), 108, 299

Douglass, Frederick (orator), 264

Downey, Robert, Jr. (actor), 68, 258

Doyle, Arthur Conan (author), 79

Dr. Dre (rapper), 135

Dr. Seuss (author), 368

Drake (rapper), 114, 199

Driver, Adam (actor), 114

Duchovny, David (actor), 297

Dunst, Kirsten (actress), 74

DuVernay, Ava (filmmaker), 99, 202, 352

dwarf planets, 20, 23, 54, 108, 155, 156, 186, 193, 201, 327

Dylan, Bob (singer-songwriter), 75, 79, 358

E

Earhart, Amelia (aviator), 94, 270

earth sign, 17, 275

Eastwood, Clint (actor/director), 79, 200

Ebertin, Elsbeth (astrologer), 55

ecliptic, 11, 43, 150

Edison, Thomas (inventor), 131, 135, 248

Edward VIII (Duke of Windsor), 292

Egypt, earliest astronomical activity in, 43

eighth house, 27, 214, 215, 217

Einstein, Albert (theoretical physicist), 24, 139–140, 244, 302

Einstein, Mileva (physicist), 302

Ejiofor, Chiwetel (actor), 88

Elba, Idris (actor), 96, 99, 246

electional astrology, 37, 389

elements, 17, 18, 275, 276

elevated planet, 280

eleventh house, 27, 214, 215, 217

Eliot, George (author) (pen name for Mary Anne Evans), 114, 201, 264

Eliot, T. S. (author), 108

Elizabeth I (queen), 10, 49

Elizabeth II (queen), 202, 258, 290

Ellington, Duke (musician), 358

Eminem (singer-songwriter), 108, 262

English, Mary (astrologer), 38

Enuma Anu Enlil, 42

equinoxes, 11, 12–13, 14, 102

Eris (dwarf planet), 193

Escher, M.C. (artist), 248

Escobar, Pablo (drug lord), 120

essential dignities, 23–24

Evans, Dale (actress), 300

Evans, Mary Anne (author), 201

exaltation (of planets), 23

exercise program, timing of start of, 396

F

fall (of planets), 23

fall equinox, 102

Fallon, Jimmy (media personality), 99

Fanning, Dakota (actress), 141

Farrell, Colin (actor), 79

Farrow, Mia (actress), 228, 257, 282, 289, 301

Farrow, Ronan (journalist), 120, 247

Fassbender, Michael (actor), 68

The Fated Sky: Astrology in History (Bobrick), 58

Federer, Roger (athlete), 376

Fellini, Federico (film director), 129

feminine signs, 16

Ferrera, America, 202

Fey, Tina (actress), 74

Ficino, Marsilio (philosopher), 49

fifth house, 27, 213, 214, 216

Finger of Fate, 282–284

fire sign, 17, 275

first house, 27, 213, 214, 215–216

Firth, Colin (actor), 99

Fischer, Bobby (chess grandmaster), 141

Fisher, Carrie (actress), 108

Fisher, Eddie (singer), 288

Fitzgerald, Ella (singer), 74, 270

Fitzgerald, F. Scott (author), 108, 281, 296

Fitzgerald, Zelda (author), 296

fixed signs, 17, 275

Flaubert, Gustave (author), 120

Fleming, Ian (author), 50, 79

Fonda, Jane (actress), 202

Ford, Betty (former US first lady), 288

Ford, Gerald (former US president), 88, 288

Ford, Harrison (actor), 88

Foucault, Jean-Pierre (media personality), 120

fourth house, 27, 213, 214, 216

Fox, Michael J. (actor), 203, 260

Foxx, Jamie (actor), 120, 301

France, earliest astronomical activity in, 42

Francis (pope), 120

Frank, Anne (diarist), 79, 359

Frankenstein (Shelley), 361

Franklin, Aretha (singer), 68, 357

Franklin, Benjamin (polymath), 53, 254

Freud, Sigmund (psychiatrist), 55, 74, 201, 357

Friedan, Betty (author), 135

Friedman, Hank (astrologer), 36–37

Frost, Robert (poet), 68, 352

Fuller, R. Buckminster (architect), 198

G

Gable, Clark (actor), 377

Gabor, Zsa Zsa (actress), 233

Gaiman, Neil (author), 114, 254, 352, 364

Galilei, Galileo (astronomer), 53, 86, 167, 181

Galle, Johann (assistant astronomer), 182

Gandhi, Indira (former India prime minister), 114

Gandhi, Mahatma (lawyer), 103, 108, 183

Gardner, Ava (actress), 299

Garland, Judy (singer/actress), 79, 377

Garner, Jennifer (actress), 288

Gates, Bill (business magnate), 110, 114, 261

Gauquelin, Michel (statistician), 224, 388

Gaye, Marvin (singer), 68

Gellar, Sarah Michelle (actress), 289

Gemini
  basic facts of, 16, 17, 18, 62, 74, 77, 78
  creativity in, 358–359
  dates of, 15, 62, 74
  described, 13
  examples of people born under sign of, 78–79
  health and wellness attributes of, 76–77
  in love, 292–293
  mythology of, 77
  relationships of, 76
  ruler of, 22, 78, 199
  sorry side of, 75
  sunny side of, 75
  symbol/glyph of, 15, 74, 78
  work attributes of, 76

Gemini Midheaven, 207

Gemini rising, 199, 204, 279

generational dates, 176

George III (king), 177

Germanotta, Stefani (aka Lady Gaga) (singer-songwriter), 67

Gershwin, George (composer), 108, 363

Gerwig, Greta (actress), 94, 361

Gilot, Françoise (artist), 300

Ginsberg, Allen (poet), 79, 204, 358

Ginsburg, Martin (lawyer), 293

Ginsburg, Ruth Bader (US Supreme Court justice), 141, 262, 281, 293, 304

Gladwell, Malcolm (author), 272

A Glance into the Future (Ebertin), 55

Glass, Philip (composer), 366

glyph, 62

Goebbels, Joseph (politician), 55

goes direct, 344

Goldberg, Whoopi (actress), 114, 203

Golding, William (author), 99

Goldman, Emma (anarchist), 183

Goldwyn, Samuel (film director), 99

Gomez, Selena (singer), 199

Goodall, Jane (primatologist), 260

Gore, Al (politician), 68

Gosling, Ryan (actor), 300

Graf, Steffi (athlete), 290

Grafton, Sue (author), 74

Graham, Martha (dancer), 358

Graham, Stedman (educator), 141, 303

Grand Cross, 239, 282, 283

Grand Sextile, 283

Grand Trine, 127, 281, 283, 360, 380

Grande, Ariana (singer), 88, 202

Grandin, Temple (professor), 99

Grant, Cary (actor), 129

Grant, Hugh (actor), 292

Grant, Ulysses S. (former US president), 74

Great Year, 12

Greece, earliest astronomical activity in, 43

Green, Hetty (businesswoman), 191–192

Griffin, Kathy (comedian), 364

Gropius, Walter (architect), 357

Guevara, Ché (revolutionary), 74, 198

Guide to Horoscope Interpretation (Jones), 268

Guiler, Hugh Parker (engraver/filmmaker), 303

Guisewite, Cathy (cartoonist), 99

H

Haddish, Tiffany (actress), 120

Hadid, Bella (model), 108

Hadid, Gigi (fashion model), 74

Hair (rock musical), 55

Halley, Edmund (astronomer), 9

Hamal (star), 66

Hamilton (musical), 126, 128

Hamilton, Alexander (US founding father), 128

Hammerstein, Oscar (librettist), 294

Hand, Robert (astrologer), 56

Hand of God, 282–284

Handler, Chelsea (comedian), 141

The Handmaid's Tale (Atwood), 363

Hanks, Tom (actor), 88, 294

Hannah, Daryl (actress), 258, 300

Hannity, Sean (commentator), 129

hard aspects, 238, 241

Haring, Keith (artist), 74

harmonious aspects, 238, 241

Harper, Ben (singer-songwriter), 300

Harris, Emmylou (singer), 68

Harrison, George (singer), 304

Harry (Duke of Sussex), 99, 202, 271, 296

Harry, Debbie (singer-songwriter), 88

Hart, Kevin (comedian/actor), 88

Haumea (dwarf planet), 193

Hawking, Stephen (physicist), 281, 282

Hawn, Goldie (actress), 301

healing hands, spotting of talent for in chart, 379–380

Heaney, Seamus (poet), 68

Hefner, Hugh, 246

Heinlein, Robert A. (author), 88

Hellenistic astrology, 56

Hemingway, Ernest (author), 88

hemisphere analysis, 268–269

Hendrix, Jimi (musician), 120, 254

Henry IV Part Ii (Shakespeare), 51

Hepburn, Audrey (actress), 74, 203

Hepburn, Katharine (actress), 74, 256, 288

Heraclitus (philosopher), 54

Herschel, William (musician/telescope maker), 54, 175, 177

Hesse, Herman (author), 88

Hickey, Isabel M. (astrology), 387

Hildegard of Bingen (saint), 352

Hill, Faith (singer), 290

Hilton, Paris (media personality), 135

A History of Western Astrology (Campion), 58

Hitchcock, Alfred (film director), 94, 361

Hitler, Adolph (ruler), 55, 70

Ho Chi Minh (former Vietnam prime minister), 70

Hockney, David (artist), 360

Hoffman, Dustin (actor), 94

Holly, Buddy (musician), 99

Holmes, Katie (actress), 294, 301

horary astrology, 37, 52

horizon line, 268

horoscope, getting yours online for free, 33–35

Houdini, Harry (magician), 68

house, timing of purchase of, 394–395

houses. *See also specific houses; specific planets*

as contributing to creativity, 369–370

determining boundaries of, 212

as distinguished from signs, 211–212

empty houses, 233–235

every horoscope as having 12, 26–27

house rulership, 234, 280

matched to elements and qualities, 278

natural houses, 33

placement of, 213, 277

significance of, 27, 213–214

Houston, Whitney (singer), 204, 272

Hudson, Jennifer (singer), 260

Hudson, Rock (actor), 114, 200

Huffman, Felicity (actress), 120, 302

Hughes, Howard (business magnate), 124, 299

Hughes, Ted (poet), 94

Hugo, Victor (author), 141, 200, 368

human body, parts of as attributable to zodiac signs, 19

Hurley, Elizabeth (businesswoman), 292

Hussein, Saddam (former Iraqi president), 70

Huston, Anjelica (actress), 88

Hyades (star cluster), 72

Hydra (constellation), 86

I

I Know Why the Caged Bird Sings (Angelou), 356

IAU measurements, 12

Ibsen, Henrik (playwright), 368

I.C. (*Imum Coeli*), 196, 206–210

icons, explained, 4

Iglesias, Julio (singer-songwriter), 99

Ihlen, Marianne (muse and girlfriend of Leonard Cohen), 290

Iman (fashion model), 296

inconjunct (or quincunx), as one of six minor aspects, 243, 283

Inferno (Dante), 48

International Astronomical Union, 156

Io programs (software), 36

Irving, Washington (author), 201

Islam, Arabic astrologers in, 46–47

Ivan the Terrible (Grand Prince of Moscow), 99

J

Jackman, Hugh (singer/actor), 108

Jackson, Jessie (activist), 108

Jackson, Michael (singer-songwriter), 99, 245, 298, 361

Jackson, Shirley (author), 120, 281

Jackson, Stonewall (general), 135

Jagger, Bianca (actress), 290

Jagger, Mick (singer-songwriter), 94, 246, 280, 290

James, Etta (singer), 135

James, LeBron (athlete), 129, 375

Janus 5 (software), 37

Jay Z (rapper), 120, 200, 298, 365

Jefferson, Thomas (former US president), 68

Jenner, Bruce (aka Caitlyn Jenner), 201, 300

Jenner, Caitlyn (media personality), 114

Jenner, Kendall (model), 114

Jenner, Kris (media personality), 114, 200, 300, 301

Jenner, Kylie (media personality), 94, 202, 290

Jeter, Derek (athlete/sports owner), 88

Jett, Joan (singer-songwriter), 99

Jim Maynard's Celestial Guide (Maynard), 308, 336

Jobs, Steve (business magnate), 139, 141, 200, 260, 368

Joel, Billy (singer-songwriter), 74

Johansson, Scarlett (actress), 120, 269

Johnson, Dakota (actress), 108

Johnson, Dwayne (actor), 74

Johnson, Lady Bird (former US first lady), 298

Johnson, Lyndon (former US president), 298

Jolie, Angelina (actress), 79, 199, 260, 293

Jonas, Nick (singer-songwriter), 294

Jones, Jim (cult leader), 70

Jones, Marc Edmund (astrologer), 268, 269

Jones, Norah (singer-songwriter), 68

Joplin, Janis (singer-songwriter), 129

Jordan, Michael (athlete), 135

Jordan, Michael B. (actor), 135

Josephine (empress), 294

Joyce, James (author), 135, 202, 366

Judd, Naomi (singer-songwriter), 129

Julius Caesar (ruler), 44

Jung, Carl G. (psychiatrist), 10, 54, 55, 94

Juno (asteroid), 54, 193

Jupiter

activating of, 314–317

attributes associated with, 167

creativity in, 369

described, 166–168

detriment of, 24

exaltation of, 24

fall of, 24

Galileo and moons of, 167

house and accidental planetary dignity of, 25

in houses, 225–226

keyword for, 21, 156

mythology of, 167

as personal planet, 155

role of in horoscope, 20

as ruler, 22, 24, 118, 139, 201, 204

as social planet, 176

symbol/glyph of, 21, 156, 167

in zodiac signs, 168

Jyotish, 56

K

Kafka, Franz (author), 360

Kahlo, Frida (artist), 86–87, 294

Kaling, Mindy (comedian), 88, 199, 244

Kardashian, Khloe (media personality), 88

Kardashian, Kim (media personality), 24, 108, 201, 257, 292, 376, 378–379, 384

Kardashian, Robert (attorney), 141, 301

Kawakubo, Rei (fashion designer), 363

Keller, Helen (author), 88

Kelley, Edward (forger), 49, 50

Kelly, Ellsworth (artist), 359

Kelly, Gene (dancer/actor), 94

Kennedy, Carolyn Bessette (publicist), 301

Kennedy, Ethel (human rights advocate), 289

Kennedy, John F. (former US president), 79, 292

Kennedy, John F., Jr. (lawyer), 301

Kennedy, Robert F. (former US attorney general), 110, 114, 289

Kennedy, Ted (former US senator), 272

Kepler, Johannes (astronomer), 45, 53, 370

Kerouac, Jack (author), 141

Kidman, Nicole (actress), 79, 200, 292, 376

Kimmel, Jimmy (media personality), 114

King, Billie Jean (athlete), 114, 270, 352

King, Coretta Scott (author), 69

King, Gayle (media personality), 302

King, Martin Luther, Jr. (minister), 124, 129, 352

King, Stephen (author), 99, 250, 254, 281, 361

Kirkland, Gelsey (dancer), 129

Kissinger, Henry (former US secretary of state), 79

Knickerbocker, Dietrich (author) (pen name for Washington Irving), 201

Knievel, Evel (daredevil), 250

Knowles, Solange (singer-songwriter), 88

Kouchner, Bernard (politician), 200, 271

Kowal, Charles (astronomer), 190

Krafft, Karl Ernst (astrologer), 55

Krasinski, John (actor), 299

Krassner, Lee (artist), 300

Kraus, Alison (singer-songwriter), 94

Kravitz, Zoë (actress), 120

Kuiper belt, 186, 193

Kunis, Mila (actress), 296

Kurosawa, Akira (film director), 65

Kusama, Yayoi (artist), 357

Kutcher, Ashton (actor), 135, 296, 300

L

La Marr, Barbara (actress), 198

Lady Gaga (singer/songwriter), 67

Lagarde, Christine (European Central Bank president), 129, 382

Lagerfeld, Karl (fashion designer), 99

Lahiri, Jhumpa (author), 88

Lakshmi, Padma (author), 99

Lamar, Kendrick (rapper), 79

Lamarr, Hedy (actress), 114

Lamb, Wally (author), 108

Lamott, Anne (author)
Bird by Bird, 356

lang, k.d. (singer-songwriter), 114, 200

Larson, Brie (actress), 108

Lauren, Ralph (fashion designer), 108

Lawrence, D. H. (author), 99

Lawrence, Jennifer (actress), 271, 360

Lawrence, T. E. (archaeologist), 94

laying low, timing of, 397

Le Guin, Ursula K. (author), 108, 198, 254

Learning Astrology with Mary English (English), 38

Ledger, Heath (actor), 288

Lee, Bruce (actor), 120, 262

Lee, Tommy (musician), 294

Leeds, Titan (publisher), 53

Legend, John (singer-songwriter), 129, 301

Leibovitz, Annie (photographer), 108, 363

Lenin, Vladimir (former Soviet Union premier), 70

Lennon, John (singer-songwriter), 103, 108, 198, 260, 299, 363

Lennox, Annie (singer-songwriter), 366

Leo
basic facts of, 16, 17, 18, 92
creativity in, 360–361
dates of, 15, 88
described, 13
exaltation of, 92–94
health and wellness attributes of, 91
in love, 295–297
mythology of, 91–92
relationships of, 90
ruler of, 22, 92, 199
sorry side of, 89
sunny side of, 89
symbol/glyph of, 15, 88, 92
work attributes of, 90–91

Leo, Alan (aka William Frederick Allan) (astrologer), 54

Leo Midheaven, 207

Leo rising, 199, 205, 279

Leonard, Elmore (author), 108

Leoni, Téa (actress), 297

Lessing, Doris (author), 108

Letterman, David (talk show host), 65, 68

Lévy, Bernard-Henri (intellectual), 114

Lewinsky, Monica (activist), 94

Lewis, Daniel Day (actor), 290

Lewis, Jerry (actor/comedian), 141

Libra
    basic facts of, 16, 17, 18, 102, 106
    creativity in, 362–363
    dates of, 15, 102
    described, 13
    examples of people born under sign of, 106–108
    health and wellness attributes of, 105
    in love, 299
    mythology of, 105–106
    relationships of, 104
    ruler of, 22, 106, 199
    sorry side of, 103–104
    sunny side of, 103
    symbol/glyph of, 15, 102, 106
    work attributes of, 104–105
Libra Midheaven, 209
Libra rising, 200, 205, 279
Lilly, William (astrologer), 52
Lin, Maya (designer), 363
Lincoln, Abraham (former US president), 131, 135, 139, 270, 301
Lincoln, Mary Todd (former US first lady), 301
Linda Goodman's Sun Signs (Goodman), 38, 55
Liu, Lucy (actress), 120
Lively, Blake (actress), 297
Lizzo (singer), 358
Llewellyn's Daily Planetary Guide (Belluomini), 308, 336, 389
locomotive, as one of seven planetary patterns, 271, 272
Lopez, Jennifer (actress), 94, 261, 295, 360
Lorde (singer-songwriter), 114
Loren, Sophia (actress), 96, 99, 202, 298
Louboutin, Christian (fashion designer), 129
Louis C. K. (comedian), 99
Louis-Dreyfus, Julia (actress), 129

Love, Courtney (singer-songwriter), 88, 295
Lowe, Rob (actor), 141
Lowell, Percival (astronomer), 187
Lucas, George (film director), 74
lunacy, 145–154
lunar deities, 333
lunar influences, making most of momentous ones, 339–340
lunar Nodes, 150–152, 217–219. See also North Node (Dragon's Head); South Node (Dragon's Tail)
Luther, Martin (professor), 167
Lynch, David (film director), 129

M
Ma, Yo-Yo (musician), 198
Macbeth (Shakespeare), 51
Machiavelli, Nicolo (diplomat), 74
Macintosh computers, astrological software for, 35–36
MacLaine, Shirley (actress), 74
MacLeod, Margaretha (aka Mata Hari), 201
Macy, William H. (actor), 302
Maddow, Rachel (media personality), 279
Madoff, Bernie (market maker), 74, 199, 290
Madoff, Ruth (wife of Bernie Madoff), 290
Madonna (singer/actress), 94
Magritte, René (artist), 364
Maher, Bill (comedian), 135
Mahler, Gustave (composer), 360
Maisani, Benjamin (night club owner), 293
Makemake (dwarf planet), 193
making money, spotting of talent for in chart, 383–384

Malcolm X (minister), 259
Malek, Rami (actor), 74
Mandela, Nelson (former South African president), 88
Manet, Edouard (artist), 135
Manson, Charles (criminal), 109
Manson, Marilyn (singer-songwriter), 129, 299
Mao Zedong (former People's Republic of China chairman), 129
Maples, Marla (actress), 292
Maplethorpe, Robert (photographer), 300
Marcus Manilius (astrologer), 19
Markle, Meghan (actress/Duchess of Sussex), 92, 296
Marley, Bob (singer-songwriter), 135, 367
Marquez, Gabriel Garcia (author), 139, 141, 198, 352, 367
marriage chart, 390–391
Mars
    aspects to, 258–262
    attributes associated with, 164
    creativity in, 369
    described, 163
    detriment of, 24
    exaltation of, 24
    fall, 24
    house and accidental planetary dignity of, 25
    in houses, 222–225
    keyword for, 21, 156
    mythology of, 164
    as personal planet, 155, 176
    in retrograde, 351, 352
    role of in horoscope, 20
    as ruler, 22, 24, 62, 66, 112, 198, 201
    symbol/glyph of, 21, 156, 164
    tracking of, 312–314
    in zodiac signs, 164–166

Mars effect, 224

Marshall, Thurgood (former US Supreme Court justice), 88

Martin, Chris (singer-songwriter), 299

Martin, George R. R. (author), 99, 352

Martin, Steve (actor), 94

Marx, Karl (philosopher), 74, 357

Mary Queen of Scots, 120

masculine signs, 16

Masha'Allan (astrologer), 47

Matalin, Mary (political consultant), 296

Matisse, Henri (artist), 129, 365

May, Theresa (member of UK Parliament), 352

Maynard, Jim (astrologer), 389

McAdams, Rachel (actress), 300

McCain, John (former US senator), 204

McCain, Meghan (columnist), 248

McCarthy, Melissa (actress), 99

McCartney, Linda (musician), 292

McCartney, Paul (singer-songwriter), 79, 259, 269, 292, 359

McCartney, Stella (fashion designer), 99

McConaughey, Matthew (actor), 114, 199

McCullers, Carson (author), 368

McDormand, Frances (actress), 88

McGraw, Tim (singer), 290

McIntyre, Reba (singer), 68

McQueen, Alexander (fashion designer), 272, 367, 368

McQueen, Steve (actor), 68, 288

medical astrology, 19

Medici, Catherine de (queen), 10, 50, 51

medicine, as looking to astrology, 19

meeting, timing of scheduling of, 393

Meier, Richard (artist), 108

Mellencamp, John (musician), 299

Melville, Herman (author), 94, 361

Mendieta, Ana (artist), 112–113

Mercury
aspects to, 252–255
attributes associated with, 158
creativity in, 368
described, 157
detriment of, 24
exaltation of, 24
fall of, 24
house and accidental planetary dignity of, 25
in houses, 219–220
keyword for, 21, 156
mythology of, 157
as personal planet, 155, 176
in retrograde, 344–349, 352
role of in horoscope, 20
as ruler, 22, 24, 200
symbol/glyph of, 21, 156, 158
in zodiac signs, 158

Meso-American astrology, 57, 349

Mesopotamia, earliest astronomical activity in, 42, 43

Michelangelo (artist), 139–140, 141, 368

Middleton, Kate. See Catherine (Duchess of Cambridge)

Midheaven (M.C.), 196, 206–210

Midler, Bette (singer), 198

A Midsummer Night's Dream (Shakespeare), 51

Miller, Arthur (playwright), 292

Miller, Henry (author), 129, 303, 352

Miller, Susan (astrologer), 39

Milne, A. A. (author), 129

Mingus, Charles (musician), 74

Minhaj, Hasan (comedian), 199

Minnesota Planetarium Society, 14

Miranda, Lin-Manuel (composer), 126–128, 198

Mirren, Helen (actress), 94

Mishima, Yukio (author), 129

Mitchell, Joni (singer-songwriter), 114, 199

modality, 16–17, 18

Modern Astrology, 54

modes, 275, 276–277

Mohammed ben Gebir al Batani (astrologer), 212

Monroe, Marilyn (actress), 79, 199, 216, 292, 293, 376

Moon
aspects to, 249–252
creativity in, 368
detriment of, 24
exaltation of, 24
fall of, 24
house and accidental planetary dignity of, 25
in houses, 215–217, 337–339
keyword for, 21
making most of momentous lunar influences, 339–340
mythology of, 146, 333
Nodes of, 150–152, 217–219. See also North Node (Dragon's Head); South Node (Dragon's Tail)
as one of three most important parts of an astrological chart, 196
as personal planet, 176
phases of, 334–335
role of in horoscope, 20
as ruler, 22, 24, 199
signs of, 145–154
symbol/glyph of, 21, 145–146

taking advantage of in signs, 336

timing your actions by phases of, 334–335

void-of-course, 340–341, 391

watching of, 335

in zodiac signs, 146–149, 336–337

Moore, Demi (actress), 114, 256, 300

Moore, Mary Tyler (actress), 129

Morissette, Alanis (singer-songwriter), 79

Morris, Jan (historian/author), 282

Morris, William (designer), 206

Morrison, Jim (singer-songwriter), 120

Morrison, Toni (author), 135, 331–332, 367, 388

Moss, Elizabeth (actress), 94

Moss, Kate (model), 129, 293

Mother Theresa (saint), 99

Mountain Astrologer, 36, 38

Mozart, Wolfgang Amadeus (composer), 135, 366, 370–371

Muhammad ibn Ahmad al-Bīrūni, 47

mundane astrology, 1, 37

Murakami, Haruki (author), 129, 366

Musgraves, Kacey (singer-songwriter), 94

Musk, Elon (SpaceX CEO), 88, 282

mutable signs, 17, 275

mutual reception, 243–244

Myss, Caroline (author), 120

N

Napoleon Bonaparte (statesman), 94, 294

natal chart, 15, 30, 34, 35, 41, 157, 196. *See also* birth chart

National Center for Health Statistics, 31

natural houses, 33

Navratilova, Martina (athlete), 108

Naylor, R. H. (astrologer), 55

negative signs, 16

Nelson, Prince Rogers (aka The Artist Formerly Known as Prince), 201

Neptune

aspects to, 264–265

attributes associated with, 182

classification of, 182

creativity in, 369

described, 181–182

detriment of, 24

discovery of, 54

exaltation of, 24

fall of, 24

house and accidental planetary dignity of, 25

in houses, 230–231

influence of, 183

keyword for, 21, 156

mythology of, 182

as nebulous, 325–327

role of in horoscope, 20

as ruler, 22, 24, 139, 204

symbol/glyph of, 21, 156, 182–183

as transpersonal planet, 176

in zodiac signs, 183–185

Nero (ruler), 46

Neruda, Pablo (poet), 88, 204, 280

Nessus (asteroid), 193

Newman, Paul (actor), 135, 303

Newton, Isaac (scientist), 9, 53, 271

Nicholas, Chani (astrologer), 39

Nichols, Mike (film director), 300

Nicholson, Jack (actor), 74

Nicks, Stevie (singer-songwriter), 79

Nietzsche, Friedrich (philosopher), 108, 249

Nin, Anais (author), 141, 303

1960s, secret of, 181

ninth house, 27, 214, 215, 217

Nixon, Cynthia (actress), 68

Nixon, Pat (former US first lady), 303

Nixon, Richard M. (former US president), 129, 303

Noah, Trevor (comedian), 141

Nodes, 150–152, 217–219. *See also* North Node (Dragon's Head); South Node (Dragon's Tail)

Nordegren, Elin, 302

North Node (Dragon's Head), 150–152, 156, 157, 217, 218–219

Nostradamus, Michel de (astrologer), 10, 50–51

Nureyev, Rudolph (dancer), 141

O

Oakley, Annie (performer), 94

Oates, Joyce Carol (author), 358

Obama, Barack (former US president), 94, 203, 272, 283, 296, 360

Obama, Michelle (former US first lady), 296

O'Brien, Conan (talk show host), 65, 68, 282

Ocasio-Cortez, Alexandria (US representative), 201, 238–239, 242, 246, 264, 271

O'Connor, Sinéad (singer-songwriter), 120, 365

Odit, Ophira (one of AstroTwins), 38

Odit, Tali (one of AstroTwins), 38

O'Donnell, Rosie (talk show host), 65, 68

Oe, Kenzaburo (author), 135

Oh, Sandra (actress), 88

O'Keeffe, Georgia (artist), 244, 300, 363

Oliver, Mary (poet), 248

"on the cusp," use of term, 15, 26, 27, 28, 122, 234–235

On the Revolutions of the Heavenly Orbs (Copernicus), 54

Onassis, Aristotle (business magnate), 296

Onassis, Jacqueline Kennedy (former US first lady), 94, 200, 292, 296

One Hundred Years of Solitude (Marquez), 367

O'Neill, Eugene (playwright), 108

Ono, Yoko (artist), 200, 299, 366

Ophiuchus the Serpent Bearer, 14

opposition, 238, 240

Ortelee, Anne (astrologer), 38

Osbourne, Kelly (singer-songwriter), 114

Oswalt, Patton (comedian), 135

outer planets, 155, 175–190, 258, 306

Oz, Mehmet (media personality), 79

P

Pacino, Al (actor), 74

Page, Jimmy (musician), 129

Page, Larry (entrepreneur), 65

Pallas (asteroid), 54, 193

Paltrow, Gwyneth (actress), 108, 204, 248, 299

Pamuk, Orham (author), 79

Parker, Bonnie (criminal), 289

Parker, Dorothy (poet), 99

Parker, Sarah Jessica (actress), 68, 288

Parker-Bowles, Camilla (duchess), 294

Parton, Dolly (singer), 129

Partridge, John (astrologer), 53

party, timing of throwing of, 393–394

Patel, Dev (actor), 74

Patrick, Danica (race car driver), 63, 68

pattern analysis, 268, 269

Paulson, Sarah (actress), 120

PCs, astrological software for, 36–37

Pei, I.M. (architect), 357

Pelosi, Nancy (Speaker of the House), 63, 68

Penn, Sean (actor), 94

Perce, Georges (author), 367

Perry, Katy (singer-songwriter), 114

personal planets, 155–174, 176, 370

Phelps, Michael (athlete), 88, 376

Philip (prince), 290

Phillippe, Ryan (actor), 288

Pholus (asteroid), 193

Piaf, Edith (singer-songwriter), 120

Picasso, Pablo (artist), 114, 300, 305, 363

Pisces

  basic facts of, 16, 17, 18, 122, 139

  creativity in, 367–368

  dates of, 16, 122, 135

  described, 14

  examples of people born under sign of, 139–141

  health and wellness attributes of, 138

  in love, 304

  modern ruler of, 22, 23, 139, 204

  mythology of, 138

  relationships of, 137

  sorry side of, 136

  sunny side of, 136

  symbol/glyph of, 16, 135, 139

  traditional ruler of, 22, 23, 139, 204

  work attributes of, 137–138

Pisces Midheaven, 210

Pisces rising, 204, 205, 279

Pitt, Brad (actor), 120, 201, 293, 301

Placidus, 212

planetary dignities, determination of, 23–25

planetary patterns, 269–274

planetary void, 277

planets. *See also specific planets*

  accidental dignities of, 24–25

  apparent backwards motion of, 344

  aspects between, 237

  as contributing to creativity, 368

  detriment of, 23

  dwarf planets. *See* dwarf planets

  essential dignities of, 23–24

  exaltation of, 23

  fall of, 23

  keywords for, 21

  locating yours, 156–157

  outer planets, 155, 175–190, 258, 306

  personal planets, 155–174, 176, 370

  as representing types of energy, 212

  in retrograde, 343–353

  role of in horoscope, 20

  ruling of zodiac signs by, 21–23

  social planets, 176

  strength in, 369

  transiting planets, 235, 265, 307, 309, 311, 331

  transpersonal planets, 176

Plath, Sylvia (author), 114, 363

Pleiades (star cluster), 72

Pliny the Elder (naturalist), 44, 45

Pluto
  in the 1960s, 181
  aspects to, 264–265
  classification of, 187
  creativity in, 369
  demotion of, 186
  described, 187
  detriment of, 24
  discovery of, 175, 186
  exaltation of, 24
  fall of, 24
  house and accidental planetary dignity of, 25
  in houses, 232–233
  influence of, 188
  keyword for, 21, 156
  mythology of, 187
  as power-hungry, 327–330
  role of in horoscope, 20
  as ruler, 22, 24, 112, 201
  symbol/glyph of, 21, 156, 187, 188
  as transpersonal planet, 176
  in zodiac signs, 188–190
Pocket Astrologer (Maynard), 308
Poe, Edgar Allen (author), 366
Poehler, Amy (actress), 99
Pol Pot (former Cambodian prime minister), 70
Polanski, Roman (film director), 296
polarity, 16, 18
Pollock, Jackson (artist), 135, 300, 366
Pollux (star), 77, 78
Ponti, Carlo (film producer), 298
Poor Richard's Almanac (Franklin), 53
Popova, Maria (author), 94
Porter, Cole (songwriter), 79
Portman, Natalie (actress), 79
positive signs, 16

Potter, Beatrix (author), 94, 361
Presley, Elvis (singer-songwriter), 129, 201, 293
Presley, Lisa Marie (singer-songwriter), 298
Presley, Priscilla (actress), 293
Previn, Andre (musician), 289
Previn, Soon-yi (actress), 299
Price, Leontyne (singer), 135
Prince (singer-songwriter), 79, 282, 358
Prinze, Freddie, Jr. (actor), 289
Project Hindsight, 56
Proust, Marcel (author), 360
Pryor, Richard (comedian), 120, 204, 258
psychic ability, spotting of in chart, 385–386
Ptolemy, Claudius (mathematician), 44, 47, 167, 212

Q

Quaid, Dennis (actor), 289
Queen Latifah (actress), 141, 198
quincunx (or inconjunct), as one of six minor aspects, 243, 283
quintile, as one of six minor aspects, 243

R

Raitt, Bonnie (singer-songwriter), 114, 198, 283
Rapinoe, Megan (athlete), 376
Reagan, Nancy (former US first lady), 56, 295
Reagan, Ronald (former US president), 135, 282, 295
Redgrave, Vanessa (actress), 135
Reed, Lou (musician), 141, 293
Reeve, Christopher (actor), 108
Reeves, Keanu (actor), 200, 228, 247

Rembrandt van Rijn (artist), 88, 360
Resnick, Judith (astronaut), 68
retrograde, 343–353
Reynolds, Debbie (actress), 288
Reynolds, Ryan (actor), 114, 297
Rhimes, Shonda (television producer), 129, 260
Rice, Condoleezza (former US secretary of state), 114
Rich, Adrienne (poet), 74, 200
Richards, Keith (musician), 120, 200
Rihanna (singer), 141, 198
Rilke, Rainer Maria (poet), 120
Rimbaud, Arthur (poet), 108
Ripa, Kelly (actress), 108, 289
rising sign, 25–26, 31, 195–205, 278, 279. *See also* Ascendant sign (rising sign)
Rivera, Diego (artist), 87, 120, 294
Rivers, Joan (comedian), 198
Roberts, Julia (actress), 114, 199
Robinson, Jackie (athlete), 135
Rodgers, Richard (composer), 294
Rodman, Dennis (athlete), 258
Rodriguez, Alex (athlete/ sportscaster), 94, 295
Rogers, Roy (actor), 300
romances (based on sign), 288–304
Romans, astrology among, 10, 44–46
Romeo and Juliet (Shakespeare), 51
Ronaldo, Cristiano (athlete), 135
Ronstadt, Linda (singer-songwriter), 88
Roosevelt, Eleanor (former US first lady), 108
Roosevelt, Franklin D. (former US president), 135, 352
Ross, Diana (singer), 68

Rossi, Portia de (model), 303

Roth, Philip (author), 141, 352

Rowling, J. K. (author), 94, 203, 360

Rudhyar, Dane (astrologer/ composer), 334

Rudolph II (emperor), 45

Ruffalo, Mark (actor), 114

rulerships, 279, 280

Rumi (poet), 363

RuPaul (drag queen), 114, 258

Rushdie, Salmon (author), 79, 198, 358

Russell, Keri (actress), 68

Russell, Kurt (actor), 301

Ruth, Babe (athlete), 281

Ryan, Meg (actress), 289, 299

Ryder, Winona (actress), 260

S

Sade, Marquis de (philosopher), 79, 200, 246

Sagittarius

  basic facts of, 16, 17, 18, 102, 114, 118

  creativity in, 364–365

  dates of, 15, 102, 114

  described, 13

  examples of people born under sign of, 118–120

  health and wellness attributes of, 117

  in love, 301–302

  mythology of, 117

  relationships of, 116

  ruler of, 22, 23, 118, 201

  sorry side of, 115

  sunny side of, 115

  symbol/glyph of, 15, 114, 118

  work attributes of, 116–117

Sagittarius Midheaven, 209–210

Sagittarius rising, 201, 205, 279

Saint-Exupery, Antoine de (author), 88

Salk, Jonas (medical researcher), 114, 379–380

Sandberg, Sheryl (Facebook COO), 99

Sanders, Bernie (US senator), 99, 352

Sarandon, Susan (actress), 108

Sargent, John Singer (artist), 366

Sartre, Jean-Paul (philosopher), 293

Saturn

  aspects to, 262–263

  attributes associated with, 171

  coping with, 318–321

  creativity in, 369

  described, 170

  detriment of, 24

  exaltation of, 24

  fall of, 24

  house and accidental planetary dignity of, 25

  in houses, 226–228

  keyword for, 21, 156

  mythology of, 170

  role of in horoscope, 20

  as ruler, 22, 24, 133, 202, 203

  as social planet, 176

  symbol/glyph of, 21, 156, 171

  in zodiac signs, 171–173

Saunders, Richard, as pseudonym for Benjamin Franklin, 53

Sawyer, Diane (journalist), 300

Scalia, Antonin (former US Supreme Court justice), 304

Schiffer, Claudia (model), 297

Schmidt, Steven (author) Astrology 14, 14

Schreiber, Liev (actor), 299

Schumer, Amy (comedian), 358

Schwarzenegger (actor/former California governor), 94, 199, 296

Schweitzer, Albert (theologian), 129

Scorpio

  basic facts of, 16, 17, 18, 102, 111, 112

  creativity in, 363–364

  dates of, 15, 102, 108

  described, 13

  examples of people born under sign of, 109, 110, 112–114

  health and wellness attributes of, 111

  in love, 300–301

  modern ruler of, 22, 23, 112, 201

  mythology of, 111

  relationships of, 109–110

  sorry side of, 109

  sunny side of, 108–109

  symbol/glyph of, 15, 108, 112

  traditional ruler of, 22, 23, 112, 201

  work attributes of, 110

Scorpio Midheaven, 209

Scorpio rising, 200–201, 205, 279

Scot, Michael (astrologer), 48

Scott, Travis (musician), 290

Seal of Solomon, 283

second house, 27, 213, 214, 216

The Secrets of the Vaulted Sky: Astrology and the Art of Prediction (Berlinski), 58

Sedgwick, Edie (socialite), 68, 256

Sedgwick, Kyra (actress), 294

Sedna (Kuiper belt object), 193

seesaw, as one of seven planetary patterns, 272

Seinfeld, Jerry (actor), 74

Seltzer, Henry (founder of Astrograph Software), 36

semi-sextile, as one of six minor aspects, 243

semi-square, as one of six minor aspects, 243

sesquiquadrate, as one of six minor aspects, 243

setting sign, 196

Seven Sisters, 72

seventh house, 27, 213, 215, 216

sextile, 238, 240, 283

Shakespeare, William (playwright), 51–52, 74, 358

Shakespeare and the Stars: The Hidden Astrological Keys to Understanding the World's Greatest Playwright (Costello), 51, 52

Shelley, Mary (author), 99, 296, 361

Shelley, Percy Bysshe (poet), 296

Shelton, Blake (singer), 292

Shields, Brooke (actress), 79, 290

Shriver, Maria (actress), 296

Silverman, Sarah (comedian), 120, 201, 365

Simon, Paul (singer-songwriter), 108, 200

Simone, Nina (singer-songwriter), 141, 368

Simpson, Wallis (socialite), 292

Sinatra, Frank (singer/actor), 120, 200, 272, 301

singleton, 271, 274

sixth house, 27, 213, 215, 216

Smith, Jada Pinkett (actress), 297

Smith, Patti (singer-songwriter), 129, 201, 300, 365

Smith, Will (actor), 108, 297

Smith, Zadie (author), 247

social planets, 176

software, for creating astrological chart, 35–37

Solar Fire Gold (software), 37

Solar Fire (software), 36

Solzhenitsyn, Aleksandr (author), 120

Sorkin, Aaron (screenwriter), 79

Sotomayor, Sonia (US Supreme Court justice), 88, 246

South Node (Dragon's Tail), 150–152, 156, 157, 217–219

Spektor, Regina (singer-songwriter), 199

Spica (star), 97, 98

Spielberg, Steven (film director), 120, 365

Spiritualism, 54

splash, as one of seven planetary patterns, 271, 272

splay, as one of seven planetary patterns, 272–273

Spock, Benjamin (doctor/author), 74

spring, signs of, 61–79

Springsteen, Bruce (singer-songwriter), 106–107

square, as one of five major aspects, 238, 240

St. Laurent, Yves (fashion designer), 94

Stallone, Sylvester (actor), 269

Star of David, 283

star sign, use of term, 13

Starr, Ringo (musician), 88, 294

Stefani, Gwen (singer-songwriter), 108, 292

Stein, Gertrude (author), 135, 305

Steinbeck, John (author), 141

Steinem, Gloria (journalist), 68, 260, 384

stelliums, 279–280

Stern, Howard (radio personality), 254

Stevenson, Robert Louis (author), 363

Stewart, Jon (comedian), 120, 262

Stewart, Kristen (actress), 199

Stieglitz, Alfred (photographer), 300

Stoker, Bram (author), 364

Stone, Oliver (filmmaker), 99

The Strange Case of Dr. Jekyll and Mr. Hyde (Stevenson), 363

Streep, Meryl (actress), 88, 199, 247, 283

Streisand, Barbra (singer/actress), 74, 290

summer, signs of, 81–99

Sun
   aspects to, 244–249
   as at the core of almost every horoscope, 61
   creativity in, 368
   detriment of, 24
   exaltation of, 24
   fall of, 24
   house and accidental planetary dignity of, 25
   in houses, 214–215
   keyword for, 21
   as one of three most important parts of an astrological chart, 196
   as personal planet, 176
   planets as orbiting, 11
   representation of, 62
   role of in horoscope, 20
   as ruler, 22, 24, 199
   symbol/glyph of, 21

Sun sign, 15, 16–19, 55, 62, 287–306

surgery, timing of, 395–396

Suvari, Mena (actress), 135

Swift, Jonathan (author), 53

Swift, Taylor (singer-songwriter), 120, 254, 271

Swinton, Tilda (actress), 114

Sykes, Wanda (actress), 254

T

Table of Houses, 30
Tan, Amy (author), 141, 198
Tarantino, Quentin (film director), 65, 68, 357
Tate, Sharon (actress), 296
Taurus
    basic facts of, 16, 17, 18, 61, 72
    creativity in, 357–358
    dates of, 15, 61, 68
    described, 13
    examples of people born under sign of, 73–74
    health and wellness attributes of, 71–72
    in love, 290–291
    mythology of, 72
    relationships of, 70
    ruler of, 22, 72, 200
    sorry side of, 69–70
    sunny side of, 69
    symbol/glyph of, 15, 68–69, 72
    work attributes of, 70–71
Taurus Midheaven, 207
Taurus rising, 198–199, 204, 279
Taylor, Elizabeth (actress), 141, 256, 301
Tebaldi, Renata (singer), 135
technology, timing of purchase of, 394
Teigen, Chrissy (model), 120, 301
tenth house, 27, 214, 215, 217
Tetrabiblos (Ptolemy), 44, 47
Tharp, Twyla (dancer/choreographer), 88, 359
Theogenes (astrologer), 44
Theron, Charlize (actress), 94, 200
third house, 27, 213, 214, 216
The 13 Signs of the Zodiac (Berg), 14
Thomas, Dylan (poet), 114, 352, 364
Thompson, Ahmir Khalib (aka Questlove) (musician), 28

Thompson, Emma (actress), 289
Thompson, Hunter S. (journalist), 247, 360
Thrasyllus (astrologer), 45
Thunberg, Greta (activist), 384–385
Tiberius (ruler), 45
Timberlake, Justin (singer-songwriter), 303
Time Cycles Research Programs, 36
TimePassages, 36, 37, 308–309
timing, art of, 389–397
Toklas, Alice B. (author), 305
Tolkien, J. R. R. (author), 129, 265, 352
Tolstoy, Leo (author), 352
Tombaugh, Clyde (amateur astronomer), 175, 187
Toobin, Jeffrey (lawyer), 79
Toro, Benicio del (actor), 141
Toro, Guillermo del (filmmaker), 260
Toth, Jim (talent agent), 288
Tracy, Spencer (actor), 288
transiting planets, 235, 265, 307, 309, 311, 331
transits, 308–332
transpersonal planets, 176
Travolta, John (actor), 135
Tretheway, Natasha (poet laureate), 74, 246
Trilling, Diana (literary critic), 294
Trilling, Lionel (literary critic), 294
trine, 238, 240
Trudeau, Justin (Canada prime minister), 260
Truffaut, Francois (film director), 135, 367
Truman, Harry (former US president), 68, 74
Trump, Donald J. (US president), 78, 199, 247, 270, 290, 292
Trump, Ivanka (businesswoman), 114

Trump, Melania (US first lady), 290
T-square, 282
Turing, Alan (mathematician), 88
Turner, Ike (singer), 300
Turner, Tina (singer), 120, 257, 300
Twain, Mark (author) (pen name for Samuel Clemens), 120, 201
twelfth house, 27, 214, 215, 217
Tyler, Steven (singer-songwriter), 68
Tyson, Mike (boxer), 88
Tyson, Neil deGrasse (astrophysicist), 108

U

Ullman, Tracey (comedian), 201
Updike, John (author), 368
Uranus
    in the 1960s, 181
    aspects to, 264–265
    creativity in, 369
    described, 176–177
    detriment of, 24
    discovery of, 54, 175
    exaltation of, 24
    fall of, 24
    house and accidental planetary dignity of, 25
    in houses, 228–230
    keyword for, 21, 156
    mythology of, 177
    role of in horoscope, 20
    as ruler, 22, 24, 133, 203
    symbol/glyph of, 21, 156, 177–178
    as transpersonal planet, 176
    understanding of, 178
    as unpredictable, 322–324
    in zodiac signs, 178–180
Urban, Keith (singer-songwriter), 292

V

Van Gogh, Vincent (artist), 26, 68, 270, 357

Vargas Llosa, Mario (writer), 68

Vedic astrology, 1, 36, 37, 57, 150, 151

Venus
  aspects to, 255–257
  attributes associated with, 161
  creativity in, 368
  described, 160
  detriment of, 24
  as Evening Star, 160
  exaltation of, 24
  fall of, 24
  house and accidental planetary dignity of, 25
  in houses, 220–221
  keyword for, 21, 156
  as Morning Star, 160
  mythology of, 160
  as personal planet, 155, 176
  in retrograde, 349–350, 352
  role of in horoscope, 20
  as ruler, 22, 24, 72, 106, 200
  symbol/glyph of, 21, 156, 161
  in zodiac signs, 161–163

Verdi, Giuseppe (composer), 108

Vermeer, Jan (artist), 364

vernal equinox, 12, 14, 61

Versace, Gianni (fashion designer), 120

Vesta (asteroid), 54, 193

Vestritius Spurinna (seer), 44

Vettius Valens (astrologer), 47

Victoria (queen), 79

Virgo
  basic facts of, 16, 17, 18, 94, 98
  creativity in, 361–362
  dates of, 15, 94
  described, 13
  examples of people born under sign of, 96, 98–99
  health and wellness attributes of, 97
  in love, 297–298
  mythology of, 97
  relationships of, 95–96
  ruler of, 23, 200
  sorry side of, 95
  sunny side of, 95
  symbol/glyph of, 15, 94, 98
  work attributes of, 96

Virgo Midheaven, 209

Virgo rising, 200, 205, 279

Vivaldi, Antonio (composer), 141, 368

void-of-course, 340–341, 391

von Furstenberg, Diane (fashion designer), 129, 295, 366

von Furstenberg, Egon (socialite), 295

von Teese, Dita (burlesque queen), 299

Vonnegut, Kurt (author), 114

W

Wagner, Robert (actor), 295

Walker, Alice (author), 367

Wang, Vera (fashion designer), 360

Warhol, Andy (artist), 94, 377

Warren, Elizabeth (US senator), 88, 247

Washington, Booker T. (educator), 68

Washington, Denzel (actor), 129, 200

Washington, George (former US president), 139, 271

water sign, 17, 275

Watson, Emma (actress), 68

Watts, Naomi (actress), 299

Wayne, John (actor), 79

Weaver, Sigourney (actress), 108

Webber, Andrew Lloyd (composer), 68, 99

The Weeknd (singer), 135

Weisz, Rachel (actress), 141, 304

Welch, Jack (former General Electric chairman/CEO), 381–382, 383

Welles, Orson (actor), 51, 199

West, Kanye (rapper), 79, 246, 292, 358

Wharton, Edith (author), 367

Whitehead, Alfred North (mathematician), 305

Whitman, Walt (poet), 216, 265

Whole Sign, 212

Wife of Bath (character in *Canterbury Tales*), 198

Wilde, Oscar (author), 108

Wilder, Laura Ingalls (author), 367

William (Duke of Cambridge), 79, 295

Williams, Michelle (singer), 99, 288

Williams, Robin (actor), 88, 200

Williams, Serena (athlete), 108, 198, 269, 309–311

Williams, Tennessee (playwright), 68

Williams, Venus (athlete), 79

Williams, Wendy (media personality), 88

Williamson, Marianne (author), 247

Wilson, Rita (actress), 294

Winehouse, Amy (singer-songwriter), 99, 199

Winfrey, Oprah (executive), 133, 271, 277, 302, 303

Winslet, Kate (actress), 108

winter, zodiac signs of, 121–141

Winterson, Jeanette (author), 99

Witchcraft Act, 54

Witherspoon, Reese (actress), 260, 288

Wonder, Stevie (singer-songwriter), 74, 200

Wood, Natalie (actress), 248, 295

Woods, Tiger (athlete), 129, 302, 375

Woodward, Joanne (actress), 303

Woolf, Virginia (author), 135, 247, 366

Wordsworth, William (poet), 68, 357

Wozniak, Steve (engineer), 94

Wright, Frank Lloyd (architect), 79, 359

writing

    spotting of talent for in chart, 388

    timing of, 396–397

Y

yang, use of term, 16

Yeats, William Butler (poet), 79, 272, 359

Yeoh, Michelle (actress), 94

yin, use of term, 16

Yod, 282–284

Yogananda, Paramahansa (yogi), 265

Young, Neil (singer-songwriter), 114, 300

Yousafzai, Malala (activist), 247

Z

Zeffirelli, Franco (film director), 366

Zelleweger, Renee (actress), 74

Zeta-Jones, Catherine (actress), 299

Zodiac Man, 19

zodiac signs. *See also specific signs*

    as compared to constellations, 11, 12–13

    as contributing to creativity, 368

    "on the cusp" of. *See* "on the cusp"

    as distinguished from houses, 211–212

    entire zodiac as residing within each of us, 15

    as geometric divisions of the ecliptic, 11

    identification of, 13–16

    modality of, 16–17, 18

    Nodes in, 152–154

    number of, 14

    parts of the body as attributable to, 19

    polarity of, 16, 18

    as representing ways of expressing energies, 212

    rulers of, 21–23

Zuckerberg, Mark (Facebook CEO), 74, 246, 381

About the Author

Rae Orion has been casting horoscopes for her entire adult life, ever since she became the court astrologer for a metaphysical bookstore in the Pacific Northwest and began to prognosticate for strangers. In addition to writing about astrology, she has written books and articles about mythology, astronomy, and many other topics. She lives in New York City.

Dedication

For George, always.

Author's Acknowledgments

Two Capricorns deserve extravagant praise: my husband, George, and my editor, Chrissy Guthrie. Both are thoughtful, serious, organized, kind, and a lot more fun than is generally advertised for that sign. I also want to thank Steven Hayes, who made it happen (Aries will do that); Tracy Boggier, who reintroduced me to the *For Dummies* way of life; the great Mary Plumb; Production Editor Siddique Shaik; and others at Wiley whose behind-the-scenes presence was always a comfort.

Publisher's Acknowledgments

Executive Editor: Steven Hayes

Editor and Project Manager: Christina N. Guthrie

Technical Editor: Mary Plumb

Production Editor: Siddique Shaik

Cover Photos: © andriano.cz/Shutterstock